Econometrics in a Formal Science of Economics

Econometrics in a Formal Science of Economics

Theory and the Measurement of Economic Relations

Bernt P. Stigum

The MIT Press
Cambridge Massachusetts
London, England

MIT Press books may be purchased at special quantity discounts for business or sales promotional use. For information, email special_sales@mitpress.mit.edu.

Set in Palatino LT Std by Toppan Best-set Premedia Limited, Hong Kong. Printed and bound in the United States of America.

Library of Congress Cataloging-in-Publication Data

Stigum, Bernt P.
Econometrics in a formal science of economics : theory and the measurement of economic relations / Bernt P. Stigum.
  pages cm
Includes bibliographical references and index.
ISBN 978-0-262-02858-5 (hardcover : alk. paper)
1. Econometrics. 2. Econometric models. I. Title.
HB139.S7575 2014
330.01'5195—dc23
2014016744

10 9 8 7 6 5 4 3 2 1

Til Fia
—for et eventyr

Contents

To the Reader

Before reading chapters 3 and 4, be sure that you have read section 2.2 of chapter 2. Before reading chapters 7 and 8, be sure that you have read chapter 6. To understand chapter 10, you should have some familiarity with rudimentary propositional calculus and you should have read chapters 3–9.

Acknowledgments

Many people have contributed ideas and helpful suggestions. Three deserve special thanks: Harald Goldstein, André Anundsen, and Olav Bjerkholt.

I have made an attempt to write an interesting book about the contrast between econometrics in the tradition of Trygve Haavelmo and formal econometrics in the tradition of Ragnar Frisch. To succeed I needed help.

I needed help to analyze time-series data. In the summer of 2005, Harald Goldstein agreed to analyze time-series data on foreign exchange along lines that formal econometrics advocates. In the summer of 2011, André Anundsen agreed to analyze the same data with the methods of David Hendry and Søren Johansen. Goldstein's and Anundsen's results enabled me to contrast present-day econometric analysis of time series with formal econometric analysis of such data. I cannot thank the two of them enough.

In addition, I needed help to find relevant information about Ragnar Frisch and Trygve Haavelmo. Olav Bjerkholt had an unending supply of such information that he was willing to share with me. It was, therefore, a real privilege for me to be Olav's colleague while I worked on this book.

Special thanks are also due to Ragnar Nymoen for his support and good advice in connection with André Anundsen's contributions, to Anne Olaug Stigum for an appendix to chapter 4 and a search for cointegrating vectors in chapter 9, and to Neil Ericsson for an extraordinarily insightful and constructive review of an early version of chapter 7.

I also benefited from both constructive criticisms and not-so-complementary comments on earlier versions of the manuscript. Aris Spanos read vesions of chapters 1 and 2. Anders Bredahl Kock and

Sigmund Ellingsrud read versions of chapters 2 and 3. Phoebus Dhrymes, Erik Bioern, Adrian Pagan, and two referees of the *Journal of Econometrics* read versions of chapter 4. Neil Ericsson, Eric Renault, and two referees of the *Journal of Financial Econometrics* read versions of chapter 7. Søren Johansen, Timo Terasvirta, Peter Phillips, and one referee of the *Journal of Econometric Theory* read versions of chapter 8. Kristoffer Midttømme, Tore Schweder, David Hendry, Arne Strøm, Tony Hall, Kevin Hoover, Grayham Mizon, and Henry McKean read and commented on various portions of the manuscript. I owe all of them heartfelt thanks.

I thank the Economics Department at the University of Oslo and Professor Wilhelm Keilhaus Minnefond for financial support, and the Norwegian Research Council for Science and the Humanities for its support. I thank Jane Macdonald for the guidance that the MIT Press provided. Finally, I want it be known that the gracious way the Department of Economics treats a professor emeritus is most appreciated.

1 Introduction

Econometrics is a study of good and bad ways to measure economic relations. This book is about the role that economic theory ought to play in such measurements. The role that theory should play depends on the researcher's ideas about the essence of an economic theory. A researcher who believes that his theory is about the actual workings of an economy can identify his theory's variables with objects in the real world of which he may or may not have accurate observations. A researcher who believes that his theory is about imaginary matters that have uncertain relations to objects in the real world has serious measurement problems that I intend to help him solve with the means that a formal science of economics can provide.

To me a branch of knowledge is a *science* if (1) it is concerned with establishing and systematizing facts and principles, (2) its arguments are based on logically consistent and precisely formulated theories whose empirical relevance can be tested with the data and the statistical methods at hand, and (3) there is a unitary methodological basis for analyzing pertinent theoretical and empirical problems. Such a science is a *formal science* if its fundamental theories and its unitary methodological basis have been given definite forms as axiomatic systems.

I begin this chapter by describing the salient parts of a formal science of economics that I have put together in this book and in earlier works (B. Stigum 1990, 2003). The parts constitute a unitary methodological basis for a science, an explication of the meaning of facts and fiction in econometrics, and a confrontation of the methods of present-day applied econometrics with the methods that my formal science advocates. I then discuss the axiomatic method of developing scientific theories and contrast it with the model-theoretic way. I apply the two methods in putting together the various parts of the science of economics and in delineating the way econometricians are to use the means which a formal science provides in their empirical analyses. The formal data confrontation of economic theories that results from these deliberations has controversial aspects. In the fourth section of the chapter, I discuss three of the controversial aspects as they relate to the application of theory in applied econometrics. One of the controversial aspects concerns the essence of an economic theory and what can be learned about social reality from empirical analyses. A second concerns the double role of theory in formal theory-data confrontations and the need for bridge principles in empirical analyses. A third concerns the reasons why theory is required both for the design of an empirical analysis and for the interpretation of its results. I conclude the chapter with a brief description of the contents of the remaining nine chapters.

1.1 A Formal Science of Economics

This is the third of three books in which I develop and demonstrate the usefulness of a formal science of economics. In the first book, *Toward a Formal Science of Economics* (1990), I use fundamental theorems in mathematical logic and model theory to construct a formal unitary methodological basis for the theoretical and empirical sides of a science. My methodological basis has two parts: $L_{t,p}$, a multi-sorted first-order language for science, and SEL, a two-sorted modal-theoretic language for talking about the meaningfulness of the assertions in $L_{t,p}$. The vocabulary of $L_{t,p}$ consists of an observational part, a theoretical part, and a dictionary. One formulates scientific theories with the theoretical vocabulary, delineates characteristic features of a universe of observable objects with the observational vocabulary, and uses the dictionary and the other two vocabularies to describe how the undefined terms of the theories and the observable objects are related to one another. The vocabulary of SEL is partly a vocabulary for discussing properties of real numbers and partly a vocabulary for describing salient characteristics of the sentences in $L_{t,p}$. The vocabulary of SEL is used to formulate statistical tests of the scientific hypotheses that are asserted in $L_{t,p}$.

Both $L_{t,p}$ and SEL are constructed as formal axiomatic systems. In parts V and VI of my 1990 book I give ample evidence of the adequacy of the pair ($L_{t,p}$, SEL) as a unitary methodological basis for the science of economics. Specifically, in chapters 26–28 I demonstrate how mathematical economists can use $L_{t,p}$ to describe situations in which the empirical relevance of their theories can be tested. I also show how $L_{t,p}$

and SEL can be used to guide applied economists and econometricians in their search for meaningful statistical models. In chapters 23 and 24 I outline a way in which $L_{t,p}$ and an extended version of SEL can be used to study the epistemological problems of econometrics. In chapter 25 I establish semantic and syntactic theorems that demonstrate that $L_{t,p}$ has all the properties one should want to require of a language for science:

• It is complete in the sense that it is impossible to derive more valid sentences by adding axioms and rules of inference.
• Any theory that is expressed in it is consistent if and only if it has a model.
• If a theory that is expressed in it has a model with an infinite universe, then it has a model with a denumerably infinite universe.[1]

In the second book, *Econometrics and the Philosophy of Economics* (Stigum 2003), I provide the philosophical underpinnings of a formal science of economics and describe the ingredients of formal theory-data confrontations in econometrics. The philosophical parts of the book constitute an essay about facts and fiction in econometrics. I begin by discussing the facts. To me that means describing the way human beings create a superstructure of things, facts, and possibilities that I designate *social reality*. Here a thing is an object in Kant's world of phenomena (see Kant 1781) or a basic element in music and mathematics. A fact is that in virtue of which a true statement is true, and the statement may be about things, about other facts, and about collections of things and facts.[2] A possibility is a future state of the world of things and facts that one or more persons believe is possible. The world of possibilities does not vary over individuals or groups of individuals. Only the probabilities that individuals assign to various future events differ among persons. I believe that economic science is systematized knowledge about the nature of social reality that pertains to economic matters.

Next I discuss the fiction in econometrics. To me that means describing my vision of the reality that philosophers of science refer to when they deliberate about the social construction of reality. The reality in question varies from one philosopher to another. According to Peter Berger and Thomas Luckmann (1966), the given reality is an ordered world of institutions that through a process of socialization receives a certain stability over time. To Karin Knorr Cetina (1981), the reality in question comprises all the artificial products that the world's scientific laboratories create. My vision of the social construction of reality is not about the construction of institutions and not about the production of scientific artifacts. It is about the social construction of "objects of thought and representation" (Sismondo 1993). Specifically, to me the reality in the philosophers' idea about a socially constructed reality is a socially constructed world of ideas that contains the references of the data with which econometricians face their theories. This world is fictional, since it has little in common with my vision of social reality.

One aspect of the production of artifacts in Knorr Cetina's laboratory is particularly interesting: The artifacts are produced in a pre-constructed artificial reality with purified chemicals, and with specially grown and selectively bred plants and rats that are equally pre-constructed. Such products cannot be part of "nature" as I understand the term. Nevertheless, scientists use such products to further their understanding of processes that are active in nature. For me, the interesting aspect is that it illustrates how knowledge of relations in one world, the laboratory, can be used to gain insight about relations that exist in another world, nature. Analogous problems arise each time an econometrician attempts to use relations among his data variables to establish properties of relations in social reality.

In Stigum 2003 the ingredients of a formal theory-data confrontation make up a unitary methodological basis for the science of economics. The place of $L_{t,p}$ is taken by two disjoint universes of real-valued variables and functions and a bridge between them. The role of SEL is assumed by a sampling scheme and two probability spaces, one for data and one for the bridge. The ingredients are designed to help applied econometricians find methodologically meaningful ways to incorporate theory in their quest to learn about interesting aspects of social reality. Here is how: Consider, for example, an economist who sets out to determine whether a given economic theory has empirical relevance. In Stigum 2003 the economist first places salient theorems of the theory in a theory universe. Then he drafts axioms that describe characteristics of his data and places them in a data universe. Finally, he formulates axioms for the bridge that relate the undefined terms of his theory to his data and delineate pertinent properties of his sampling scheme. Whether the two universes, the bridge, and the two probability spaces provide sufficient means to determine the empirical relevance of the theory, is not obvious. The theory is about symbols, and the data have references in a socially constructed world of ideas. Neither have much in common with social reality. Still, in Stigum 2003 I claim that the econometrician with the means I have given him can determine the empirical relevance of his theories and in that way learn about characteristics of social reality that are interesting from an economist's point of view.

In this book, I develop a new unitary methodological basis for the science of economics that differs in essential details from the one I presented in Stigum 2003. In Stigum 2003 the data I used in the empirical analysis were generated by a stratified random sampling scheme. The new basis is designed for the analysis of data that are either time series of observations of a vector-valued random process or cross-section data that are generated by a random sampling scheme. In the new formulation, the place of $L_{t,p}$ is taken by two disjoint universes of real-valued variables and functions and a bridge between them. The role of SEL is assumed by two probability spaces, one for theory and one for data. Also, the sampling scheme is described in axioms that concern the probability distributions of theory and data variables.

In the formulation of the methodological basis in this book, as in Stigum 2003, the bridge principles play two roles. In one role, the bridge principles translate the theory so that it becomes a statement about relations among variables in the data universe. In the other role, the bridge principles convert the probability distributions of variables in the theory universe into probability distributions of variables in the data universe that are to be used in the empirical analysis. I designate the latter family of probability distributions by the acronym MPD, and I read the acronym as the marginal probability distribution of the data variables. The double role of the bridge principles depicts the way theory is incorporated in the empirical-analysis part of my methodological basis.

The purpose of this book is to contrast formal econometrics in the tradition of Ragnar Frisch with present-day applied econometrics in the tradition of Trygve Haavelmo. Frisch and Haavelmo were two of the founding fathers of econometrics. They had a vision of a science of economics in which the theoretical-quantitative and the empirical-quantitative approaches to economic problems were to be unified. In his 1944 treatise *The Probability Approach in Econometrics*, Haavelmo showed how a non-formal (that is, non-axiomatized) version of such a science could be developed. His ideas were adopted by his fellow econometricians and are still fundamental pillars of econometrics. Frisch was an extraordinary mathematical economist and an extraordinary mathematical statistician. His idea of a science of economics must have been a formal science in which mathematical economics and mathematical statistics are conjoined. However, he did not know how to put such a science together. He missed the bridge and the MPD, probably, because he considered the gap between empirical laws and rational laws to be unbridgeable. (See Bjerkholt and Qin 2010, p. 34.) My three books show how it can be done. The necessary mathematical foundations can be found in my 1990 book, the philosophical underpinnings in my 2003 book; the present volume presents a formal unitary methodological basis for the science of economics that Frisch may have had in mind in his 1931 draft of the constitution of the Econometric Society.[3]

My new formal methodological basis for the science of economics makes it possible to describe the contrast between formal econometrics and present-day applied econometrics in one simple scenario: The data variables constitute a vector-valued random process, $Y = \{y(t, \omega_P); t \in N\}$, on a probability space, $(\Omega_P, \aleph_P, P_P(\cdot))$, where $N = \{0, 1, 2, \dots\}$, Ω_P is a subset of a vector space, $\aleph_P$ is a σ field of subsets of Ω_P, and $P_P(\cdot):\aleph_P \rightarrow [0, 1]$ is a probability measure. The family of finite-dimensional probability distributions of the members of Y relative to $P_P(\cdot)$ is the true probability distribution (TPD) of the data variables. The MPD is, also, a family of finite-dimensional probability distributions of the members of Y. With an MPD I can associate a probability measure, $P_M(\cdot):\aleph_P \rightarrow [0, 1]$, such that Y has the probability distribution MPD relative to $P_M(\cdot)$, and such that Y can be thought of as a vector-valued random process on the probability space, $(\Omega_P, \aleph_P, P_M(\cdot))$. A researcher has two options: He can assume that his observations of the $y(t, \cdot)$ were generated by the TPD version of the data-generating process and analyze his data with present-day econometric methods. He can, also, assume that his observations were generated by the MPD version of the data-generating process and analyze his data with the methods of my formal econometrics. The results of the two analyses provide me with the means I need to contrast present-day econometric analysis with the empirical analysis which my formal econometrics advocates.

The probability measures, $P_P(\cdot)$ and $P_M(\cdot)$, are probability measures on one and the same measurable space, $(\Omega_P, \aleph_P)$. For pedagogical reasons it is useful to think of $(\Omega_P, \aleph_P, P_P(\cdot))$ and $(\Omega_P, \aleph_P, P_M(\cdot))$ as forming part of two different data universes: an upper data universe for $(\Omega_P, \aleph_P, P_P(\cdot))$ and a lower data universe for $(\Omega_P, \aleph_P, P_M(\cdot))$. The picture I have in mind looks roughly like figure 1.1. Here, the bridge connects the theory universe with the lower data universe. The two data universes

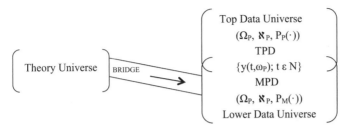

Figure 1.1
A theory universe and two data universes for an empirical contrast.

share the pair, $(\Omega_P, \aleph_P)$ and the random process, Y. The probability distribution of Y is TPD in the upper data universe and MPD in the lower one. I picture in my mind that present-day econometric analyses take place in the upper data universe and empirical analyses in formal econometrics happen in the lower one.

Variants of figure 1.1 play a central role in every chapter of this book. In chapter 2 I use such a variant to describe how the ideas of Frisch and Haavelmo fit in a formal methodological analysis of the problems of econometrics. In chapters 3–5 and 7–9 I apply the underlying ideas of figure 1.1 in case studies in which I compare results of present-day econometric analyses with results of my formal econometric methods. The case studies confront an economic theory with cross-section data and time-series data. The theory is sometimes static and other times dynamic. The results display significant and provocative contrasts between present-day econometric analysis and the methods that my formal science advocates. Both the analyses and the results are very different. Finally, in chapter 10 I use figure 1.1 to discuss the role of congruence and encompassing in formal econometrics. There I show that congruence and encompassing may play a role in formal econometrics that is analogous to the role truth and the Real World play in applied economics. This observation is akin to David Hendry's idea that congruence and encompassing can substitute for truth in the evaluation of econometric models. (See chapter 9 of Hendry 1995.) David Hendry's idea pertains to empirical analyses in the upper data universe in figure 1.1, whereas my result pertains to empirical analyses in the lower data universe.

I conclude the book by discussing what the case studies have taught me about econometric methodology and about the importance of theory in applied econometrics.

The lessons about econometric methodology are of three kinds. I have discovered a novel and theoretically sound way to analyze positively valued time series with currently available software programs. I have, also, learned that the standard ways of analyzing qualitative response models are suspect, and I have found a novel and theoretically sound way of analyzing them. Finally, I have observed that current ways of analyzing cointegrated economic time series leave little room for economic theory in the empirical analysis. This aspect of present-day econometrics hampers a researcher's ability to draw meaningful inferences about social reality from a statistical analysis of such data.

The lessons about the importance of theory in applied econometrics are of two kinds. Lessons of one kind pertain to the behavior characteristics of variables in the two data universes. I have discovered that the behavior characteristics of the data variables in the two universes differ, and I have determined the causes of the differences. The implications that these differences have for applied econometrics, I discuss in chapter 10. Lessons of the other kind concern the information about social reality that the statistical analyses in the two data universes confer. I have discovered that in the upper data universe the statistical analysis establishes relations among Haavelmo's true variables.[4] In the lower data universe the statistical analysis together with the pertinent bridge principles establishes relations among variables in Frisch's model world.[5] The established relations among true variables and among Frischian theory variables, in turn, confer information about interesting characteristics of events and phenomena in social reality. The information about social reality that the statistical analyses in the two data universes convey may, but need not, be the same. When they differ, who is one to believe in—the econometrician in the upper data universe, or his colleague in the lower one? I attend to that question in chapter 10.

1.2 The Axiomatic Method

The axiomatic method is a systematic way of developing a concept, such as consumer choice, from propositions—axioms—about a few undefined terms using only generally accepted logical rules of inference. It plays a pivotal role in my three books. I use the method to construct the sought-for formal unitary methodological basis of a science. Also, I envision that a scientist who accepts the basis will apply the means it provides and the axiomatic method to develop his theories and to formulate the required tests of the empirical relevance of these theories. The power and weaknesses of the axiomatic method as well as its uses in mathematical economics and statistics are detailed in the first book. The way leading econometricians today apply the method to gain knowledge about characteristic features of social reality is exemplified in the second book. And in this book I will utilize the method to examine the consequences of adopting Frisch and Haavelmo's vision of a science of economics.

The uses of the axiomatic method in mathematical economics and statistics have many aspects that are interesting from an applied econometrician's point of view. For example, a consistent axiomatized theory can be used to talk about different matters just by giving the undefined terms different interpretations; the same concept can be derived from many different sets of axioms; and seemingly very different theories may be empirically equivalent. Here I am content to discuss one particular aspect: The extraordinary sensitivity of theories to minor variations in their axioms. Two examples—one from mathematical economics and one from mathematical statistics—will attest to that.

First, mathematical economics: The predominant part of microeconomics that is presented in current undergraduate and first-year graduate courses is a theory in which individuals make their choices with complete knowledge of present and future prices. Such a theory is a theory about choice in an imaginary world that has little in common with the one most humans experience today. It is, therefore, interesting that minor changes to the basic axioms can change the theory into a theory about choice in an uncertain world.

Consider, for example, the certainty theory of consumer choice. It is a theory about four undefined terms, *commodity bundle*, *price*, *consumer*, *and consumption bundle*, whose characteristics are as described in five axioms. The first four axioms claim that a commodity bundle is a vector, $x \in R_+^n$; a price is a vector, $p \in R_{++}^n$; a consumer is a pair, $(V(\cdot), A)$, where $V(\cdot):R_+^n \to R_+$ and $A \in R_{++}$, and a consumption bundle is a commodity bundle that maximizes the value of $V(x)$ subject to the consumer's budget constraint, $px \le A$. The fifth axiom insists that $V(\cdot)$ is continuous, strictly increasing, and strictly quasi-concave with differentiable level sets in $(R_+^n - R_{++}^n) - \{0\}$. If I add a sixth axiom which claims that $V(\cdot)$ is an integral, e.g., when $n = 2$,

$$V(x_1, x_2) = \int_{R_+} U(x_1 + rx_2)f(r)dr, \tag{1.1}$$

where

$U'(\cdot) > 0,$

$U''(\cdot) < 0,$

and

$\int_{R_+} f(r)dr = 1,$

I end up with six axioms from which I can develop Kenneth Arrow and John Pratt's theory of choice among safe and risky assets. (See Arrow 1965 and Pratt 1964.) Thus, by adding an axiom concerning properties of $V(\cdot)$, I turn the certainty theory of consumer choice into an interesting theory of choice under uncertainty. Details are given in chapters 10 and 12 of my 1990 book.

There is an interesting aspect of my formulation of Arrow and Pratt's theory that is relevant here. In the integral representation of $V(\cdot)$ in equation 1.1, the pair $(1, r)$ is the price of a safe asset, x_1, and a risky asset, x_2, which the consumer expects to face in the next period. To me the fact that the probability distribution of r is independent of the current price of (x_1, x_2) is disconcerting since it is likely that an individual's expectation of future prices depend on current prices. If I let the distribution of r depend on (p_1, p_2), an integral representation of $V(\cdot)$ makes $V(\cdot)$ a function of (p_1, p_2) as well as of x_1 and x_2; e.g., with $F(\cdot \,|\, p_1, p_2)$ as the conditional distribution of r given p_1 and p_2,

$$V(p_1, p_2, x_1, x_2) = \int_{R_+} U(x_1 + rx_2)dF(r \,|\, p_1, p_2)), \qquad (1.2)$$

where

$$\int_{R_+} dF(r \,|\, p_1, p_2) = 1.$$

But if that is so, it may be possible to turn the certainty theory of consumer choice into a theory of choice under uncertainty simply by insisting that $V(\cdot)$ is a function of both p and x, and by changing the fifth axiom so that it specifies a characteristic of $V(p, \cdot)$ for each value of p. Theorems T30.2 and T30.3 on pages 801–802 of my 1990 book demonstrates that the idea is a good one provided I assume that $V(\cdot)$ is continuous and that $V(p, \cdot)$ is increasing and strictly concave for each value of p. In the uncertainty version of consumer choice the x-vector may record so many units of $n - 2$ currently available commodities, the number of units of account in cash, and the number of shares in some company.[6]

If small variations in axioms can change the certainty theory of consumer choice into a theory about choice in an uncertain environment, an important question arises: What difference does it make? In the certainty theory of consumer choice one derives Paul Samuelson's fundamental theorem about income and substitution effects and establishes the relation between revealed preference and consistent choice. In Arrow and Pratt's theory one discovers wonderful theorems about absolute and proportional risk aversion and investments in safe and risky assets. However, these theorems are not valid in an uncertain environment in which an individual's expectations depend on current prices. In fact Microeconomics in an uncertain world in which consumers' and entrepreneurs' price expectations depend on current and past prices is very different from microeconomics in Samuelson's and Arrow and Pratt's world. The behavior of individual consumers and firms differs, and fundamental ideas about competitive equilibria and resource allocation are no longer valid. (See Stigum 1969a, 1969b, 1972.) Consequently, minor changes in axioms may lead to changes in the pertinent theory that really matter. The specifics of these observations are given in theorems T 10.9 and T 10.16 in chapter 10, T 12.5 and T 12.6 in chapter 12, and T 30.2–T 30.7 in chapter 30 of my 1990 book.

Next, mathematical statistics: Non-informative improper priors play an important role in Bayesian econometrics. They are improper because they cannot be rationalized as the probability distributions of ordinary random variables. It is, therefore, interesting that minor changes to Andrei Kolmogorov's fundamental axioms of probability will allow such priors to have a role to play in probability theory as well.

Kolmogorov's probability theory is a theory about two undefined terms, an *experiment* and *probability*, that satisfy six axioms. (See Kolmogorov 1933.) The first three axioms insist that an experiment is a pair, $(\Omega, \aleph)$, where Ω is a non-empty set of objects; e.g., the outcomes of an experiment, and $\aleph$ is a σ field of subsets of Ω. The last three axioms insist that probability is the value of a function, $P(\cdot):\aleph \rightarrow [0, 1]$, that is a σ-additive probability measure on $(\Omega, \aleph)$. I can use the two undefined terms to define three useful concepts, a *probability space*, *conditional probability*, and a *conditional probability space*. A probability space is a triple, $(\Omega, \aleph, P(\cdot))$, where $(\Omega, \aleph)$ is an experiment and $P(\cdot)$ is a σ-additive probability measure on $(\Omega, \aleph)$. A conditional probability is the value of a function, $P(\cdot \mid \cdot)$, on the cross-product, $\aleph \times £$, where $£$ designates the family of subsets of Ω that contains all members of $\aleph$ with positive probability. Specifically, $P(\cdot \mid \cdot):\aleph \times £ \rightarrow [0, 1]$, and for all

$B \in \pounds$ and $A \in \aleph$, $P(\cdot \,|\, B)$ is a σ-additive probability measure on $(\Omega, \aleph)$ that satisfies the condition $P(A \,|\, B) = P(A \cap B)/P(B)$. Finally, a conditional probability space is a quadruple, $(\Omega, \aleph, \pounds, P(\cdot \,|\, \cdot))$, whose components are as described above. In the vernacular of probabilists, this quadruple is the full conditional probability space generated by $P(\cdot)$. The finiteness of the generator $P(\cdot)$ ensures that there is no room for improper priors in Kolmogorov's axiom system.

Alfred Rényi's probability theory is a theory about three undefined terms, Kolmogorov's experiment, $(\Omega, \aleph)$, a *bunch of events*, and a *conditional probability space*. (See Rényi 1970.) A bunch of events is a subset of $\aleph$, N, that satisfies three conditions: (1) ϕ does not belong to N; (2) if B_1 and B_2 belong to N, their union also belongs to N; and (3) there is a sequence of members of N, B_i, $i = 1, 2, \dots$ whose union contains Ω. A conditional probability space is a quadruple, $(\Omega, \aleph, N, Q(\cdot \,|\, \cdot))$, where N is a bunch of events and $Q(\cdot \,|\, \cdot){:}\aleph \times N \to [0, 1]$ is a function that for each $B \in N$, $C \in N$, and $A \in \aleph$, satisfies three conditions: (1) $Q(\cdot \,|\, B)$ is a σ-additive probability measure on $(\Omega, \aleph)$, (2) $Q(B \,|\, B) = 1$, and (3) if $C \subset B$, $Q(C \,|\, B) > 0$, and $Q(A \,|\, C) = Q(A \cap C \,|\, B)/Q(C \,|\, B)$. For us the important fact to observe is that if $(\Omega, \aleph, N, Q(\cdot \,|\, \cdot))$ is a conditional probability space, there exists a σ-additive measure, $V(\cdot){:}\aleph \to R_+$, such that for each $B \in N$ and $A \in \aleph$, $0 < V(B) < \infty$, and $Q(A \,|\, B) = V(A \cap B)/V(B)$. $V(\cdot)$ is determined up to a multiplicative constant and σ-finite, that is, there exists a sequence of members of $\aleph$, A_i, $i = 1, 2, \dots$ whose union equals Ω and whose V values are finite. When N contains all sets of finite positive V measure, $(\Omega, \aleph, N, Q(\cdot \,|\, \cdot))$ is the full conditional probability space generated by $V(\cdot)$. Also, when $\Omega \in N$, $V(\cdot)$ can be chosen so that $V(\Omega) = 1$. Then $V(\cdot)$ becomes an ordinary σ-additive probability measure on $(\Omega, \aleph)$. Thus, by choosing conditional probability rather than probability to be an undefined term and by introducing the idea of a bunch of events, Rényi has enlarged upon the scope of Kolmogorov's probability theory. The fact that $V(\cdot)$ need not be bounded ensures that there is plenty of room for the Bayesian improper priors in Rényi's axiom system. Details of all this are given in chapter 18 of my 1990 book.

From a methodological point of view the use of priors in Bayesian econometrics is interesting. In econometrics the probability distributions of the random variables being studied, usually, belong to well-defined classes whose extent is determined by the range of values assumed by certain parameters; e.g., $x(\cdot)$ is normally distributed with mean μ and variance σ^2, where $\mu \in R$ and $\sigma^2 \in R_{++}$. Econometricians, often, assume that—conditional on the true values of these parameters—sequences of the random variables in question are independently and identically distributed. Classical econometricians treat them as independently and identically distributed regardless of whether they know the values of the parameters. Bayesian econometricians assign a prior distribution to the parameters and treat the variables as exchangeable random variables. The two procedures are justifiable if the random variables in question constitute a subset of an infinite sequence of integrable exchangeable random variables with a σ field of tail events that has pertinent characteristics. In the classical case the procedure is justifiable if the σ field of tail events is degenerate (that is, if each of the relevant parameters has a true value). In the Bayesian case the procedure is justifiable if the σ field of tail events contains a sub-σ field with three important properties: (1) It is generated by a function, M. (2) Conditional on the σ field generated by M, the random variables are independently and identically distributed. (3) The distribution of M is in accord with the prior distribution that the Bayesians have assigned. In Kolmogorov's axiom system the distribution of M is a probability distribution. In Rényi's axiom system the distribution of M may be improper in the usual sense of the term. The specifics underlying these observations are given in theorems T 18.4, T 18.6, T 18.7, and T 18.10 in chapter 18 of my 1990 book.[7]

1.3 Model-Theoretic Characterizations of Theories

There are philosophers of science who believe that the best way to think of a scientific theory is to picture it as a set-theoretic predicate that prescribes the conditions that the models of the theory must satisfy. (See, for example, Balzer, Molines, and Sneed 1987.) Some of these conditions determine the conceptual framework within which all the models of the theory must lie. Others describe law-like properties of the entities about which the theory speaks. If one adopts this view of scientific theories, one can think of the scientist as formulating his theory in two steps. He begins by writing down the assertions that characterize the conceptual framework of the theory. He then makes simplifying assumptions about the law-like properties of the elements that play an essential role in its development. The latter assumptions determine a family of models of the original assertions that I take to constitute the searched for theory. In this book I will refer to this two-step way of constructing a scientific theory as *model-theoretic*.[8]

A scientific theory that is constructed in the axiomatic way may be thought of as a set-theoretic predicate as well. Here is an example to fix ideas: The theory of consumer choice under certainty is, in the view of Balzer et al., a predicate, *consumer*, where "consumer" is any quadruple, (X, β, V, C), that satisfies seven conditions. Four of them describe the conceptual framework of the predicate: $X = R_+^n$; β is a family of compact, convex subsets of X; V is a continuous function, $V(\cdot):X \to R_+$; C is a function, $C(\cdot):\beta \to X$. The remaining three conditions list the simplifying assumptions of the theory: $B \in \beta$ if and only if there is a p $\in R_{++}^n$ and an $A \in R_+$ such that $B = \{x \in X: px \leq A\}$; $V(\cdot)$ is strictly increasing, strictly quasi-concave, and has differentiable level sets in $(R_+^n - R_{++}^n) - \{0\}$; if $B \in \beta$, then $C(B) \in B$, and if $x \in B$ and $x \neq C(B)$, then $V(x) < V(C(B))$. Evidently, the conditions that a "consumer" must satisfy are identical to the conditions I listed in the axioms of the theory of consumer choice under certainty.

The preceding example demonstrates that I can formulate a theory as an axiomatic system and think and talk of the theory as a family of models of the axioms. Note, therefore, that in this book a theory is always taken to be a family of models of an axiomatic system. Also, the intended interpretation of an axiomatic system designates the subfamily of models for which the system was developed.

It is important that a reader have a good understanding of the model-theoretic way of formulating economic theories. For that reason, I will present a second example of a set-theoretic predicate. The example I have in mind is a set-theoretic formulation of Maurice Allais' 1988 (U, θ) theory of choice among uncertain prospects. I designate the required predicate by the name, *investor in random prospects A*, where A is short for Allais. An "investor in random prospects A" is any seven-tuple, $(a, P, f_P, u, \theta, W, C)$, that satisfies ten conditions. The first seven conditions describe the conceptual framework: $a \in R_{++}$; $P = \{[(x_1, p_1), \ldots, (x_n, p_n)] \in ([0, a] \times [0, 1])^n; 0 \leq x_1 \leq x_2 \leq \cdots \leq x_n$, and $\Sigma_{1 \leq i \leq n}\, p_i = 1\}$; f_P is the family of all finite subsets of P; u is a function, $u(\cdot):[0, a] \to R_+$; θ is a function, $\theta(\cdot):[0, 1] \to [0, 1]$; W is a function, $W(\cdot):P \to R_+$; and C is a function, $C(\cdot):f_P \to P$. In the intended interpretation, P is a set of random prospects; the value of $u(x)$ is a measure of the utility of a certain return, x; $\theta(\cdot)$ is Allais' specific probability function; $W(z)$ measures the utility of a random prospect, z; and $C(B)$ is the investor's preferred choice among random prospects in B. The simplifying assumptions of the predicate are threefold: $u(\cdot)$ and $\theta(\cdot)$ are continuous and strictly increasing with $\theta(0) = 0$ and $\theta(1) = 1$; if $z = [(x_1, p_1), \ldots, (x_n, p_n)]$ and $z \in P$,

$$W(z) = u(x_1) + \theta(p_2 + \cdots + p_n)(u(x_2) - u(x_1)) + \cdots$$
$$+ \theta(p_n)(u(x_n) - u(x_{n-1})),$$

(1.3)

and if $B \in f_P$ and $z \in B$, $C(B) \in B$ and $W(z) \leq W(C(B))$. The given ten conditions provide a set-theoretic formulation of Allais' (U, θ) theory.

Allais' (U, θ) theory was developed for uncertain situations in which investors typically do not act in accordance with the expected-utility hypothesis. It is, therefore, interesting that the predicate, *investor in uncertain prospects A*, has models in which the utility function, i.e., the $W(\cdot)$ in equation 1.3, ranks prospects according to their expected utility. I can formulate such models of $W(\cdot)$, simply, by insisting that $\theta(r) = r$ for all $r \in [0, 1]$.

In 1952 Allais engaged several illustrious proponents of the expected-utility hypothesis in an experiment in which they were asked to choose between the components of two pairs of random prospects. All of them made choices that could not be rationalized by the expected-utility hypothesis. The next example exhibits a model of an "investor in random prospects A," where the investor in an analogue of Allais' 1952 experiment ranks the prospects in the same way Allais' subjects did.

E1.3.1

Consider an urn in which there are 100 balls that differ only in color, and assume that there are 89 red balls, ten black balls, and one white ball. The urn is shaken well and a blindfolded man is to pull a ball from it. A decision maker is asked to rank the components of the following pairs of prospects:

a_1: $1,000 regardless of which ball is drawn.
a_2: Nothing, $1,000, or $5,000 depending on whether the ball drawn is white, red, or black.
b_1: Nothing if the ball is red; $1,000 otherwise.
b_2: Nothing if the ball is either red or white; $5,000 if the ball is black.

The choice situation that the decision maker faces can be formulated as a choice of investment by "an investor in random prospects A." To see how, observe first that the four prospects can be expressed as a model of four random prospects. To wit: $a_1 = \{(\$1,000, 0.89), (\$1,000, 0.10), (\$1,000, 0.01)\}$; $a_2 = \{(0, 0.01), (\$1,000, 0.89), (\$5,000, 0.10)\}$; b_1: = $\{(0, 0.89), (\$1,000, 0.10), (\$1,000, 0.01)\}$; and $b_2 = \{(0, 0.01), (0, 0.89), (\$5,000, 0.10)\}$. Next, note that I can choose as a model of Allais' specific probability function a function that satisfies the equations, $\theta(0.10) =$ 0.14, $\theta(0.11) = 0.15$, and $\theta(0.99) = 0.97$. Finally, I may choose as a model of $u(\cdot)$ a function that satisfies the equations, $u(0) = 0$, $u(\$1,000) = 0.85$, and $u(\$5,000) = 1$. With $u(\cdot)$ and $\theta(\cdot)$ as described, I can use equation 1.3 to compute the values of $W(\cdot)$ at the given prospects: W at $a_1 = 0.85$, W at $a_2 = 0.837$, W at $b_1 = 0.1275$, and W at $b_2 = 0.14$. But if that is so, the present "investor in random prospects A," like Allais' subjects, orders the components of the given pairs of prospects in a way that cannot be rationalized by the expected-utility hypothesis.

A risky situation is a situation in which the probabilities of the events in question can be calculated. In contrast an uncertain situation is a situation in which the probabilities of the events in question cannot be calculated with reason alone. A long time ago, William Fellner (1961) and Daniel Ellsberg (1961) claimed that decision makers in uncertain situations tended to shade their probabilities when choosing among uncertain prospects. It is, therefore, interesting that there are models of an "investor in random prospects A" in which the investor shades his probabilities of uncertain events, overvalues low probabilities, under-values high probabilities, and makes choices that are controversial. The following example describes a case in point.

E1.3.2
Consider an urn with 90 colored balls. Thirty of the balls are red; the other 60 are either yellow or black. No one knows how many of the sixty balls are yellow. The urn is shaken well, and a blindfolded man is to pull a ball from the urn. The decision maker is asked to choose among the components of two pairs of random prospects that can be expressed as follows:

a_1: \$100 if the ball is red and otherwise nothing.
a_2: \$100 if the ball is black and otherwise nothing.
b_1: \$100 if the ball is either red or black, and otherwise nothing.
b_2: \$100 if the ball is either yellow or black, and otherwise nothing.

The present investor in random prospects has a utility function $u(\cdot)$ that satisfies the equations, $u(0) = 0$ and $u(\$100) = 100$. Also he overvalues low probabilities and undervalues high probabilities. His subjective probability distribution and specific probability function are displayed in table 1.1. There, ω_i designates a ball that has the color i, i = red, yellow, or black. The probability assignments indicate that Allais'

Table 1.1
A probability measure and a specific probability function.

A	Φ	$\{\omega R\}$	$\{\omega Y\}$	$\{\omega B\}$	$\{\omega R, \omega Y\}$	$\{\omega R, \omega B\}$	$\{\omega Y, \omega B\}$	Ω
$p(A)$	0	$1/3 + \tau$	$1/3 - \tau/2$	$1/3 - \tau/2$	$2/3 + \tau/2$	$2/3 + \tau/2$	$2/3 - \tau$	1
$\theta(p(A))$	0	$(2 + \tau)/6$	$(2 + \tau/2)/6$	$(2 + \tau/2)/6$	$(8 - \tau)/12$	$(8 - \tau)/12$	$(8 - 2\tau)/12$	1

investor shades his probabilities of uncertain events, overvalues a low probability, $1/3$, and undervalues a high probability, $2/3$.[9] The given four prospects can be expressed as random prospects as follows:

$a_1 = \{(0, 1/3 - \tau/2), (0, 1/3 - \tau/2), (\$100, 1/3 + \tau)\}$,

$a_2 = \{(0, 1/3 + \tau), (0, 1/3 - \tau/2), (\$100, 1/3 - \tau/2)\}$,

$b_1 = \{(0, 1/3 - \tau/2), (\$100, 1/3 - \tau/2), (\$100, 1/3 + \tau)\}$,

$b_2 = \{(0, 1/3 + \tau), (\$100, 1/3 - \tau/2), (\$100, 1/3 - \tau/2)\}$.

Here τ is taken to be a small number that is much smaller than $1/12$. By using the table and the definition of $W(z)$ in equation 1.3, it is easy to verify that $W(a_1)) = 100(2 + \tau)/6$, $W(a_2) = 100(2 + \tau/2)/6$, $W(b_1) = 100(8 - \tau)/12$, and $W(b_2) = 100(8-2\tau)/12$. Hence the present "investor in random prospects A" prefers a_1 to a_2 and b_1 to b_2. That he prefers a_1 to a_2 is as expected. However, it is controversial that an investor who shades his probabilities in the present uncertain situation can prefer b_1 to b_2 when he prefers a_1 to a_2.

1.4 The Essence of an Economic Theory and the Role of Theory in Theory-Data Confrontations

In this section I will discuss the essence of an axiomatized economic theory, the role of theory in the construction of data, and the difference theory makes in applied econometrics.

1.4.1 The Underlying Ideas of a Theory-Data Confrontation
Figure 1.2 illustrates the underlying ideas of a data confrontation of an economic theory. On the left side of the figure are boxes that contain information pertaining to the theory whose empirical relevance the researcher in charge is studying. There is a box for the theory itself and a box for the subfamily of models of the theory that is at stake in the empirical analysis. The latter box comprises the ingredients by which

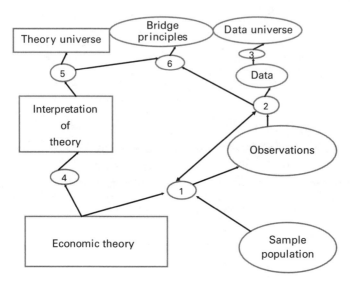

Figure 1.2
A methodological framework for applied econometrics.

the theory-universe box is constructed. On the right-hand side of the figure are boxes that contain information concerning the data-generating process. There is a box for the sample population of whose characteristics the researcher's observations are based, a box for the observations, and a box for the data that the researcher has constructed. The latter box provides the ingredients by which the data-universe box is constructed. The two universes are disjoint and connected by a bridge. The bridge consists of assertions, called bridge principles, that describe how variables in the theory universe are related to variables in the data universe.

It may be difficult to intuit the contents of the various boxes in figure 1.2. Hence, an example to fix ideas is called for.

E1.4.1
A researcher wants to establish the empirical relevance of the standard theory of consumer choice under certainty (TCCC), and he puts the theory in the Economic-Theory box. TCCC is a theory about four undefined terms—*commodity bundle, price, consumer, and consumption bundle*—that has five axioms and a huge family of models. Three subfamilies of models that can be put in the Interpretation-of-Theory box are Franco

Modigliani and Richard Brumberg's Life-Cycle Hypothesis, Milton Friedman's Permanent Income Hypothesis, and Kenneth Arrow and John Pratt's Theory of Risk Aversion. In my 1990 book I confronted the three subfamilies with data. The Sample-Population box comprised US consumers who were alive in 1960, and the Observations box contained information about their disposable incomes and balance sheets in 1962 and 1963. I used the observations to create data for the respective theory-data confrontations. Some of these data provided accurate observations of the associated theory variables (e.g., of a consumer's age). The values of others differed from the values of the corresponding theoretical variables by an additive error term (e.g., observed disposable income equaled the sum of the theory's permanent and transitory income). Friedman's theory failed the test; the other two theories passed.

1.4.2 The Essence of an Axiomatized Economic Theory
An axiomatized economic theory is an abstract idea. What might be the essence of such a theory? There are, probably, many different answers to this question. I believe that Frisch would have claimed that an axiomatized theory pictures "those indefinable things in the real world which we might call 'essentials,' meaning by that essentials with regard to our own ends" (Bjerkholt and Qin 2010, p. 32). I also believe that Haavelmo might have insisted that an economic theory is a system of equations whose members depict economic relations that are autonomous to changes in variables and functions outside the part of social reality to which they themselves pertain (Haavelmo 1944, p. 29). To me an economic theory of choice or development delineates the positive analogies that the originator of the theory considered sufficient to describe the kind of situation that he had in mind.[10]

Analogy is a process of reasoning in which objects and events that are similar in one respect are judged to resemble each other in certain other respects as well. A *positive analogy* for a group of individuals (or a family of events) is a characteristic that the members of the group (family) share. A *negative analogy* is a characteristic that only some of the members of the group (family) possess. For example, I have a theory about Frenchmen: They drink wine. All the Frenchmen I know drink wine. Thus, for the reference group—all the Frenchmen I know—my theory describes a positive analogy. For a larger reference group—e.g., all Frenchmen in France—my theory depicts a negative analogy.

E1.4.2

In an economic theory of the firm, one learns that the manager of a firm chooses his input–output strategy so as to maximize the firm's profits. This characterization provides a succinct description of an important characteristic feature of firm behavior in the theory's reference group of firms in social reality. The firms in the given reference group may produce different products with different combinations of labor and capital. They may be privately owned or public enterprises. Also, they need not all be successful in their search for the technically and allocatively most efficient combination of labor and capital. However, all of them have an input output strategy that aims to make their firm's profits as large as possible.

In this example the firm in the given theory operates in a Frischian model world. The theory may be static or dynamic. Also, from its axioms and theorems one may deduce characteristics of firm behavior besides profit maximization that might be positive analogies in the theory's reference group of firms in social reality. To find reference groups for which characteristics of firm behavior are positive analogies is the task of an applied econometrician.

In reading my characterization of the meaning of economic theories, it is important to keep in mind the following observations:

(1) To say that profit maximization is a positive analogy of firm behavior is very different from saying that the firm behaves *as if* it were maximizing profits. The managers of the firms in the theory's reference group do, by hypothesis, choose their input–output vectors so as to maximize their firms' profits.
(2) Even though an accurate description of the behavior of a particular firm in the theory's reference group would exhibit many negative analogies of firm behavior, the positive analogies that the theory identifies must not be taken to provide an *approximate* description of firm behavior.
(3) The hypotheses that a theory's basic postulates and theorems comprise are valid in the theory's intended universe. One's understanding of the theory and the data that one possesses determine what kind of questions about social reality one can answer in a theory-data confrontation.

With the first point and the third I rule out of court the instrumentalistic view of economic theories expounded by Friedman (1953). With the second and third point I distance my view from the idea that the theorems of an economic theory are tendency laws in the sense John Stuart Mill (1836) gave to this term.

Kevin Hoover (2010) disagrees with my dismissal of Mill's tendency laws. His reasons for that are relevant in the context of this book. Hoover claims that Mill was "an *apriorist* with respect to economic theory," and that his tendency laws can be understood in a way that is consistent with Nancy Cartwright's (1989) notion of causal capacities. Specifically, a *tendency* in Mill's economic theory is the product of a pertinent set of capacities without the interference of other capacities. If in the real world interfering capacities are not too strong, the observed regularities need not differ much from the regularities in the theory. "We might even say," Hoover writes (2010, p. 301), "that [the observed] regularity is approximately [in accord with theory], but the [tendency] *law* is not this regularity but the outcome of the interactions of the [given] capacities in a world without interference."

In *Nature's Capacities and Their Measurement* (1989), Cartwright does not say explicitly what she means by capacity. However she gives many examples; e.g., aspirin has the capacity to relieve headaches (ibid., 3). She also claims that her idea of a causal capacity is akin to Frisch and Haavelmo's idea of an autonomous factor (ibid., pp. 155–156). Finally, in her discussion of Mill's economics she tells the reader that he can take "tendency" to be a synonym for "capacity" or for "the product of a finite number of interacting capacities" as the case may be (ibid., p. 170). Whatever the capacities of nature might be in Social Reality, Mill's 1843 *principle of the uniformity of nature* and Keynes' 1921 *principle of the limited variability of nature* that I postulated for the Social World in Stigum 2003 ensure that there are at most a finite number of capacities in Social Reality.

Hoover's objection is interesting. However, for the purposes of this book my understanding of an economic theory is all right. There are several reasons for this. First, the idea that an axiom or a theorem of economic theory expresses a tendency law is much too vague for applied econometrics. Second, Cartwright's capacities live and function in the real world. Consequently, if a tendency *law* is taken to be the outcome of interactions of pertinent capacities without interference, a tendency law expresses characteristic features of some phenomenon or event in social reality. My theories are about objects in Frisch's model world. Third, it is far from obvious how the capacities of nature can be used effectively in confronting economic theories with data. Therefore, in this book I will insist on using my own understanding of the essence of an economic theory when I deliberate about the problems of econometrics. Also, I will feel free to use tendency, not about laws, but in describing my knowledge of an empirically relevant theoretical hypothesis. Then tendency accounts for the fact that I have analyzed a sample of members of a given population and not the whole population.

1.4.3 Bridge Principles and the Role of Theory in the Construction of Data

One's understanding of the essence of the theory and the data one possesses determine the questions about social reality that one can ask in a theory-data confrontation. In that context, it is important to be aware of the role theory plays in the construction of data in figure 1.2. This role of theory in a theory-data confrontation must be accounted for in the bridge principles.

In some cases, the theory at stake in a theory-data confrontation may determine the content of all three boxes on the right side of figure 1.2. The theory describes the characteristics of a relevant population, imposes restrictions on the kind of information to extract from members of the population, and delineates the way observations are to be used to create data for the empirical analysis. Here is a good example.

E1.4.3

Consider John von Neumann and Oskar Morgenstern's theory of choice under uncertainty. It is a theory about three undefined terms, a *universe*, an *operation*, and a *preference relation*, whose characteristics are as described in five axioms. I put this theory in the Economic Theory box in figure 1.2. In the Interpretation of Theory box I put a subfamily of the models of the theory that are also models of three axioms that delineate the characteristics of the undefined terms, an *option*, a *decision maker*, and a *choice function*.[11]

In accordance with a theorem of von Neumann and Morgenstern's theory, I observe that in the Interpretation of Theory box individual decision makers order random prospects according to their expected utility. To test this hypothesis, I decide to confront a randomly selected member of a given population with a finite number, M, of random prospects, $1,000 with probability q_i and $0 with probability $(1 - q_i)$, i = 1, ... , M. When presenting the various prospects, I begin by asking my subject to record the least number of dollars, z, that he would be willing to receive instead of participating in the prospect. In that way I obtain M values of z, z_i, i = 1, … , M. I use them and the von Neumann-Morgenstern theorem to calculate M + 2 values of the subject's utility function, $W(\cdot):[0, 1{,}000] \to [0, 1]$, with the equations, $W(0) = 0$, $W(1{,}000) = 1$, and $W(z_i) = q_i$, i =1, … , M. Finally, I put the given population of subjects in the Sample Population box; I put 0, 1,000, and the pairs, (q_i, z_i), i = 1, … , M, in the Observations box; and I put (0, W(0)), (1,000, W(1,000)) and the triples, $(q_i, z_i, W(z_i))$, i = 1, … , M, in the Data box.

To complete my description of the present theory-data confrontation I must reveal the contents of the Theory Universe, the Data Universe, and the Bridge Principles box. In the Data Universe I find the pairs and triples that I left in the Data box; i.e., (0, W(0)), (1,000, W(1,000)), and $(q_i, z_i, W(z_i))$, i = 1, … , M, that satisfy the conditions, $W(0) = 0$, $W(1{,}000) = 1$, and $W(z_i) = q_i$, i = 1, … , M. In the Theory Universe I find the pairs, (0, U(0)) and (1,000, U(1,000)), and the triples, $(p_i, x_i, U(x_i))$, i = 1, … , M, that satisfy the equations, $p_i \in (0, 1)$, $x_i \in [0, 1{,}000]$, $U(\cdot):[0, 1{,}000] \to [0, 1]$, $U(0) = 0$, $U(1{,}000) = 1$, and $U(x_i) = p_i$, i = 1, … , M. These pairs and triples I have gathered from the Interpretation of Theory box. I interpret the function $U(\cdot)$ as my decision maker's utility function and the x_i as my decision maker's certainty equivalent of a random prospect: winning $1,000 with probability p_i and $0 with probability $1 - p_i$.

I know that the pairs and triples that I have gathered for the theory universe actually roam around in the theory universe. Also, due to the fact that I have applied von Neumann and Morgenstern's theory to both the theory variables and the data variables, the relations that p_i, x_i, and $U(\cdot)$ satisfy in the theory universe are identical to the relations that the z_i, q_i, and $W(\cdot)$ satisfy in the data universe. Still, there is a fundamental difference. I can observe the z_i, q_i, and the values of $W(\cdot)$ in the data universe. The elements in the theory universe are unobservable. To carry out any kind of empirical analysis with my data, I must describe how the theoretical variables are related to the data variables; i.e., I must specify the bridge principles in the present theory-data confrontation.

When specifying the bridge principles for the present theory-data confrontation I have many options. I can, for example, insist that I have accurate observations of the p_i and the x_i and claim that $U(\cdot)$ and $W(\cdot)$ are alike. That will put a glorious end to the empirical analysis. I can, also, insist that I have accurate observations of the x_i and claim that my subject tends to overvalue low probabilities and undervalue high probabilities. If I do, I may end up with the following bridge principles:

$$x_i = z_i, \ p_i = 0.5 + 4(q_i - 0.5)^3, \quad i = 1, \dots, M. \tag{1.4}$$

Here each p_i is taken to measure my subject's perception of the value of the corresponding prospect's q_i. The given bridge principles imply that

$$W(z_i) = 0.5 + [(U(z_i) - 0.5)/4]^{1/3}, \quad i = 1, \dots, M \tag{1.5}$$

which is an equation I can use as a basis for an empirical analysis of the expected-utility hypothesis. In chapter 9 I will use variants of equations 1.4 and 1.5 to give a scientific explanation of some of the stylized facts that Maurice Allais has observed in his many tests of the expected-utility hypothesis.[12]

In other cases, the theory at stake in the theory-data confrontation and the availability of data determine the content of the Sample-Population and the Observations boxes, while preconceived theoretical ideas determine the way the researcher is to use his observations to create data for the empirical analysis. Here is a good example.

E1.4.4
Consider the certainty theory of the firm in microeconomics. It is a theory about six undefined terms, *input, output, wage, revenue, firm,* and *input-output strategy* whose characteristics are as described in eight axioms. I put this theory in the Economic Theory box.[13] In the Interpretation of Theory box I put a subfamily of models of the theory in which (1) the firm produces one output, y, with three inputs, x_1, x_2, and x_3, in accord with a production function that satisfies the equations, $y^b e^{dy} = A x_1^\alpha x_2^\beta x_3^\gamma$, $y \geq 0$, and $x_i \geq 0$, $i = 1, 2, 3$, where b, d, A, α, β, and γ are positive constants; and (2) the firm's revenue equals the value of y at a given market price, and the wage; i.e., the unit cost of each input, that the firm pays, is a given positive triple, w_1, w_2, and w_3. According to a theorem of the chosen subfamily of models of the theory, the firm will, to minimize the cost of producing a given value of y, choose its inputs so that they satisfy the following equations:

$$y^b e^{dy} = A x_1^\alpha x_2^\beta x_3^\gamma,$$

$$\alpha x_2 / \beta x_1 = w_1 / w_2, \tag{1.6}$$

$$\gamma x_2 / \beta x_3 = w_3 / w_2.$$

I decide to check whether a randomly selected bus transportation company in Norway is a firm that acts in accord with the prescriptions of the theory in the Interpretation of Theory box. In Norway the Norwegian Department of Commerce fixes the outputs and fares of the bus companies and, supposedly, the bus companies always provide their services at minimum costs. So, let y denote the number of kilometers of transportation that the buses of a randomly selected bus transportation company provide during a given period. Let x_1 denote the liters of gasoline, let x_2 denote the hours of labor, and let x_3 denote the units of account of capital that the buses use to produce y. I have data on the kilometers of transportation that the selected bus company provided in Norway during 1991 and the costs of this service; i.e., the cost of gasoline, c_1, labor, c_2, and capital, c_3, that the company incurred in providing the service. Specifically, I have observed the values y^*, x_1^*, x_2^*, x_3^*, c_1^*, c_2^*, and c_3^*, respectively, for y, x_1, x_2, x_3, c_1, c_2, and c_3. I place the bus companies in Norway in 1991 in the Sample Population box. Also, I place my observations, y^*, x_1^*, x_2^*, x_3^*, c_1^*, c_2^*, and c_3^*, in the Observations box. Then, with the given observations, I use the simplest of all index functions to create observations of the price of gasoline, $w_1^* = c_1^*/x_1^*$, the wage rate of labor, $w_2^* = c_2^*/x_2^*$, and the rental price of capital, $w_3^* = c_3^*/x_3^*$, that the bus company paid. Finally, I place y^*, x_1^*, x_2^*, x_3^*, c_1^*, c_2^*, c_3^*, w_1^*, w_2^*, and w_3^* in the Data box.

For the present theory-data confrontation, I place in the theory universe the values of the variables, y, x_1, x_2, x_3, w_1, w_2, w_3, u, v_1, and v_2, that pertain to the selected bus transportation company . I assume that they satisfy equation 1.6 and the equations $u \in R_+$, $v_1 \in R$, and $v_2 \in R$. Also, I transfer the variables in the Data box to the Data Universe. As in E1.4.2 the variables in the data universe are observable. The elements in the theory universe, however, are unobservable. To carry out any kind of empirical analysis with my data, I must describe how the values of the theoretical variables are related to the data variables; i.e., I must specify the pertinent bridge principles.

In confronting my theory with the given data, I postulate the following bridge principles:

$$y = y^*, \tag{1.7}$$

$$y^b e^{dy} = A x_1^{*\alpha} x_2^{*\beta} x_3^{*\gamma} e^{-u}, \tag{1.8}$$

$$x_1/x_2 = x_1^*/x_2^* e^{v_1}, \tag{1.9}$$

$$x_3/x_2 = x_3^*/x_2^* e^{v2}, \tag{1.10}$$

$$w_1 = w_1^*, \quad w_2 = w_2^*, \quad w_3 = w_3^*. \tag{1.11}$$

Here a positive u suggests that the production in the given bus company is technically inefficient. Similarly, non-zero values of v_1 and v_2 indicate that the production of y in the bus company is allocatively inefficient.

The preceding sketch of a formal theory-data confrontation was used by Harald Dale-Olsen in 1994 and Harald Goldstein in 2003 to assess the technical and allocative efficiency of a sample of bus companies in Norway. In the context of this book it is interesting to note that, although Dale-Olsen and Goldstein analyzed the same data and based their analyses on my sketch, their statistical analyses of the data differ significantly. That goes to show that a formal theory-data confrontation need not constrict the ingenuity of an applied econometrician.

1.4.4 Why Theory? What Difference Does It Make in Empirical Analyses?

Finding variables and interesting relations among them that can help us understand the economics of social reality is difficult. There are thousands of possible variables and a gargantuan number of possible relations among them. To do meaningful empirical research an economist needs economic theory to help him pick relevant variables and divine interesting ways to combine them. Also, once he has found the variables and determined their relations empirically, he needs theory to interpret his results and to suggest new ways to combine the given variables with new variables. Finally, theory might help him determine whether an empirical relation is autonomous or not. I will give four examples to explain what I have in mind.

It is not difficult to depicture a theory's role in the interpretation of empirical results, but valid interpretations need not come to mind easily. For example, consider an economist who is out to explore the effect of years of schooling, s, on a person's annual earnings, Y_s. He has obtained a random sample of observations of the pair (Y_s, s), and he decides to estimate the parameters in the equation $\log Y_s = \alpha + \beta s + \eta$, where η is an error term. To interpret his results, he picks a model of Jacob Mincer's (1974, pp. 9–11) "Schooling Model" and assumes that he has accurate observations of Y_s and s. In the resulting interpretation the economist's estimate of α becomes an estimate of $\log Y_0$, and the estimate of β becomes an estimate of the rate of return to schooling of a person who does not invest in human capital beyond his s years of schooling. Evidently, the economist's interpretation is valid only if the model of Mincer's theory, which he chose, is relevant in the given empirical context.

Here is a less obvious example of the role of economic theory in the interpretation of empirical results.

E1.4.5

In 1857 Ernest Engel studied the budgets of 153 Belgian families. The results led him to proclaim his famous law: The poorer a family, the greater the proportion of its total expenditure that must be devoted to the provision of food. Since then applied economists have estimated all sorts of Engel curves; that is, curves that depict the relationship between consumers' expenditures on various commodities and their incomes. (See, for example, Aasnes et al. 1993.) Under the assumption that the certainty theory of consumer choice is empirically relevant, such estimates have an interesting bearing on the relationship between consumer demand for commodities and their prices. To wit, Samuelson's (1953, p. 2) fundamental theorem of consumer choice: "Any good (simple or composite) that is known always to increase in demand when money income alone rises must definitely shrink in demand when its price alone rises."

Samuelson's theorem illustrates how an empirically relevant economic theory can be used to gain insight about relations among one set of variables on the basis of observed relations among a different set of variables. Samuelson's theorem is a fundamental theorem in consumer choice under certainty. The "always" in Samuelson's theorem is short for "in all relevant empirical contexts." If that is correct, it is interesting here that the theorem is not relevant in the uncertain world I described in section 1.2. In an uncertain world the relationship between an Engel curve and the pertinent price change is relevant only in empirical contexts in which the price change does not affect consumers' expectations of future prices.

Empirical analyses of an interesting economic relation may lead to thought-provoking controversies. Here is a good example.

E1.4.6

In 1936 John Maynard Keynes launched his *General Theory of Employment, Interest and Money*. It is a theory about seven undefined terms, *national income, consumption, net investment, interest rate, price level, money,* and *labor,* whose characteristics are as described in seven axioms.[14] One of the axioms insists that consumption, C, is an increasing function of national income, Y, and that changes in Y always result in less than proportionate changes in C. For the purposes of this example, I will insist that the relation between C and Y is linear—i.e., that $C = a + bY$, $a > 0$, $0 < b < 1$, and $(C, Y) \in R_+^2$.

Empirical studies of Keynes' consumption function raised an interesting problem: Cross-section analyses of consumer budgets supported the empirical relevance of Keynes' ideas; i.e., consumer expenditures tended to increase with income and the ratio of consumption to income tended to decrease with income. (See, for example, chart 2A in Brady and Friedman 1947.) Yet time-series data on aggregate consumption and national income suggested that the ratio of consumption to income did not vary much even during periods when national income increased considerably. (See, for example, table 1 in Kuznets 1952.) How can the characteristics of the cross-section data be reconciled with the characteristics of the corresponding time-series data?

Given the role of the consumption function in macroeconomics and in economic policy making, this was a problem that required an explanation. The important thing to notice here is that the problem called for a scientific explanation; i.e., an explanation in which an economic theory plays an essential role. James Duesenberry's (1949) Relative Income Hypothesis, Modigliani and Brumberg's (1955) Life-Cycle Hypothesis, and Friedman's (1957) Permanent Income Hypothesis are examples of economic theories about consumer choice that were conceived to resolve the consumption function controversy. The authors give good arguments for the empirical relevance of their theories, and the three resolutions of the cross-section time-series problem are interesting.[15]

Researchers often experience that the relations which their theoretical models depict are much more complicated than the relations that their data reveal. According to Haavelmo (1944, p. 26), the puzzlement is "a result of confusing two different kinds of variations of economic variables, namely hypothetical *free* variations, and variations which are restricted by a system of simultaneous relations."

The following example presents a case in point and illustrates how economic theory can be used to question the autonomy of an empirical relation.

E1.4.7
I have put an economic theory in the Economic Theory box in figure
1.2. In the Interpretation of Theory box I have put a certain subfamily
of models of the theory. The subfamily concerns four real-valued variables, y, u, z, and w, that satisfy the equation

$$y = a + bu + cz + dw, \tag{1.12}$$

where a, b, c, and d are constants. I have, also, obtained a finite random
sample of values of the four variables. My observations of u, z, and w
are accurate, while my observations of y are marred by an additive
error, η. Hence my bridge principles insist that

$$\hat{y} = y + \eta, \qquad \hat{u} = u, \quad \hat{z} = z, \text{ and } \quad \hat{w} = w. \tag{1.13}$$

From equations 1.12 and 1.13 I infer that

$$\hat{y} = a + b\hat{u} + c\hat{z} + d\hat{w} + \eta. \tag{1.14}$$

I assume that η is normally distributed with mean 0 and finite variance,
that $\hat{u}$, $\hat{z}$, and $\hat{w}$ have finite variances, and that η is orthogonal to $\hat{u}$, $\hat{z}$,
and $\hat{w}$. If these assumptions are correct, I can obtain good maximum-
likelihood estimates of the constants a, b, c, and d.

Suppose, now, that in the given sample population $\hat{u}$, $\hat{z}$, and $\hat{w}$ satisfy
two additional linear equations:

$$\hat{z} = \alpha + \beta\hat{u} + \varphi\hat{w} \tag{1.15}$$

and

$$\hat{w} = \gamma + \psi\hat{u} + \delta\hat{z}. \tag{1.16}$$

From these equations it follows that

$$(\hat{z},\hat{w}) = (1 - \delta\varphi)^{-1}[(\alpha + \varphi\gamma) + (\beta + \varphi\psi)\hat{u}, (\gamma + \alpha\delta) + (\psi + \alpha\beta)\hat{u}]. \tag{1.17}$$

Hence, if $1 \neq \delta\varphi$, in the given sample population

$$\hat{y} = A + B\hat{u} + \eta, \tag{1.18}$$

where

$$A = a + (1 - \delta\varphi)^{-1}[c(\alpha + \varphi\gamma) + d(\gamma + \alpha\delta)]$$

and

$$B = b + (1 - \delta\varphi)^{-1}[c(\beta + \varphi\psi) + d(\psi + \alpha\beta)].$$

I do not know about equations 1.15 and 1.16, and my maximum-likelihood estimates of equation 1.14 need not look like equation 1.18. Be that as it may. My example provides an illustration of Haavelmo's observation on free variations and variations within a simultaneous system of equations. This is so regardless of whether the relations in equations 1.12, 1.15, and 1.16 form part of a larger economic system, like a system that Haavelmo might have had in mind, or whether equations 1.15 and 1.16 depict relations that prevail only in the given sample population.

The illustration comes with an interesting twist. Equation 1.14 is deduced from equation 1.12, which depicts an unobservable relation that is valid in my model world. Still, if the empirical relevance of equation 1.12 has been established in other empirical contexts, I can use equation 1.14 to question the autonomy of the relation in equation 1.18. In that way my example illustrates how an empirically relevant theory can be used to question the autonomy of an empirical relation.

1.5 A Preview of the Book

In this section I will give a brief description of the contents of the remaining nine chapters. My goal for the book has been to provide ideas for a meaningful discussion of the best way to incorporate economic theory in empirical analyses. In pursuing this goal I have followed in the footsteps of many illustrious economists and econometricians. In addition to Frisch and Haavelmo, I have in mind Wassily Leontief for his input-output analysis, Gottfried von Haberler, Jan Tinbergen, and John Maynard Keynes for their contributions to the Tinbergen debate; Arthur Burns and Wesley Mitchell, Tjalling Koopmans, and Kenneth Wolpin for their contributions to the measurement-without-theory debate; and Paul Samuelson, Robert Solow, Maurice Allais, and Gerard Debreu for their contributions to mathematical economics. Those authors' understandings of the essence of an economic theory and their views of econometrics are very different from mine. However, they agree with me that the role of theory in applied econometrics deserves a serious discussion.[16]

Chapter 2 has three purposes: to present Frisch and Haavelmo's ideas about a science of economics, to explicate in simple terms the meaning of a formal theory-data confrontation, and to describe and resolve an interesting riddle in applied econometrics. Frisch and

Haavelmo's idea of a unified theoretical-quantitative and empirical-quantitative approach to economic problems can be realized in several ways. In one way the researcher identifies his theory variables with Haavelmo's true variables and carries out his empirical analysis the way present-day econometricians do. In the other way the researcher identifies his theory variables with variables in Frisch's model world and carries out his empirical analysis as depicted in a formal theory-data confrontation. The intricacies of a formal theory-data confrontation are not easy to grasp. Therefore, I devote many pages to describing the component parts of a formal theory-data confrontation and explaining how the parts interact in a pertinent empirical analysis. I give many examples that ought to make it possible for a reader to understand and appreciate the various empirical analyses in chapters 3 and 4. In the last section of chapter 2 I pose and resolve a riddle: How is it possible to learn about interesting aspects of social reality with theories about objects in Frisch's model world and data whose references belong in a socially constructed world of ideas? My resolution of the riddle provides motivation for my deliberations in the ensuing chapters.

In chapter 3 I set out to explain and illustrate what it means for an economic theory to be empirically relevant in the two data universes of figure 1.1. The outcome of a test of a theory's empirical relevance depends both on the empirical context in which the theoretical hypothesis is tested and on the pertinent explication of empirical relevance. In figure 1.1 the empirical context in the upper data universe is determined by the characteristics of the TPD. In the lower data universe the empirical context is determined by the bridge principles and the relevant family of models of the MPD. The explication of empirical relevance in the upper data universe is like a description of a test of hypothesis in mathematical statistics. In the lower data universe the explication is different because the pertinent theory whose relevance one searches is located in the theory universe and not in the given data universe. I show how different the explication is in examples of theory-data confrontations from four fields of economics, experimental economics, consumer choice under certainty, simultaneous equations, and risk aversion and choice of risky assets. The examples illustrate interesting aspects of the ideas of empirical relevance that I am trying to convey. In the experimental-economics example, the researcher in charge has accurate observations of his theory variables. In the consumer-choice example the theory axioms have only one model. In the simultaneous-equations example the theory axioms have any number of models that are interrelated in interesting ways. Finally, the risk-aversion example presents an empirical analysis in which the empirical relevance of a single theorem of a theory is at stake. The examples demonstrate that the outcome of a test of the empirical relevance of a theoretical hypothesis need not be the same in the two data universes of figure 1.1.

In chapter 4 I discuss current econometric analyses of qualitative response models. A *qualitative response model* is an econometric model in which the dependent variable is either discrete or half-discrete and half-continuous. Such models are interesting in the context of this book for several reasons. Theory-data confrontations of qualitative response models prescribe an empirical analysis of inaccurate observations with distinctive bridge principles. Also, each prototype of such models prescribe two seemingly equivalent empirical analyses, one for the upper data universe in figure 1.1 and one for the lower data universe. I demonstrate that an empirical analysis of a qualitative response model must be interpreted with care. Maximum-likelihood estimates of the parameters of a qualitative response model may be empirically irrelevant. Also, the fact that the empirical analysis of the two seemingly equivalent models happen in different universes has an interesting consequence: the empirical relevance of one of the models need not mean that the other is empirically relevant.

Chapter 5 begins with a discussion of formal theory-data confrontations in which the sample population plays a significant role. Cross-section analyses with data that are generated by a stratified random sampling scheme are good examples. The formalism differs from the theory-data confrontations in chapters 3 and 4, but the fundamental ideas of the empirical analysis are the same. The chapter presents two cases in point. First, the empirical relevance of Friedman's Permanent Income Hypothesis (PIH) in the 1963 population of US consumers is tested in accord with the prescriptions of a formal theory-data confrontation. Then, the preceding test is contrasted with a test that an econometrician in the spirit of Frisch 1934 and Haavelmo 1944 might have carried out with the same data. The contrast throws new light on the use of theory in the measurement of economic relations.

In the context of the book the two empirical analyses in the present chapter become especially interesting when compared with the analyses in section 3.3. The effect which a small change in the axioms of section 3.3 has on the analysis in this chapter is dramatic. In section 3.3 it was not possible to formulate a meaningful alternative hypothesis to

Friedman's null hypothesis that permanent consumption is proportional to permanent income. With a minor change in the axioms of section 3.3, I subject Friedman's hypothesis to a stringent statistical test.

Chapter 6 provides an introduction to formal theory-data confrontations with time-series data. It begins with the axioms of an empirical analysis in which the vectors in section 2.2 become vector-valued sequences and the vector-valued random variables become vector-valued random processes. Then it describes salient characteristics of ARIMA processes. Of these there are two that matter the most. First, ARIMA processes tend to display long positive and negative sojourns. This long-run property of ARIMA processes is used to demonstrate that a meaningful empirical analysis of positively valued time series can be carried out with the help of auxiliary variables. Secondly, any multi-dimensional ARIMA process can be written as an error-correction model on the basis of which the degree of cointegration of the component processes is determined. This search for cointegrated processes is exclusive. It fails to consider the possibility that other theoretically meaningful cointegrating relations may exist. The chapter describes one such relation.

Chapter 7 has two purposes: to study methodological problems that arise in analyzing positively valued time series in foreign exchange and to contrast the analysis of time series that a formal theory-data confrontation prescribes with the analysis of time series that present-day econometric theory prescribes.

The methodological problems occur in a study of the dynamics of foreign exchange because exchange rates are positively valued variables whereas pertinent statistical programs are designed for the analysis of time series of variables that assume both positive and negative values. One can solve the problems in one of two ways. The standard way is to formulate axioms for a data confrontation of log transforms of the actual theory variables with log transforms of the data variables. A different way is to formulate axioms for the theory-data confrontation in which actual and auxiliary theory and data variables interact in such a way that the problem disappears. I prefer the second way, and in this chapter I explain why and present a case study of spot and forward exchange to show how the second way is carried out.

To contrast my axiomatic way of analyzing economic time series with the present-day econometric way of doing it, I begin by formulating a data confrontation of a theory of the dynamics of spot and forward rates in foreign exchange. The data I have consist of observations of spot and forward rates in the market for Swiss francs and US dollars. In section 6.3 Harald Goldstein carries out the analysis of the data that my theory-data confrontation prescribes; in section 6.4 André Anundsen analyzes the same data with David Hendry's and Søren Johansen's methods. My theory is empirically relevant in the empirical context that my bridge principles and Goldstein's estimate of the pertinent MPD determine. Under the assumption that my observations of the theory variables are accurate, my theory is, also, empirically relevant in the empirical context that Anundsen's analysis creates. It is, therefore, interesting that the dynamics of spot and forward rates in Goldstein's universe are very different from their dynamics in Anundsen's universe.

In chapter 8 I have two aims. On the one hand, I want to develop a novel theory of non-linear cointegration among second-order random processes. On the other, I want to present a second demonstration of how different time-series analysis in a formal theory-data confrontation is from the time-series analysis which present-day econometrics prescribes.

I begin by explaining why the accepted characterization of integrated second-order random processes is inadequate for the analysis of non-linearly cointegrated economic systems. Then, I propose alternative characterizations of integrated processes and describe how the new concepts differ from analogous concepts that Clive Granger (1991, 1995) and F. M. Aparicio Acosta et al. (2002) have proposed. Finally, I develop novel ideas of non-linearly cointegrated and non-linearly polynomially cointegrated second-order random processes that generalize upon ideas of Terje Myklebust et al. (2002), Juan-Carlos Escanciano and Alvaro Escribano (2009), and Stéphane Gregoir and Guy Laroque (1993).

In section 8.2, for the purpose of checking the empirical relevance of my mathematical concepts of non-linear cointegration, I develop an economic theory of foreign exchange whose variables have behavior characteristics like the random processes in the mathematical theory. In sections 8.3 and 8.4 I confront this economic theory with data from the Swiss franc, euro, and US dollar market. Harald Goldstein carries out the empirical analysis in section 8.3. His estimates of the MPD distribution of my data demonstrate that my economic theory has empirical relevance in the given currency market. In doing that, Goldstein's analysis, also, establishes the empirical relevance of my mathematical concepts of non-linear cointegration. In section 8.4, André

Anundsen, in the spirit of Haavelmo's Treatise and with Hendry and Johansen's methods, analyzes the same data to establish characteristics of their TPD distribution. It turns out that the dynamics of foreign exchange in the TPD distribution are very different from the dynamics of foreign exchange in the estimated MPD distribution. Also, under the assumption that my observations of the theory variables are accurate, my theory is not empirically relevant in the empirical context that Anundsen creates.

In chapter 9 I give two formal characterizations of logically and empirically adequate scientific explanations—one (SE1) for economics and one (SE2) for econometrics. I exemplify them with scientific explanations of interesting observed regularities in experimental economics and in the dynamics of financial markets. For motivation and for ease of reference I begin by discussing relevant aspects of Carl Hempel's fundamental ideas as they appear in chapters 10 and 12 of his 1965 book *Aspects of Scientific Explanation* and in Wesley Salmon's interesting 1989 survey article "Four Decades of Scientific Explanation."

According to Hempel's (1965, pp. 245–251) *deductive-nomological scheme* (DNS), a scientific explanation of an event or a phenomenon must have four elements: a sentence E that describes the event or the phenomenon; a list of relevant antecedent conditions, $C_1, C_2, \ldots , C_n$; a list of general laws $L_1, L_2, \ldots , L_k$; and arguments that demonstrate that E is a logical consequence of the C's and the L's. From my perspective, the DNS is a theory-data confrontation in reverse that, superficially, is not too different from my SE1 scheme for scientific explanation in economics. With the proper translation, SE1, can be made to look like a DNS explanation. However, there is a fundamental difference. Hempel's L's are laws. My L's are economic theories of limited empirical relevance.

The situation envisaged in Hempel's DNS and in my SE1 is similar to the experimental tests of physical theories that Pierre Duhem described on pages 144–147 of his 1954 book *The Aim and Structure of Physical Theory*. However, it differs from the situations econometricians usually face when they search for the empirical relevance of economic theories. In SE1 and in a DNS, E is a family of sentences each of which has a truth value in every model of the data universe. In contrast, in econometrics E is often a family of statistical relations. For example, an E might insist that "on the average, families with high incomes save a greater proportion of their incomes than families with low incomes." Such assertions make claims about properties of the data-generating process that need not have a truth value in a model of the data universe. Thus, for the purposes of a scientific explanation in econometrics, SE1 is inadequate.

In subsection 9.2.1 I formulate SE2, a scheme for scientific explanations in econometrics. In sections 9.3 and 9.4 I present an example in which I provide a scientific explanation of a regularity in the market for US Treasury Bills (Hall et al. 1992). My scientific explanation of the observed regularity in financial markets has several interesting aspects. The observed regularity describes a characteristic of the TPD in the upper data universe of a pertinent formal theory-data confrontation. My explanation establishes the existence in the corresponding lower data universe of an MPD that has the observed characteristics of the TPD. The MPD is different from the TPD, and the empirical context that the MPD determines in the lower data universe is different from the empirical context that the TPD determines in the upper data universe. How different the empirical contexts are is borne out in two interesting statistical analyses by Geir Storvik and Heather Anderson. Storvik's estimates establish the empirical adequacy of my scientific explanation in the lower data universe. Heather's analysis finds no reason to reject the conjecture of Hall et al. in the upper data universe. The differences in the empirical contexts that Storvik and Anderson's analyses create raise an interesting question about the adequacy of my scientific explanation of the conjecture of Hall et al.

I begin chapter 10 with a discussion of the status of bridge principles in applied economics. I then show how the ideas of encompassing and congruence can be used to determine the status of bridge principles in formal theory-data confrontations in econometrics. I conclude with a discussion of what the contents of the book have taught me about econometric methodology and about the use of theory in applied econometrics.

2 A Vision of a Science of Economics

Economic science is systematized knowledge about the nature of social reality that pertains to economic matters. Economists derive such knowledge from theories about toys in toy economies and sophisticated statistical analyses of data whose references belong in a socially constructed world of ideas. The toy economies and economists' world of ideas have little in common with social reality—a fact that renders successful searches for knowledge about economic aspects of social reality questionable.[1]

The scientific work that economists carry out is a varied lot with a common problem. Economists develop theories and collect data to determine the empirical relevance of their theories; they provide scientific explanations for regularities that they observe in their data; and they use their theories and data to make predictions about the future of relevant economic phenomena and events. In such endeavors economists face a special problem: What is the best way to incorporate economic theory in the empirical analysis when the variables of the theory have no obvious counterparts among the data variables?

In this book I shall use case studies to contrast the way researchers in present-day econometrics and formal econometrics incorporate economic theory in their empirical analyses. The various case studies confront the researcher's theory with cross-section data and time-series data, and the theory is sometimes static and other times dynamic. In present-day econometrics, theory and data variables reside in the same universe, and empirical analysis is carried out in accord with postulated characteristics of the data-generating process. In formal econometrics, theory and data variables reside in two disjoint universes that are connected by a bridge. Then the empirical analysis is carried out in accord with the characteristics of a probability distribution that differs in uncertain ways from the pertinent data-generating process. These differences in statistical inference have interesting consequences. They cause the concepts of congruence and encompassing to assume different meanings in present-day and formal econometrics. Also, a theory may be empirically relevant in present-day econometrics but not in formal econometrics, and vice versa.

The ideas that I present in the book originated in the works of two of the founding fathers of econometrics, Ragnar Frisch and Trygve Haavelmo. Therefore, I will begin the non-introductory part of the book with a chapter that describes how the ideas of Frisch and Haavelmo fit in a formal methodological analysis of the problems of econometrics and asks whether they left us with the means one needs to obtain knowledge about interesting economic aspects of social reality. My answer to the question is yes. With the proper understanding of the essence of an economic theory, applied econometricians have the means to learn about characteristic features of the economics of social reality. The ensuing chapters, each in its own way, lend support to my contention.

2.1 Frisch and Haavelmo's Vision of a Science of Economics

Ragnar Frisch and Trygve Haavelmo had a vision of economics as a science. In this vision the theoretical-quantitative and the empirical-quantitative approaches to economic problems were to be unified. Frisch formulated the idea in drafting the Constitution of the Econometric Society (1931), and Haavelmo demonstrated the possibility of creating such a science in his treatise *The Probability Approach in Econometrics* (1944). In this section and the next I will discuss some of the unforeseen consequences for applied econometrics of adopting the vision of Frisch and Haavelmo.

The respective component parts of their vision of a science of economics differed. They agreed that theoretical "models are necessary tools in our attempts to understand and "explain" events in real life" (Haavelmo 1944, p.1). However, to Frisch a theory comprised a finite number of non-contradictory axioms about relations in a model world and all the logical consequences of the axioms (Bjerkholt and Qin 2010, pp. 32–33). To Haavelmo, a theoretical model was, instead, a system of (ordinary or functional) equations that express definitional identities, technical relations, or relations depicting behavior (1944, p. 2).

They agreed that one lends meaning to an economic theory by describing the elements in real life to which the variables of the theory correspond. However, Frisch insisted that an economic theory, like a theory in the natural sciences, received its concepts from the relations that the originator of the theory had observed in real life (1926, p. 302). In contrast, Haavelmo insisted that assigning names to theoretical variables was like imagining an experiment in which one would measure those quantities in real economic life that were thought "to obey the laws imposed on their theoretical namesakes" (1944, p. 6).

They agreed that the world of observations is disjoint from the model world, and that the relationship between observations and theory-related elements in the real world is complicated. In his 1934 treatise *Statistical Confluence Analysis by Means of Complete Regression Systems*, Frisch discussed both errors in variables and errors in equations without relating them to a model world. In his 1930 Yale lectures, published as *A Dynamic Approach to Economic Theory*, he insisted that the regularities that were discovered in the world of observations, the *empirical laws*, and the mental pictures of these regularities in the model world, the *rational laws*, were fundamentally different: "Between them there exists a gap, which can never be bridged." (Bjerkholt and Qin 2010, p. 34) In the treatise, Haavelmo distinguished between three kinds of variables, theoretical, true, and observational variables. The *theoretical* variables were variables in the researcher's theory. The *true* variables were variables in the real world with which the researcher identified his theory variables. And the *observational* variables were variables in the researcher's world of observations. If the denotation of the available observational variables differed from the denotation of the true variables, Haavelmo would bridge the gap between theory and observations by correcting his observations and/or adjusting the theory so as to make the facts, which he considered to be the true variables, relevant to his theory (Haavelmo 1944, p. 7).

The respective contours of Frisch and Haavelmo's vision of a science of economics differed. Frisch was an extraordinary mathematical economist. (See Frisch 1933 and lectures 1 and 2 in Bjerkholt and Dupont-Kieffer 2009.) He was also an extraordinary mathematical statistician. (See Frisch 1929, 1934.) To judge from his published works, Frisch's vision of a science of economics must have been a vision of a formal science of economics, a science in which the fields of mathematical economics and mathematical statistics are conjoined. However, as his Poincaré Lectures (Bjerkholt and Dupont-Kieffer 2009) and his Yale lectures (Bjerkholt and Qin 2010) demonstrate, he did not know how to put such a science together.

Now, Haavelmo was an extraordinary econometrician. (See, for instance, Haavelmo 1943, 1947a, and 1947b.) He was also a philosopher of science with novel ideas. His 1944 treatise bears witness to that. In it, Haavelmo showed a way in which the theoretical-quantitative and the empirical-quantitative approaches to economic problems can be unified. In doing that he demonstrated the possibility of creating a science of economics.

Economics in 1944 satisfied two of three conditions for a branch of knowledge to be called a science: (1) it was concerned with establishing and systematizing facts and principles and (2) its arguments were based on logically consistent and precisely formulated theories whose empirical relevance could be tested with the data and the statistical methods at hand. Haavelmo's Treatise provided the ingredients for satisfying the third condition—the existence of a unitary methodological basis for analyzing pertinent theoretical and empirical problems.[2] In doing that, Haavelmo's treatise, in fact, established economics as a science. The resulting science of economics was not formal the way Frisch envisioned it, but its vitality has been amply demonstrated in the last 70 years.

2.2 A Formal Unitary Methodological Basis for the Science of Economics

Haavelmo's treatise was extraordinarily influential. Its insights were absorbed so thoroughly that it became difficult to think of them as insights (Aldrich 1989). Yet a question remains in my mind: Is it possible that Haavelmo's ideas were accepted too quickly? Many econometricians must believe that they were. To wit: (1) Aris Spanos' observation that, unfortunately for econometrics, Haavelmo's remarkable monograph became a classic much too early (Spanos 1989, p. 409), and (2) the Econometric Society's decision in 2009 to establish a new journal, *Quantitative Economics*, that was to provide a home for papers that fulfilled Frisch's vision of a science of economics. I believe that the answer to my question is Yes, and in this section I will show why by exhibiting how Haavelmo's ideas appear in the context of a formal unitary methodological basis for the science of economics.

A unitary methodological basis for analyzing the theoretical and empirical problems of a science is formal if it has been given definite form as an axiomatic system. I shall, in this section, present a formal unitary methodological basis for the science of economics that I believe is the kind Frisch may have envisioned when he drafted the constitution of the Econometric Society.

2.2.1 Modeling Theory-Data Confrontations in Econometrics

Modeling theory-data confrontations in econometrics is problematic. There is no accepted formalism, and applied econometricians are at odds about the use of bridge principles in empirical analyses. Here, I will write axioms for a theory-data confrontation in agreement with the ideas that I depicted in figure 1.2.

Strictly speaking, the data confrontation of a theory takes place in the three top boxes of figure 1.2. Hence, I may picture a formal theory-data confrontation as being carried out in one of two abstract scenarios: In one of them, the researcher in charge identifies his theory variables with *true* variables in the real world (Haavelmo 1944, p. 8), and he may or may not assume that he has accurate observations on all the relevant theoretical variables. The researcher sees no need for bridge principles in empirical analysis. He formulates his theory, describes his data, and carries out the empirical analysis in the data universe. Then the theory-data confrontation reduces to the data universe alone. I believe that this abstract scenario depicts the way most applied and theoretical econometrics are carried out today.

In the other scenario, the researcher, like Frisch (Bjerkholt and Qin 2010, p. 34), believes that there is a definite divide between his model world and the world of observations, and that his data need not provide accurate measurements of the undefined terms of his theory. He formulates his theory in a theory universe and uses bridge principles to describe how his theoretical variables are related to his data variables. Then the theory-data confrontation becomes a triple of two disjoint universes—one for theory and one for data—and a bridge between them.

The two abstract scenarios of a theory-data confrontation leave out many details. Although it is true that the first scenario pictures the way most applied econometrics is carried out today, it is also true that there are many different methodologies that provide guiding hands to the various practitioners—among them the error-statistical reformulation of Haavelmo's methodology that Aris Spanos presented in 1989 and 2012, Ragnar Frisch's 1934 confluence analysis, the London School of Economics (LSE) approach to time-series analysis (Mizon 1995; Hendry and Krolzig 2003), and Bayesian econometrics (Stigum 1967; Zellner 1971). Similarly, the second scenario is exemplified in one way in time-series analyses and in another in cross-section analyses with data that are generated by a stratified random sampling scheme.

The ideas underlying the empirical analysis that the second scenario envisions are my own. Judging from the response they have received, I must take time to spell them out in simple terms with many examples. I will do that in three steps. I begin in this section by discussing theory-data confrontations in which the data have been obtained in a purely random sampling scheme. In chapter 5 I present a cross-section analysis of data that have been obtained in a stratified random sampling scheme, and in chapter 6 I delineate the ideas underlying a formal theory-data confrontation with time-series data. Case studies to go with the three steps are given in chapters 3 and 4 for the first step, in chapter 5 for the second step, and in chapters 7–9 for the third step.

2.2.2 Theory-Data Confrontations with Two Disjoint Universes and a Bridge

Theory-data confrontations in which the data are obtained in a purely random sampling scheme depict a formal empirical analysis in which the sample population plays no central role. To simplify my arguments, I formulate axioms for a case in which the researcher samples at random only once in the Observations box in figure 1.2. My discussion ends with a formal theory-data confrontation in which I contrast my kind of empirical analysis with the kind of empirical analysis that Spanos' error-statistical reformulation of Haavelmo's methodology prescribes.

The Data Universe

Formally, the data universe in an axiomatized theory-data confrontation is a triple, $(\Omega_P, \Gamma_p, (\Omega_P, \aleph_P, P_P(\cdot)))$, where Ω_P is a subset of a vector space, Γ_p is a finite set of axioms that vectors in Ω_P must satisfy, and $(\Omega_P, \aleph_P, P_P(\cdot))$ is a probability space, where $\aleph_P$ is a σ field of subsets of Ω_P and $P_P(\cdot):\aleph_P \to [0, 1]$ is a probability measure. In the applications that I have in mind for this section there are two axioms in Γ_P that concern the conceptual framework of the data-generating process. One insists that $\Omega_P \subset R^k$. Thus $\omega_P \in \Omega_P$ only if $\omega_P = y$ for some $y \in R^k$. The other lets $y(\cdot): \Omega_P \to R^k$ be a vector-valued function that is defined by the equations $y(\omega_P) = \omega_P$ and $\omega_P \in \Omega_P$, and insists that $y(\cdot)$ is measurable with respect to $\aleph_P$ and that $y(\cdot)$, subject to the conditions on which Γ_P insists, has a well-defined probability distribution relative to $P_P(\cdot)$. This probability distribution is the true probability distribution of $y(\cdot)$. I denote it by TPD, where T stands for true, P for probability, and D for distribution.

In reading this description of the data universe there are several characteristics to notice. The Ω_P that appears in two places is one and the same subset of a vector space. Also, $\aleph_P$ is a family of subsets of the given vector space, and $P_P(\cdot)$ assigns numbers to these subsets. Moreover, that $y(\cdot): \Omega_P \to R^k$ is a vector-valued function means that, at any ω_P in the domain of $y(\cdot)$, $y(\omega_P) = (y_1(\omega_P), \ldots, y_k(\omega_P))$. For such a function, $y(\omega_P) = \omega_P$ is short for $(y_1(\omega_P), \ldots, y_k(\omega_P)) = \omega_P$. In the present theory-data confrontation y plays two roles: that of a vector in Ω_P and that of a vector-valued random variable on $(\Omega_P, \aleph_P)$. The components of y can be observed, and the values that $P_P(\cdot)$ assigns to the members of $\aleph_P$ can (ideally, at least) be calculated. Here is an example.

E2.2.1
Consider a city, called OS, that has a million inhabitants. Let a consumer be an individual living alone or a family living together and having a common budget. Suppose that there is a uniform way of measuring each consumer's disposable income, y, and that there are 200,000 consumers in OS. According to a knowledgeable demon, the last year 10,000 consumers had seven units of account in disposable income, 40,000 had five units, 100,000 had three units, and 50,000 had one unit. If I let $\Omega_P = \{1, 3, 5, 7\}$, $\omega_P \in \Omega_P$ only if $\omega_P = y$ for some $y \in \{1, 3, 5, 7\}$. Also, if I let $\aleph_P$ be the field of all subsets of Ω_P, I find that I can calculate the values that $P_P(\cdot)$ assigns to the members of $\aleph_P$. To wit: $P_P(A) = 1/4, 1/2\ 1/5$, and $1/20$ according as $A = \{1\}, \{3\}, \{5\}$, or $\{7\}$. Finally, if I let $y(\cdot): \Omega_P \to \{1, 3, 5, 7\}$ be defined by the equations $y(\omega_P) = \omega_P$ and $\omega_P \in \Omega_P$, I find that $y(\cdot)$ is measurable with respect to $\aleph_P$, and that I can calculate interesting probabilities concerning the values of y; e.g., $P_P(\{\omega_P \in \Omega_P: y(\omega_P) > 1\}) = 3/4$ and $P_P(\{\omega_P \in \Omega_P: y(\omega_P) < 7\}) = 19/20$. Thus, if I were to sample at random among consumers in OS, the probability of my observing a consumer with disposable income greater than 1 unit of account equals 3/4, and the probability of my observing one with a disposable income of fewer than seven units is 19/20.

The Theory Universe
Formally, the theory universe in an axiomatized theory-data confrontation is a triple, $(\Omega_T, \Gamma_T, (\Omega_T, \aleph_T, P_T(\cdot)))$, where Ω_T is a subset of a vector space, Γ_T is a finite set of assertions that the vectors in Ω_T must satisfy, $\aleph_T$ is a σ field of subsets of Ω_T, and $P_T(\cdot): \aleph_T \to [0, 1]$ is a probability measure. In the applications that I have in mind for this section, there are two assertions in Γ_T that describe the researcher in charge's idea of a conceptual

framework for the theory he confronts with data. One insists that $\Omega_T \subset R^{h+k}$. Thus $\omega_T \in \Omega_T$ only if $\omega_T = (x, u)$ for some $x \in R^h$, $u \in R^k$, and $(x, u) \in R^{h+k}$. The other lets $x(\cdot): \Omega_T \to R^h$ and $u(\cdot): \Omega_T \to R^k$ be defined by the equations $(x(\omega_T), u(\omega_T)) = \omega_T$ and $\omega_T \in \Omega_T$, and insists that the vector-valued function $(x, u)(\cdot)$ is measurable with respect to $\aleph_T$ and that $(x, u)(\cdot)$, subject to the conditions on which Γ_T insists, has a well-defined probability distribution relative to $P_T(\cdot)$. I denote this probability distribution by RPD, where R stands for researcher, P for probability, and D for distribution. I assume that the researcher is its originator.

As in the case of the data universe, the Ω_T that appears in two places is one and the same subset of a vector space. Also, $\aleph_T$ is a family of subsets of the given vector space, and $P_T(\cdot)$ assigns numbers to these subsets. Moreover, for the vector-valued function $(x, u)(\cdot)$ the equation $(x(\omega_T), u(\omega_T)) = \omega_T$ is short for $(x_1(\omega_T), \ldots, x_h(\omega_T), u_1(\omega_T), \ldots, u_k(\omega_T)) = \omega_T$. In the present theory-data confrontation (x, u) plays the role of a vector in Ω_T and also the role of a vector-valued random variable on $(\Omega_T, \aleph_T)$. The components of (x, u) are theoretical variables and their values are not observable. Also, the probability measure, $P_T(\cdot)$, exists in the mind of the pertinent researcher and cannot, even ideally, be calculated by an outsider. Here is an example.

E2.2.2
Consider OS again. The researcher has a good idea of the possible values of y, but not much of an idea of the values of $P_P(\cdot)$. He believes that a consumer's disposable income, y, has two components—permanent income, y_p, and transitory income, y_t—and that y_p and y_t are independently distributed. Specifically, with the unit of account being the same as in E2.2.2, the researcher believes that $\Omega_T = \{2, 4, 6\} \times \{-1, 1\}$. Thus $\omega_T \in \Omega_T$ only if $\omega_T = (y_p, y_t)$ for some $y_p \in \{2, 4, 6\}$, $y_t \in \{-1, 1\}$, and $(y_p, y_t) \in \{2, 4, 6\} \times \{-1, 1\}$. He lets $\aleph_T$ be the field of all subsets of Ω_T, and he lets $P_T(\cdot): \aleph_T \to [0, 1]$ be a probability measure whose values he is to assign. Also, he lets $y_p(\cdot): \Omega_T \to \{2, 4, 6\}$ and $y_t(\cdot): \Omega_T \to \{-1, 1\}$ be defined by the equations $(y_p(\omega_T), y_t(\omega_T)) = \omega_T$ and $\omega_T \in \Omega_T$, and observes that the vector-valued function $(y_p, y_t)(\cdot)$ is measurable with respect to $\aleph_T$. Finally, he assigns the P_T probabilities that are displayed in table 2.1 to the values of $(y_p, y_t)(\cdot)$. (In that table, mp_x is short for the marginal probability of x.)

The Bridge
In an axiomatized theory-data confrontation, Ω_P is disjoint from Ω_T. I assume that the researcher's sample of observations consists of pairs of vectors, (ω_T, ω_P), where $\omega_T \in \Omega_T$, and $\omega_P \in \Omega_P$. The observations of

Table 2.1

y_t	y_P			
	2	4	6	mp_{yt}
−1	1/8	1/4	1/8	1/2
1	1/8	1/4	1/8	1/2
mp_{yp}	¼	1/2	1/4	1

the components of ω_T are unobservable, whereas the observations of the components of ω_P can be seen and recorded. For example, two of the components of ω_T might record "observations" of a consumer's permanent and transitory income while the corresponding component of ω_P records the same consumer's actual disposable income. I assume, also, that the σ fields, $\aleph_T$ and $\aleph_P$, are stochastically independent. This assumption reflects Frisch's insistence that the empirical laws exist in the real world and must be discovered, whereas the rational laws exist in the model world and are created by the mind of the investigator (Bjerkholt and Qin 2010, p. 34).

When $\aleph_T$ and $\aleph_P$ are stochastically independent, the probability spaces in the theory universe and the data universe induce a uniquely determined probability measure on $\Omega_T \times \Omega_P$. To see how, let $\varkappa$ denote the family of all sets in $\Omega_T \times \Omega_P$ of the form $E_T \times E_P$ with $E_T \in \aleph_T$ and $E_P \in \aleph_P$, and let $\aleph$ denote the smallest σ field in $\Omega_T \times \Omega_P$ containing $\varkappa$. There is a uniquely determined probability measure, $P(\cdot):\aleph \rightarrow [0, 1]$, such that for all $E \in \varkappa$, $P(E) = P_T(E_T)P_P(E_P)$ (Dunford and Schwartz 1957, pp. 183–189). Here is an example to fix ideas.

E2.2.3
In OS $\Omega_T = \{(2, -1), (2, 1), (4, -1), (4, 1)\ (6, -1), (6, 1)\}$ and $\Omega_P = \{1, 3, 5, 7\}$. Hence,

$\Omega_T \times \Omega_P =$

$$\begin{pmatrix} ((2,-1),1), & ((2,1),1), & ((4,-1),1), & ((4,-1),1) & ((6,-1),1), & ((6,-1),1) \\ ((2,-1),3), & ((2,1),3), & ((4,-1),3), & ((4,1),3) & ((6,-1),3), & ((6,1),3) \\ ((2,-1),5), & ((2,1),5), & ((4,-1),5), & ((4,1),5) & ((6,-1),5), & ((6,1),5) \\ ((2,-1),7), & ((2,1),7), & ((4,-1),7), & ((4,1),7) & ((6,-1),7), & ((6,1),7) \end{pmatrix}.$$

The probabilities that $P(\cdot)$ assigns to these triples are given in table 2.2. In reading that table, notice that $\{((2, -1), 3)\} = \{(2, -1)\} \times \{3\}$. Hence $P(\{((2, -1), 3)\} = P_T(\{(2, -1)\}) \cdot P_P(\{3\}) = \frac{1}{8} \cdot \frac{1}{2} = (1/16)$. Also, the

Table 2.2

y	(y_p, y_t)						mp_y
	$\{(2, -1)\}$	$\{(2.1)\}$	$\{(4, -1)\}$	$\{(4, 1)\}$	$\{(6, -1)\}$	$\{(6, 1)\}$	
$\{1\}$	1/32	1/32	1/16	1/16	1/32	1/32	1/4
$\{3\}$	1/16	1/16	1/8	1/8	1/16	1/16	1/2
$\{5\}$	1/40	1/40	1/20	1/20	1/40	1/40	1/5
$\{7\}$	1/160	1/160	1/80	1/80	1/160	1/160	1/20
$pm_{(yp, yt)}$	1/8	1/8	1/4	1/4	1/8	1/8	1

Table 2.3
The values $P(\cdot)$ assigns to the basic subsets of Ω. Here $P(\Omega) = 48/160 = 3/10$.

$\{\omega\} \in \aleph$	$\{((2, -1), 1)\}$	$\{((2, 1), 3)\}$	$\{((4, -1), 3)\}$	$\{((4, 1), 5)\}$	$\{((6, -1), 5)\}$	$\{((6, 1), 7)\}$
$P(\cdot)$	1/32	1/16	1/8	1/20	1/40	1/160

marginal probability that $y = 3$ is given by $P(\{3\} \times \Omega_T) = P_P(\{3\}) \cdot P_T(\Omega_T)$ $= P_P(\{3\}) = \frac{1}{2}$.

Formally, the Bridge is a pair, $(\Omega, \Gamma_{T,P})$, where Ω is a subset of $\Omega_T \times \Omega_P$, and $\Gamma_{T,P}$ is a finite number of assertions that the elements in Ω must satisfy. The first three of the axioms in $\Gamma_{T,P}$ describe conceptual properties of the relationship between theoretical and observational variables. The other assertions describe law-like properties of this relationship. The first two assertions concerning the conceptual properties of the bridge between theory and data are that observations come in pairs, (ω_T, ω_P), all of which belong to Ω, and that $\Omega \subset \Omega_T \times \Omega_P$. The third assertion, which refers to the given product probability space on $\Omega_T \times \Omega_P$, is that $\Omega \in \aleph$ and $P(\Omega) > 0$. In some applications I will also insist that $\Omega_T \subset \{\omega_T \in \Omega_T$ for which there is an $\omega_P \in \Omega_P$ with $(\omega_T, \omega_P) \in \Omega\}$. The remaining assertions in $\Gamma_{T,P}$ describe how the components ω_T and ω_P in Ω are related to one another. In the present context, there is only one such assertion. It claims that there exists a k-by-h dimensional matrix H such that $y(\omega_P) = Hx(\omega_T) + u(\omega_T)$ for all $(\omega_T, \omega_P) \in \Omega$.

E2.2.4
Back to OS again. In OS the fourth bridge principle insists that $y(\omega_P) = y_p(\omega_T) + y_t(\omega_T)$. From this and E2.2.1–E2.2.3 I deduce that

$$\Omega = \{((2, -1), 1), ((2, 1), 3), ((4, -1), 3), ((4, 1), 5), ((6, -1), 5), ((6, 1), 7)\}$$

and that the values $P(\cdot)$ assigns to the basic subsets of Ω are as in table 2.3. In this case,

$$\Omega_T \subset \{\omega_T \in \Omega_T \text{ for which there is an } \omega_P \in \Omega_P \text{ with } (\omega_T, \omega_P) \in \Omega\}.$$

The MPD

In the first scenario of a theory-data confrontation that I described above, the researcher in charge formulates his theory in terms of variables that live and function in his data universe and tests its empirical relevance in the same data universe. In the second scenario, the researcher formulates his theory in a theory universe and tests its empirical relevance in a data universe that is disjoint from the theory universe. In this scenario the bridge principles play two roles. In one role, the bridge principles translate the theory so that it becomes a statement about relations among variables in the data universe. In the other role, the bridge principles convert the RPD distribution of variables in the theory universe into the probability distributions of variables in the data universe that are to be used in the empirical analysis. I designate the probability distribution of the data variables that is derived from the RPD and the bridge principles MPD, where M stands for marginal, P for probability, and D for distribution. I refer to it as the marginal probability distribution of the data variables.

Formally, the MPD is the probability distribution of the components of ω_P that is induced by the bridge principles and the probability distribution of the components of ω_T that $P_T(\cdot)$ determines. Suppose that $\Gamma_{T,P}$ comprises only the four assertions mentioned above. Then

$$MPD(y(\omega_P) = \acute{y})$$

$$= \frac{P_T(\{\omega_T \in \Omega_T \text{ with } Hx(\omega_T) + u(\omega_T) = \acute{y}\} \cap \{\omega_T \in \Omega_T \text{ with } \omega_P \in \Omega_P \text{ and } (\omega_T, \omega_P) \in \Omega\})}{P_T(\{\omega_T \in \Omega_T \text{ with } \omega_P \in \Omega_P \text{ and } (\omega_T, \omega_P) \in \Omega\})}.$$

The MPD may be very different from the TPD. Since it is not easy to intuit how different the MPD can be from the TPD, an example to fix ideas is called for.

E2.2.5

From table 2.1 I deduce that in OS the MPD of y is given by the following equations:

Table 2.4

$\{y\} \in \aleph_P$	$\{1\}$	$\{3\}$	$\{5\}$	$\{7\}$
TPD($\cdot$)	1/4	1/2	1/5	1/20
MPD($\cdot$)	1/8	3/8	3/8	1/8

$MPD(y(\omega_P) = j)$

$$= \frac{P_T(\{\omega_T \in \Omega_T \text{ with } y_p(\omega_T) + y_t(\omega_T) = j\}) \cap}{P_T(\{\omega_T \in \Omega_T \text{ with } \omega_p \in \Omega_p \text{ and } (\omega_T, \omega_P) \in \Omega\})}$$

$= \frac{1}{8}, \frac{3}{8}, \frac{3}{8}, \text{ and } \frac{1}{8} \text{ according as } j = 1, 3, 5, \text{ or } 7,$

$MPD(\{y = j\}) = 0$ for $j \neq 1, 3, 5,$ or 7.

Table 2.4 shows how different these values are from the corresponding TPD values.

E2.2.1–E2.2.4 have several special features; for example, the support of MPD is all of Ω_P and $\Omega_T \subset \{\omega_T \in \Omega_T$ for which there is an $\omega_P \in \Omega_P$ with $(\omega_T, \omega_P) \in \Omega\}$. Hence, a second example is required. In reading the example, note that it describes a model of all the axioms of the theory-data confrontation that I have discussed above.

E2.2.6
In this example, k = h = H = 1 and Ω_P, Ω_T, and Ω are discrete.

The Γ_T axioms
$\Omega_T = \{-2, 2\} \times \{-1, 1\}$, $\aleph_T$ is the field of all subsets of Ω_T, and $P_T(\cdot):\aleph_T \to [0, 1]$ is a probability measure. Also, $x(\cdot): \Omega_T \to \{-2, 2\}$ and $u(\cdot): \Omega_T \to \{-1, 1\}$are defined by the equations $(x(\omega_T), u(\omega_T)) = \omega_T$, and $\omega_T \in \Omega_T$, and the vector-valued function $(x, u)(\cdot)$ is measurable with respect to $\aleph_T$ and has a well-defined probability distribution relative to $P_T(\cdot)$. In this probability distribution, x and u are distributed independently with $P_T(x = -2) = \frac{1}{4}$, $P_T(x = 2) = \frac{3}{4}$, $P_T(u = -1) = \frac{1}{2}$, and $P_T(u = 1) = \frac{1}{2}$. Hence, $\Omega_T = \{(-2, -1), (-2, 1), (2, -1), (2, 1)\}$, and the $P_T(\cdot)$ probabilities of the basic sets in $\aleph_T$ are displayed in table 2.5.

The Γ_P axioms
$\Omega_P = \{-2, -1, 0, 1, 2\}$. $\aleph_P$ is the field of all subsets of Ω_P, and $P_P(\cdot):\aleph_P \to [0, 1]$ is a probability measure. Also, $y(\cdot): \Omega_P \to\{-2, -1, 0, 1, 2\}$ is defined

Table 2.5

	x		
u	-2	2	mp_u
-1	1/8	3/8	1/2
1	1/8	3/8	1/2
mp_x	1/4	3/4	1

by the equations $y(\omega_P) = \omega_P$, and $\omega_P \in \Omega_P$, and $y(\cdot)$ is measurable with respect to $\aleph_P$, and has a well-defined probability distribution relative to $P_P(\cdot)$. In this probability distribution $P_P(\{\omega_P \in \Omega_P: y(\omega_P) = j\}) = 1/3$ for $j \in \{-2, -1\}$, and $1/9$ for $j \in \{0, 1, 2\}$. Consequently,

$TPD(y = j) = 1/3$ for $j \in \{-2, -1\}$ and $1/9$ for $j \in \{0, 1, 2\}$.

The Bridge
$\Omega \subset \Omega_T \times \Omega_P$. Also $(\omega_T, \omega_P) \in \Omega$ if and only if $\omega_T \in \Omega_T$, $\omega_P \in \Omega_P$, and $y(\omega_P) = x(\omega_T) + u(\omega_T)$. Hence,

$\Omega = \{((-2, 1), -1), ((2, -1), 1)\}$

and

$P(\{((-2, 1), -1)\}) = 1/24$; $P(\{((2, -1), 1)\}) = 1/24$; and $P(\Omega) = 1/12$.

From these axioms I deduce that

$MPD(y(w_P) = j)$

$$= \frac{P_T(\{\omega_T \in \Omega_T \text{with } x(\omega_T) + u(\omega_T) = j\} \cap}{P_T(\{\omega_T \in \Omega_T \text{with } \omega_P \in \Omega_P \text{ and } (\omega_T, \omega_P) \in \Omega\})}$$
$$\frac{\{\omega_T \in \Omega_T \text{with } \omega_P \in \Omega_P \text{ and } (\omega_T, \omega_P) \in \Omega\})}{}$$

$$= ⅛/½ = ¼ \text{ for } j = -1$$

and

$⅜/½ = ¾$ for $j = 1$.

Also,

$MPD(y = j) = 0$ for $j = -2, 0, 2$ and for $j \neq -2, -1, 0, 1, 2$.

Hence, as table 2.6 shows, the MPD is very different from the TPD.

Table 2.6

$\{y\} \in \Omega_P$	$\{-2\}$	$\{-1\}$	$\{0\}$	$\{1\}$	$\{2\}$
TPD($\cdot$)	1/3	1/3	1/9	1/9	1/9
MPD($\cdot$)	0	1/4	0	3/4	0

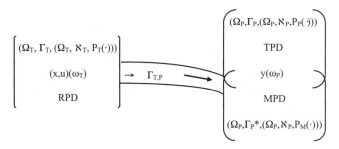

Figure 2.1
Theory-data confrontation with a bridge.

The MPD, a New Data Universe, and the Conditional Measure $P(\cdot \mid \Omega)$ on $(\Omega_P, \aleph_P)$

The properties of the MPD imply that there exists a probability measure, $P_M(\cdot):\aleph_P \to [0, 1]$, relative to which the probability distribution of $y(\cdot)$ equals the MPD. Consequently, one can think of the empirical analysis as being carried out in a data universe, $(\Omega_P, \Gamma_P^*, (\Omega_P, \aleph_P, P_M(\cdot)))$, that differs from the original universe in characteristic ways. In the latter triple, the Ω_P and $\aleph_P$ components are identical with the Ω_P and $\aleph_P$ components of the original data universe. The Γ_P^* component differs from Γ_P in two ways: $P_M(\cdot)$ is substituted for $P_P(\cdot)$ and MPD is substituted for TPD. Evidently, the probability measure, $P_M(\cdot)$, that determines the probability distribution of $y(\omega_P)$ in the new universe may be very different from $P_P(\cdot)$.

The ideas that I presented in the last paragraph are illustrated in figure 2.1, with one theory universe, two data universes, and one bridge. The data universes have the same pair $(\Omega_P, \aleph_P)$ and share the function $y(\cdot)$. The probability distribution of $y(\cdot)$ is TPD in the upper data universe and MPD in the lower data universe. The bridge connects the theory universe with the lower data universe.[4]

In E2.2.5 and E2.2.6 I used the RPD and the bridge principles to derive the MPD distribution of y. In the present context, it is important to observe that there is another way of using the bridge principles to

Table 2.7

$\{y\} \in \aleph_P$	{1}	{3}	{5}	{7}
$P(y \mid \Omega)$	5/48	30/48	12/48	1/48
MPD(y)	1/8	3/8	3/8	1/8

derive a probability distribution of y for the empirical analysis. Here, to prove my point, is a follow-up on E2.2.5 and E2.2.6.

E2.2.7
Looking back at E2.2.4 and table 2.3, I obtain all the data I need to compute the conditional distribution of y in Ω. Recall that the marginal probability that y = 3 is equal to $P(\{3\} \times \Omega_T) = P_P(\{3\}) \cdot P_T(\Omega_T) = P_P(\{3\})$. Hence,

$P(y(\omega_P) = j \mid \Omega)$

$\quad = P(\{(\omega_T, \omega_P) \in \Omega_T \times \Omega_P : y(\omega_P) = j\} \cap \Omega) / P(\Omega)$

$\quad = P(\{(\omega_T, \omega_P) \in \Omega_T \times \Omega_P : y(\omega_P) = j \text{ and } x(\omega_T) + u(\omega_T) = j\}) / P(\Omega)$

$\quad = P_T(\{(\omega_T \in \Omega_T : x(\omega_T) + u(\omega_T) = j\}) \cdot P_P(\{\omega_P \in \Omega_P : y(\omega_P) = j\}) / P(\Omega)$

$\quad = 5/48, 30/48, 12/48, \text{ and } 1/48 \text{ according as } j = 1, 3, 5, \text{ and } 7.$

Table 2.7 shows how different the MPD and $P(\cdot \mid \Omega)$ are.

Similarly, looking back at E2.2.3. I can compute the conditional distribution of y there:

$P(y(\omega_P) = j \mid \Omega)$

$\quad = P(\{(\omega_T, \omega_P) \in \Omega_T \times \Omega_P : y(\omega_P) = j\} \cap \Omega) / P(\Omega)$

$\quad = P(\{(\omega_T, \omega_P) \in \Omega_T \times \Omega_P : y(\omega_P) = j \text{ and } x(\omega_T) + u(\omega_T) = j\}) / P(\Omega)$

$\quad = P_T(\{(\omega_T \in \Omega_T : x(\omega_T) + u(\omega_T) = j\}) \cdot P_P(\{\omega_P \in \Omega_P : y(\omega_P) = j\}) / P(\Omega)$

$\quad = \frac{1}{2} \text{ for } j = -1, 1, 0 \text{ for } j = -2, 0, 2.$

Table 2.8 shows how different MPD and $P(\cdot \mid \Omega)$ are.

It is important to observe that that the numbers that MPD($\cdot$) and $P(\cdot \mid \Omega)$ assign to members of $\aleph_P$ differ. It is equally important to notice how the formulas I use in the computation of these numbers differ. Consider, for example, the pertinent formulas in E2.2.5 and E2.2.7. In E2.2.5,

Table 2.8

$\{y\} \in \aleph_P$	$\{-2\}$	$\{-1\}$	$\{0\}$	$\{1\}$	$\{2\}$
$P(y \mid \Omega)$	0	1/2	0	1/2	0
$MPD(y)$	0	1/4	0	3/4	0

$MPD(y(\omega_P) = j)$

$$= \frac{P_T(\{\omega_T \in \Omega_T \text{ with } y_p(\omega_T) + y_t(\omega_T) = j\} \cap \{\omega_T \in \Omega_T \text{ with } \omega_P \in \Omega_P \text{ and } (\omega_T, \omega_P) \in \Omega\})}{P_T(\{\omega_T \in \Omega_T \text{ with } \omega_P \in \Omega_P \text{ and } (\omega_T, \omega_P) \in \Omega\})}.$$

In E2.2.7,

$P(y(\omega_P) = j \mid \Omega)$

$\quad = P(\{(\omega_T, \omega_P) \in \Omega_T \times \Omega_P : y(\omega_P) = j\} \cap \Omega)/P(\Omega)$

$\quad = P(\{(\omega_T, \omega_P) \in \Omega_T \times \Omega_P : y(\omega_P) = j \text{ and } x(\omega_T) + u(\omega_T) = j\})/P(\Omega)$

$\quad = P_T(\{\{\omega_T \in \Omega_T : x(\omega_T) + u(\omega_T) = j\}) \cdot P_P(\{\omega_P \in \Omega_P : y(\omega_P) = j\})/P(\Omega).$

In the MPD formula, the set $\{\omega_T \in \Omega_T \text{ with } \omega_P \in \Omega_P \text{ and } (\omega_T, \omega_P) \in \Omega\}$, plays the role that Ω plays in the $P(\cdot \mid \Omega)$ formula. Also, $P_P(\cdot)$ is not involved in the computation of MPD, whereas it plays a fundamental role in the computation of $P(\cdot \mid \Omega)$.

To me the MPD is the correct choice of probability distribution for the statistical analysis of $y(\cdot)$. The MPD is the distribution of $y(\cdot)$ that is induced by the pertinent researcher's RPD and his bridge principles. In that way the MPD depicts the researcher's vision of how his data were generated. By using the MPD in his statistical analysis of the data, the researcher incorporates economic theory in his empirical analysis in a theoretically meaningful way.

The Contrast: Empirical Analyses in the Two Data Universes

I have observed that the TPD differs from the MPD and given several examples in support of my contention. It remains to demonstrate how this difference affects the empirical analysis in the two data universes in figure 2.1. In chapters 3–5 and chapters 7–9 I will present detailed case studies, each of which exhibits different aspects of the way empirical analysis in the two data universes differs. Here I will be content to present a model of the preceding axioms that exemplifies an idea that

I learned from reading Aris Spanos' 1989 and 2012 deliberations about the legacy of Trygve Haavelmo's 1944 treatise *The Probability Approach in Econometrics*.

When reading E2.2.9, it is good to keep in mind that a theory is a family of models of an axiomatic system. An axiomatic system has many different families of models. The family of models for which the system was developed is designated *the intended interpretation* of the system. For instance, in the given example, I postulate that $\Omega_T \subset (R^5 \times (R^2 \times \{0,0\}))$ and that the five x components of the vectors in Ω_T satisfy the conditions in equation 2.1. Besides, I insist that the theory is about commodities and prices in a competitive market. In social reality commodities and prices assume only positive values. Yet the postulate allows the components of ω_T that pertain to commodities and prices— that is x_1, x_2, and x_3—to be negative. In other words, the postulate has models in which prices and commodities assume negative values. Note, therefore, that in the intended interpretation of the axioms, prices and commodities are positive. Equations 3.33–3.35, figure 3.1, equations 3.41–3.43, and figure 3.2 in chapter 3 demonstrate that the subfamily of models of the axioms that constitutes the intended interpretation of the axioms is not empty.

E2.2.9
Consider a family of models of the preceding axioms in which $k = 4$, $h = 5$, u has only two non-zero components, and $H_{ij} = 1$ if $(i, j) = (1, 1)$, $(2, 3)$, $(3, 4)$, or $(4, 5)$. Otherwise, $H_{ij} = 0$. The intended interpretation of the axioms depicts a data confrontation of a theory of a competitive commodity market in which the pertinent researcher is to sample at random once in the Observations box in figure 1.2.

The Γ_T axioms
In this case $\Omega_T \subset (R^5 \times (R^2 \times \{0,0\}))$ $\aleph_T$ is a σ field of subsets of Ω_T, and $P_T(\cdot){:}\aleph_T \to [0, 1]$ is a probability measure. Also, $x(\cdot): \Omega_T \to R^5$ and $u(\cdot): \Omega_T \to R^2 \times \{0, 0\}$ are defined by the equations $(x(\omega_T), u(\omega_T)) = \omega_T$ and $\omega_T \in \Omega_T$. Moreover, the vector-valued function $(x, u)(\cdot)$ is measurable with respect to $\aleph_T$, and has, subject to the conditions on which Γ_T insists, a well-defined probability distribution relative to $P_T(\cdot)$. In this probability distribution, $x(\omega_T)$ has finite means and covariances, and the covariance matrix of $x_4(\omega_T)$ and $x_5(\omega_T)$ is invertible; $(u_1, u_2)(\omega_T)$ has zero means and finite positive variances; $x(\omega_T)$ and $(u_1, u_2)(\omega_T)$ are distributed independently of each other; and $u_1(\omega_T)$ and $u_2(\omega_T)$ are independently

distributed. Finally, there are six constants, $\alpha_0 > 0$, $\alpha_1 < 0$, $\alpha_2 \in R$, $\beta_0 < \alpha_0$, $\beta_1 > 0$, and $\beta_2 \in R$, such that, for all $\omega_T \in \Omega_T$,

$$x_1 = \alpha_0 + \alpha_1 x_3 + \alpha_2 x_4, \ x_2 = \beta_0 + \beta_1 x_3 + \beta_2 x_5, \text{ and } x_1 = x_2. \tag{2.1}$$

In the intended interpretation of the axioms, the first of equations 2.1 describes the market participants' intended demand for a given commodity, x_1, as a function of its price, x_3, and some explanatory variable, x_4. The second equation describes the market participants' intended supply of the given commodity, x_2, as a function of its price, x_3, and an explanatory variable, x_5, different from x_4. The third of equations 2.1 insists that the market is in equilibrium; i.e., that the market is in a state in which the price of a given commodity and the values of the explanatory variables are such that the intended demand for the commodity equals the intended supply of the commodity. Finally, the means and covariances of $x(\cdot)$ and $u(\cdot)$ are their means and covariances in the RPD distribution.

For present purposes it is interesting that I can use equations 2.1 to express x_1 and x_3 as linear functions of the two explanatory variables, x_4 and x_5. To wit: Let

$$\gamma_0 = [(\alpha_1\beta_0 - \alpha_0\beta_1)/(\alpha_1 - \beta_1)],$$

$$\gamma_1 = -[\alpha_2\beta_1/(\alpha_1 - \beta_1)], \tag{2.2}$$

$$\gamma_2 = [\alpha_1\beta_2/(\alpha_1 - \beta_1)],$$

and

$$\varphi_0 = [(\beta_0 - \alpha_0)/(\alpha_1 - \beta_1)]; \ \varphi_1 = -[\alpha_2/(\alpha_1 - \beta_1)], \ \varphi_2 = [\beta_2/(\alpha_1 - \beta_1)] \tag{2.3}$$

and observe the following.

T1
Suppose that Γ_T is valid, and let γ_i and φ_i, i= 0, 1, 2 be as defined in equations 2.2 and 2.3. For all $\omega_T \in \Omega_T$, it is the case that

$$x_1 = \gamma_0 + \gamma_1 x_4 + \gamma_2 x_5 \quad \text{and} \quad x_3 = \varphi_0 + \varphi_1 x_4 + \varphi_2 x_5. \tag{2.4}$$

The Γ_T axioms have many models. The models vary with the values of the α and β constants, with the means and covariances of the components of x, and with the variances of u_1 and u_2. The models must heed the sign constraints on the α and β constants and the condition that the covariance matrix of x_4 and x_5 is invertible. In addition, they must heed an interesting consistency condition on the constants and the RPD distribution of x.

To describe the consistency condition, I must introduce several new symbols that pertain to the RPD distribution of x:

$\Sigma_{22}(RPD) = RPD.cov((x_4, x_5)'(x_4, x_5))$,

$\Sigma_{11}(RPD) = RPD.cov((x_1, (x_4, x_5))$,

$\Sigma_{13}(RPD) = RPD.cov(x_3, (x_4, x_5))$,

$\mu_i = RPD.mean(x_i)$, $i = 1, 3, 4, 5$.

With these symbols in hand, I find that

$(\gamma_1, \gamma_2) = \Sigma_{11}(RPD)\Sigma_{22}(RPD)^{-1}$,

$(\varphi_1, \varphi_2) = \Sigma_{13}(RPD)\Sigma_{22}(RPD)^{-1}$,
(2.5)

$\gamma_0 = \mu_1 - \gamma_1\mu_4 - \gamma_2\mu_5$,

$\varphi_0 = \mu_3 - \varphi_1\mu_4 - \varphi_2\mu_5$.
(2.6)

Thus the mean and covariance structure of x in RPD and equations 2.5 and 2.6 determine the values of the γ_i and φ_i, $i = 0, 1, 2$. The latter values and equations 2.2 and 2.3 determine the values of the α_i and β_i, $i = 0, 1, 2$, without regard to the sign conditions that the Γ_T axioms impose on them. Similarly, the values of α_i and β_i, $i = 0, 1, 2$, and equations 2.2 and 2.3 determine the values of γ_i and φ_i, $i = 0, 1, 2$, without regard to whether the latter values satisfy equations 2.5 and 2.6.

The Γ_P axioms
In this case, $\Omega_P \subset R^4$, $\aleph_P$ is a σ field of subsets of Ω_P, and $P_P(\cdot):\aleph_P \to [0, 1]$ is a probability measure. Also, $y(\cdot): \Omega_P \to R^4$ is defined by the equations $y(\omega_P) = \omega_P$ and $\omega_P \in \Omega_P$, is measurable with respect to $\aleph_P$, and has, subject to the conditions on which Γ_P insists, a well-defined probability distribution relative to $P_P(\cdot)$. In this probability distribution, $y(\omega_P)$ has finite means and covariances and the covariance matrix of $y_3(\omega_P)$ and $y_4(\omega_P)$ is invertible.

In the intended interpretation of these axioms, y_1 denotes the actual purchases of the given commodity, y_2 denotes the actual value of the price of the commodity, and y_3 and y_4 represent the actual values of the explanatory variables, x_4 and x_5. Also, the means and covariances of $y(\cdot)$ are the means and covariances of the components of $y(\cdot)$ in the TPD distribution. In the present formal theory-data confrontation, as elsewhere in the book, I assume that there is a true probability distribution of the data variables and, hence, that the TPD has only one model.

The Bridge

In this case, $\Omega \subset \Omega_T \times \Omega_P$. Also, $(\omega_T, \omega_P) \in \Omega$ if and only if $\omega_T \in \Omega_T$, $\omega_P \in \Omega_P$,

$$y_1(\omega_P) = x_1(\omega_T) + u_1(\omega_T),$$
$$y_2(\omega_P) = x_3(\omega_T) + u_2(\omega_T),$$
(2.7)

$$y_3(\omega_P) = x_4(\omega_T),$$
$$y_4(\omega_P) = x_5(\omega_T).$$
(2.8)

Finally,

$$\Omega_T \subset \{(x, u) \in \Omega_T \text{ for which there is a } y \in \Omega_P \text{ with } ((x, u), y) \in \Omega\}. \quad (2.9)$$

From T1, from the Γ_T and Γ_P axioms, and from the Bridge, it follows that the bridge principles and each model of the Γ_T axioms induce an MPD distribution of y with characteristic features.

The MPD and the $P_M(\cdot)$ measure on $(\Omega, \aleph_P)$

To describe the MPD distribution in the present case, a preliminary remark is called for. I must introduce a pair of random variables on $(\Omega_P, \aleph_P)$, $(\eta_1, \eta_2)(\omega_P)$, that is to take the place of $(u_1, u_2)(\omega_T)$ in the empirical analysis. Here it is:

For all $(\omega_T, \omega_P) \in \Omega$, $(\eta_1, \eta_2)(\omega_P) = (u_1, u_2)(\omega_T)$. $\qquad (2.10)$

From this definition, equations 2.7–2.9, and equation 2.4 I find that

$$y_1(\omega_P) - \gamma_0 - \gamma_1 y_3(\omega_P) - \gamma_2 y_4(\omega_P) = \eta_1(\omega_P) \qquad (2.11)$$

and

$$y_2(\omega_P) - \varphi_0 - \varphi_1 y_3(\omega_P) - \varphi_2 y_4(\omega_P) = \eta_2(\omega_P). \qquad (2.12)$$

Hence, the pair $(\eta_1, \eta_2)(\cdot)$ is well defined and measurable with respect to $\aleph_P$. But if that is so, for any $A \subset R^2$ and $B \subset R^2$,

$$\text{MPD}((\eta_1, \eta_2, y_3, y_4) \in A \times B) = P_T(\{\omega_T \in \Omega_T: (u_1, u_2, x_4, x_5) \in A \times B\}),$$

which goes to show that the MPD distribution of $(\eta_1, \eta_2, y_3, y_4))$ equals the RPD distribution of (u_1, u_2, x_4, x_5). In that way it justifies the role (η_1, η_2) plays in T3.

The properties of the MPD distribution of $(y_1, \ldots, y_4, \eta_1, \eta_2)$ and Kolmogorov's consistency theorem (see Stigum 1990, p. 347, T 15.23) determine a probability measure, $P_M(\cdot):\aleph_P \rightarrow [0, 1]$, relative to which the probability distribution of the given variables is the MPD distribution. With that observation in mind, I can characterize the MPD distribution of y as follows.

T3

Suppose that Γ_T and $\Gamma_{T,P}$ are valid. In an MPD-determined $P_M(\cdot)$ measure there is a pair $(\eta_1, \eta_2)(\cdot)$ that is measurable with respect to $\aleph_P$, has the same means and variances as (u_1, u_2), is distributed independently of y_3 and y_4, and of each other, and satisfies the equations

$$y_1 = \gamma_0 + \gamma_1 y_3 + \gamma_2 y_4 + \eta_1 \quad \text{and} \quad y_2 = \varphi_0 + \varphi_1 y_3 + \varphi_2 y_4 + \eta_2. \quad (2.13)$$

Also, the γ_i and the φ_i, $i = 0, 1, 2$, satisfy the following equations:

$$(\gamma_1, \gamma_2) = \Sigma_{11}(MPD)\Sigma_{22}(MPD)^{-1}, \quad (\varphi_1, \varphi_2) = \Sigma_{12}(MPD)\Sigma_{22}(MPD)^{-1}, \quad (2.14)$$

$$\gamma_0 = \delta_1 - a_1\delta_3 - a_2\delta_4, \quad \text{and} \quad \varphi_0 = \delta_2 - b_1\delta_3 - b_2\delta_4, \quad (2.15)$$

where

$$\Sigma_{22}(MPD) = MPD.cov.((y_3, y_4)'(y_3, y_4)),$$

$$\Sigma_{11}(MPD) = MPD.cov((y_1, (y_3, y_4)),$$

$$\Sigma_{12}(MPD) = MPD.cov.(y_2, (y_3, y_4)),$$

and

$$\delta_i = MPD.mean(y_i), \quad i = 1, 2, 3, 4.$$

In reading the preceding theorem, note that, with the exception of the variances of y_1 and y_2, the mean and covariance structure of y in the MPD distribution is identical with the corresponding mean and covariance structure of (x_1, x_3, x_4, x_5) in the RPD distribution. That justifies my using γ_i and φ_i, $i = 0, 1, 2$, in equations 2.13 and 2.14.

Recall, now, the two abstract scenarios that I described in discussing the meaning of figure 1.2. Without spelling out the details, I can use the model of the axioms in E2.2.9 to describe how empirical analyses of simultaneous-equations models differ in the two scenarios.

Consider the first scenario, and suppose that the researcher in charge has obtained a finite number of observations of y in a random sampling scheme. He adopts the Γ_P axioms as stated. From them and a standard theorem in mathematical statistics he deduces the validity of the following theorem.

T2.3
Suppose that Γ_P is valid. Then there exist six constants, a_0, a_1, a_2, b_0, b_1, and b_2, and two random variables, ξ_1, and ξ_2 with means zero and finite covariance matrix, Π, such that, relative to $P_P(\cdot)$,

$$y_1 = a_0 + a_1y_3 + a_2y_4 + \xi_1; \quad y_2 = b_0 + b_1y_3 + b_2y_4 + \xi_2 \tag{2.16}$$

and

$$\text{TPD.cov}((\xi_1, \xi_2)'(y_3, y_4)) = 0. \tag{2.17}$$

The constants in equation 2.16 have a meaningful interpretation. Let $\Sigma_{22}(\text{TPD}) = \text{TPD.cov.}((y_3, y_4)'(y_3, y_4))$; $\Sigma_{11}(\text{TPD}) = \text{TPD.cov}((y_1,(y_3, y_4))$; $\Sigma_{12}(\text{TPD}) = \text{TPD.cov.}(y_2,(y_3, y_4))$, and $\upsilon_i = \text{TPD.mean}(y_i)$, $i = 1, 2, 3, 4$. Then

$$(a_1, a_2) = \Sigma_{11}(\text{TPD})\Sigma_{22}(\text{TPD})^{-1},$$
$$(b_1, b_2) = \Sigma_{12}(\text{TPD})\Sigma_{22}(\text{TPD})^{-1}, \tag{2.18}$$

$$a_0 = \upsilon_1 - a_1\upsilon_3 - a_2\upsilon_4,$$
$$b_0 = \upsilon_2 - b_1\upsilon_3 - b_2\upsilon_4. \tag{2.19}$$

These characteristics are the characteristics of a TPD that is, formally, independent of the RPD.

In accord with the Haavelmo-Spanos blueprint (Spanos 1989, pp. 414–418; Spanos 2012, pp. 7–10), the researcher assumes that he has accurate observations of x_1, x_3, x_4, x_5 and takes the parameters in equations 2.16 and 2.17 to be purely statistical parameters that are unrelated to the structural parameters in equation 2.1. Consequently, he has no need for the Γ_T and the $\Gamma_{T/P}$. He throws the axioms out, but he keeps a record of equations 2.2 and 2.3. For the statistical analysis he assumes that the covariance matrix of the error terms in equation 2.16, Π, is the identity matrix. Then he estimates the parameters in equations 2.16 and 2.17, and ascertains that the estimated statistical model is statistically adequate.[5] At last, he uses the given estimates and equations 2.2 and 2.3 to obtain an estimate of a structural model in which the components of y play the roles that the corresponding components of x play in equation 2.1.[6] The structural model is theoretically meaningful only if all the members of a 95-percent-confidence band around the estimated parameters in equations 2.16 and 2.17—when combined with equations 2.2 and 2.3—determine α and β constants that heed the sign constraints that I listed in the Γ_T axioms.[7]

Here two arresting remarks are in order. A theoretically meaningful structural model relates actual purchases of a given commodity to the observed values of the price of the commodity and the auxiliary variables. The structural model in equation 2.1 relates the intended demand and supply of a commodity to hypothetical values of the price of the commodity and the explanatory variables. Also, the probability distribution of the variables in a theoretically meaningful structural model is the TPD distribution. The probability distribution of the variables in the structural model in equation 2.1 is the RPD distribution. The TPD distribution of the y vector may be very different from the RPD distribution of the corresponding x vector.

Consider next the second scenario, and suppose again that the researcher in charge has obtained a finite number of "observations" of the pairs, ((x,u),y) in a random sampling scheme. The components of (x,u) are unobservable, Hence, only the components of y are observed. In this case the purpose of the empirical analysis is to determine whether the Γ_T axioms are empirically relevant.

The Γ_T is taken to be empirically relevant if it has a model that together with a model of the Bridge determines a model of the MPD in a 95-percent-confidence band around a statistically meaningful estimate of the MPD.

The researcher begins by estimating the parameters of equations 2.13 and makes sure that the estimated model is statistically adequate. Then he delineates a 95-percent-confidence band around the estimated parameters. To establish the empirical relevance of Γ_T he needs the following theorem: T 2.4: Suppose that Γ_T and $\Gamma_{T,P}$ are valid. Then the Γ_T axioms are empirically relevant if and only if at least one member of this confidence band together with equations 2.2 and 2.3 determines α and β constants that satisfy the sign constraints listed in the Γ_T axioms.

The "only if" part of T2.4 is obviously valid. To establish the "if" part, the researcher proceeds as follows: He supposes that $(\gamma^o, \varphi^o) \in R^6$ is a member of the given confidence band and lets (α^o, β^o) be the α and β parameters that (γ^o, φ^o) and equations 2.2 and 2.3 determine. He supposes, also, that (α^o, β^o) satisfies the sign constraints in Γ_T, and lets η^o

be the error term in equations 2.13 that $(\gamma^\circ, \varphi^\circ)$ determines. Then, for all $\omega_P \in \Omega_P$,

$$y_1(\omega_P) = \gamma_0^\circ + \gamma_1^\circ y_3(\omega_P) + \gamma_2^\circ y_4(\omega_P) + \eta_1^\circ(\omega_P) \qquad (2.20)$$

and

$$y_2(\omega_P) = \varphi_0^\circ + \varphi_1^\circ y_3(\omega_P) + \varphi_2^\circ y_4(\omega_P) + \eta_2^\circ(\omega_P). \qquad (2.21)$$

Also, by hypothesis, the x components of ω_T satisfy the equations $x_1 = \alpha_0^\circ + \alpha_1^\circ x_3 + \alpha_2^\circ x_4$, $x_2 = \beta_0^\circ + \beta_1^\circ x_3 + \beta_2^\circ x_5$, and $x_1 = x_2$. Hence, to establish his claim the researcher need only show that the RPD distribution of the vector-valued random variable, $(x_1, x_2, x_3, x_4, x_5, u_1, u_2)$, satisfies the conditions on which Γ_T insists. To do that, he lets ω_P be a vector in the support of the pertinent MPD distribution and observes that the MPD distribution of the right-hand sides of the equations

$$(u_1, u_2) = (\eta_1^\circ, \eta_2^\circ)(\omega_P), \qquad (2.22)$$

$$x_1 = \gamma_0^\circ + \gamma_1^\circ y_3(\omega_P) + \gamma_2^\circ y_4(\omega_P), \qquad (2.23)$$

$$x_3 = \varphi_0^\circ + \varphi_1^\circ y_3(\omega_P) + \varphi_2^\circ y_4(\omega_P), \qquad (2.24)$$

$$x_4 = y_3(\omega_P), \qquad (2.25)$$

and

$$x_5 = y_4(\omega_P) \qquad (2.26)$$

determines an RPD distribution of $(x_1, x_3, x_4, x_5, u_1, u_2)$ that satisfies the conditions on which Γ_T insists. This fact and the equation $x_1 = x_2$ conclude the proof.

The researcher in the lower data universe can now conclude his empirical analysis by checking whether there is a member of the confidence band around his estimate of the MPD parameters that together with equations 2.2 and 2.3 determines α and β constants that satisfy the sign constraints listed in the Γ_T axioms.

The preceding example demonstrates that the TPD and the MPD in figure 2.1 are not just different families of finite-dimensional probability distributions of the components of ω_P. TPD and MPD are fundamentally different in another way as well. There is one and only one true TPD. In contrast, there are as many MPDs as there are members of the intended families of models of Γ_T and $\Gamma_{T,P}$. Each pair of models of Γ_T and $\Gamma_{T,P}$ determines a mathematical model of MPD, and different pairs of models of Γ_T and $\Gamma_{T,P}$ determine different mathematical models of MPD. This difference between the TPD and the MPD in figure 2.1 causes the empirical analyses in the lower data universe to be fundamentally different from the empirical analyses that present-day econometric theory prescribes. The ensuing chapters—each in its own way—bear witness to that. In doing so, they exhibit in cross-section analyses, in the analysis of qualitative response models, in time-series analyses, and in scientific explanations the unforeseen consequences of adopting Frisch and Haavelmo's vision of a science of economics.

2.2.3 Frisch and Haavelmo's Unitary Methodological Bases for the Science of Economics

Haavelmo's unitary methodological basis for economics was not formal. When formalized, his basis reduces to a data universe in my sense of the term. In that data universe, Haavelmo's researcher formulates his theory, describes his data, and carries out the empirical analysis. To wit: According to Haavelmo (1944, p. 14), there are two classes of experiments:

(1) experiments that we *should like to make* to see if certain real economic phenomena—when *artificially isolated* from "other influences"—would verify certain hypotheses, and (2) the stream of experiments that Nature is steadily turning out from her own enormous laboratory, and which we merely watch as passive observers. In the first case we can make the agreement and disagreement between theory and facts depend on *two* things: the facts we choose to consider, as well as our theory about them. In the second case we can only try to adjust our theories to reality as it appears before us. And what is the meaning of a design of experiments in this case? It is this: We try to choose a theory and a design of experiments to go with it, in such a way that the resulting data *would be* those which we get by passive observation of reality.

Thus, Haavelmo saw no need for a bridge and an MPD in applied econometrics. In fact, he believed that the whole problem of quantitative inference could be viewed as a problem of gathering information about some unknown probability law. To make this search "a rational problem of statistical inference," one must "start out by an axiom, postulating that every set of observable variables has associated with it one particular 'true,' but unknown, probability law" (Haavelmo 1944, p. 49). Aris Spanos (1989, p. 415) refers to this probability law as the Haavelmo Distribution. To me it is the TPD in the upper data universe of figure 2.1, and the upper data universe in that figure is the universe in which Haavelmo's researcher formulates his theory and carries out his empirical analysis.[8]

The axiomatized theory-data confrontation in subsection 2.2.2 is a formal unitary methodological basis for the science of economics that Frisch may have envisioned when he drafted the constitution of the Econometric Society. His model world was a theory universe in my sense of the term. Also, the universe in which Frisch (1934) carried out his statistical analysis was a data universe in my sense of the term. However, Frisch failed to see the role that a bridge between the two universes may play in applied econometrics. He missed the bridge and the MPD, most likely because he considered the gap between *empirical laws* and *rational laws* to be unbridgeable (Bjerkholt and Qin 2010, p. 34).

I believe that Haavelmo's ideas were adopted too quickly. The universal acceptance of Haavelmo's blueprint for econometrics ended the search for the missing elements in Frisch's idea of a formal science of economics. In fact, since 1944 both theoretical and applied econometrics have, for the most part, been carried out in a world in which figure 2.1 reduces to the upper data universe alone. That has hampered the development of econometrics by making it difficult for econometricians to perceive the logical consequences of adopting Frisch and Haavelmo's vision of a science of economics that I illustrated in figure 2.1.

2.3 A Riddle and Its Resolution

I have described a formal unitary methodological basis for the science of economics and attributed the underlying ideas to Frisch and Haavelmo. Now a question arises: What is the purpose of creating such a formidable structure? I believe that Frisch would have insisted that the purpose of creating such a methodological basis for the science of economics is to help us obtain control over nature and the social institutions we face (Bjerkholt and Qin 2010, p. 32). Haavelmo would have said that its purpose is to provide the tools we need to gain insight into the happenings in real economic life (Haavelmo 1944, pp. 2 and 6). To me the purpose is to facilitate the search for knowledge about interesting economic aspects of social reality.

Obtaining knowledge about interesting economic aspects of social reality is difficult and it is far from obvious that an economist with the given methodological basis will be equal to the task. Frisch and Haavelmo did not doubt their ability to obtain such knowledge. So let's see what they thought about their tools—that is, about economic theory and the data produced by their fellow researchers.

.

According to Frisch, the "observational world, taken as a whole in its infinite complexity and with its infinite mass of detail, is impossible to grasp. [It resembles] a jelly-like mass on which the mind cannot get a grip. In order to create points where the mind can get a grip, we make an intellectual trick: in our mind we create a little *model world* of our own, [and] then we analyse this little model world instead of the real world. This mental trick is the thing which constitutes the rational method, that is, theory." (Bjerkholt and Qin 2010, p. 32) Thus, to Frisch economic theory is a theory about objects in a model world with uncertain relations to objects in social reality.

According to Haavelmo (1944, p. 4), it is "never possible—strictly speaking—to avoid ambiguities in classifications and measurements of real phenomena. Not only is our technique of physical measurements imprecise, but in most cases we are not even able to give an unambiguous description of the *method* of measurement to be used, nor are we able to give precise rules for the choice of *things to be measured* in connection with a certain theory." Thus, to Haavelmo the references of most of the observations that economists have are not well defined. In the words of Sergio Sismondo (1993, p. 516), the references belong in a socially constructed world of ideas—a world that has little in common with social reality.

With such attitudes toward economic theory and data, Frisch and Haavelmo leave us with a riddle that they seem to have overlooked: How is it possible to obtain knowledge about interesting economic aspects of social reality with theories about variables in a model world and with data whose references belong in a socially constructed world of ideas? To solve this riddle it is necessary to have a good idea of the contents of the boxes in figure 2.2.

I discussed the contents of the top three boxes at length in sections 1.4 and 2.2, and there is no need to say more about them here. In chapters 2 and 3 of Stigum 2003 I explicated the meaning of social reality and that of a socially constructed world of ideas. My deliberations in those chapters, and the summary I gave of them in section 1.1 suffice to give the interested reader a good idea of the contents of the socially-constructed-world-of-ideas box and the social-reality box. Finally, the model-world box contains an axiomatized economic theory about variables in Frisch's model world. I discussed the essence of such a theory in section 1.4. There is no need to add further details about the content of the model-world box here.

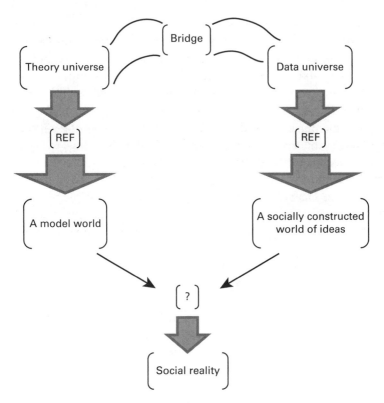

Figure 2.2
A riddle.

2.3.1 The Resolution

In chapters 23 and 24 of my 1990 book I discussed the possibility of knowledge about interesting aspects of social reality. I described the kind of knowledge one can hope to obtain without experience, what we may know by acquaintance and description of things and other minds, and the possibility of knowledge of variable hypotheticals. A variable hypothetical is a for-all sentence that cannot be written as a finite conjunction. Some of them one can know because they are true by definition; e.g., all widows have had a husband. Others one may know by analysis; e.g., Walras' Law. Still others one may know because they describe its instances in terms of a finite number of characteristics that are independent of the state of the world; e.g., a human being is a rational animal. Finally, there are the so-called derivative variable hypotheticals that are axioms or theorems in a scientific theory; here is an example.

APT

A consumer's absolute risk aversion is a decreasing function of his net worth if and only if his holdings of risky assets are an increasing function of his net worth.

This variable hypothetical is a (roughly formulated) theorem in Arrow's 1965 theory of risk aversion that I discussed in chapter 12 of my 1990 book. The possibility of knowing that such a variable hypothetical is a fact is problematic. I ended up my discussion in the 1990 book by saying that the best I can hope for is to know that such a variable hypothetical has empirical relevance. To provide a resolution of the riddle in figure 2.2, I must explicate the meaning of having knowledge of the empirical relevance of a derivative variable hypothetical.

Consider the theory-data confrontations box in figure 2.3 and recall the various boxes in figure 1.2. I presume that I have put a certain theory in the theory box in figure 1.2 and that I have decided on the subfamily of models of the theory that I am going to confront with data. If I identify theory variables with true variables in the real world, I use the chosen family of models of the theory and the data I have to formulate axioms for a data universe. Then I put this data universe in the theory-data confrontations box in figure 2.3. If I do not identify the undefined terms of my theory with true variables in the real world, I use my data to formulate axioms for a data universe and the chosen models of the theory to formulate axioms for a theory universe. At last I formulate bridge principles that relate the theory variables to the data variables, and put the two universes and the bridge in the theory-data confrontation box in figure 2.3.

The purpose of the theory-data confrontation is to check whether the chosen subfamily of models of the theory has empirical relevance. A plus sign in the empirical-relevance box indicates that the theory has empirical relevance. A minus sign indicates that it failed the test. A failure calls for a diagnosis in accord with the discussion of diagnosis in chapter 20 of Stigum 2003. Such a diagnosis may cause changes in the theory axioms and bridge principles or in the data axioms, all of which are formulated inside the theory-data-confrontations box. For the purpose of the present deliberations, I presume that the diagnosis loop results in a theory-data-confrontations box in which the theory has empirical relevance.

Suppose now that we have hit a plus in the empirical-relevance box. Then two things happen. The empirical results; i.e., the estimated models

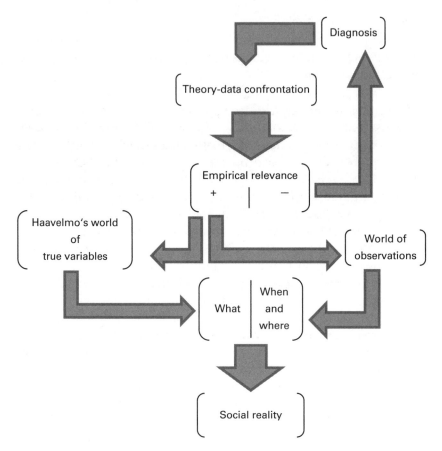

Figure 2.3
Resolution of the riddle.

are transferred to the world-of-observations box. Also, the translation of the empirically relevant theory is transferred to the Haavelmo's-world-of-true-variables box. If we have accurate observations of the theory variables, the estimated models that are transferred to the world-of-observations box are like the models that are transferred to the Haavelmo box. When we have inaccurate observations of the theory variables, the model of the empirically relevant theory may be very different from the estimated models in the world-of-observations box. In this case it is the translated version of the empirically relevant theory that is transferred to the Haavelmo box. I presume that the researcher is able to point out the true variables that corresponds to his theory variables. Hence there is no formal bridge between Frisch's model world and Haavelmo's world of true variables.

In the next step, the world-of-observations box provides information about when and where the theory is deemed empirically relevant. Also, the Haavelmo box confers information about what characteristics of social reality are empirically relevant. Together the two boxes confer information on the basis of which I can claim that I know that there is a situation in social reality in which certain economic aspects have interesting and well-documented characteristics.

A good example of the preceding analysis is the empirical analysis of Arrow and Pratt's theory that I carried out in my 1990 book. There I found that among the consumers who were alive and living in the United States in 1960, those with large net worth in 1963 had lower absolute risk aversion and invested more of their funds in risky assets than those with less net worth. On the basis of that observation, I can make the following assertion:

I know that in the 1960 population of consumers in the U.S.A. those with much net worth in 1963 tended to have lower absolute risk aversion and invest more in risky assets than those with less net worth.

(I write "tended to" because I have analyzed a sample of consumers in the United States, not the whole population.) That formulation explicates what it means to know a derivative variable hypothetical and depicts the extent to which I have solved the riddle I posed in figure 2.3.

My resolution of the riddle applies to the upper data universe of figure 2.1 as well as to the lower data universe. That raises an important question: Does it make a difference for my knowledge of the empirical relevance of a derivative variable hypothetical whether I established it in the upper or lower data universe of figure 2.1? I will discuss and answer this question in the last chapter of this book.

2.4 Concluding Remarks

In this chapter I have described how Frisch and Haavelmo's ideas about a unified theoretical-quantitative and empirical-quantitative approach to economic problems fit in a formal unitary methodological basis for the science of economics. I have also demonstrated that applied econometricians, with the proper understanding of the essence of an economic theory, can learn about characteristic features of the economics of social reality. The ensuing chapters, each in its own way, will lend support to my contention.

3   Empirical Relevance

In this chapter I intend to explain and illustrate what it means for an economic theory to be empirically relevant in the two data universes illustrated in figure 2.1. The need for such an explication is clear—the term "empirical relevance" does not appear in the subject indexes of leading textbooks in econometrics. The 1997 edition of William Greene's *Econometric Analysis* and the 1993 edition of Russell Davidson and James MacKinnon's *Estimation and Inference in Econometrics*, for instance, deal with confidence regions and hypothesis testing in depth but have nothing to say about the empirical relevance of the hypotheses in a test.

3.1 Confidence Regions and Hypothesis Tests

Confidence regions and statistical tests of theoretical hypotheses are fundamental ingredients in my explication of empirical relevance. So, a few words about them are called for. First confidence intervals: A random interval, $I \subset R$, is a mapping of a finite sample, $x_1, \ldots, x_m$, of observations of a random variable, x, to the family of interval subsets of R. A confidence interval is a quadruple, $(I, \beta, \beta^o, \alpha)$, where I is a random interval, β is a parameter whose value is unknown, β^o is an estimate of β that resides in I, $\alpha \in (0, 1)$, and I is structured so that there are good reasons to believe that $\beta \in I$ in $(1 - \alpha)$ percent of all possible samples $x_1, \ldots, x_m$. A confidence region in R^k, $(I, \beta, \beta^o, \alpha)$, is a k-dimensional analogue of a confidence interval where $I \subset R^k$ is a mapping of a finite sample $x_1, \ldots, x_m$ of observations of a vector-valued random variable x to the family of subsets of R^k, $\beta \in R^k$ is a parameter vector whose value is unknown; β^o is an estimate of β that resides in I, $\alpha \in (0, 1)$; and I is structured so that there are good reasons to believe that $\beta \in I$ in $(1 - \alpha)$ percent of all possible samples $x_1, \ldots, x_m$.

The idea of a confidence interval, or a confidence region as the case may be, is well known to econometricians. Even so, for the purpose of explicating the notion of empirical relevance, a simple example that clarifies the concept will be useful.

E3.1
Suppose that x is a normally distributed variable with a mean of β and a known variance of σ^2. Also, suppose that I have a random sample of m observations of x, $x_1, \dots, x_m$, and let β° be the maximum-likelihood estimate of β. Then $\beta^\circ = m^{-1}\Sigma_{1 \le i \le m}x_i$, and $(\beta^\circ - \beta)/(\sigma/\sqrt{m})$ is normally distributed with mean 0 and variance 1. Consequently, if I let $\alpha = 0.05$ and consult a table of areas under the standard normal distribution, I find that in the standard normal distribution the probability is $1 - \alpha$ that $-1.96 \le (\beta^\circ - \beta)/(\sigma/\sqrt{m}) \le 1.96$ and, hence, that $\beta^\circ - 1.96(\sigma/\sqrt{m}) \le \beta \le \beta^\circ + 1.96(\sigma/\sqrt{m})$. From this I conclude that the random interval [$\beta^\circ - 1.96(\sigma/\sqrt{m}), \beta^\circ + 1.96(\sigma/\sqrt{m})$)] is a confidence interval that in 95 percent of all random samples, $x_1, \dots, x_m$, of observations of x contains the true value of β.

Next, hypothesis tests: Roughly speaking, a hypothesis test in an econometric textbook is a triple, $\{H_0, H_1, T\}$, where H_0 represents a null hypothesis, H_1 an alternative hypothesis, and T a pertinent test statistic. It is assumed that the distribution of T under the null hypothesis is known at least approximately, and it is agreed that the range of T is to be divided into an acceptance region A and a rejection region R^*. A researcher begins the test by assigning a number α (for example, 0.05) to the probability of T falling in R^* when H_0 is true. The value of α is referred to as the *significance level* of the test. Thereafter, the researcher chooses R^* and A in such a way that the probability of T falling in R^* when H_0 is false is maximized subject to the condition that the significance level of the test equals α. When the actual value of T is known, the researcher is to reject H_0 if $T \in R^*$. If $T \in A$, the researcher may accept H_0 or assert that the test gives him no reason to reject H_0.

The idea of a hypothesis test is well known to econometricians, but a simple example that clarifies the concept will be useful for the purpose of explicating the notion of empirical relevance.

E3.2
Suppose that x is a normally distributed variable with mean β and known variance σ^2. Also, suppose that I have a random sample of m

observations of x, x_1, ... , x_m, and let β° be the maximum-likelihood estimate of β. Then $\beta^\circ = m^{-1}\Sigma_{1 \leq i \leq m}x_i$. Let H_0 insist that $\beta = 0.1$, let H_1 claim that $\beta \neq 0.1$, and choose as a test statistic $T = (\beta^\circ - 0.1)/(\sigma/\sqrt{m})$. Under the null hypothesis, T is normally distributed with mean 0 and variance 1. If $\alpha = 0.05$ is the significance level of the test, the appropriate choices of A and R^* are $A = [-1.96, 1.96]$ and $R^* = R - A$. I am to reject H_0 if $|T| > 1.96$, and to accept T if $|T| \leq 1.96$.

The relationship between hypotheses tests and confidence regions is important in the present context. One way to depict the relationship is as follows: Let x be a vector-valued random variable on a probability space, $\{\Omega, £, P_\theta(\cdot)\}$, where $\theta \in \Phi$ and $\Phi \subset R^k$ for some positive integer k. Suppose that the hypotheses in a given test are about the true value of θ. Let $T(\cdot)$ be a real-valued function on Ω that is measurable with respect to £, and suppose that $T(\cdot)$ is a test statistic for the given test. Let $S(\cdot)$ be a mapping of Ω to subsets of Φ. Then the family of subsets of Φ, $\{S(x), x \in \Omega\}$, constitutes a family of confidence sets at confidence level $1 - \alpha$ if

$$P_\theta(\{\theta \in S(x)\}) \geq 1 - \alpha \text{ for all } \theta \in \Phi \tag{3.1}$$

—that is, if the random set, $S(x)$, covers the true value of θ with probability $\geq 1 - \alpha$. In a hypothesis test, (H_0, H_1, T), the characterization of $S(\cdot)$ is as follows (see Lehman 1986, pp. 89–91): For each $\theta^\circ \in \Phi$, let $A(\theta^\circ)$ be the subset of the range of $T(\cdot)$ that denotes the acceptance region of a significance-level α test of the null hypothesis, $\theta = \theta^\circ$. Let $S(x) = \{\theta: T(x) \in A(\theta), \theta \in \Phi\}$. Then $S(x)$ is a family of confidence sets for θ at confidence level $1 - \alpha$. This is so because, by definition,

$$\theta \in S(x) \text{ if and only if } T(x) \in A(\theta), \tag{3.2}$$

and hence

$$P_\theta(\{\theta \in S(x)\}) = P_\theta(\{T(x) \in A(\theta)\}) \geq 1 - \alpha. \tag{3.3}$$

Here is an example.

E3.3
Let x, x_1, ... , x_m, I, β, β°, and α be as in E3.1 and suppose that $\sigma = 3$, $\alpha = 0.05$, $\beta^\circ = 0.01$, and $m = 900$. Suppose that

$$H_0 \text{ insists that } \beta = 0.1 \text{ and } H_1 \text{ claims that } \beta \neq 0.1. \tag{3.4}$$

With the given numerical values of the parameters in E3.1, the confidence interval, $S(x_1, \ldots, x_n)$, is

$$[\beta^\circ - 0.196, \beta^\circ + 0.196] = [-0.186, 0.206]. \tag{3.5}$$

According to my understanding of confidence intervals, the given interval suggests that it is perfectly possible that the true value of β equals 0.1. My reading of a hypothesis test agrees. In this case, the test statistic, $T(x_1, \ldots, x_n)$, equals $(\beta^\circ - 0.1)/(3/30)$. Hence, the value of T is -0.9. According to E3.2, I am to reject H_0 only if $|T| > 1.96$. Consequently, I accept H_0.

3.2 Empirical Relevance in Figure 2.1—An Explication

The outcome of a given test of a theoretical hypothesis depends both on the empirical context in which the theoretical hypothesis is tested and on the pertinent explication of empirical relevance. In figure 2.1 the empirical context in the upper data universe differs from the empirical context in the lower data universe. Also, the explication of empirical relevance in the upper data universe differs from its explication in the lower data universe. I describe how below.

First, empirical context. In the upper data universe in figure 2.1, the empirical context has two components: (1) axioms and loosely formulated assumptions that the pertinent researcher uses to delineate the characteristics of the data-generating process and (2) the prescriptions that underlie the statistical analysis. The second component details, for example, the way the researcher is to search for a data-admissible econometric model that parsimoniously encompasses the so-called local data-generating process (Bontemps and Mizon 2003, pp. 356, 359, and 366; Hendry and Krolzig 2003, pp. 380 and 386–391).

In the lower data universe, the empirical context has, also, two components: (1) the prescriptions that underlie the statistical analysis and (2) a description of the characteristics of a data-admissible mathematical model of the MPD. The prescriptions that underlie the statistical analysis detail the way the researcher is to obtain a consistent estimate of a mathematical model of the MPD. Also, a mathematical model of MPD is data admissible if (1) the estimated mathematical model of MPD satisfies the strictures on which the non-stochastic axioms of the data universe and the prescriptions that underlie the statistical analysis insist; (2) the values that the given model assigns to the parameters of MPD satisfy the strictures on which the theory axioms, the non-stochastic data axioms, and the axioms of the bridge insist; and (3) the model lies within a 95-percent-confidence region of the estimated mathematical model of MPD.

Next, empirical relevance. In the upper data universe, the empirical relevance of a theoretical hypothesis is, with my reading of the outcome of hypothesis tests, determined the way a null hypothesis is tested in mathematical statistics. The theoretical hypothesis is taken to be empirically relevant if and only if the test gives the researcher no reason to reject the hypothesis. In the lower data universe, a family of mathematical models of the theory axioms is empirically relevant if and only if there is a member of the given family that, together with a model of the non-stochastic data axioms and the bridge principles, determines a model of the MPD that belongs to a 95-percent-confidence band of a meaningful statistical estimate of the MPD.

Why the explications in the two data universes differ in empirical relevance is important. I insist throughout the book that there is only one model of the TPD in figure 2.1. Since the pertinent axioms in the upper data universe delineate characteristics of the TPD, it follows that these axioms also have just one true model. In contrast, there are as many "true" models of the pertinent theory axioms as there are members of a specified family of models of these axioms. A model of the MPD is a model that is determined by the non-stochastic axioms of the data universe, the bridge principles, and one of the many "true" models of the pertinent theory axioms. Hence, there are as many models of the MPD in the lower data universe of figure 2.1 as there are members of a specified family of models of the axioms in the pertinent theory universe and the bridge principles. These models are data admissible only if they lie in a 95-percent-confidence band of an estimated model of the MPD. An estimated model of MPD, in turn, is an estimate of a model of an MPD that the non-stochastic data axioms, the bridge principles, and any one of the "true" models of the theory axioms determine.

In the remainder of the chapter I will give four examples from different fields of economics: experimental economics, consumer choice under certainty, simultaneous equations, and risk aversion and choice of risky assets. The examples illustrate four interesting aspects of the ideas of empirical context and empirical relevance that I have tried to convey above. In the example from experimental economics, the researcher has accurate observations of his theory variables. In the example from consumer choice, the theory axioms have only one model. In the simultaneous-equations example, the theory axioms have any number of models that are interrelated in interesting ways. The risk-aversion example presents an empirical analysis in which the empirical relevance of a single theorem of a theory is at stake. In the four examples—and in the rest of the book—I take, without saying so, the α in a confidence interval and the significance level of a hypothesis test to equal 0.05.

In reading the examples, note that they have a definite design. I first present the axioms for a theory-data confrontation with two universes and a bridge between them. I then present the axioms for an empirical analysis in which the same theory-data confrontation is reduced to a data universe alone. The axioms of the data universe in the first formulation play two roles—one as part of the empirical analysis in the lower data universe of figure 2.1 and another as the basic axioms for the empirical analysis in the upper data universe. For the upper data universe these basic axioms delineate, in the terminology of Grayham Mizon and David Hendry, an identifiable and low-level-theory-consistent structure of the empirical analysis. The low-level theory is taken to "provide a framework within which the high-level theory can be tested" (Bontemps and Mizon 2003, p. 365).

In the examples in this chapter the researcher will add elements of his high-level theory to the axioms of the upper data universe before he commences the analysis of his data. Adding elements of the high-level theory to the low-level theory in the upper data-universe may involve adding components to ω_P, adding axioms to Γ_P, and reformulating the triple $(\Omega_P, \aleph_P, P_P(\cdot))$. Whatever the changes may be, they will add interesting details to the low-level characteristics of the TPD in the original upper data universe.

3.3 An Example from Experimental Economics

Consider an urn with 1,000 identical balls. Some of the balls are red. The others are blue. It is unknown how many blue balls there are. A blindfolded man is to pull 250 balls at random from the urn. After each draw, the color of the ball will be recorded, the drawn ball will be returned to the urn, and the urn will be shaken well before the next ball is drawn.

Before the blindfolded man gets started, I figure that the probability, p, of pulling a red ball from the urn is no less than 0.5 and no more than 0.6; i.e., that $p \in [0.5, 0.6]$. I intend to confront this hypothesis with the results of the blindfolded man's draws.

I begin by formulating axioms for the theory universe, the data universe, and the bridge that I need for the empirical analysis in the lower data universe of figure 2.1. First the axioms for the theory universe.

The Γ_T axioms
$\Omega_T = \{r, b\}$, where r is short for red and b is short for blue, $\aleph_T$ is the field of all subsets of Ω_T, and $P_T(\cdot):\aleph_T \to [0, 1]$ is a probability measure. Thus $\omega_T \in \Omega_T$ only if $\omega_T = x$ for some $x \in \{r, b\}$. Also, $x(\cdot): \Omega_T \to \{r, b\}$ is defined by the equations $x(\omega_T) = \omega_T$, and $\omega_T \in \Omega_T$, and is measurable with respect to $\aleph_T$. Finally, $P_T(x(\omega_T) = r) = \beta$, $P_T(x(\omega_T) = b) = 1 - \beta$, and $\beta \in [0.5, 0.6]$.

Then the axioms for the data universe.

The Γ_P axioms
$\Omega_P = \{r, b\}$, where r is short for red and b is short for blue, $\aleph_P$ is the field of all subsets of Ω_P, and $P_P(\cdot):\aleph_T \to [0, 1]$ is a probability measure. Thus $\omega_P \in \Omega_P$ only if $\omega_P = y$ for some $y \in \{r, b\}$. Also, $y(\cdot): \Omega_P \to \{r, b\}$ is defined by the equations $y(\omega_P) = \omega_P$, and $\omega_P \in \Omega_P$, and is measurable with respect to $\aleph_P$. Finally, $P_P(y(\omega_P) = r) = p$, $P_P(y(\omega_P) = b) = 1 - p$, and $p \in (0, 1)$.

Finally the axioms for the bridge.

The $\Gamma_{T,P}$ axioms
$\Omega \subset \Omega_T \times \Omega_P$, Ω_T and Ω_P are disjoint, and $\aleph_T$ and $\aleph_P$ are stochastically independent. Also, $\Omega \in \aleph$, and $P(\Omega) > 0$, where $\aleph$ and $P(\cdot)$ are as defined in section 2.2. Finally, $(\omega_T, \omega_P) \in \Omega$ if and only if $\omega_T \in \Omega_T$, $\omega_P \in \Omega_P$, and $y(\omega_P) = x(\omega_T)$.

The MPD
From the Γ_T and $\Gamma_{T,P}$ axioms it follows that

$\Omega_T \subset \{\omega_T \in \Omega_T$ for which there is an $\omega_P \in \Omega_P$ with $(\omega_T, \omega_P) \in \Omega\}$.

Hence, the MPD must be as described by equations:

$$\text{MPD}(y(\omega_P) = r) = P_T(\{\omega_T \in \Omega_T \text{ and } x(\omega_T) = r\}) = \beta \qquad (3.6)$$

and

$$\text{MPD}(y(\omega_P) = b) = P_T(\{\omega_T \in \Omega_T \text{ and } x(\omega_T) = b\}) = 1 - \beta. \qquad (3.7)$$

The statistical analysis

The prescriptions underlying my statistical analysis insist that I obtain a maximum-likelihood estimate of β. From equations 3.6 and 3.7 I deduce that the likelihood function in the MPD distribution of y takes the form

$$L(\beta \mid y_1, \ldots, y_{250}) = \prod_{1 \leq i \leq 250} \beta^{yi}(1 - \beta)^{(1 - yi)}, \qquad (3.8)$$

where y_i is a random variable that assumes the value 1 if the ball in the ith draw is red and the value 0 if the ball is blue. The result of the sampling process is 140 red balls and 110 blue balls. Consequently, the maximum-likelihood estimate of β is

$$\beta^\circ = 140/250 = 0.56. \qquad (3.9)$$

The maximum-likelihood estimator in this case is consistent in the MPD-determined P_M measure on $(\Omega_P, \aleph_P)$. Hence, the estimate in equation 3.9 satisfies the prescriptions underlying my statistical analysis. Besides, the given estimate satisfies the pertinent conditions in the Γ_T axioms. From this it follows that β° determines a data-admissible mathematical model of the MPD.

A data-admissible mathematical model of the MPD marks off one empirically relevant model of the theory axioms. It is interesting to see how many such empirically relevant models of Γ_T there are. For that purpose I must delineate a 95-percent-confidence interval around β°. The negative, $H(\cdot)$, of the Hessian of the likelihood function evaluated at 0.56 is

$$H(0.56) = \begin{pmatrix} (62,500 / 140) & 0 \\ 0 & (62,500 / 110) \end{pmatrix}. \qquad (3.10)$$

I presume that

$$(\beta - \beta^\circ, (1 - \beta) - (1 - \beta^\circ)) \cdot (H(\beta^\circ)) \cdot (\beta - \beta^\circ, (1 - \beta) - (1 - \beta^\circ))'$$

is approximately χ^2 distributed with one degree of freedom. The critical value for a 95-percent-confidence interval for β is then 3.84, and the confidence interval for which I am looking is

$$\beta \in [0.498826, 0.621174]. \qquad (3.11)$$

This confidence interval does not vary with the models of MPD, but it depends on the observed value of β°.

The fact that the interval [0.5, 0.6] is a proper subset of the confidence interval in equation 3.11 implies that all the points in [0.5, 0.6] are empirically relevant. The remaining points in the confidence interval are not. The same fact provides an example of a confidence region around the estimate of MPD that contains mathematical models of the MPD that are not data admissible.

It is relevant here to observe that in the present case I have accurate observations of the theory variables. Even so, as I will show next, the analysis in the lower data universe is very different from the analysis in the upper data universe.

For the empirical analysis in the upper data universe I adopt the Γ_P axioms that I listed above, and I add an axiom that insists that $p \in [0.5, 0.6]$. From the axioms I deduce that the likelihood function of the data-generating process is

$$L(p \mid y_1, \dots, y_{250}) = \Pi_{1 \leq i \leq 250} \, p^{y_i}(1 - p)^{(1 - y_i)}. \tag{3.12}$$

I intend to apply the method of maximum likelihood to estimate the value of p. Also, I use a standard 95-percent-confidence interval around the estimate to test the empirical relevance of my theory.

Since the result of the sampling process is 140 red balls and 110 blue balls, the maximum-likelihood estimate of p is

$$p^{\circ} = 140/250 = 0.56. \tag{3.13}$$

The maximum-likelihood estimator in the upper data universe is consistent in P_P measure. Also, with the negative of the Hessian as described in equation 3.10, the 95-percent-confidence interval around the estimate of p is given by $p \in [0.498826, 0.621174]$—the same confidence interval as the confidence interval around the estimate of β in the lower data universe. According to my reading of the meaning of confidence intervals, the confidence interval that I have computed will in 95 percent of all random samples contain the true value of p. Consequently, since the given confidence interval contains values of p that are not allowed by my theoretical hypothesis, the sampling results imply that my theory about the proportion of red balls in the urn is not empirically relevant in the upper data universe of figure 2.1.

It is significant for the import of the present example that the implications of the confidence interval in the upper data universe are so different from its implications in the lower data universe. In the upper data universe I reject the empirical relevance of my theory because the confidence interval contains too many points. In the lower data universe I accept the empirical relevance of my theory because [0.5, 0.6] has a non-empty intersection with the confidence interval.

3.4 An Example from Consumer Choice under Certainty

Now let us return to our imaginary city, OS, to study formal characteristics of consumer income and consumption. As before, the theory
universe, the data universe, and the bridge are $(\Omega_T, \Gamma_T, (\Omega_T, \aleph_T, P_T(\cdot)))$,
$(\Omega_P, \Gamma_P, (\Omega_P, \aleph_P, P_P(\cdot)))$, and $(\Omega, \Gamma_{T,P})$ with h = 2, k = 2, and H = I—the 2
× 2 identity matrix. I assume throughout that Ω_T and Ω_P are disjoint,
that $\aleph_T$ and $\aleph_P$ are stochastically independent, and that $\Omega \in \aleph$ and $P(\Omega)$
> 0 in the probability space $(\Omega_T \times \Omega_P, \aleph, P(\cdot))$, which I described in
chapter 2. To simplify my arguments, I formulate axioms for a case in
which the researcher samples at random only once in the observations
box in figure 1.2. In the intended interpretation of the axioms, y, y_P, and
y_t denote, respectively, a consumer's disposable income, permanent
income, and transitory income, and c, c_p, and c_t denote, respectively,
consumption, permanent consumption, and transitory consumption,
where consumption is short for a consumer's outlays on consumer
goods. It is understood that in the present case the object of the empirical analyses in the two data universes in figure 2.1 is to ascertain
whether Milton Friedman's Permanent Income Hypothesis is empirically relevant in OS.

I begin by writing down axioms for a theory-data confrontation with
two disjoint universes and a bridge between them. First, the data
universe.

The Γ_P axioms
$\Omega_P = \{1, 3, 5, 7\} \times \{0.5, 1.5, 2.5, 3.5, 4.5\}$, $\aleph_P$ is the field of all subsets of
Ω_P, and $P_P(\cdot):\aleph_P \rightarrow [0, 1]$ is a probability measure. Thus $\omega_P \in \Omega_P$ only if
$\omega_P = (y,c)$ for some y $\in \{1, 3, 5, 7\}$, c $\in \{0.5, 1.5, 2.5, 3.5, 4.5\}$, and (y,c) $\in$
$\{1, 3, 5, 7\} \times \{0.5, 1.5, 2.5, 3.5, 4.5\}$. Also, $y(\cdot): \Omega_P \rightarrow \{1, 3, 5, 7\}$ and $c(\cdot):$
$\Omega_P \rightarrow \{0.5, 1.5, 2.5, 3.5, 4.5\}$ are defined by the equations $(y(\omega_P), c(\omega_P))$
$= \omega_P$ and $\omega_P \in \Omega_P$, and the vector-valued function $(y, c)(\cdot)$ is measurable
with respect to $\aleph_P$. Finally, relative to $P_P(\cdot)$, the pair (y, c) has finite
means, finite positive variances, and positive covariance.

Next the theory universe.

The Γ_T axioms
$\Omega_T = \{2, 4, 6\} \times \{-1, 1\} \times \{1, 2, 3\} \times \{-0.5, 0.5\}$, $\aleph_T$ is the field of all subsets
of Ω_T, and $P_T(\cdot):\aleph_T \rightarrow [0, 1]$ is a probability measure. Thus $\omega_T \in \Omega_T$ only
if $\omega_T = (y_p, y_t, c_p, c_t)$ for some $y_p \in \{2, 4, 6\}$, $y_t \in \{-1, 1\}$, $c_p \in \{1, 2, 3\}$,

$c_t \in \{-0.5, 0.5\}$, and $(y_p, y_t, c_p, c_t) \in \{2, 4, 6\} \times \{-1, 1\} \times \{1, 2, 3\} \times \{-0.5, 0.5\}$. Also, $y_p(\cdot): \Omega_P \to \{2, 4, 6\}$, $y_t(\cdot): \Omega_P \to \{-1, 1\}$, $c_p(\cdot): \Omega_P \to \{1, 2, 3\}$, and $c_t(\cdot): \Omega_P \to \{-0.5, 0.5\}$ are defined by the equations $(y_p(\omega_T), y_t(\omega_T), c_p(\omega_T), c_t(\omega_T)) = \omega_T$, and $\omega_T \in \Omega_T$, and the vector-valued function (y_p, y_t, c_p, c_t) $(\cdot)$ is measurable with respect to $\aleph_T$. Moreover, for all $\omega_T \in \Omega_T$,

$$c_p(\omega_T) = 0.5 \cdot y_p(\omega_T), \tag{3.14}$$

and relative to $P_T(\cdot)$, y_p, y_t, and c_t are distributed independently of each other. Finally, $P_T(\{\omega_T \in \Omega_T: y_p(\omega_T) = j\}) = \frac{1}{4}, \frac{1}{2}, \frac{1}{4}$ according as $j = 2, 4, 6$: $P_T(\{\omega_T \in \Omega_T; y_t(\omega_T) = -1\}) = P_T(\{\omega_T \in \Omega_T; y_t(\omega_T) = 1\}) = \frac{1}{2}$; and $P_T(\{\omega_T \in \Omega_T: c_t(\omega_T) = -0.5\}) = P_T(\{\omega_T \in \Omega_T: c_t(\omega_T) = 0.5\}) = \frac{1}{2}$.

Finally, the Bridge.

The $\Gamma_{T,P}$ axioms
$\Omega \subset \Omega_T \times \Omega_P$. Also, $(\omega_T, \omega_P) \in \Omega$ if and only if $\omega_T \in \Omega_T$, $\omega_P \in \Omega_P$, $y_p(\omega_T)$ $+ y_t(\omega_T) = y(\omega_P)$, and $c_p(\omega_T) + c_t(\omega_T) = c(\omega_P)$.

It follows from the axioms that in the given bridge $\Omega_T = \{(y_p, y_t, c_p, c_t) \in \Omega_T$ for which there is a pair $(y, c) \in \Omega_P$ such that $(y_p, y_t, c_p, c_t, y, c\} \in \Omega\}$.

The MPD
In Ω_P, the pairs with positive MPD probabilities are restricted. To see how, observe that in the given bridge the possible values of $y(\omega_P)$ are 1, 3, 5, and 7 and the possible values of $c(\omega_P)$ are 0.5, 1.5. 2.5, and 3.5. There are no values of $c_p(\omega_T)$ and $c_t(\omega_T)$ in Ω_T such that $c_p(\omega_T) + c_t(\omega_T)$ $= 4.5$. Hence, the set $\{\omega_T \in \Omega_T$ for which there is a pair $(y, c) \in \{1, 3, 5, 7\} \times \{4.5\}$ such that $y_p(\omega_T) + y_t(\omega_T) = y$ and $c_p(\omega_T) + c_t(\omega_T) = c\}$ is empty. In fact, if I let

$$A = \{(y,c) \in (\{1\} \times \{2.5, 3.5\} \cup \{3\} \times \{3.5\} \cup \{5\} \times \{0.5\} \cup \{7\} \times \{0.5, 1.5\})$$

I find that

$$\mathrm{MPD}(A) = P_T(\{\omega_T \in \Omega_T: (y_p(\omega_T) + y_t(\omega_T), c_p(\omega_T) + c_t(\omega_T)) = (y, c)$$

and

$$(y, c) \in A\}) = 0.$$

The MPD probabilities of the remaining (y, c) pairs are given in table 3.1.
With the given MPD probabilities, I find that $E_{\mathrm{MPD}}(c) = 2$, $E_{\mathrm{MPD}}(y) = 4$, $E_{\mathrm{MPD}}(y - 4)^2 = 3$, $E_{\mathrm{MPD}}(c - 2)^2 = 0.75$, and $E_{\mathrm{MPD}}(c - 2)(y - 4) = 1$.

Table 3.1

| | c | | | | | |
y	{0.5}	{1.5}	{2.5}	{3.5}	{4.5}	mp_y
{1}	1/16	1/16	0	0	0	1/8
{3}	1/16	3/16	1/8	0	0	3/8
{5}	0	1/8	3/16	1/16	0	3/8
{7}	0	0	1/16	1/16	0	1/8
Pm_c	1/8	3/8	3/8	1/8	0	1

Consequently, the least-squares regression line of c on y in $P_M(\cdot)$ measure is given by

$$c = (2/3) + (1/3)y + \xi, \tag{3.15}$$

where

$$\xi_{ij} = c_i - (2/3) - (1/3)y_j$$

with

$$(c_i, y_j) \in (\{0.5\} \times \{1,3\} \cup \{1.5\} \times \{1,3,5\} \cup \{2.5\} \times \{3,5,7\} \cup \{3.5\} \times \{5,7\}).$$

The MPD probabilities of the ξ_{ij} are equal to the MPD probabilities of the associated (c_i, y_j) pairs in table 3.1. The variance of ξ, denoted by $E\xi^2$, is 0.4167.

Recall, now, the two abstract scenarios that I described in section 2.2. Without spelling out the details, I shall pick a model of the given axioms and describe how the empirical analyses of Friedman's Permanent Income Hypothesis in the two scenarios differ. Also, I shall use OxMetrics' uniform random number generator to design a purely random sampling scheme for observations of the pair (y, c) based on the probabilities in table 3.2.

My sampling scheme and the table delineate the characteristics of the data-generating process in the present case. The details of this data-generating process are unknown to the researcher in charge.

From the table I deduce that $E_{TPD}(c) = 2.05$, $E_{TPD}(y) = 3.1$, $E_{TPD}(c - 2.05)^2 = 0.8975$, $E_{TPD}(y - 3.1)^2 = 2.59$, and $E_{TPD}(c - 2.05) \cdot (y - 3.1) = 1.260625$. Consequently, the regression line of c on y in the TPD distribution is given by

$$c = 0.5418442 + 0.4867277 \cdot y + \zeta, \tag{3.16}$$

Table 3.2

y	c {0.5}	{1.5}	{2.5}	{3.5}	{4.5}	mp$_y$
{1}	1/8	1/8	0	0	0	1/4
{3}	0	1/4	¼	0	0	1/2
{5}	0	0	1/10	1/10	0	1/5
{7}	0	0	0	1/40	1/40	1/20
Pm$_c$	1/8	3/8	7/20	1/8	1/40	1

where

$$\zeta_{ij} = c_i - 0.5418442 - 0.4867277 \cdot y_j$$

with

$$(c_i, y_j) \in \{\{0.5\} \times \{1\} \cup \{1.5\} \times \{1,3\} \cup \{2.5\} \times \{3,5\} \times \{5,7\} \cup \{4.5\} \times \{7\}$$

The TPD probabilities of the ζ_{ij} are equal to the TPD probabilities of the associated (c_i, y_j) pairs in table 3.2. The variance of ζ, denoted by $E\zeta^2$, is 0.5114.

Consider the first scenario, and suppose that the researcher in charge, with my help, has obtained a finite random sample of observations of (y, c). He accepts the Γ_P axioms of the data universe that I listed above, but he has no use for the Γ_T and $\Gamma_{T,P}$ axioms and throws them out.

Next, he adds four variables, $\acute{y}_p, \acute{y}_t, \acute{c}_p, \acute{c}_t$, to the components of ω_P, and designates the new data universe by the triple, $(\Omega^*_P, \Gamma^*_P, (\Omega^*_P, \aleph^*_P, P^*_P(\cdot))$. Then, $\Omega^*_P = \Omega_P \times \{2, 4, 6\} \times \{-1, 1\} \times \{1, 2, 3\} \times \{-0.5, 0.5\}$, $\aleph^*_P$ is the field of all subsets of Ω^*_P, and $P^*_P(\cdot): \aleph^*_P \to [0, 1]$ is a probability measure. Thus $\omega_P \in \Omega^*_P$ only if $\omega_P = (y, c, \acute{y}_p, \acute{y}_t, \acute{c}_p, \acute{c}_t)$ for some $(y, c) \in \Omega_P, \acute{y}_p \in \{2, 4, 6\}, \acute{y}_t \in \{-1, 1\}, \acute{c}_p \in \{1, 2, 3\}, \acute{c}_t \in \{-0.5, 0.5\}$, and $((y, c), \acute{y}_p, \acute{y}_t, \acute{c}_p, \acute{c}_t) \in \Omega_P \times \{2, 4, 6\} \times \{-1, 1\} \times \{1, 2, 3\} \times \{-0.5, 0.5\}$. Also, $y(\cdot): \Omega^*_P \to \{1, 3, 5, 7\}, c(\cdot): \Omega^*_P \to \{0.5, 1.5, 2.5, 3.5, 4.5\}, \acute{y}_p(\cdot): \Omega^*_P \to \{2, 4, 6\}, \acute{y}_t(\cdot): \Omega^*_P \to \{-1, 1\}, \acute{c}_p(\cdot): \Omega^*_P \to \{1, 2, 3\}$, and $\acute{c}_t(\cdot): \Omega^*_P \to \{-0.5, 0.5\}$ are defined by the equations $(y(\omega_P), c(\omega_P), \acute{y}_p(\omega_P), \acute{y}_t(\omega_P), \acute{c}_p(\omega_P), \acute{c}_t(\omega_P)) = \omega_P$, and $\omega_P \in \Omega^*_P$, and the vector-valued function $(y, c, \acute{y}_p, \acute{y}_t, \acute{c}_p, \acute{c}_t)(\cdot)$ is measurable with respect to $\aleph^*_P$.

The researcher identifies his theory variables, $\acute{y}_p$, and $\acute{c}_p$ with Haavelmo's true variables in the real world, and adds an axiom that details how they are related to each other and to y and c. The new axiom postulates the validity in Ω^*_P of the following three equations:

$$y(\omega_P) = \acute{y}_p(\omega_P) + \acute{y}_t(\omega_P),$$

$$c(\omega_P) = \acute{c}_p(\omega_P) + \acute{c}_t(\omega_P),$$ (3.17)

$$\acute{c}_p(\omega_P) = \alpha + \beta \; \acute{y}_p (\omega_P).$$

When the researcher accepts Γ_P, I take it to mean that he assumes that the variables c and y relative to $P^*_P(\cdot)$ have finite means, positive variances, and positive covariance. He adds a second axiom to the effect that, relative to $P^*_P(\cdot)$, the means of $\acute{y}_t$ and $\acute{c}_t$ are 0, the variances of $\acute{y}_t$ and $\acute{c}_t$ are positive, and $\acute{y}_p$, $\acute{y}_t$, and $\acute{c}_t$ are distributed independently. Their distribution is the same as the distribution of their name sakes in the RPD distribution. The researcher's axioms leave him with a serious problem: Estimates of α and β cannot be identified.

To test the validity of the Permanent Income Hypothesis, the researcher uses a variant of an idea that he has learned from reading Yngve Willassen's 1984 article on unidentified structural parameters in errors-in-variable models. His test is based on the validity of the following theorem.

T3.1
Suppose that the assumptions in Γ_P concerning the probability distribution of y and c are valid in the new data universe. Suppose also that the researcher's assumptions concerning the relations in equation 3.17, the means and variances of $\acute{y}_t$ and $\acute{c}_t$, and the distribution of $\acute{y}_p$, $\acute{y}_t$, and $\acute{c}_t$ are valid. Let

$$c = \alpha_{cy} + \beta_{cy} \cdot y + \eta_c \text{ and } y = \alpha_{yc} + \beta_{yc} \cdot c + \eta_y$$ (3.18)

be, respectively, the least-squares regression lines of c on y and y on c. Then

$$0 < \beta_{cy}; \; 0 < \beta_{yc} \text{ and } \beta_{cy} < \beta < 1/\beta_{yc}; \; \alpha < \alpha_{cy}; \; (\alpha/\beta) < \alpha_{yc}.$$ (3.19)

The first three inequalities in equation 3.19 present a strict-inequality version of one of Frisch's theorems. (See equation 9.11 on page 60 of Frisch 1934.) The strict inequalities involved follow easily from the assumption that the covariance of c and y is positive and the variances of $\acute{y}_t$ and $\acute{c}_t$ are positive. The last two inequalities in equation 3.19 follow from the first three inequalities and the equation (mean of c) = α + β(mean of y) and need no further proof.

To provide an empirical test of the Permanent Income Hypothesis, the researcher uses my data to ascertain whether T3.1 has empirical

Table 3.3
OLS-CS (ordinary least-squares–compound symmetric) modeling of CIV.

	Coefficient	SE	t value	t probability	Part.R^2
Constant	0.495629	0.04505	11.0	0.0000	0.1683
INCIV	0.497626	0.01306	38.1	0.0000	0.7081
sigma	0.500685	RSS	149.910056		
R^2	0.708133	F(1, 598) =	1451 [0.000]**		
Adj.R^2	0.707645	log-likelihood	−435.295		
no. of observations	600	no. of parameters	2		
mean(CIV)	2.025	se(CIV)	0.925997		
Normality test:	Chi^2(2) =	847.79	[0.0000]**		
Hetero test:	F(2, 597) =	0.073904	[0.9288]		
Hetero-X test:	F(2, 597) =	0.073904	[0.9288]		
RESET23 test:	F(2, 596) =	0.60438	[0.5467]		

relevance in the empirical context that my data determine. In the present case, H_0 insists that the inequalities in equation 3.19 are valid, and H_1 claims that at least one of them does not hold. The researcher begins by regressing c (= CIV) on y (= INCIV) and y on c.[1] The results of the researcher's regressions are as shown in tables 3.3–3.5.

The two asterisks in table 3.4 are disconcerting, but the estimated linear relation between y and c is not statistically different from the true relation, $y = 0.2206 + 1.4046c + \eta$, where η is the pertinent error term. Thus, I will ignore the two asterisks here.

The values of α and β are not identifiable in the researcher's model. However, whatever their values are, they must satisfy the equation (mean of c) = α + β(mean of y). Among the possible (α, β) pairs there is one in which $\alpha = 0$ and β = (mean of c)/(mean of y), so the researcher lets $\alpha = 0$. His estimate of β is then $\beta^* = 2.0250/3.0733 = 0.6589$. With this estimate of β, the researcher's regression results satisfy all the inequalities in equation 3.19:

$$\alpha_{cy} = 0.495629, \alpha_{yc} = 0.191713, \beta_{cy} = 0.497626, 1/\beta_{yc} = 1/1.42302 = 0.7027.$$

Since all the parameter estimates are significantly different from 0, the researcher does not seem to have reasons to reject his null hypothesis.[2]

If the researcher's arguments for choosing 0 as the value of α are valid, the outcome of his test has an important bearing on the empirical

Table 3.4
Modeling INCIV by OLS-CS.

	Coefficient	SE		t value	t probability	Part.R^2
Constant	0.191713	0.08317		2.30	0.0215	0.0088
CIV	1.42302	0.03736		38.1	0.0000	0.7081
sigma	0.84668	RSS		428.686091		
R^2	0.708133	F(1, 598) =		1451 [0.000]**		
Adj.R^2	0.707645	log-likelihood		−750.502		
no. of observations	600	no. of parameters		2		
mean(INCIV)	3.07333	se(INCIV)		1.5659		
Normality test:	Chi^2(2) =	36.814		[0.0000]**		
Hetero test:	F(2, 597) =	41.552		[0.0000]**		
Hetero-X test:	F(2, 597) =	41.552		[0.0000]**		
RESET23 test:	F(2, 596) =	8.8999		[0.0002]**		

Table 3.5
Means, standard deviations, and correlations.

Means

CIV	INCIV
2.0250	3.0733

Standard deviations (using T − 1)

CIV	INCIV
0.92600	1.5659

Correlation matrix

	CIV	INCIV
CIV	1.0000	0.84151
INCIV	0.84151	1.0000

relevance of Friedman's Permanent Income Hypothesis. With $\alpha = 0$, the researcher's axioms are the axioms of Friedman's theory. Consequently, if $\alpha = 0$, the outcome of the test demonstrates that the researcher has no reason to reject Friedman's hypothesis. In other words, the Permanent Income Hypothesis is empirically relevant in the empirical context the theory faces in the upper data universe in OS.

Next, consider the second scenario, and suppose that the researcher in charge, with my help, has obtained a finite number of "observations" of $((y_p, y_t, c_p, c_t), (y, c))$. The components of (y_p, y_t, c_p, c_t) are unobservable. Hence, only the components of (y, c) are observed. The observations of y and c are the same as the observations of y and c that the researcher in the upper data universe had. In this case the purpose of the empirical analysis is to determine whether the Γ_T axioms are empirically relevant. The researcher begins by estimating the parameters of equations 3.15 and makes sure that the estimated model is statistically adequate. Then he delineates a 95-percent-confidence band around the estimated parameters. The Γ_T axioms are empirically relevant only if at least one member of the confidence band has parameters from which one can deduce the relation (mean of c) = 0.5(mean of y) and ascertain that equations 3.15 depict a data-admissible model of the MPD. In this case there is only one model of the Γ_T axioms. Also, equations 3.15 and 3.16 are formally equivalent. From this and from the statistical results listed in tables 3.1–3.3 it follows that the Γ_T and $\Gamma_{T,P}$ version of the Permanent Income Hypothesis is not empirically relevant in OS.

3.5 A Simultaneous-Equations Example

In this example I carry out the empirical analysis that was missing in example E2.2.9 in chapter 2. The theory universe, the data universe, and the bridge are, as always, designated by $(\Omega_T, \Gamma_T, (\Omega_T, \aleph_T, P_T(\cdot)))$, $(\Omega_P, \Gamma_P, (\Omega_P, \aleph_P, P_P(\cdot)))$, and $(\Omega, \Gamma_{T,P})$. Also, vectors in the theory universe function as vectors in Ω_T and as vector valued random variables on $(\Omega_T, \aleph_T)$. Similarly, vectors in the data universe function as vectors in Ω_P and as vector valued random variables on $(\Omega_P, \aleph_P)$. I assume throughout that Ω_T and Ω_P are disjoint, that $\aleph_T$ and $\aleph_P$ are stochastically independent, and that $\Omega \in \aleph$ and $P(\Omega) > 0$ in the probability space, $(\Omega_T \times \Omega_P, \aleph, P(\cdot))$, that I described in chapter 2.

For ease of reference I repeat the axioms and much of the commentaries that I presented in the original example. Also, here as there, the intended interpretation of the axioms depicts a data confrontation of a theory of a competitive commodity market in which the researcher is to sample at random once in the Observations box in figure 1.2.[3]

I begin with the axioms for a theory-data confrontation in which there are two disjoint universes and a bridge between them. First, the axioms of the theory universe.

The Γ_T axioms

In this case $\Omega_T \subset (R^5 \times (R^2 \times \{0,0\}))$, $\aleph_T$ is a σ field of subsets of Ω_T, and $P_T(\cdot):\aleph_T \to [0, 1]$ is a probability measure. Thus $\omega_T \in \Omega_T$ only if $\omega_T = (x,u)$ for some $x \in R^5$, $u \in (R^2 \times \{0,0\})$, and $(x,u) \in (R^5 \times (R^2 \times \{0,0\}))$. Also, $x(\cdot)$: $\Omega_T \to R^5$ and $u(\cdot): \Omega_T \to R^2 \times \{0, 0\}$ are defined by the equations $(x(\omega_T), u(\omega_T)) = \omega_T$, and $\omega_T \in \Omega_T$. Moreover, the vector-valued function $(x, u)(\cdot)$ is measurable with respect to $\aleph_T$, and has, subject to the conditions on which Γ_T insists, a well-defined probability distribution relative to $P_T(\cdot)$. In this probability distribution, $x(\omega_T)$ has finite means and covariances and the covariance matrix of $x_4(\omega_T)$ and $x_5(\omega_T)$ is invertible; $(u_1, u_2)(\omega_T)$ has zero means and finite positive variances; $x(\omega_T)$ and $(u_1, u_2)(\omega_T)$ are distributed independently of each other; and $u_1(\omega_T)$ and $u_2(\omega_T)$ are independently distributed. Finally, there are six real-valued constants, $\alpha_0 > 0$, $\alpha_1 < 0$, $\alpha_2 \in R$, $\beta_0 < \alpha_0$, $\beta_1 > 0$, and $\beta_2 \in R$, such that, for all $\omega_T \in \Omega_T$,

$$x_1 = \alpha_0 + \alpha_1 x_3 + \alpha_2 x_4, \ x_2 = \beta_0 + \beta_1 x_3 + \beta_2 x_5, \text{ and } x_1 = x_2. \tag{3.20}$$

In the intended interpretation of the axioms, the first of equations 3.20 describes the market participants' intended demand for a given commodity, x_1, as a function of its price, x_3, and some explanatory variable, x_4. The second equation describes the market participants' intended supply of the given commodity, x_2, as a function of its price, x_3, and an explanatory variable, x_5, different from x_4. The third equation insists that the market is in equilibrium. Finally, the means and covariances of $x(\cdot)$ and $u(\cdot)$ are their means and covariances in the RPD distribution.

For present purposes, it is interesting that I can use equations 3.20 to express x_1 and x_3 as linear functions of the two explanatory variables, x_4 and x_5. To wit: Let

$$\gamma_0 = [(\alpha_1\beta_0 - \alpha_0\beta_1)/(\alpha_1 - \beta_1)]; \ \gamma_1 = -[\alpha_2\beta_1/(\alpha_1 - \beta_1)]; \ \gamma_2 = [\alpha_1\beta_2/(\alpha_1 - \beta_1)] \tag{3.21}$$

and

$$\varphi_0 = [(\beta_0 - \alpha_0)/(\alpha_1 - \beta_1)], \ \varphi_1 = -[\alpha_2/(\alpha_1 - \beta_1)], \text{ and } \varphi_2 = [\beta_2/(\alpha_1 - \beta_1)] \tag{3.22}$$

and observe that the following theorem is valid.

T3.2

Suppose that Γ_T is valid and let γ_i and φ_i, i= 0, 1, 2 be as defined in equations 3.21 and 3.22. For all $\omega_T \in \Omega_T$, it is the case that

$$x_1 = \gamma_0 + \gamma_1 x_4 + \gamma_2 x_5 \text{ and } x_3 = \varphi_0 + \varphi_1 x_4 + \varphi_2 x_5. \tag{3.23}$$

The Γ_T axioms have many models. The models vary with the values of the α and β constants, with the means and covariances of the components of x, and with the variances of u_1 and u_2. The models must heed the sign constraints on the α and β constants and the condition that the covariance matrix of x_4 and x_5 is invertible. In addition, they must heed an interesting consistency condition on the constants and the RPD distribution of x.

To describe the consistency condition, I must introduce several new symbols that pertain to the RPD distribution of x: $\Sigma_{22}(RPD)$ = RPD.cov. $((x_4, x_5)'(x_4, x_5))$; $\Sigma_{11}(RPD)$ = RPD.cov$((x_1, (x_4, x_5))$; $\Sigma_{13}(RPD)$ = RPD.cov. $(x_3, (x_4, x_5))$, and μ_i = RPD.mean(x_i), i = 1, 3, 4, 5. With these symbols in hand, I find that

$$(\gamma_1, \gamma_2) = \Sigma_{11}(RPD)\Sigma_{22}(RPD)^{-1},$$
$$(\varphi_1, \varphi_2) = \Sigma_{13}(RPD)\Sigma_{22}(RPD)^{-1}, \tag{3.24}$$

and

$$\gamma_0 = \mu_1 - \gamma_1\mu_4 - \gamma_2\mu_5, \quad \varphi_0 = \mu_3 - \varphi_1\mu_4 - \varphi_2\mu_5. \tag{3.25}$$

Thus the mean and covariance structure of x in RPD and equations 3.24 and 3.25 determine the values of the γ_i and φ_i, i = 0, 1, 2. The latter values and equations 3.21 and 3.22 determine the values of the α_i and β_i, i = 0, 1, 2, without regard to the sign conditions that the Γ_T axioms impose on them. Similarly, the values of α_i and β_i, i = 0, 1, 2, and equations 3.21 and 3.22 determine the values of γ_i and φ_i, i = 0, 1, 2, without regard to whether the latter values satisfy equations 3.24 and 3.25.

Next the axioms of the data universe.

The Γ_P axioms

In this case, $\Omega_P \subset R^4$, $\aleph_P$ is a σ field of subsets of Ω_P, and $P_P(\cdot):\aleph_P \to [0, 1]$ is a probability measure. Thus $\omega_P \in \Omega_P$ only if $\omega_P = y$ for some $y \in R^4$. Also, the vector-valued function $y(\cdot): \Omega_P \to R^4$ is defined by the equations $y(\omega_P) = \omega_P$, and $\omega_P \in \Omega_P$, is measurable with respect to $\aleph_P$, and has, subject to the conditions on which Γ_P insists, a well-defined probability distribution relative to $P_P(\cdot)$. In this probability distribution,

$y(\omega_P)$ has finite means and covariances and the covariance matrix of $y_3(\omega_P)$ and $y_4(\omega_P)$ is invertible.

In the intended interpretation of these axioms, y_1 denotes the actual purchases of the given commodity, y_2 denotes the value of the actual price of the commodity, and y_3 and y_4 are the actual values of the explanatory variables, x_4 and x_5. Also, the means and covariances of $y(\cdot)$ are the means and covariances of the components of $y(\cdot)$ in the TPD distribution. In the present formal theory-data confrontation, as else-where in the book, I assume that there is a true probability distribution of the data variables and, hence, that the TPD has only one model.

The Bridge
In this case, $\Omega \subset \Omega_T \times \Omega_P$. Also, $(\omega_T, \omega_P) \in \Omega$ if and only if

$\omega_T \in \Omega_T,$

$\omega_P \in \Omega_P,$

$y_1(\omega_P) = x_1(\omega_T) + u_1(\omega_T),$

$y_2(\omega_P) = x_3(\omega_T) + u_2(\omega_T),$

$y_3(\omega_P) = x_4(\omega_T),$

and

$y_4(\omega_P) = x_5(\omega_T).$

Finally,

$\Omega_T \subset \{(x, u) \in \Omega_T \text{ for which there is a } y \in \Omega_P \text{ with } ((x, u), y) \in \Omega\}.$

From T3.2, from the Γ_T and Γ_P axioms, and the Bridge, it follows that the bridge principles and each model of the Γ_T axioms induce an MPD distribution of y. The MPD distribution and Kolmogorov's consistency theorem determine a probability measure, $P_M(\cdot):\aleph_P \rightarrow [0, 1]$, relative to which the distribution of $y(\cdot)$ is the given MPD.[4] With the $P_M(\cdot)$ in hand, I can characterize the MPD distribution of $y(\cdot)$ as follows.

T3.3
Suppose that Γ_T and $\Gamma_{T,P}$ are valid. In an MPD-determined $P_M(\cdot)$ measure there is a pair $(\eta_1, \eta_2)(\cdot)$ that is measurable with respect to $\aleph_P$, has the same means and variances as (u_1, u_2), is distributed independently of y_3 and y_4, and of each other, and satisfies the following equations:

$$y_1 = \gamma_0 + \gamma_1 y_3 + \gamma_2 y_4 + \eta_1, \quad y_2 = \varphi_0 + \varphi_1 y_3 + \varphi_2 y_4 + \eta_2. \tag{3.26}$$

Also, the γ_i and the φ_i, $i = 0, 1, 2$, satisfy the following equations:

$$(\gamma_1, \gamma_2) = \Sigma_{11}(\text{MPD})\Sigma_{22}(\text{MPD})^{-1}, \quad (\varphi_1, \varphi_2) = \Sigma_{12}(\text{MPD})\Sigma_{22}(\text{MPD})^{-1}, \tag{3.27}$$

$$\gamma_0 = \delta_1 - a_1\delta_3 - a_2\delta_4, \quad \varphi_0 = \delta_2 - b_1\delta_3 - b_2\delta_4, \tag{3.28}$$

where

$$\Sigma_{22}(\text{MPD}) = \text{MPD.cov.}((y_3, y_4)'(y_3, y_4)),$$

$$\Sigma_{11}(\text{MPD}) = \text{MPD.cov}((y_1, (y_3, y_4)),$$

$$\Sigma_{12}(\text{MPD}) = \text{MPD.cov.}(y_2, (y_3, y_4)),$$

and

$$\delta_i = \text{MPD.mean}(y_i), \quad i = 1, 2, 3, 4.$$

In reading the preceding theorem, note that, with the exception of the variances of y_1 and y_2, the mean and covariance structure of y in the MPD distribution is identical with the corresponding mean and covariance structure of (x_1, x_3, x_4, x_5) in the RPD distribution. That justifies my using γ_i and φ_i, where $i = 0, 1, 2$, in equations 3.27 and 3.28.

Recall, now, the two abstract scenarios that I described in section 2.2. Without spelling out all the details, I can use the simultaneous-equations model presented above to describe how empirical analyses of simultaneous-equations models differ in the two scenarios.

Consider the first scenario, and suppose that the researcher, with my help, has obtained a finite number of observations of y in a random sampling scheme. He adopts the Γ_P axioms as stated. From them and a standard theorem in mathematical statistics he deduces the validity of the following theorem.

T3.4
Suppose that Γ_P is valid. Then there exist six constants, $a_0, a_1, a_2, b_0, b_1,$ and b_2, and two random variables, $\xi_1,$ and ξ_2 with means 0 and finite covariance matrix, Π, such that, relative to $P_P(\cdot)$,

$$y_1 = a_0 + a_1 y_3 + a_2 y_4 + \xi_1,$$
$$y_2 = b_0 + b_1 y_3 + b_2 y_4 + \xi_2, \tag{3.29}$$

and

$$\text{TPD.cov}((\xi_1, \xi_2)'(y_3, y_4)) = 0. \tag{3.30}$$

The constants in equations 3.29 have a meaningful interpretation. Let

$$\Sigma_{22}(\text{TPD}) = \text{TPD.cov}((y_3, y_4)'(y_3, y_4)),$$

$$\Sigma_{11}(\text{TPD}) = \text{TPD.cov}((y_1, (y_3, y_4)),$$

$$\Sigma_{12}(\text{TPD}) = \text{TPD.cov}(y_2, (y_3, y_4)),$$

and

$$\upsilon_i = \text{TPD.mean}(y_i), \qquad i = 1, 2, 3, 4.$$

Then

$$(a_1, a_2) = \Sigma_{11}(\text{TPD})\Sigma_{22}(\text{TPD})^{-1}, \qquad (b_1, b_2) = \Sigma_{12}(\text{TPD})\Sigma_{22}(\text{TPD})^{-1}, \tag{3.31}$$

$$a_0 = \upsilon_1 - a_1\upsilon_3 - a_2\upsilon_4, \quad b_0 = \upsilon_2 - b_1\upsilon_3 - b_2\upsilon_4. \tag{3.32}$$

Equations 3.29–3.32 list characteristics of the TPD—a TPD that is, formally, independent of the RPD. If the researcher were to substitute a_i for γ_i and b_i for φ_i, $i = 0, 1, 2$, in equations 3.21 and 3.22, the values of the α and β constants that they determine would not necessarily satisfy the sign constraints on which the Γ_T axioms insist.

In accord with the Haavelmo-Spanos blueprint (Spanos 1989, pp. 414–418; Spanos 2012, pp. 7–10), the researcher assumes that he has accurate observations of x_1, x_3, x_4, and x_5 and takes the parameters in equation 3.29 to be purely statistical parameters not related to the structural parameters in equation 3.20. Consequently, he has no need for the Γ_T and the $\Gamma_{T,P}$. So he throws the axioms out, but he keeps a record of equations 3.21 and 3.22. For the statistical analysis he assumes that the co-variance matrix of the error terms in equation 3.16, Π, is the identity matrix. Then he estimates the parameters in equations 3.29 and 3.30 and ascertains that the estimated model is statistically adequate. At last he uses equations 3.21 and 3.22 to obtain an estimate of a structural model in which the components of y play the roles that the corresponding components of x play in equation 3.20. The structural model is theoretically meaningful only if all the members of a 95-per-cent-confidence band around the estimated parameters in equations 3.29 and 3.30—when combined with equations 3.21 and 3.22—determine α and β constants that heed the sign constraints that I listed in the Γ_T axioms.[5]

The requirement the researcher's estimates must satisfy in order that they be declared theoretically meaningful sounds daunting. To show that it is reasonable, I will describe the data I gave the researcher and record the results of his statistical analysis.

In generating the data, I presumed that the x's in equation 3.20 satisfy the equations

$$x_1 = 10 - 2x_3 + x_4 \quad \text{and} \quad x_2 = 1 + 2x_3 + 0.5x_5. \tag{3.33}$$

Also, I began by generating four independent sequences of random numbers with the OxMetrix 6 normal number generator, rann(): GENN1, GENN2, GENN3, and GENN4. Then I let RAIN = 2 · GENN2 + GENN3 and SUN = GENN2 + 2 · GENN3, where RAIN and SUN, respectively, are to play the roles of y_3 and y_4. Finally, I let

$$\text{SALESYY} = 5.5 + 0.5 \cdot \text{RAIN} + 0.25 \cdot \text{SUN} + \text{GENN1} \tag{3.34}$$

and

$$\text{PRICEY} = 2.25 + 0.25 \cdot \text{RAIN} - 0.125 \cdot \text{SUN} + \text{GENN4}. \tag{3.35}$$

I have generated these data without insisting that the sales of the given commodity and its price must be positive. It is, therefore, significant for the import of the empirical analysis that the data are as pictured in figure 3.1.[6]

With the given data and OxMetrics' PcGive the researcher estimates the parameters in equations 3.29 and 3.30 with three methods, Autometrics, FIML, and OLS. His results were the same in all three cases. So, it suffices that I display the researcher's Autometrics results. They are recorded in tables 3.6–3.9.[7]

The researcher does not know the TPD, but he believes that in 95 percent of all samples the Wald 95-percent-confidence intervals around the estimated parameters will cover the true values of the parameters of the data-generating process that produced the data I gave him. They do in fact, as equations 3.34 and 3.35 and tables 3.6 and 3.7 demonstrate. Also, the estimate of Π in table 3.9 is close enough to the true value of Π.

The researcher decides that the parameter estimates are statistically significant, so the only interesting question left is whether the estimates determine a theoretically meaningful model of the theory model in the data universe. To answer that question, the researcher must solve

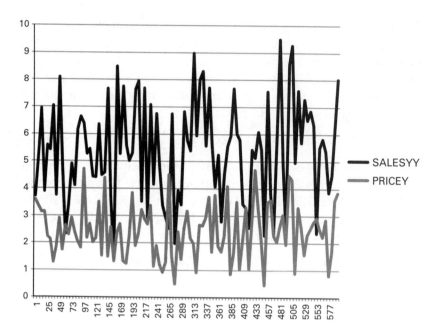

Figure 3.1
Price and sales of a commodity in the data universe.

Table 3.6
The URF (unrestricted reduced form) equation for SALESYY.

	Coefficient	SE	t value	t probability
RAIN	0.526485	0.02928	18.0	0.0000
SUN	0.230415	0.02885	7.99	0.0000
Constant U	5.48361	0.04073	135.	0.0000
Sigma = 0.995482	RSS = 591.6178465			

Table 3.7
The URF equation for PRICEY.

	Coefficient	SE	t value	t probability
RAIN	0.273825	0.02918	9.38	0.0000
SUN	−0.155221	0.02875	−5.40	0.0000
Constant U	2.29816	0.04058	56.6	0.0000
Sigma = 0.991902	RSS = 587.3700132			

Table 3.8
Sundry test results.

log-likelihood	−1692.11128	−T/2log|Omega| =	10.6149588
|Omega|	0.965235471	log|Y′Y/T| =	1.36547127
R^2(LR)	0.753614	R^2(LM) =	0.403447
no. of observations	600	no. of parameters	6

F-test on regressors except unrestricted

$F(4, 1192) = 302.355 \ [0.0000]$ **

F-tests on retained regressors, F(2, 596)

RAIN	206.369	[0.000]**		SUN	46.1142	[0.000]**
Constant U	206.369	[0.000]**				

Table 3.9
Correlation of URF residuals (standard deviation on diagonal).

	SALESYY	PRICEY
SALESYY	0.99548	−0.0063047
PRICEY	−0.0063047	0.99190
Correlation between actual and fitted		
	SALESYY	PRICEY
	0.85303	0.37574

equations 3.21 and 3.22 for the pertinent α and β constants. In short, the solution looks like this:

$$\alpha_1 = \gamma_2/\varphi_2,$$

$$\beta_1 = \gamma_1/\varphi_1,$$

$$\alpha_2 = ((\alpha_1 - \beta_1)/\beta_1)\gamma_1,$$

$$\beta_2 = ((\alpha_1 - \beta_1)/\alpha_1)\gamma_2, \tag{3.36}$$

$$\beta_0 = \gamma_0 - \beta_1\varphi_0,$$

$$\alpha_0 = \gamma_0 - \alpha_1\varphi_0.$$

With these equations and the preceding list of test results, it is easy to see that all the sets of γ and φ constants in the confidence region that Wald's confidence intervals determine result in estimates of α and β that satisfy the sign constraints that the Γ_T axioms impose on the α and β constants. Hence, the estimated parameters determine a theoretically meaningful model of the theory model in the data universe:

$$y_1 = 8.89507 - 1.48443 \ y_2 + 0.93296 \ y_3, \qquad\qquad (3.37)$$

$$y_1 = 1.06491 + 1.92271 \ y_2 + 0.52886 \ y_4. \qquad\qquad (3.38)$$

Next, consider the second scenario. Suppose, again, that the researcher, with my help, has obtained a finite number of "observations" of $((x,u),y)$ in a random sampling scheme. The components of (x,u) are unobservable. Hence, only the components of y are observed. The observations of y are the same as the ones I gave the researcher in the upper data universe in figure 2.1. In the lower data universe the purpose of the empirical analysis is to determine whether the Γ_T axioms are empirically relevant. The researcher begins by estimating the parameters of equations 3.26 and makes sure that the estimated model is statistically adequate. Then he delineates a 95-percent-confidence band around the estimated parameters. According to T2.4 the Γ_T axioms are empirically relevant if and only if at least one member of the confidence band together with equations 3.21 and 3.22 determines α and β constants that satisfy the sign constraints listed in the Γ_T axioms.[8]

Equations 3.26 and 3.29 are formally identical. Hence, the estimates of the parameters of the MPD distribution are identical to the researcher's estimates of the parameters of the TPD and listed in tables 3.6–3.9. From this it follows that the structural model in the theory universe, which the estimates of the parameters in equations 3.26, 3.21, and 3.22 determine, is identical to the model in equations 3.37 and 3.38 with the appropriate x's in place of the y's. Here it is:

$$x_1 = 8.89507 - 1.48443x_3 + 0.93296x_4, \qquad\qquad (3.39)$$

$$x_2 = 1.06491 + 1.92271x_3 + 0.52886x_5. \qquad\qquad (3.40)$$

The researcher's parameter estimates in equations 3.37 and 3.38 are theoretically meaningful. Consequently, it must also be the case that each and every sixtuple of parameters in Wald's confidence region determines an empirically relevant model of the Γ_T axioms. For the import of this result it is significant that the confidence region that Wald's confidence intervals determine, depend on the estimated values of the pertinent parameters in equation 3.26, but it is independent of the MPD model itself.

It is particularly interesting in this case that I can use the parameters of a data-admissible mathematical model of MPD and the bridge both

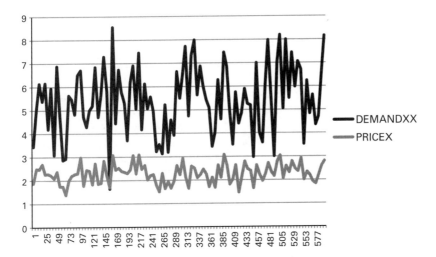

Figure 3.2
Price and demand for a commodity in the theory universe.

to delineate the values of the parameters of an empirically relevant model of the Γ_T axioms and to create meaningful observations of all five components of x. Here is how I do so: With the estimated parameters of the MPD in tables 3.6 and 3.7 and in equation 3.40, I obtain observations of x_1, x_3, and x_2 where x_1 = DEMANDXX, x_3 = PRICEX, and x_2 = SUPPLYXX:

$$\text{DEMANDXX} = 5.48361 + 0.526485 \cdot \text{RAIN} + 0.230415 \cdot \text{SUN}, \quad (3.41)$$

$$\text{PRICEX} = 2.29816 + 0.273825 \cdot \text{RAIN} - 0.155221 \cdot \text{SUN}, \quad (3.42)$$

$$\text{SUPPLYXX} = 1.06491 + 1.92271 \cdot \text{PRICEX} + 0.52886 \cdot \text{SUN}. \quad (3.43)$$

The observations of x_1 and x_3 are displayed in figure 3.2. Note that all my observations of x_1 and of the price of x_1; i.e., of x_3, are positive.

With the observations of x_1 and x_3 and with the given observations of x_4 and x_5; i.e., of RAIN and SUN, I can regress x_1 on x_3 and x_4 and x_2 on x_3 and x_5. The single-equation OLS results are given in tables 3.10 and 3.11.

The coefficients of the estimated model have appropriate values. What about the observations of x? Do they satisfy the condition $x_1 = x_2$ in equation 3.20? They do, as table 3.12 demonstrates.

For the import of this example, it is relevant that I have carried out the statistical analysis in the upper data universe in the spirit of Aris

Table 3.10
Modeling DEMANDXX by OLS-CS.

	Coefficient	SE	t value	t probability	Part.R^2
Constant	8.89507	1.331e − 0156	.685e+015	0.0000	1.0000
PRICEX	−1.48443	5.783e − 016	−2.567e+015	0.0000	1.0000
RAIN	0.93296	1.036e − 0169	.007e+015	0.0000	1.0000

sigma = 3.09722e − 015   RSS = 5.72688365e − 027
no. of observations 600   no. of parameters 3
mean(DEMANDXX) 5.40952   se(DEMANDXX) 1.62451

Table 3.11
Modeling SUPPLYX X by OLS-CS

	Coefficient	SE	t value	t probability	Part.R^2
Constant	1.06491	5.720e − 0161	.862e+015	0.0000	1.0000
PRICEX	1.92271	2.480e − 0167	.752e+015	0.0000	1.0000
SUN	0.52886	4.377e − 0171	.208e+016	0.0000	1.0000

sigma = 2.30884e − 015   RSS = 3.18246211e − 027
no. of observations 600   no. of parameters 3
mean(SUPPLYXX) ? 5.40952   se(SUPPLYXX) = 1.62451

Table 3.12
Descriptive statistics: means, standard deviations, and correlations.

Means

DEMANDXX	SUPPLYXX	PRICEX
5.4095	5.4095	2.2720

Standard deviations (using T − 1)

DEMANDXX	SUPPLYXX	PRICEX
1.6245	1.6245	0.40150

Correlation matrix:

	DEMANDXX	SUPPLYXX	PRICEX
DEMANDXX	1.0000	1.0000	0.71254
SUPPLYXX	1.0000	1.0000	0.71254
PRICEX	0.71254	0.71254	1.0000

Spanos' error-statistical reformulation of Haavelmo's methodology. My data represent a typical realization of the data-generating process. Also, equations 3.34 and 3.35 can be viewed as a parameterization of the data-generating process. Finally, the structural model in equations 3.37 and 3.38 is a theoretically meaningful model in Spanos' sense of the term. To compare Spanos' methodology with mine, I have used the same data to estimate pertinent MPD parameters. Also, I have used the estimated MPD parameters and the bridge principles to generate two different kinds of estimates for the theory universe: (1) an estimate of a structural model for the theory universe that I describe in equations 3.39 and 3.40; and (2) estimates of series of quintuples of observations of the unobservables, x_1, x_2, and x_3, and of the explanatory variables, x_4 an x_5. Each quintuple in the series records the intended demand and supply of the commodity in response to a given value of the price of the commodity and to given values of the auxiliary variables. I used the series to estimate a model of equations 2.1. My results are recorded in tables 3.10–3.12. The values of the structural parameter-estimates in equations 3.37 and 3.38 are the same as the values of the corresponding structural parameter-estimates in equations 3.39 and 3.40. Note, therefore, that the probability distribution of the data variables in equations 3.37 and 3.38 is different from the probability distribution of the theory variables in equations 3.39 and 3.40. Also, the confidence region around the parameters in equations 3.37 and 3.38 covers with high probability the true values of the structural parameters. In contrast, each and every member of the confidence region around the parameters in equations 3.39 and 3.40 constitutes parameters of an empirically relevant structural model.

3.6 An Example of Risk Aversion and Choice of Risky Assets

Take another look at figure 1.2. In this example the economic theory in question is the standard theory of consumer choice under certainty that I described in section 1.2 of this book and developed in chapter 10 of my 1990 book. I have put the five axioms of the theory of consumer choice under certainty in the economic-theory box and the subfamily of models of the theory that constitutes Arrow's 1965 theory of risk aversion in the interpretation-of-theory box. In the given subfamily of models, a commodity vector is a pair $(\mu, m) \in R_+^2$ and a price vector is a pair $(1, a)$, where $a \in R_{++}$. A consumer is a pair $(V(\cdot), A)$, where

$A \in R_+$,

$V(\cdot): R_+^2 \to R_+$,

$V(\mu, m) = \int_{(0,\infty)} U(\mu + rm)f(r)dr$

with

$U(\cdot): R_+ \to R_+,$

$U'(\cdot) > 0, U''(\cdot) < 0,$

and

$\int_{(0,\infty)} f(r)dr = 1.$

Finally, a consumption bundle is a pair, (μ, m), that maximizes $V(\cdot)$ subject to the conditions $(\mu, m) \geq 0$ and $\mu + am \leq A$. Here μ is taken to be a safe asset, m is a risky asset, and A is the consumer's net worth.

The purpose of the present example is to formulate a theory-data confrontation in which the empirical relevance of the variable hypothetical APT that I described in subsection 2.3.2 is at stake. If I let $(\mu, m)(\cdot)$: $R_{++} \times R_+ \to R_+ \times R_+$ denote the consumer's demand function for (μ, m), and let $R(A) = -U''(A)/U'(A)$, where $A \geq 0$, be the consumer's absolute risk-aversion function, I can formulate APT precisely as follows.

APT
In the region $\{(a, A) \in R_{++} \times R_+: (\mu, m)(a, A) > 0\}$, $m(a, \cdot)$ is a strictly increasing (constant (strictly decreasing)) function of A if and only if $R(\cdot)$ is a strictly decreasing (constant (strictly increasing)) function of A.

Arrow (1965, p. 43) established the sufficiency part of APT, and Pratt (1964, p. 136) established the necessity part.

3.6.1 An Interesting Aggregation Problem in Applied Econometrics
In the sample-population box of figure 1.2 I have put the consumers in the United States who were alive in 1960. In the observations box I have put observations of the sampled consumers' income in 1962 and 1963 and of the level of their assets and liabilities at the end of 1962 and 1963. In the data box I have put estimates of the value of the respective consumers' investments in safe and risky assets at the end of 1963, μ^* and m^*, and their net worth at the end of 1963, A^*. The given observations were obtained in a re-interview survey of consumer finances by the Federal Reserve Board. (See Projector and Weiss 1966 and Projector 1968.) Also, in the survey a consumer was taken to be either a family living together and having a common budget or a single individual living alone. Finally, for the purposes of this example, I presume that

the given re-interview survey sampled consumers in accord with a purely random sampling scheme.

My data pose an interesting problem for my empirical analysis: Arrow and Pratt's theorem is not valid for a pair, (μ, am), in which a $\in R_{++}{}^n$, $m \in R_+{}^n$, and $n > 1$. For such a pair, APT is valid only if the consumer's utility function, $U(\cdot)$, has the separation property—that is, only if the utility function has one or the other of the following two forms:

$U'(A) = d(\alpha + \beta A)^\gamma$, $A \in R_+$, where d, α, β, and γ are appropriately chosen constants

$U'(A) = be^{gA}$, $A \in R_+$, where b and g are appropriately chosen constants.

In formulating the axioms for the theory universe, I presume implicitly that every member of the subfamily of models that I have put in the interpretation-of-theory box in figure 1.2 has a utility function that has the first of the exhibited two forms with $d > 0$, $\gamma \in [-1, 0)$, $\alpha > 0$, $\beta > 0$, and $U(\cdot): [0, \infty) \to R_+$. The corresponding absolute risk-aversion function, $R(\cdot)$, is a decreasing function of A. (For details concerning the present aggregation problem, see pages 225–236 of B. Stigum 1990.)

3.6.2 A Formal Theory-Data Confrontation

With this much said about the contents in the various boxes in figure 1.2, I can begin writing down axioms for a theory-data confrontation of Arrow's theory of risk aversion in which there are two universes—one for theory and one for data—and a bridge between them. The theory universe, the data universe, and the bridge are, as before, designated $(\Omega_T, \Gamma_T, (\Omega_T, \aleph_T, P_T(\cdot)))$, $(\Omega_P, \Gamma_P, (\Omega_P, \aleph_P, P_P(\cdot)))$, and $(\Omega, \Gamma_{T,P})$. Also, vectors in the theory universe function as vectors in Ω_T and as vector valued random variables on $(\Omega_T, \aleph_T)$. Similarly, vectors in the data universe function as vectors in Ω_P and as vector valued random variables on $(\Omega_P, \aleph_P)$. I assume throughout that Ω_T and Ω_P are disjoint, that $\aleph_T$ and $\aleph_P$ are stochastically independent, and that $\Omega \in \aleph$ and $P(\Omega) > 0$ in the probability space $(\Omega_T \times \Omega_P, \aleph, P(\cdot))$, which I described in chapter 2. To simplify my arguments, I formulate axioms for a case in which the pertinent researcher samples at random only once in the observations box in figure 1.2. In the intended interpretation of the axioms, μ and m, respectively, denote a consumer's investment in safe and risky assets; a and A denote, respectively, the price of m and the consumer's net worth; and η plays the role of an error of measurement. Also, μ^*, m^*, and A^* are the observational counterparts of μ, am, and A.

First the theory universe.

The Γ_T axioms

$\Omega_T \subset R_+^{n+2} \times R$, $\aleph_T$ is a σ field of subsets of Ω_T, and $P_T(\cdot):\aleph_T \to [0, 1]$ is a probability measure. Thus $\omega_T \in \Omega_T$ only if $\omega_T = (\mu,m,A,\eta)$ for some $\mu \in R_+$, $m \in R_+^n$, $A \in R_+$, $\eta \in R$, and $(\mu,m,A,\eta) \in R_+^{n+2} \times R$. Also, $\mu(\cdot):\Omega_T \to R_+$, $m(\cdot):\Omega_T \to R_+^n$, $A(\cdot):\Omega_T \to R_+$, and $\eta(\cdot):\Omega_T \to R$, are defined by the equations $(\mu(\omega_T), m(\omega_T), A(\omega_T), \eta(\omega_T)) = \omega_T$, and $\omega_T \in \Omega_T$, and the vector-valued function $(\mu, m, A, \eta)(\cdot)$ is measurable with respect to $\aleph_T$, and has, subject to the conditions on which Γ_T insists, a well-defined probability distribution relative to $P_T(\cdot)$. In this distribution, $\eta(\omega_T)$ has mean zero and finite variance; the triple, $(\mu, am, A)(\omega_T)$, has a positive mean vector and a finite covariance matrix, Π, with positive diagonal elements; and $\eta(\omega_T)$ and $(\mu, am, A)(\omega_T)$ are distributed independently of each other. Finally, for all $\omega_T \in \Omega_T$, there exist a positive constant, c, a set, $D \subset R_{++}^n$, two functions, $\varphi(\cdot):D \to R_{++}$ and $\psi(\cdot):D \to R_{++}$, and a function, $h(\cdot): R_{++}^n \times R_+ \to R_+$, such that, for all $a \in D$,

$c\psi(a) = \varphi(a)$,

$0 < h(a, A) < A$,

$h(a, A) = \varphi(a) + \psi(a)A$,

$\mu + am = A$,

and

$am = h(a, A)$.[9]

Next, the data universe.

The Γ_P axioms

$\Omega_P \subset R_+^3$, $\aleph_P$ is a σ field of subsets of Ω_P, and $P_P(\cdot):\aleph_P \to [0, 1]$ is a probability measure. Thus $\omega_P \in \Omega_P$ only if $\omega_P = (\mu^*,m^*,A^*)$ for some $\mu^* \in R_+$, $m^* \in R_+$, $A^* \in R_+$, and $(\mu^*,m^*,A^*) \in R_+^3$. Also, $\mu^*(\cdot):\Omega_P \to R_+$, $m^*(\cdot):\Omega_P \to R_+$, and $A^*(\cdot):\Omega_P \to R_+$ are defined by the equations $(\mu^*(\omega_P), m^*(\omega_P), A^*(\omega_P)) = \omega_P$, and $\omega_P \in \Omega_P$, and the vector-valued function $(\mu^*, m^*, A^*)(\cdot)$ is measurable with respect to $\aleph_P$, and has, subject to the conditions on which Γ_P insists, a well-defined probability distribution relative to $P_P(\cdot)$. In this distribution, the triple, $(\mu^*, m^*, A^*)(\omega_P)$, has a positive mean vector and a finite covariance matrix, Ξ, with positive diagonal elements. Finally, for all $\omega_P \in \Omega_P$,

$$\mu^* + m^* = A^*. \tag{3.44}$$

At last the bridge.

The $\Gamma_{T,P}$ axioms

$\Omega \subset \Omega_T \times \Omega_P$. Also, $(\omega_T, \omega_P) \in \Omega$ only if

$\omega_T \in \Omega_T$, $\omega_P \in \Omega_P$, $m^*(\omega_P) = h(a, A(\omega_T)) + \eta(\omega_T)$, and $A^*(\omega_P) = A(\omega_T)$. (3.45)

Finally, $\Omega_T \subset \{\omega_T \in \Omega_T$ for which there is an $\omega_P \in \Omega_P$ such that $(\omega_T, \omega_P) \in \Omega\}$.[10]

With the help of the Γ_T axioms, the $\Gamma_{T,P}$ axioms, and Kolmogorov's consistency theorem, I can now deduce the characterization of the MPD distribution of (μ^*, m^*, A^*) that I describe in T3.5. In the statement of the theorem, I make use of one new variable, $\xi(\omega_P)$, which I define as follows:

$$\text{For all } (\omega_T, \omega_P) \in \Omega, \xi(\omega_P) = \eta(\omega_T). \tag{3.46}$$

From this definition and equations 3.45 I find that $\xi(\omega_p) = m^*(\omega_P) - h(a, A^*(\omega_P))$. Hence, $\xi(\cdot)$ is well defined and measurable with respect to $\aleph_P$. But, if that is so, for any $B \subset R$ and $C \subset R$,

$MPD(\xi, A^*)(\omega_p) \in B \times C) = P_T(\{\omega_T \in \Omega_T: (\eta, A)(\omega_T) \in B \times C\}),$

which goes to show that the MPD distribution of (ξ, A^*) equals the RPD distribution of (η, A). In that way it justifies the role ξ plays in T3.5.

T3.5

Suppose that Γ_T, $\Gamma_{T,P}$, and the non-stochastic axiom of the data universe are valid. Then there exists a probability measure, $P_M(\cdot):\aleph_P \to [0, 1]$, and a random variable, ξ, that relative to $P_M(\cdot)$ has mean 0 and the same variance as η. Relative to $P_M(\cdot)$, (μ^*, m^*, A^*) satisfies the stochastic equations

$$\mu^* + m^* = A^* \text{ a.e.} \tag{3.47}$$

and

$$m^* = \varphi(a) + \psi(a)A^* + \xi \text{ a.e.} \tag{3.48}$$

and the orthogonality condition

$EA^*\xi = 0.$ (3.49)

(The abbreviation a.e. stands for "almost everywhere" and means "with probability 1." It means that something is the case almost everywhere as seen from the point of view of a given probability measure.)

3.6.3 The Empirical Analysis

In the empirical analysis. I assume that I have obtained a random sample of "observations" of the pairs of triples, $((\mu,m,A),(\mu^*,m^*,A^*))$. The components of (μ,m,A) are unobservable. Hence only the components of (μ^*,m^*,A^*) have been observed. The purpose of my analysis is to demonstrate how a test of the empirical relevance of APT in the lower data universe in figure 2.1 differs from a test of the empirical relevance of APT in the upper data universe. As before, I envision two scenarios for the empirical analysis—one for the upper data universe and one for the lower data universe. The components of (μ,m,A) play no role in the empirical analysis in the upper data universe. They play an essential role in the empirical analysis in the lower data universe.

The Lower Data Universe in Figure 2.1

This time I begin with the test in the lower data universe. There I presume that the sample consumers have faced the same price vector, a, and that this price vector belongs to D. Also, since equation 3.47 is true by design, equations 3.48 and 3.49 suggest that I let "the prescriptions that underlie my statistical analysis" instruct me to obtain maximum-likelihood estimates of the parameters in the linear equation

$$m^*(t) = \alpha + \beta A^*(t) + \varsigma(t), \qquad t = 1, 2, \dots, M. \tag{3.43}$$

Here M is the number of observations and the error process, $\{\varsigma(t); t = 1, \dots, M\}$, is taken to be a purely random, normally distributed process that is orthogonal to the $A^*(t)$ and has mean 0 and the variance of $\xi(t)$. I suppose that the data do not reject the hypothesis that $\varsigma(t)$ is normally distributed. Then the maximum-likelihood estimates of α and β, α° and β°, and the estimate of the variance of $\varsigma(t)$, Ψ° are the parameters of a data-admissible mathematical model of MPD only if $\alpha^\circ > 0$ and $1 > \beta^\circ > 0$.[11]

From the point of view of this book it is an important fact that the Γ_T axioms are empirically relevant if the maximum-likelihood estimates of the parameters in equation 3.50 are positive and $\beta^\circ < 1$. To establish this fact proceed as follows: Let α°, β°, and Ψ° be the maximum-likelihood estimates of the parameters in equation 3.50. Suppose that they are positive with $\beta^\circ < 1$ and that the data do not reject the hypothesis that $\varsigma(t)$ is normally distributed. Pick an $a^\circ \in D$, insist that $\varphi(a^\circ) = \alpha^\circ$, $\psi(a^\circ) = \beta^\circ$, and $c = \alpha^\circ / \beta^\circ$, and choose σ_ξ^2 so that it satisfies the equation $\sigma_\xi^2 = \Psi^\circ$. Finally, for an ω_P in the support of the pertinent MPD, define $\xi^\circ(\omega_P)$ by the equation

$$\xi^\circ(\omega_P) = m^*(\omega_P) - \alpha^\circ - \beta^\circ A^*(\omega_P). \tag{3.51}$$

Then the MPD distribution of the right-hand sides of the equations

$$\eta = \xi^\circ(\omega_P), \tag{3.52}$$

$$A = A^*(\omega_P), \tag{3.53}$$

$$am = \alpha^\circ + \beta^\circ A^*(\omega_P) - \xi^\circ(\omega_P), \tag{3.54}$$

and

$$\mu = \mu^*(\omega_P) + \xi^\circ(\omega_P) \tag{3.55}$$

induces an RPD distribution of (μ, am, A, η) that satisfies the conditions of Γ_T. This RPD distribution together with the vector, $(\varphi(a^\circ), \psi(a^\circ), c, \sigma_\xi^2)$, determines an empirically relevant model of the Γ_T axioms.

Suppose, now, that $\alpha^\circ < 0$ and $\beta^\circ > 0$. Then α°, β°, and Ψ° do not constitute parameters of a data-admissible mathematical model of the MPD. However, there may exist another triple, $(\alpha^*, \beta^*, \Psi^*)$, within the 95-percent-confidence region of $(\alpha^\circ, \beta^\circ, \Psi^\circ)$, whose components are positive with $\beta^* < 1$ and constitute parameters of a data-admissible mathematical model of the MPD. If such a triple exists, and if I choose σ_ξ^2 so that it satisfies the equation $\sigma_\xi^2 = \Psi^*$, then $(\varphi(a^\circ), \psi(a^\circ), c^*, \sigma_\xi^2)$ with $\varphi(a^\circ) = \alpha^*$, $\psi(a^\circ) = \beta^*$, and $c^* = \alpha^* / \beta^*$ and an obvious analogue of equations 3.51–3.55 determine an empirically relevant mathematical model of the Γ_T axioms. If a triple with the characteristics of $(\alpha^*, \beta^*, \Psi^*)$ does not exist in the 95-percent-confidence region of $(\alpha^\circ, \beta^\circ, \Psi^\circ)$, I will deem the Γ_T axioms empirically irrelevant in the empirical context that I consider in this example.

The Upper Data Universe in Figure 2.1

Here I assume that I have accurate observations of the theory variables; i.e., that $(\mu^*, m^*, A^*) = (\mu, am, A)$. That means that I have no need for the Γ_T and $\Gamma_{T,P}$ axioms. To formulate the axioms for the upper data universe, Γ_{PTOP}, I begin by adding a fourth variable, χ, to the ω_P vector, and by letting $(\Omega^*_P, \Gamma^*_P, (\Omega^*_P, \aleph^*_P, P^*_P(\cdot))$ be the new data universe. Then

$\Omega^*_P \subset R_+^3 \times R$, $\aleph^*_P$ is a σ field of subsets of Ω^*_P, and $P^*_P(\cdot):\aleph^*_P \to [0, 1]$ is a probability measure. Thus $\omega_P \in \Omega^*_P$ only if $\omega_P = ((\mu^*,m^*,A^*),\chi)$ for some triple $(\mu^*,m^*,A^*) \in R_+^3$, $\chi \in R$, and $((\mu^*,m^*,A^*),\chi) \in R_+^3 \times R$. Also, $\mu^*(\cdot):\Omega^*_P \to R_+$, $m^*(\cdot):\Omega^*_P \to R_+$, $A^*(\cdot):\Omega^*_T \to R_+$, and $\chi(\cdot):\Omega^*_P \to R$ are defined by the equations, $(\mu^*(\omega_P), m^*(\omega_P), A^*(\omega_P), \chi(\omega_P)) = \omega_P$, and $\omega_P \in \Omega^*_P$, and the vector-valued function $(\mu^*, m^*, A^*, \chi)(\cdot)$ is measurable with respect to $\aleph^*_P$. Relative to $P^*_P(\cdot)$ χ has mean 0 and positive finite variance and is distributed independently of the triple (μ^*, m^*, A^*). The probability distribution of (μ^*, m^*, A^*) relative to $P^*_P(\cdot)$ is as described in Γ_P. Finally, I assume that there exists a monotonic function, $h(\cdot): R_+ \to R_+$, such that, for all $\omega_P \in \Omega^*_P$,

$$\mu + {}^*m^* = A^*$$

and

$$m^* = h(A^*) + \chi.$$

Moreover, there exist positive constants c, φ, and ψ such that, for all $\omega_P \in \Omega^*_P$, $c\psi = \varphi$, $0 < h(A^*) < A^*$, and $h(A^*) = \varphi + \psi A^*$.

I deduce from the Γ_{PTOP} assumptions about the components of ω_P in the upper data universe that there exists a true pair of positive constants, α and β, with $\beta < 1$ such that m^* and A^* satisfy equation 3.50 with $\varsigma(t)$ replaced by $\chi(t)$. For the purpose of estimating α and β, I assume that the error term is normally distributed and proceed to compute maximum-likelihood estimates of α, β, and σ (say, $\alpha^\wedge$, $\beta^\wedge$, and $\sigma^\wedge$) and a 95-percent-confidence region, E, around these estimates. If the data do not reject my hypothesis that the $\chi(t)$ are normally distributed, and if the triples in E are positive with $\beta^\wedge < 1$, I deem the axioms that I have postulated for the upper data universe empirically relevant in the empirical context that I have designed for the empirical analysis. Otherwise I deem the given axioms empirically irrelevant in the same empirical context.

Empirical Relevance in the Two Data Universes in Figure 2.1
My reading of empirical relevance in the upper data universe in figure 2.1 accords with my reading of a textbook hypothesis test: A theory is empirically relevant in a given empirical context if and only if it cannot be rejected. In the present example the axioms that I have postulated for the upper data universe, Γ_{PTOP}, are empirically relevant only if all the triples in the 95-percent-confidence region, E, are positive with $\beta < 1$. The reason is as follows: According to the theoretical hypotheses,

there is a true triple (α, β, σ) such that the components of $(\varphi, \psi, c, \sigma)$ with $\varphi = \alpha$, $\psi = \beta$, and $c = \alpha/\beta$ are parameters of the true TPD distribution of (μ^*, m^*, A^*, χ). In 95 percent of all samples, the confidence region, E, around the maximum-likelihood estimate of (α, β, σ) will contain the true values of these parameters. Since the given axioms are valid only if the true values of these parameters are positive and $\beta < 1$, I can be 95 percent certain of the empirical relevance of the axioms only if all the $(\alpha, \beta, \sigma) \in E$ are positive with $\beta < 1$.

My reading of empirical relevance in the lower data universe is fundamentally different. There I search for a data-admissible mathematical model of the associated MPD by estimating the parameters of equation 3.50 and by delineating a 95-percent-confidence region around the parameter estimates. If the confidence region contains values of the pertinent parameters that are parameters of a data-admissible mathematical model of MPD, I use these parameters and the bridge principles to formulate a mathematical model of the Γ_T axioms that is empirically relevant. It is irrelevant whether the 95-percent-confidence region contains (α, β, Ψ) triples that are not positive and/or has a β whose value is not smaller than 1.

3.7 Concluding Remarks

In a given theory-data confrontation, I may find many mathematical models of Γ_T that are empirically relevant. Ideally, I would like to delineate the largest family of empirically relevant models of the theory. The possibility of my doing that depends on my ability to identify all the parameter values in the confidence region around the estimated model of MPD that constitute parameters of a data-admissible mathematical model of the MPD. For an example of such a search in a different setting, see subsection 5.2.5a, where I try to delineate the largest family of empirically relevant models of the axioms of Friedman's Permanent Income Hypothesis. For a different kind of search, see subsection 4.2.1c and the appendix to chapter 4, where Anne Olaug Stigum searches for an empirically relevant qualitative response model.

4 Qualitative Response Models

Maximum-likelihood estimators and asymptotic theory play important roles in classical econometrics. This is so because maximum-likelihood estimates have attractive statistical properties and because asymptotic theory can be used to establish the meaningfulness of estimators. Besides, asymptotic theory provides the approximate probability distributions of estimated parameters that are needed in statistical tests of hypotheses. In the present chapter, the finite sample properties and the asymptotic values of maximum-likelihood estimates are in focus.

Maximum-likelihood estimation is a search for the value of a pertinent parameter that would maximize the likelihood of a given sample of observations. For example, if $x_1, \ldots, x_n$ are observations of a family of independently and identically distributed random variables with density function, $f(x, \theta)$, the likelihood of the observed sample is equal to the product $f(x_1, \theta) \cdot f(x_2, \theta) \cdots f(x_n, \theta)$, and the maximum-likelihood estimate of θ is a value of θ that maximizes the value of this product.

Under reasonable conditions on $f(\cdot)$, a maximum-likelihood estimate of θ has attractive statistical properties; that is, it is consistent and asymptotically normally distributed. It is also asymptotically efficient. However, a maximum-likelihood estimate of θ may be biased and need not be empirically relevant. In this chapter I will show that the maximum-likelihood estimates prescribed by the standard Probit analysis of qualitative response models may be empirically irrelevant, and the limiting values of such parameter estimates need not be well defined. For the study of qualitative response models my results raise serious questions concerning the meaningfulness of the relations between dependent and explanatory variables described by an estimated qualitative response model.

4.1 Qualitative Response Models

A qualitative response model is an econometric model in which the range of the dependent variable is either discrete or half-discrete and half-continuous. Such models surface in analyses of situations in which individuals are asked to choose from among a finite set of alternatives—for example, when an addict is asked to choose whether or not to participate in a rehabilitation program. They come in many disguises. Some are univariate, others are multivariate, and still others are multinomial. They may also be aliases of sample selection models. In the present context the qualitative response models are interesting because each prototype of such models can be viewed as prescribing two seemingly equivalent empirical analyses, one for the upper data universe in figure 2.1 and one for the lower data universe.

Excellent introductions into the intricacies of estimating parameters in qualitative response models can be found in Davidson and MacKinnon 1993, in Greene 1997, in Gourieroux 2000, and in Hendry and Nielsen 2007; interesting surveys of the last thirty years' theoretical and applied work with such models can be found in Heckman 2001, in Dhrymes 1986, and in McFadden 1984. In this chapter I will question the meaningfulness of the empirical analyses that these authors advocate. With the help of their two main univariate qualitative response models, I will give a novel illustration of how present-day econometric analysis differs from formal econometric analysis.

4.1.1 A Standard Univariate Qualitative Response Model with Accurate Observations

Consider a researcher who is studying behavior characteristics of women in the United States. As a result of a properly conducted random survey, he has observations of a finite number of women in the 1980 US population. The observations contain information about the subjects' salient socioeconomic characteristics and about whether they have chosen to enter the labor force. The researcher's present problem is to ascertain how a woman's socioeconomic characteristics influence her choice of entering or not entering the labor force.

The researcher develops a standard univariate qualitative response model with k + 1 variables, $y^* \in \{0, 1\}$ and $x^* \in R^k$, and the following two equations:

$$\Pr.\{y^* = 1 \,|\, x^*\} = F(\alpha + \beta x^*), \tag{4.1}$$

$\Pr.\{y^* = 0 \mid x^*\} = 1 - F(\alpha + \beta x^*)$. (4.2)

Here y^* equals 1 if a woman has entered the labor force and 0 otherwise. The components of x^* record the woman's socioeconomic characteristics, $F(\cdot): R \to [0, 1]$ is a cumulative probability distribution function, and $\alpha \in R$ and the components of $\beta \in R^k$ are constants. The researcher assumes that his observations of y^* and x^* are accurate and decides to identify $F(\cdot)$ with the normal distribution, $\Phi(\cdot)$, whose mean is 0 and whose variance is 1. Thereafter he uses Greene's (2007) LIMDEP 9.0 software program for Probit models to obtain maximum-likelihood estimates of the values of α and the components of β. These estimates and the derivatives $\partial F(\alpha + \beta x^*)/\partial x^*_i = F'(\alpha + \beta x^*)\beta_i$, where $i = 1, \ldots, k$, provide him with answers to the questions he is asking.

The researcher is carrying out his empirical analysis in accord with the prescriptions of the authors I mentioned in the introduction to this section. Still, I question the adequacy of his analysis. Here is why. The likelihood function the researcher uses to obtain his maximum-likelihood estimates of α and β is given by the equation

$L(\alpha, \beta \mid (y^*_1, x^*_1), \ldots, (y^*_M, x^*_M))$
$= \Pi_{1 \le i \le M}\Phi(\alpha + \beta x^*_i)^{y^*_i}(1 - \Phi(\alpha + \beta x^*_i))^{(1 - y^*_i)}$. (4.3)

His choice of $\Phi(\cdot)$ for $F(\cdot)$ in equations 4.1 and 4.2 is arbitrary, and it is unlikely that $L(\cdot \mid (y^*_1, x^*_1), \ldots, (y^*_M, x^*_M))$, when evaluated at the maximum-likelihood estimates of α and β, is a good measure of the conditional likelihood of the sample.[1] If the estimate of the conditional likelihood is bad, the researcher's results concerning the import of socioeconomic characteristics for a woman's choice to enter or not to enter the labor force may be meaningless.

The researcher's results are meaningful only if his maximum-likelihood estimates of α and β are empirically relevant. In the present case, the pair (y^*, x^*) for the United States in 1980 has a well-defined probability distribution, $P(\cdot)$. The components of x^* can assume only a finite number of values. Consequently, $P(\cdot)$ is discrete, and the true likelihood of the sample, $TL(\cdot)$, is given by the equation

$T\,L((y^*, x^*)_1, \ldots, (y^*, x^*)_M) = \Pi_{1 \le i \le M}P((y^*, x^*) = (y^*, x^*)_i)$. (4.4)

To see if the researcher's estimates are empirically relevant, I would calculate an estimate of $P(\cdot)$ and of $mpr(\cdot)$, the marginal probability distribution of x^*, and delineate a 95-percent-confidence region around my estimate of $P(\cdot)$. The researcher's estimates of α and β are empirically relevant only if the probability distribution of (y^*, x^*) that the estimated values of $\Phi(\cdot)$ and the mpr$(\cdot)$ determine belongs to the given confidence region.

4.1.2 A Standard Univariate Qualitative Response Model with Inaccurate Observations

Suppose that a woman's choice of whether to enter the labor force in the United States in 1980 depended on the difference y between the wage rate that a woman could expect to earn in the market and her reservation wage. Then the researcher can reformulate his statistical model as a standard univariate latent variable model for his data with $(3 + 2k)$ variables, $y \in R$, $x \in R^k$, $u \in R$, $y^* \in \{0, 1\}$, $x^* \in R^k$, and four basic assertions:

$$y = \alpha + \beta x + u, \tag{4.5}$$

u is a random variable with mean 0 and variance 1, x is a random vector with finite means and a covariance matrix with strictly positive diagonal elements, and u and x are independently distributed, $\qquad (4.6)$

$$y^* = 1 \text{ if } y > 0 \text{ and } y^* = 0 \text{ if } y \leq 0, \tag{4.7}$$

and

$$x^* = x. \tag{4.8}$$

Here the components of x record a woman's socioeconomic characteristics, u is an error term, and equation 4.5 describes how the researcher imagines that the socioeconomic characteristics in the United States in 1980 influence a woman's income expectations. The given researcher takes for granted that a woman will enter the labor force if and only if y is positive. Consequently, according to equations 4.7 and 4.8 the interpretation of y^* and x^* in the latent variable model is the same as the interpretation of the pair in equations 4.1 and 4.2.

The triple y, x, u consists of theoretical variables. They are, in principle, unobservable. The pair y^*, x^* consists of data variables whose values the researcher can observe. Equations 4.7 and 4.8 describe how the theoretical variables are related to the data variables. They insist that the values of the components of x^* provide accurate observations of the components of x, and that the value of y^* equals 1 or 0 according as the value of y in the pertinent woman's mind is positive or not.[2] In his statistical analysis of the data, the researcher may assume that u is normally distributed, derive the resulting conditional distribution of y* given x*, and obtain maximum-likelihood estimates of α and β as prescribed in the texts cited above.

4.1.3 The Empirical Equivalence of the Two Qualitative Response Models

On the surface, the two qualitative response models are not too different. For example, if the probability distribution of u is symmetric around 0 and has the cumulative distribution function $G(\cdot)$. Then

$$\text{Pr.}\{y^* = 1 \mid x^*\} = \text{Pr.}\{u > -\alpha - \beta x \mid x = x^*\} = G(\alpha + \beta x^*) \qquad (4.9)$$

and

$$\text{Pr.}\{y^* = 0 \mid x^*\} = \text{Pr.}\{u \leq -\alpha - \beta x \mid x = x^*\} = 1 - G(\alpha + \beta x^*). \qquad (4.10)$$

If $F(\cdot)$ is chosen to be $G(\cdot)$, equations 4.1 and 4.2 reduce to equations 4.9 and 4.10. In particular, if u in the latent variable model is normally distributed with mean 0 and variance 1, the $G(\cdot)$ in equations 4.9 and 4.10 is identical with the normal distribution that the researcher employed in his data analysis in subsection 4.1.1.

The seeming equivalence of the two models overlooks the fact that the empirical analysis of the first model is carried out in the upper data universe in figure 2.1, whereas the empirical analysis of the latent variable model is carried out in the lower data universe. The probability distribution of (y*, x*) that $G(\cdot)$, the probability distribution of x, and equations 4.7 and 4.8 determine in the lower data universe is different from the probability distribution of (y*, x*) that $G(\cdot)$ and the estimated mpr(·) determine in the upper data universe. Because of this dissimilarity and the fact that the meaning of empirical relevance differs in the two universes, checking for the empirical relevance of parameter estimates in the latent variable model differs from checking for the empirical relevance of parameter estimates in the researcher's original qualitative response model. The results also may differ. One of the models may be empirically relevant and the other may be empirically irrelevant. I will explain how in section 4.5.

4.1.4 A Remark

Before presenting the axioms of the present theory-data confrontation, a word about the mean and the variance of u in equation 4.6 is required. If I multiply equation 4.5 with a positive constant, k^*, I obtain

$k^*y = (k^*\alpha) + (k^*\beta)x + k^*u.$

The family of models that constitutes the theory of the latent variable model with the equation for k^*y and equations 4.6–4.8 is the same as the family of models that constitute the theory of the latent variable model with equations 4.5–4.8.[3] In the axiom system in this chapter I will insist on equation 4.5 and assume that u has finite mean and variance. The resulting family of models of the axioms contains all the models of the latent variable model in subsection 4.1.2 and many more. It is, therefore, significant that in the applications of the axioms that I envision it is always a subfamily of the models that is confronted with data. In subsection 4.2.3, for example, $u \in \{-3, 3\}$, $Pr(u = -3) = 1/3$, $Pr(u = 3) = 2/3$, and the mean and the variance of u are, respectively, 1 and 8. In the Probit family of models of the axioms in subsection 4.2.4, u is normally distributed with mean 0 and variance 1.

4.2 Formal Theory-Data Confrontations of a Latent Variable Model

In this chapter I treat the two qualitative response models as two different theories about one phenomenon in social reality, and I disregard their possible observational equivalence. I do so to contrast as clearly as I can the empirical analysis of a latent variable model in the lower data universe of figure 2.1 with the empirical analysis of a standard qualitative response model in the upper data universe. Also, I will formulate a formal data confrontation of qualitative response models that have many families of models, two of which I described in subsections 4.1.1 and 4.1.2. In subsection 4.2.4 a particular family of models of the given theory-data confrontation constitutes the basis for a case study of women's participation in the US labor force. I will refer to this family of models as the intended interpretation of the axioms.[4]

4.2.1 A Formalized Latent Variable Model
In this section I formulate the axiomatic version of the latent variable model, describe the ingredients of a meaningful empirical analysis of the model, and discuss its empirical relevance in two case studies. I begin with the axioms.

The theory universe, the data universe, and the bridge are, as before, designated $(\Omega_T, \Gamma_T, (\Omega_T, \aleph_T, P_T(\cdot)))$, $(\Omega_P, \Gamma_P, (\Omega_P, \aleph_P, P_P(\cdot)))$, and $(\Omega, \Gamma_{T,P})$. Also, vectors in the theory universe function as vectors in Ω_T and as vector-valued random variables on $(\Omega_T, \aleph_T)$. Similarly, vectors in the data universe function as vectors in Ω_P and as vector-valued random variables on $(\Omega_P, \aleph_P)$. I assume throughout that Ω_T and Ω_P are disjoint, that $\aleph_T$ and $\aleph_P$ are stochastically independent, and that the probability space $(\Omega_T \times \Omega_P, \aleph, P(\cdot))$ is as I described it in chapter 2. To simplify my arguments, I formulate axioms for a case in which the pertinent researcher samples at random only once in the observations box in figure 1.2.

First the Γ_T axioms for the theory universe. A1 and A2 describe pertinent characteristics of the conceptual framework of the theory that is at stake in a given theory-data confrontation. In the intended interpretation of the two axioms, (y, x, u) are vectors whose components are taken to record the values of some woman's net income expectations, y, her socioeconomic characteristics, x, and an associated error term, u. The value of the net-income variable, y, is taken to be a measure of the difference between the wage rate that the woman expects to earn in the market and her reservation wage.

A1
$\Omega_T \subset R \times Q \times R$, and Q is a finite discrete k-dimensional subset of R^k. Thus, $\omega_T \in \Omega_T$ only if $\omega_T = (y, x, u)$ for some $y \in R, x \in Q, u \in R$, and $(y,x,u) \in R \times Q \times R$.

A2
$\aleph_T$ is a σ field of subsets of Ω_T, $P_T(\cdot):\aleph_T \to [0, 1]$ is a probability measure, and $y(\cdot): \Omega_T \to R, x(\cdot): \Omega_T \to Q$, and $u(\cdot): \Omega_T \to R$ are defined by the equations $(y(\omega_T), x(\omega_T), u(\omega_T)) = \omega_T, \omega_T \in \Omega_T$. The vector-valued function $(y, x, u)(\cdot)$ is measurable with respect to $\aleph_T$, and the probability distribution of the $(y, x, u)(\cdot)$ that $P_T(\cdot)$ determines is the probability distribution that the researcher assigns to the given function. I designate this probability distribution RPD.

It follows from the two axioms that the subsets of Ω_T that might belong to $\aleph_T$ can be described in two different ways. For example, let C_1 be the set of all (y, x, u) vectors in Ω_T whose components record a positive income expectation, and let C_2 be the set of all (y, x, u) vectors in Ω_T whose components' record of socioeconomic characteristics belong to A. Then

$$C_1 = \{(y, x, u) \in \Omega_T: y > 0, x \in Q, \text{ and } u \in R\}$$

and

$C_2 = \{(y, x, u) \in \Omega_T : y \in R, x \in A, \text{ and } u \in R\}.$

The two sets can also be described by the equations

$C_1 = \{\omega_T \in \Omega_T : y(\omega_T) > 0\}$

and

$C_2 = \{\omega_T \in \Omega_T : x(\omega_T) \in A\}$, where A is a subset of Q.

Whatever description I use, $P_T(C_1)$ is the number that the researcher assigns to the probability that a woman in a draw of a random sample has positive income expectations. Also, $P_T(C_2)$ is the number the researcher assigns to the probability that a draw of a random sample contains a woman whose socioeconomic characteristics belong to A.

In addition to A1 and A2, the Γ_T contains four axioms that describe how the components of ω_T are related to one another, and what the salient characteristics of the RPD are.

A3
There are an $\alpha \in R$ and a $\beta \in R^k$ such that, for all $\omega_T \in \Omega_T$, $y = \alpha + \beta x + u$. Also, $\alpha \leq 0$ and $\alpha + \beta x > 0$ for some $x \in Q.$[5]

A4
Relative to $P_T(\cdot)$, the probability distribution of $u(\cdot)$ has finite mean and variance, and may or may not be symmetric around 0.

A5
Relative to $P_T(\cdot)$, $x(\cdot)$ is a vector-valued random variable with a finite mean vector, μ_x, and a covariance matrix, Σ_x, with finite, strictly positive diagonal elements.

A6
Relative to $P_T(\cdot)$, $u(\cdot)$ and $x(\cdot)$ are distributed independently of each other.

Next, the Γ_P axioms for the data universe. D1 and D2, describe characteristic features of the conceptual framework of the data-generating process. In the intended interpretation of the two axioms, (y^*, x^*) is a vector whose components are taken to record whether or not, according to the 1980 US census, some woman has entered the labor force, and what her socioeconomic characteristics are.

D1

$\Omega_P \subset \{0, 1\} \times Q$. Thus, $\omega_P \in \Omega_P$ only if $\omega_P = (y^*, x^*)$ for some, and (y^*, x^*) $\in \{0, 1\} \times Q$.

D2

$\aleph_P$ is a σ field of subsets of Ω_P, $P_P(\cdot):\aleph_P \rightarrow [0, 1]$ is a probability measure, and $y^*(\cdot): \Omega_P \rightarrow \{0, 1\}$ and $x^*(\cdot): \Omega_P \rightarrow Q$ are defined by the equations $(y^*(\omega_P), x^*(\omega_P)) = \omega_P$, $\omega_P \in \Omega_P$. The vector-valued function $(y^*, x^*)(\cdot)$ is measurable with respect to $\aleph_P$, and the probability distribution of $(y^*, x^*)(\cdot)$ that $P_P(\cdot)$ determines is the true probability distribution of the given function. I designate this probability distribution TPD.

It follows from the two axioms that the subsets of Ω_P that might belong to $\aleph_P$ can be described in two different ways. For example, let D_1 be the set of all (y^*, x^*) vectors in Ω_P whose components record that a woman has entered the labor force, and let D_2 be the set of all (y^*, x^*) vectors in Ω_P whose component's record of socioeconomic characteristics belong to A. Then

$D_1 = \{(y^*, x^*) \in \Omega_P: y^* = 1, \text{ and } x^* \in Q\}$

and

$D_2 = \{(y^*, x^*) \in \Omega_P: y^* \in \{0, 1\} \text{ and } x^* \in A\}.$

The two sets can also be described by the equations

$D_1 = \{\omega_P \in \Omega_P: y^*(\omega_P) = 1\}$

and

$D_2 = \{\omega_P \in \Omega_P: x^*(\omega_P) \in A\}$, where A is a subset of Q.

Whatever description I use, $P_P(D_1)$ is the true probability that a woman in a draw in a random sample has entered the labor force. Also, $P_P(D_2)$ is the true probability that a draw in a random sample contains a woman whose socioeconomic characteristics belong to A.

   In addition to D1 and D2, Γ_P contains one axiom that describes characteristics of the TPD.

D3

Relative to $P_P(\cdot)$, the pair $(y^*, x^*)(\cdot)$ has a finite mean vector, (μ_{y^*}, μ_{x^*}), and a covariance matrix, Σ_{y^*, x^*}, with finite, strictly positive diagonal elements.

Now the $\Gamma_{T,P}$ axioms for the Bridge. The first four of the axioms in $\Gamma_{T,P}$ describe conceptual properties of the relationship between theoretical and observational variables.

G1

Observations come in pairs, (ω_T, ω_P), all of which belong to the sample space.

G2

The sample space, Ω, is a subset of $\Omega_T \times \Omega_P$; i.e., $\Omega \subset \Omega_T \times \Omega_P$, and $\Omega_T \times \Omega_P \subset ((R \times Q \times R) \times (\{0, 1\} \times Q))$.

G3

Let $(\Omega_T \times \Omega_P, \aleph, P(\cdot))$ be the product probability space that I described in chapter 2. It is the case that $\Omega \in \aleph$ and $P(\Omega) > 0$.

G4

It is the case that $\Omega_T \subset \{(y, x, u) \in \Omega_T$ with $(y, x, u, y^*, x^*) \in \Omega$ for some $(y^*, x^*) \in \Omega_P\}$.

In addition to these four axioms, $\Gamma_{T,P}$ contains two assertions that are characteristic of a theory-data confrontation with qualitative response models.

G5

For all $(\omega_T, \omega_P) \in \Omega$, $y^* = 0$ if $y \le 0$, $y^* = 1$ if $y > 0$; i.e., for all $(\omega_T, \omega_P) \in \Omega$, $y^*(\omega_P) = 0$ if $y(\omega_T) \le 0$, $y^*(\omega_P) = 1$ if $y(\omega_T) > 0$.

G6

For all $(\omega_T, \omega_P) \in \Omega$, $x^* = x$; i.e., for all $(\omega_T, \omega_P) \in \Omega$, $x^*(\omega_P) = x(\omega_T)$.

In G5 and G6, I assume that the researcher in charge can, without fail, infer from an observation of y whether y is positive or not. The actual value of y is unobservable. Also, I assume that any observation of x that the researcher may obtain is accurate, and that the ranges of values of x and x^* in Q are equal. Finally, in G4 I rule out of court uninteresting models of the axioms. Assumption G4 implies that $P_T(\{(y, x, u) \in \Omega_T$ with $(y, x, y^*, x^*) \in \Omega$ for some $(y^*, x^*) \in \Omega_P\}) = 1$, a fact that facilitates the computation of the MPD below.

The MPD
The RPD distribution of ω_T and the bridge principles, $\Gamma_{T,P}$, induce a probability distribution of the $(y^*, x^*)(\cdot)$ that I denote by MPD and read as the *marginal probability distribution of the components of* ω_P . In the present case, for a $v \in Q$,

$\mathrm{MPD}(y^* = 0, x^* = v)$

$$= \frac{\begin{array}{c}P_T(\{(y,x,u) \in \Omega_T : y \leq 0, x = v\} \cap \{(y,x,u) \in \Omega_T \\ \text{with } (y,x,u,y^*,x^*) \in \Omega \text{ for some}(y^*,x^*) \in \Omega_P\})\end{array}}{P_T(\{(y,x,u) \in \Omega_T \text{with } (y,x,y^*,x^*) \in \Omega \text{ for some } (y^*, x^*) \in \Omega_P\})},$$

from which it follows that, for $v \in Q$,

$\mathrm{MPD}(y^* = 0, x^* = v) = P_T(\{(y, x, u) \in \Omega_T: y \leq 0 \text{ and } x = v\}).$

In the same way, I find that

$\mathrm{MPD}(y^* = 1, x^* = v) = P_T(\{(y, x, u) \in \Omega_T: y > 0 \text{ and } x = v\}),$

$\mathrm{MPD}(x^* = v) = P_T(\{(y, x, u) \in \Omega_T: x = v\}),$

$\mathrm{MPD}(y^* = 1 \,|\, x^* = v) = P_T(\{(y, x, u) \in \Omega_T: y > 0\} \,|\, x = v),$

and

$\mathrm{MPD}(y^* = 0 \,|\, x^* = v) = P_T(\{(y, x, u) \in \Omega_T: y \leq 0\} \,|\, x = v).$

The properties of the MPD and Kolmogorov's Consistency Theorem (see B. Stigum 1990, p. 347, T 15.23) imply that there is a probability measure, $P_M(\cdot): \aleph_P \to [0, 1]$, relative to which the probability distribution of $(y^*, x^*)(\cdot)$ equals the MPD. Consequently, one can think of the researcher's empirical analysis as being carried out in a data universe, $(\Omega_P, \Gamma_P^*, (\Omega_P, \aleph_P, P_M(\cdot)))$, that differs from the original universe in characteristic ways. In the latter triple, the Ω_P and $\aleph_P$- components are identical with the Ω_P and $\aleph_P$ components in the original data universe. The Γ_{P^*} component differs from Γ_P in two ways. The D2 component of Γ_P^* differs from the D2 component of Γ_P in that $P_M(\cdot)$ is substituted for $P_P(\cdot)$ and MPD is substituted for TPD. Finally, in the third component of the data universe $P_M(\cdot)$ is substituted for $P_P(\cdot)$. These ideas are depicted in figure 4.1 for ease of reference. Figure 4.1 is, for this chapter, an appropriate analogue of figure 2.1.

With $P_M(\cdot)$ in hand, I can describe the salient characteristics of the MPD in two useful theorems.

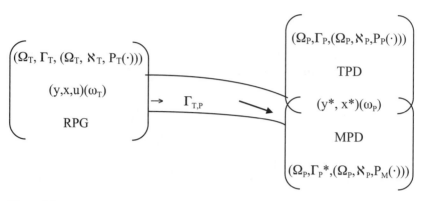

Figure 4.1
A theory-data confrontation with inaccurate observations.

T4.1

Suppose that A1–A6, D1, and G1–G6 are valid. For all $v_j \in Q$ such that $P_T(x = v) \neq 0$,

$$MPD(y^* = 0, x^* = v)$$

$$= MPD(y^* = 0 \mid x^* = v) \cdot MPD(x^* = v)$$

$$= P_T(\{(y, x, u) \in \Omega_T : y \leq 0\} \mid x = v) \cdot P_T(\{(y, x, u) \in \Omega_T : x = v\})$$

$$= P_T(\{(y, x, u) \in \Omega_T : u \leq -\alpha - \beta x\} \mid x = v) \cdot P_T(\{(y, x, u) \in \Omega_T : x = v\})$$

$$= P_T(\{(y, x, u) \in \Omega_T : u \leq -\alpha - \beta v\}) \cdot P_T(\{(y, x, u) \in \Omega_T : x = v\})$$

$$(4.11)$$

and

$$MPD(y^* = 1, x^* = v)$$

$$= MPD(y^* = 1 \mid x^* = v) \cdot MPD(x^* = v)$$

$$= P_T(\{(y, x, u) \in \Omega_T : y > 0\} \mid x = v) \cdot P_T(\{(y, x, u) \in \Omega_T : x = v\})$$

$$= P_T(\{(y, x, u) \in \Omega_T : u > -\alpha - \beta x\} \mid x = v) \cdot P_T(\{(y, x, u) \in \Omega_T : x = v\})$$

$$= P_T(\{(y, x, u) \in \Omega_T : u > -\alpha - \beta v\}) \cdot P_T(\{(y, x, u) \in \Omega_T : x = v\}).$$

$$(4.12)$$

T4.2

Suppose that axioms A1–A6, D1, and G1–G6 are valid. Then, relative to an MPD determined $P_M(\cdot)$, the pair, $(y^*, x^*)(\omega_P)$, is a vector-valued random variable that has a finite mean vector and a finite covariance matrix with strictly positive diagonal elements that depend on the values of α and β.

4.2.2 Empirical Analyses of a Latent Variable Model

In this section I shall discuss the kind of empirical analysis of a univariate qualitative response model that the preceding formal theory-data confrontation prescribes. A1–A6, D1–D3, and G1–G6 are written for an experiment in which the researcher samples at random only once in the observations box in figure 1.2. Now I shall use them as a basis for an empirical analysis of a random sample of observations of members of a population at a given point in time. In the empirical analysis the population is taken to be finite. Also, the number of observations equals M, a finite integer, and the observations are presumed to be obtained in a random sampling scheme with replacement. To simplify my discussion, I assign numbers to the members of Q. Specifically, I suppose that there are m members in Q, and I number them from 1 to m and mark their values by v_j, where $j = 1, \ldots , m$.

My empirical deliberations in this case center on three fundamental ideas that describe the prescriptions underlying the statistical analysis, delineate the salient characteristics of a data-admissible mathematical model of MPD, and describe what it means for a theory to be empirically relevant. In the present context, the prescriptions that underlie the statistical analysis detail the way I am to obtain a consistent estimate of a mathematical model of the MPD. Also, a mathematical model of MPD is data admissible if (1) the estimated mathematical model of MPD satisfies the strictures on which D1 and the prescriptions that underlie the statistical analysis insist, (2) the values that the given model assigns to the parameters of MPD satisfy the strictures on which the A axioms, D1, and the G axioms insist, and (3) the model lies within a 95-percent-confidence region of the estimated mathematical model of MPD. Finally, a family of mathematical models of axioms A1–A6 is empirically relevant if and only if there is at least one member of the family which—with a corresponding mathematical model of D1 and G1–G6—determines a data-admissible mathematical model of the MPD.

The Prescriptions That Underlie the Statistical Analysis

Since in this case the probability distribution of the MPD is determined by a finite number of probability assignments, the prescriptions that underlie the statistical analysis can be described in the following way: I assume that all the observed values of the x^* belong to $\{v_1, \ldots , v_m\}$, that I have observed the values of the pairs, $(y^*, x^*)(1), \ldots , (y^*, x^*)(M)$, and that the P_T probability that x will assume the observed value of $x^*(t)$ is positive for all $t = 1, \ldots , M$. I assume, also, that the family of random pairs $\{(y^*, x^*)(t); t \in M\}$, in $P_M(\cdot)$ measure, are independently and identically distributed with the same means, variances, and covariance. In P_M measure these are the means, variances, and covariance of the MPD in T4.2. Finally, I let m_{ij} denote the number of observed pairs $(y^*, x^*)(t)$ with $y^*(t) = i$ and $x^*(t) = v_j$, $i = 0, 1$, and $j = 1, \ldots , m$, and observe that T4.2 implies that, in terms of the MPD, the probability of the sample observations being what they are is given by a constant multiple of the likelihood function

$$L_{MPD}(p_{01}, \ldots , p_{0m}, p_{11}, \ldots , p_{1m} \mid (y^*, x^*)(1), \ldots , (y^*, x^*)(M)) = \Pi_{1 \leq j \leq m} \, p_{0j}{}^{m0j} p_{1j}{}^{m1j},$$
(4.13)

where $p_{ij} = MPD((y^*, x^*)(t) = (i, v_j))$, $i = 0, 1$ and $j = 1, \ldots , m$, and where $m_{ij} \in \{0, \ldots , M\}$, $i = 0, 1$, $j = 1, \ldots , m$, and $\Sigma_{1 \leq j \leq m}(m_{0j} + m_{1j}) = M$.

The prescriptions that underlie my statistical analysis direct me to obtain maximum-likelihood estimates of the p_{ij} by maximizing the logarithmic transform of the likelihood function subject to the constraint $\Sigma_{1 \leq j \leq m} p_{0j} + p_{1j} = 1$. The resulting estimates are uniquely determined and given by the equations

$$p_{ij}{}^0 = m_{ij}/M, \text{ where } i = 0, 1 \text{ and } j = 1, \ldots , m.$$
(4.14)

Since the m_{ij}/M are non-negative, add to 1, and represent a maximum of the log-likelihood function, my estimates of the p_{ij} satisfy D1 and the prescriptions that underlie my statistical analysis.

The estimates in equation 4.14 are consistent. To wit: in the lower data universe in figure 4.1, $(\Omega_P, \Gamma_P{}^*, (\Omega_P, \aleph_P, P_M(\cdot)))$, my assumption concerning my data implies that, with respect to $P_M(\cdot)$ and, hence, in terms of the MPD distribution of $y^*(t)$ and $x^*(t)$ (i.e., in P_M measure), for $i = 0, 1$ and $j = 1, \ldots , m$,

$$\text{Lim}_{M \to \infty} \, m_{ij}/M = P_M(y^*(t) = i, x^*(t) = v_j) = MPD(y^*_t = i, x^*_t = v_j) \text{ a.e.}$$
(4.15)

A Confidence Region for Data-Admissible Models of the MPD

Next I must describe the region, D, in which the data-admissible mathematical models of the MPD must reside. In the present case I identify this region with a 95-percent-confidence region around my maximum-likelihood estimates of the p_{ij} in equation 4.14. Consequently, to delimit D, I let $\phi = (p_{01}, \ldots , p_{0m}, p_{11}, \ldots , p_{1m})$ and I let ϕ^0 be the

maximum-likelihood estimates in equation 4.14. I define the function
H(·) as the negative of the Hessian of the logarithmic transform of the
likelihood function in equation 4.13,

$$H(\phi) = -(\partial^2 \log L_{\text{MPD}}(\phi \mid (y^*, x^*)(1), \ldots, (y^*, x^*)(M))/\partial\phi_i\partial\phi_j), \quad (4.16)$$

and observe that in P_M measure $(\phi - \phi^\circ)H(\phi^\circ)(\phi - \phi^\circ)'$ is, for large M,
approximately χ^2 distributed with $2m - 1$ degrees of freedom. (See
chapter 13 of Davidson and MacKinnon 1993.). Hence, I can define D
as follows:

$$D = \left\{ \phi \in R_+^{2m} : \sum_{1 \leq i \leq 2m} \phi_i = 1 \text{ and } (\phi - \phi^\circ)H(\phi^\circ)(\phi - \phi^\circ)' \leq \chi^2(2m-1) \right\}, \quad (4.17)$$

where ϕ and ϕ° are as described above, and where, with $2m - 1$ degrees
of freedom, 0.95 is the χ^2 measure of the interval, $[0, \chi^2(2m - 1]$.

The Empirical Relevance of a Family of Models of A1–A6
To determine whether a given family of models of A1–A6 is empirically
relevant, I must estimate the theoretical version of the MPD that I
described on the right-hand sides of equations 4.11 and 4.12, and delineate an appropriate confidence region around the estimate. Here an
appropriate confidence region is a statistical confidence band that
heeds the restrictions that the researcher has imposed on the values of
pertinent parameters in A3. If this confidence region contains a data-
admissible mathematical model of the MPD (that is, if this region has
a non-empty intersection with D), I judge axioms A1–A6 to be empirically relevant.[6] Otherwise I judge them not to be empirically relevant.

   In looking back at my explication of empirical relevance, an explanatory remark is in order. According to T4.1 and T4.2, the MPD distribution of (y^*, x^*) depends on the values of α and β. Hence there are as
many MPDs as there are relevant values of α and β. From this it follows
that the limit in equation 4.15 varies with the chosen model of MPD. It
is, therefore, important to observe that the limiting distribution of $(\phi - \phi^\circ)H(\phi^\circ)(\phi - \phi^\circ)'$ is the same for all relevant models of the MPD.
Consequently, the confidence region D depends on ϕ° but not on any
particular one of the possible "true" versions of the MPD.

**4.2.3 A Case Study in Which Axioms A1–A6 Have Only One
Model**
Axioms A1–A6 have many models. In the present case their undefined
terms are k, m, α, β, and the parameters of the probability distribution

of x and u. I obtain a family of models of A1–A6 with just one member by fixing the values of these parameters. The one-member family of mathematical models of A1–A6 that I have in mind has the following characteristics: $k = 1$, $m = 2$, $\alpha = -1$, $\beta = 2$, $u \in \{-3, 3\}$ and $x \in \{1/2, 3/2\}$. Also, relative to $P_T(\cdot)$, x and u are independently distributed. Finally, $P_T(u = -3) = 1/3$, $P_T(u = 3) = 2/3$; $P_T(x = 1/2) = 1/2$, and $P_T(x = 3/2) = 1/2$.

From the preceding description of the given mathematical model of A1–A6 and from G1–G6 I deduce that

$$\begin{pmatrix} \text{MPD}(y^* = 0, x^* = \frac{1}{2}) & \text{MPD}(y^* = 1, x^* = \frac{1}{2}) \\ \text{MPD}(y^* = 0, x^* = \frac{3}{2}) & \text{MPD}(y^* = 1, x^* = \frac{3}{2}) \end{pmatrix} = \begin{pmatrix} \frac{1}{6} & \frac{1}{3} \\ \frac{1}{6} & \frac{1}{3} \end{pmatrix}. \tag{4.18}$$

The following theorem is also valid.

T4.4

In the given mathematical model of A1–A6, it is the case that, relative to $P_M(\cdot)$, the pair $(y^*, x^*)(\omega_P)$ has a mean of $(2/3, 1)$, a variance of $(2/9, 1/4)$, and a covariance of 0.

An Empirical Analysis with Generated Data

For the purposes of this example I let the given one-member family of models of A1–A6 face a mathematical model of the data universe in which $x^* \in \{1/2, 3/2\}$, and in which the value of $\text{DGP}(y^* = i, x^* = j)$ is set equal to $1/6$ if $(i, j) = (0, 1/2)$ or $(0, 3/2)$ and to $1/3$ if $(i, j) = (1, 1/2)$ or $(1, 3/2)$. I generated 999 observations of the values of the pair (y^*, x^*) with a random number generator for a multinomial distribution. The four parameters of the given distribution were chosen so that $p_{01/2} = 1/6$, $p_{11/2} = 1/3$, $p_{03/2} = 1/6$, and $p_{13/2} = 1/3$, where the first subscript denotes the value of y^* and the second denotes the value of x^*. With this sample, I obtained estimates of the MPD probabilities by maximizing the logarithmic transform of the analogue of the likelihood function in equation 4.13 subject to the condition $p_{01/2} + p_{11/2} + p_{03/2} + p_{13/2} = 1$. The estimates are the following:

$$p_{01/2}{}^\circ = 0.175175, \quad p_{11/2}{}^\circ = 0.323323,$$
$$p_{03/2}{}^\circ = 0.156156, \quad p_{13/2}{}^\circ = 0.345345. \tag{4.19}$$

The negative of the Hessian matrix of the likelihood function in equation 4.13, when evaluated at the maximum-likelihood estimates in equation 4.19, is given below with $p^\circ = (p_{01/2}{}^\circ, p_{11/2}{}^\circ, p_{03/2}{}^\circ, p_{13/2}{}^\circ)$:

$$H(p^\circ) = \begin{pmatrix} 5702.869 & 0 & 0 & 0 \\ 0 & 3089.789 & 0 & 0 \\ 0 & 0 & 6397.449 & 0 \\ 0 & 0 & 0 & 2892.759 \end{pmatrix}.$$

This matrix and equation 4.17 determine the following 95-percent-confidence region around p°:

$$D = \{p \in R_+^4: p_{01/2} + p_{11/2} + p_{03/2} + p_{13/2} = 1,$$
$$\text{and } (p - p^\circ)\, H(p^\circ)(p - p^\circ)' \leq 7.81\}, \tag{4.20}$$

where $p^\circ = (0.175175, 0.323323, 0.156156, 0.345345)$. With three degrees of freedom, the χ^2 probability of the interval $[0, 7.81]$ is 0.95. Let $p^* = (0.166667, 0.333333, 0.166667, 0.333333)$ be the mathematical model of MPD in equation 4.18 that the given one-member family of mathematical models of A1–A6 determines. Since $(p^* - p^\circ)\, H(p^\circ)(p^* - p^\circ)' = 1.846593$, p^* does belong to D and is, therefore, data admissible. Consequently, the given one-member family of mathematical models of A1–A6 is empirically relevant in the empirical context that my sample of observations determines.

The example has several interesting aspects. First, the estimated mathematical model of MPD is not data admissible, since it does not heed the restrictions on which the model of A1–A6, D1, and G1–G6 insists. Also, in the 95-percent-confidence interval around the estimated model of the MPD there is only one data-admissible model of MPD, namely the model determined by the axioms and given in equation 4.18. Finally, the TPD is the data-generating model in the example, and this model is equal to the MPD in equation 4.18; i.e., $MPD(y^*, x^*) = TPD(y^*, x^*)$ for $y^* = 0, 1$ and $x^* = 1/2, 3/2$. Consequently, the one and only data-admissible mathematical model of the MPD is in this case a congruent model of the TPD.

4.2.4 A Case Study with a Probit Family of Models of A1–A6
The Probit family of mathematical models of A1–A6 comprises models in which $k > 1$, m is the number of elements in Q, $\alpha \in R$, $\beta \in R^k$, and u is normally distributed with mean 0 and variance 1. I mark the values of the m members of Q by $v_1, \ldots, v_m$ and designate the corresponding probabilities $P_T(x = v_j) = p_j, j = 1, \ldots, m$. Finally, x and u are distributed independently of each other. In the new family of mathematical models of A1–A6 the MPD is as described in T4.5 and T4.6.

T4.5

Consider the Probit family of mathematical models of A1–A6. For all $v_j \in Q$ such that $P_T(x_t = v_j) \neq 0$,

$MPD(y^* = 0, x^* = v_j)$

    $= MPD(y^* = 0 \mid x^* = v_j) \cdot MPD(x^* = v_j)$

    $= P_T(\{(y, x, u) \in \Omega_T: y \leq 0\} \mid x = v_j) \cdot P_T(\{(y, x, u) \in \Omega_T : x = v_j\})$

    $= P_T(\{(y, x, u) \in \Omega_T: u \leq -\alpha - \beta x\} \mid x = v_j) \cdot P_T(\{(y, x, u) \in \Omega_T: x = v_j\})$

    $= [(1/\sqrt{2\Pi}) \int_{(-\infty, -\alpha - \beta v_j)} \exp. -\frac{1}{2}u^2 \, du] \cdot P_T(\{(y, x, u) \in \Omega_T: x = v_j\})$

and

$MPD(y^* = 1, x^* = v_j)$

    $= MPD(y^* = 1 \mid x^* = v_j) \cdot MPD(x^* = v_j)$

    $= P_T(\{(y, x, u) \in \Omega_T: y > 0\} \mid x = v_j) \cdot P_T(\{(y, x, u) \in \Omega_T: x = v_j\})$

    $= P_T(\{(y, x, u) \in \Omega_T: u > -\alpha - \beta x\} \mid x = v_j) \cdot P_T(\{(y, x, u) \in \Omega_T: x = v_j\})$

    $= [(1/\sqrt{2\Pi}) \int_{(-\alpha - \beta v_j, \infty)} \exp. -\frac{1}{2}u^2 \, du] \cdot P_T(\{(y, x, u) \in \Omega_T: x = v_j\}).$

T4.6

In the Probit family of mathematical models of A1–A6 it is the case that, relative to an MPD determined $P_M(\cdot)$, the pair, $(y^*, x^*)(\omega_P)$, is a vector-valued random variable with finite means, variances, and covariances that depend on the values of α and β.

In the vernacular of econometricians, the Probit family of mathematical models of A1–A6 together with D1 and G1–G6 constitutes a formal version of the so-called Probit qualitative response model. To ascertain whether the Probit family of models of A1–A6 has empirical relevance, I must check whether there is at least one member of the family and a corresponding model of D1 and G1–G6 that determine a data-admissible mathematical model of the MPD. To do that I proceed as follows: I let

$\Phi(-\alpha - \beta x^*(t)) = (1/\sqrt{2\Pi}) \int_{(-\infty, -\alpha - \beta x^*(t)]} \exp. -\frac{1}{2}u^2 \, du$

and

$\phi(u) = (1/\sqrt{2\Pi}) \exp. -\frac{1}{2}u^2.$

I let m_{ij}, be the number of t values of the pairs $(y^*, x^*)(t)$ with $y^*(t) = i$, and $x^*(t) = v_j$, $i = 0, 1, j = 1, \ldots, m$, and I note that $\Sigma_{1 \leq j \leq m} (m_{0j} + m_{1j}) = M$. Also, I let $p_{ij} = P_M((y^*, x^*)(t, \omega_P)) = (i, v_j))$, $i = 0, 1$, and $j = 1, \ldots, m$. Then I appeal to T4.5 and my assumption that my sample of observations of (y^*, x^*) is random, and claim that, in terms of the MPD, the likelihood function of the sample can be expressed as follows:

$$L_{MPD}(\alpha, \beta, p_{01}, \ldots, p_{0m}, p_{11}, \ldots, p_{1m} \mid (y^*, x^*)(1), \ldots, (y^*, x^*)(M))$$

$$= \Pi_{1 \leq j \leq m} \Phi(-\alpha - \beta v_j)^{m_{0j}} \Pi_{1 \leq j \leq m} (1 - \Phi(-\alpha - \beta v_j))^{m_{1j}} \Pi_{1 \leq j \leq m} p_{0j}^{m_{0j}} p_{1j}^{m_{1j}}.$$

$$(4.21)$$

In the statistical analysis, I obtain estimates of α, β, and the p_{ij}, $i = 0$, 1, and $j = 1, \ldots, m$, by maximizing the logarithmic transform of the $L_{MPD}(\cdot)$ with respect to the given parameters subject to the constraint that $\Sigma_{1 \leq j \leq m} (p_{0j} + p_{1j}) = 1$. The estimates of α and β are uniquely determined since the maximum in the pertinent part of the log-likelihood function is a global maximum. (See Greene 1997, p. 884.) The estimates of the p_{ij} are also uniquely determined and equal to the estimates displayed in equation 4.14.

My maximum-likelihood estimates of α and β are consistent. (See Davidson and MacKinnon 1993, pp. 255–257 and 517–518.) The maximum-likelihood estimates of the p_{ij} in equation 4.14 are also consistent with the limiting values displayed in equation 4.15. Together these estimates determine a mathematical model of the MPD in T4.4. To see if this model is data admissible, I proceed as follows. I denote the maximum-likelihood estimates of the respective parameters by $\alpha°$, $\beta°$, and $p_{ij}°$, where $i = 0, 1$, and $j = 1, \ldots, m$, and I let $p_j° = p_{0j}° + p_{1j}°$, $j = 1$, $\ldots, m$. Then I check whether the m pairs

$$(p_{0j}^*, p_{1j}^*) = [(1 - \Phi(\alpha° + \beta° v_j)) p_j°, \Phi(\alpha° + \beta° v_j) p_j°], \quad j = 1, \ldots, m \quad (4.22)$$

belong to D in equation 4.17.[7] If they do, I judge the mathematical model of MPD that the given maximum-likelihood estimates determine to be data admissible, and the associated member of the Probit family of mathematical models of A1–A6 to be empirically relevant.

If the pairs in equation 4.22 do not belong to D, I cannot use them to infer that A1–A6 are empirically irrelevant. There may exist another pair of parameters, (α^*, β^*), in the appropriate 95-percent-confidence band around the maximum-likelihood estimates of α and β, that satisfies the conditions in A3 and determines a data-admissible mathematical model of the MPD, i.e., an m-tuple of pairs,

$$[(1 - \Phi(\alpha^* + \beta^* v_j))p_j^{\,\circ}, \ \Phi(\alpha^* + \beta^* v_j)p_j^{\,\circ}], \qquad j = 1, \ldots, m \qquad (4.23)$$

that belongs to D. If such a pair of values of α and β exists, the associated member of the Probit family of mathematical models of A1–A6 is empirically relevant. Otherwise it is not.

An Empirical Analysis with Data from Women's Participation in the US Labor Force

In the present study, y measures the difference between the wage rate that a woman can expect to earn in the market and her reservation wage, $k = 2$, $m = 9$, and the components of x measures a woman's age (x_1) and her number of years of schooling (x_2). The values of x_1 belong to {30, 45, 60}; the values of x_2 belong to {6, 9, 12}. Finally, y^* equals 1 or 0 according as y is positive or not, and x_1^* and x_2^* belong, respectively, to {30, 45, 60} and {6, 9, 12}. The data consist of observations of a randomly selected subset of women in the 1980 census of the US population of women between the ages 18 and 65 whose years of education ranged from 0 to 20. I have assigned 30 to the age of all women of age smaller or equal to 30, 45 to the age of women of ages between 30 and 45 including 45, and 60 to the age of women of age greater than 45. Similarly, I have assigned 6 to the schooling of women with 7 or less years of education, 9 to the schooling of women with 8 or 9 years of education, and 12 to the schooling of women with more than 9 years of education. The source of the census data is the Integrated Public Use Microdata Series at http://www.ipums.org. D. F. Hendry and B. Nielsen (2007, p. xi) are responsible for the selection of the subsample of women that I use in my study.

To carry out the empirical analysis of the data, I begin by assigning v_js to the members of the present Q. (See table 4.1.) Thereafter I use equation 4.14 to obtain maximum-likelihood estimates of the $P_M(\cdot)$ probabilities of the triples in {0, 1}× Q. (See table 4.2.) Finally, to delineate the confidence region D in equation 4.17, I use equation 4.16 to obtain estimates of the diagonal elements of $H(\varphi^\circ)$, where $\varphi^\circ = (p_{01}^{\,\circ}, \ldots , p_{0m}^{\,\circ}, p_{11}^{\,\circ}, \ldots , p_{1m}^{\,\circ})$. (See table 4.3.[8])

It remains to estimate the probabilities in equation 4.22 and to check whether they belong to the D in equation 4.17. I begin by estimating α and the two β's with the help of PcGive's Probit program. The results are given in table 4.4.

Next, I use the estimates of α and β and the estimates of the p_{ij} in table 4.2 to calculate the probabilities in equation 4.22. They are displayed in table 4.5.

Table 4.1
Assignment of values to the members of Q.

(30, 12)	(45, 9)	(60, 12)	(60, 6)	(60, 9)	(45, 12)	(45, 6)	(30, 9)	(30, 6)
v_1	v_2	v_3	v_4	v_5	v_6	v_7	v_8	v_9

Table 4.2
Maximum-likelihood estimates of the p_{ij}, with $i = 1, 0$ and $j = 1, \ldots, 9$.

p_{01}^{o}	p_{02}^{o}	p_{03}^{o}	p_{04}^{o}	p_{05}^{o}	p_{06}^{o}	p_{07}^{o}	p_{08}^{o}	p_{09}^{o}
0, 1133	0, 0113	0, 1156	0, 0240	0, 0283	0, 0872	0, 0074	0, 0105	0, 0053

p_{11}^{o}	p_{12}^{o}	p_{13}^{o}	p_{14}^{o}	p_{15}^{o}	p_{16}^{o}	p_{17}^{o}	p_{18}^{o}	p_{19}^{o}
0, 2310	0, 0110	0, 1320	0, 0104	0, 0178	0, 1778	0, 0053	0, 0080	0, 0037

Table 4.3
The diagonal members of $H(\varphi^o)$.

$H_{1,1}$	$H_{2,2}$	$H_{3,3}$	$H_{4,4}$	$H_{5,5}$	$H_{6,6}$	$H_{7,7}$	$H_{8,8}$	$H_{9,9}$
392388	3932457	384605	1850351	1567374	509800	5994017	4235601	8453101

$H_{10,10}$	$H_{11,11}$	$H_{12,12}$	$H_{13,13}$	$H_{14,14}$	$H_{15,15}$	$H_{16,16}$	$H_{17,17}$	$H_{18,18}$
192565	4028565	336972	4290728	2503830	250098	83814655	55876433	121351277

Table 4.4
Probit estimates of α and β with PcGive.

	Coefficient	S.E.	t value	t probability
A	−0.623402	0.05436	−11.5	0.0000
β_1	−0.0111428	0.00049341	−22.6	0.000
β_2	0.119870	0.003987	30. 01	.0000

loglik = −29102.50578 for three parameters and 44,475 observations
Standard errors based on numerical second derivatives, BFGS/warm-up using numerical derivatives (eps1 = 0.0001; eps2 = 0.005): Strong convergence

Table 4.5
Estimates of the probabilities in equation 4.22.

p_{01}^*	p_{02}^*	p_{03}^*	p_{04}^*	p_{05}^*	p_{06}^*	p_{07}^*	p_{08}^*	p_{09}^*
0, 10858	0, 01158	0, 10939	0, 0247	0, 0270	0, 09991	0, 00837	0, 00834	0, 005304

p_{11^*}	p_{12}^*	p_{13}^*	p_{14}^*	p_{15}^*	p_{16}^*	p_{17}^*	p_{18}^*	p_{19}^*
0, 23573	0, 01076	0, 13823	0, 0097	0, 01918	0, 16516	0, 00436	0, 01012	0, 003622

Finally, with the estimates in tables 4.2, 4.3, and 4.5 and with $\varphi^* = (p_{01}^*, \dots, p_{0m}^*, p_{11}^*, \dots, p_{1m}^*)$, I find that

$$(\varphi^* - \varphi^\circ)H(\varphi^\circ)(\varphi^* - \varphi^\circ)' = 233.2177. \tag{4.24}$$

The 0.05 critical value of the χ^2 distribution with 17 degrees of freedom is 27.6. Hence, it is a fact that my Probit maximum-likelihood estimates of α and β and my assumption that u is normally distributed with mean 0 and variance 1 determine a Probit mathematical model of A1–A6 that is not empirically relevant.

It remains to be checked whether I can find a triple $(\alpha^*, \beta_1^*, \beta_2^*)$ in an appropriate 95-percent-confidence region around the maximum-likelihood estimates in table 4.4 that satisfy the conditions in A3 and determine estimates of the MPD that are data admissible. Anne Olaug Stigum conducted an extensive search for such triples in the confidence region determined by the three standard errors in table 4.4. Relevant Excel tables and a brief description of her analysis and results are presented in an appendix to this chapter. Her best result (i.e., minimum χ^2 value), 232.974, indicates that the given confidence region does not contain triples of parameters with the required properties. Hence I feel confident in concluding that the present family of models of A1–A6 is not empirically relevant in the given empirical context.

It is relevant here that Anne Olaug searched the whole confidence region for possible empirically relevant values of α and β. Consequently, in her search the "appropriate" confidence region was taken to equal the standard confidence region.

4.3 A Formalized Qualitative Response Model

In this section I will formulate an axiomatized version of subsection 4.1.1's qualitative response model to be used in an empirical analysis in which it is irrelevant whether the model has an equivalent latent variable model.

In the present case I assume that I have accurate observations of y^* and x^*, throw out the A and G axioms, and reformulate the D axioms so that I can proceed to analyze the data in the upper data universe in figure 4.1. There is no need to add new components to ω_P. Therefore, when I reformulate the D axioms, I can adopt D1–D3 as stated and just give them new names: D*1, D*2, and D*3. I then add the following axiom, which is a simple rewrite of equations 4.1 and 4.2.

D*4
Let $\alpha \in R$, and $\beta \in R^k$, be constants, and suppose that $\alpha \leq 0$ and $\alpha + \beta x > 0$ for some $x \in Q.^9$ Let $G(\cdot):R \to [0, 1]$ be a cumulative probability distribution function that may or may not be symmetric around 0. Then, relative to $P_P(\cdot)$, the probability distribution of the pair (y^*, x^*) (ω_P) satisfies the following conditions: For all $x^* \in Q$,

$$P_P\{y^* = 1 \,|\, x^*\} = G(\alpha + \beta x^*) \tag{4.25}$$

and

$$P_P\{y^* = 0 \,|\, x^*\} = 1 - G(\alpha + \beta x^*). \tag{4.26}$$

In line with the standard formulation of qualitative response models, I refrain from including a fifth axiom that specifies the probability distribution of x^*. The proper analogues of equations 4.11 and 4.12 are, therefore, equations 4.27 and 4.28.

T4.6
Suppose that axioms D*1–D*4 are valid. Then, relative to $P_P(\cdot)$, the probability distribution of the pair $(y^*, x^*)(\omega_P)$ satisfies the following conditions: For all $x \in Q$,

$$P_P\{y^* = 1, x^* = x\} = G(\alpha + \beta x) \cdot P_P\{x^* = x\} \tag{4.27}$$

and

$$P_P\{y^* = 0, x^* = x\} = (1 - G(\alpha + \beta x)) \cdot P_P\{x^* = x\}. \tag{4.28}$$

When $G(\cdot)$ is the probability distribution of u in axioms A3, A4, and A6, the conditions prescribed in equations 4.27 and 4.28 differ from the conditions specified in equations 4.11 and 4.12 to the extent that the P_T distribution of x differs from the P_P distribution of the x^*. There is a second difference that, in the context of this book, is more important. My assumption that there is only one model of the TPD in the upper data universe of figure 4.1 must be taken to mean that there is a true model of the axioms D*1–D*4. Consequently, in the upper data universe the researcher insists that there is a true value of the pair (α, β) and that there is a true value of $G(\cdot)$. In contrast, in the lower data universe in figure 4.1 there are no true values of these variables; they are free to vary within a specified family of models of A1–A6. I explore the effect of these differences on the empirical analysis of A1–A6 and D*1–D*4 below.

4.3.1 The Empirical Relevance of Axioms D*1–D*4

As in subsection 4.2.1, my empirical deliberations center on three fundamental ideas that describe the prescriptions underlying the statistical analysis, delineate the salient characteristics of a data-admissible mathematical model of TPD, and describe what it means for a theory to be empirically relevant. In the present context, the prescriptions that underlie the statistical analysis detail the way I aim to obtain a consistent estimate of the pertinent mathematical model of the TPD. Also, a mathematical model of TPD is data admissible if (1) the estimated mathematical model of TPD satisfies the strictures on which D*1 and the prescriptions that underlie the statistical analysis insist, (2) the values that the given model assigns to the parameters of TPD satisfy the strictures on which the D* axioms insist, and (3) the model lies within a 95-percent-confidence region of the estimated mathematical model of TPD. Finally, the true model of TPD is with 95 percent certainty a data-admissible model of TPD. Consequently, I have no reason to reject the empirical relevance of axioms D*1–D*4. The theoretical model of TPD—described on the right-hand sides of equations 4.27 and 4.28—satisfies two conditions: that the values of the (α, β) pairs in the region satisfy the conditions on which D*4 insists and that there is at least one (α, β) pair in the region that constitutes parameters of a data-admissible mathematical model of the TPD. Thus, D*1–D*4 are empirically relevant in the empirical context that I have created for the upper data universe if and only if a 95% confidence band around an estimate of the theoretical model of TPD has the required two properties.

The Prescriptions That Underlie the Statistical Analysis

Since the probability distribution of the TPD in this case is determined by a finite number of probability assignments, the prescriptions that underlie the statistical analysis can be described as follows: I assume that I have observed the values of the pairs $(y^*, x^*)(1), \ldots, (y^*, x^*)(M)$, that all the observed x*(t) belong to {$v_1, \ldots, v_m$}, and that the P_P probability that x* will assume the observed value of x*(t) is positive for all $t = 1, \ldots, M$. I assume, also, that the sampling scheme was random and, hence, that the random pairs in {(y*(t), x*(t); $t \in M$} are independently and identically distributed, with the same means, variances, and covariance. In P_P measure these are the means, variances, and covariance of the TPD in T4.6. Finally, I let m_{ij} denote the number of observed pairs (y*, x*)(t) with y*(t) = i and x*(t) = v_j, i = 0, 1, and j = 1, \ldots, m, and observe that T4.6 implies that, in terms of the TPD, the probability of the sample observations being what they are is given by a constant multiple of the likelihood function

$$L_{TPD}(p_{01}, \ldots, p_{0m}, p_{11}, \ldots, p_{1m} \mid (y^*, x^*)(1), \ldots, (y^*, x^*)(M))$$
$$= \Pi_{1 \leq j \leq m} \, p_{0j}^{m0j} p_{1j}^{m1j}, \tag{4.29}$$

where $p_{ij} = TPD((y^*, x^*)(t) = (i, v_j))$, i = 0, 1 and j = 1, \ldots, m, and where $m_{ij} \in \{0, \ldots, M\}$, i = 0, 1, j = 1, \ldots, m, and $\Sigma_{1 \leq j \leq m} (m_{0j} + m_{1j}) = M$.

The prescriptions that underlie my statistical analysis direct me to obtain maximum-likelihood estimates of the p_{ij} by maximizing the logarithmic transform of the likelihood function subject to the constraint that $\Sigma_{1 \leq j \leq m} p_{0j} + p_{1j} = 1$. The resulting estimates are uniquely determined and given by the equations

$$p_{ij}^{\circ} = m_{ij}/M, \tag{4.30}$$

where i = 0, 1 and j = 1, \ldots, m.

Since the m_{ij}/M are non-negative, add to 1, and represent a maximum of the log-likelihood function, my estimates of the p_{ij} satisfy D*1 and the prescriptions that underlie my statistical analysis.

The estimates in equation 4.30 are consistent. To wit: The assumption that the sampling scheme was random and T4.6 imply that, with respect to $P_P(\cdot)$ and hence in terms of the TPD distribution of y*(t) and x*(t) (i.e., in P_P measure), for i = 0, 1 and j = 1, \ldots, m,

$$Lim_{M \to \infty} m_{ij}/M = P_P(y^*(t) = i, x^*(t) = j) = TPD(y^* = i, x^* = j) \text{ a.e.} \quad (4.31)$$

A Confidence Region for Data-Admissible Models of the TPD

Next I must describe the region, D, in which the data-admissible mathematical models of TPD must reside. In the present case I identify this region with a 95-percent-confidence region around my maximum-likelihood estimates of the p_{ij} in equation 4.30. Consequently, to delimit D,

I let $\varphi = (p_{01}, \ldots, p_{0m}, p_{11}, \ldots, p_{1m})$ and let φ° be the maximum-likelihood estimates in equation 4.30. Also, I define the function $H(\cdot)$ as the negative of the Hessian of the logarithmic transform of the likelihood function in equation 4.29,

$$H(\varphi) = -(\partial^2 \log L_{\mathrm{TPD}}(\varphi \mid (y^*, x^*)(1), \ldots, (y^*, x^*)(M))/\partial\varphi_i\partial\varphi_j), \qquad (4.32)$$

and observe that in P_P measure $(\varphi - \varphi^\circ)H(\varphi^\circ)(\varphi - \varphi^\circ)'$ is, for large M, approximately χ^2 distributed with $2m - 1$ degrees of freedom. (See chapter 13 of Davidson and MacKinnon 1993.) Hence, I can define D as follows:

$$D = \left\{ \varphi \in R_+{}^{2m} : \sum_{1 \le i \le 2m} \varphi_i = 1 \text{ and } (\varphi - \varphi^\circ)H(\varphi^\circ)(\varphi - \varphi^\circ)' \le \chi^2(2m-1) \right\}, \qquad (4.33)$$

where φ and φ° are as described above, and where, with $2m - 1$ degrees of freedom, 0.95 is the χ^2 measure of the interval $[0, \chi^2(2m - 1)]$.

The Empirical Relevance of D*1–D*4
To determine the empirical relevance of D*1–D*4, I must estimate the theoretical model of the TPD that I described on the right-hand sides of equations 4.27 and 4.28 and delineate a confidence region around the estimate. If the (α, β) pairs in this confidence region heed the restrictions on which D*4 insists, and if one of them constitutes the parameters of a data-admissible mathematical model of the TPD; i.e., if the confidence region has a non-empty intersection with D, I consider the axioms D*1–D*4 empirically relevant. Otherwise I do not.

It is relevant that the TPD has one true model. In this model the limit in equation 4.31 is well defined. So is D.

4.3.2 A Case Study in Which Axioms D*1–D*4 Have Only One Model
Axioms D*1–D*4 have many models. In the present case their undefined terms are m, α, β, $G(\cdot)$, and the parameters of the probability distribution of $x^*(t)$. By fixing the values of these parameters, I obtain a family of models of D*1–D*4 with only one member. The one-member family of mathematical models of D*1–D*4 that I have in mind has the following characteristics: $m = 2$, $\alpha = -1$, $\beta = 2$, $x^* \in \{1/2, 3/2\}$, and $G(x) = 0$ for $x < 0$, $2/3$ for $x \in [0, 2]$, and 1 for $x > 2$. Also, $P_P(x^* = 1/2) = 1/3$ and $P_P(x^* = 3/2) = 2/3$. Finally, $P_P(y^* = 1 \mid x^*) = G(-1 + 2x^*)$ and $P_P(y^* = 0 \mid x^*) = 1 - G(-1 + 2x^*)$. From these relations it follows that the TPD distribu-

tion of y* and x* in equations 4.27 and 4.28 has the following characteristics:

$$P_P(y^* = 1, x^* = 1/2) = G(-1 + 1) \cdot 1/3 = (2/3)(1/3) = 2/9,$$
$$P_P(y^* = 1, x^* = 3/2) = G(-1 + 3) \cdot 2/3 = (2/3)(2/3) = 4/9,$$
(4.34)

$$P_P(y^* = 0, x^* = 1/2) = (1 - G(-1 + 1)) \cdot 1/3 = (1/3)(1/3) = 1/9,$$
$$P_P(y^* = 0, x^* = 3/2) = (1 - G(-1 + 3)) \cdot 2/3 = (1/3)(2/3) = 2/9.$$
(4.35)

Note that the probabilities in these equations differ from the probabilities in equation 4.18 because the $P_P(\cdot)$ distribution of x* differs from the $P_T(\cdot)$ probability distribution of x. Since I do not know the $P_P(\cdot)$ probability distribution of x*, in the empirical analysis I must replace the true $P_P(\cdot)$ probabilities with an estimate of them.

For the purposes of this example, I will face the given one-member family of models of D*1–D*4 with the same data with which I faced the one-member family of models of A1–A6 in subsection 4.2.3. The data consisted of 999 observations of the values of the pair (y*, x*) that I obtained with a random number generator for a multinomial distribution. The four parameters of the given distribution were chosen so that $p_{01/2} = 1/6$, $p_{11/2} = 1/3$, $p_{03/2} = 1/6$, and $p_{13/2} = 1/3$, where the first subscript denotes the value of y* and the second the value of x*. With this sample, I obtained estimates of the TPD probabilities in equations 4.27 and 4.28 by maximizing the logarithmic transform of the analogue of the likelihood function in equation 4.29 subject to the condition, $p_{01} + p_{11} + p_{03} + p_{13} = 1$. The estimates were as follows:

$$p_{01}{}^\circ = 0.175175, \quad p_{11}{}^\circ = 0.323323,$$
$$p_{03}{}^\circ = 0.156156, \quad p_{13}{}^\circ = 0.345345.$$
(4.36)

In this case the $H(\cdot)$ in equation 4.32 becomes the $H(\cdot)$ in subsection 4.2.3, and the confidence region of equation 4.33 becomes the confidence region in equation 4.37:

$$D = \{p \in R_+{}^4: p_{01}+p_{11}+p_{03}+p_{13} = 1, \text{ and } (p - p^\circ)H(p^\circ)(p - p^\circ)' \le 7.81\},$$
(4.37)

where $p^\circ = (0.175175, 0.323323, 0.156156, 0.345345)$ and with three degrees of freedom the χ^2 probability of the interval [0, 7.81] is 0.95.

Now, with the maximum-likelihood estimates of the $P_P(\cdot)$ probabilities of the events, x* = 1/2 and x* = 3/2, equal to 1/2 and 1/2, respectively, the probabilities in equations 4.38 and 4.39 become estimate of $P_P (y^* = 0, x^* = 1/2) = (1 - G(-1 + 1)) \cdot 1/2 = 1/6$,

estimate of $P_P (y^* = 1, x^* = 1/2) = G(-1 + 1) \cdot 1/2 = 1/3$ (4.38)

estimate of $P_P(y^* = 0, x^* = 3/2) = (1 - G(-1 + 3)) \cdot 1/2 = 1/6$,

estimate of $P_P(y^* = 1, x^* = 3/2) = G(-1 + 3) \cdot 1/2 = 1/3$.   (4.39)

With $p^* = (0.166667, 0.333333, 0.166667, 0.333333)$, I find that $(p^* - p^\circ) H(p^\circ)(p^* - p^\circ)' = 1.846593$. Consequently, p^* does belong to D and is, therefore, data admissible. From this it follows that the given one-member family of mathematical models of D*1–D*4 is empirically relevant in the empirical context that my sample of observations determines.

4.3.3 A Case Study with Data from Women's Participation in the US Labor Force

The axioms in the upper data universe of figure 4.1 are observationally equivalent to A1–A6 as stated in section 4.2. when $G(\cdot)$ is replaced by $\Phi(\cdot)$. The corresponding TPD probabilities in equations 4.27 and 4.28 differ from the MPD probabilities in T4.4 only to the extent that the $P_P(\cdot)$ probabilities of x^* differ from the corresponding $P_T(\cdot)$ probabilities of x. However, that is an inessential difference for the empirical analysis of women's participation in the US labor force, since the estimates of the TPD probabilities in equation 4.30 are identical to the estimates of the MPD probabilities in equation 4.14. Thus, it seems that the question of the empirical relevance of D*1–D*4 must be answered in a way that is almost an analogue of the way I answered the question of the empirical relevance of A1–A6. To wit: A second look at equations 4.13–4.16 and 4.29–4.32 reveals that the confidence region, D, in equation 4.17 is identical with the confidence region, D, in equation 4.33, and that equation 4.17 is as much an equation for testing the empirical relevance of D*1–D*4 as it is an equation for testing the empirical relevance of A1–A6. But if that is so, then it must be the case that the maximum-likelihood estimates of the α and β determine an empirically relevant model of A1–A6 if they determine an empirically relevant model of D*1–D*4. However, the converse is not valid. In order that the maximum-likelihood estimates of α and β determine an empirically relevant model of D*1–D*4, it must be the case that all the (α, β) pairs in the standard confidence region around the estimates satisfy the restrictions on which D*4 insists. In the present case they do not. It is easy to demonstrate that there are values of (α, β) in the given confidence region for which no x in the pertinent Q satisfies the inequality $\alpha + \beta x > 0$. Consequently, in the present case I can insist that D*1–D*4 is empirically irrelevant without searching for alternative values of α and β in the way Anne Olaug searched for alternative values of α and β in the lower data universe.[10]

4.4 Empirical Relevance, Misspecification Tests, and Generalizations

In sections 4.2 and 4.3 I developed axioms for data confrontations of qualitative response models, and I presented two case studies: one with generated data and one with data from the US labor force. The purpose of my deliberations was to demonstrate the usefulness of my formal econometrics and to contrast its methods with the methods of present day econometrics. Also, my analysis focused on one aspect of qualitative response models: their empirical relevance.

Note that I tested the empirical relevance of two different families of qualitative-response models. The failure of the Probit family leaves interesting questions unanswered. For example: Do the omitted variables make a difference? Is the cumulative probability distribution that I chose the right one? My explanatory variables consist of age and schooling and the cumulative probability distribution is normal. I could have included variables for marriage, number of children, and location. Also, I could have chosen the Logit or the Weibull distribution as the cumulative probability distribution for equations 4.27 and 4.28. From a formal point of view, these questions and the possible answers to them constitute a search for a different family of models of the A axioms and a different empirical context in which the new family of models of the A axioms might be empirically relevant.

A final remark about generalizations: The examples I gave of univariate qualitative response models were based on several fundamental assumptions concerning the value of k and the ranges of the x and x* in axioms A1 and D1. These examples can be generalized in obvious ways to cases where k is a finite integer greater than 2 and the ranges of the components of x and x* are finite and discrete. Moreover, with some obvious changes, the ideas that I have developed in section 4.2 can be extended to the empirical analysis of multivariate and multinomial qualitative response models as well as to sample selection models. (See Stigum 2003, p. 248.)

Table 4.6
Til R, csv (that is, ingredients in search for empirically relevant Probit parameters).

Id	kombinasjon	Antall	0/1	Grade	Age	v_j	p_j
1	(1;9;60)	790	1	9	60	0.0177628	0.0461383
2	(1;9;45)	491	1	9	45	0.0110399	0.0223496
3	(1;9;30)	354	1	9	30	0.0079595	0.0184598
4	(1;6;60)	461	1	6	60	0.0103654	0.0344014
5	(1;6;45)	236	1	6	45	0.0053064	0.0127263
6	(1;6;30)	163	1	6	30	0.003665	0.0089264
7	(1;12;60)	5870	1	12	60	0.1319843	0.2476223
8	(1;12;45)	7909	1	12	45	0.1778302	0.2650702
9	(1;12;30)	10272	1	12	30	0.2309612	0.3443058
10	(0;9;60)	1262	0	9	60	0.0283755	0.0461383
11	(0;9;45)	503	0	9	45	0.0113097	0.0223496
12	(0;9;30)	467	0	9	30	0.0105003	0.0184598
13	(0;6;60)	1069	0	6	60	0.024036	0.0344014
14	(0;6;45)	330	0	6	45	0.0074199	0.0127263
15	(0;6;30)	234	0	6	30	0.0052614	0.0089264
16	(0;12;60)	5143	0	12	60	0.115638	0.2476223
17	(0;12;45)	3880	0	12	45	0.08724	0.2650702
18	(0;12;30)	5041	0	12	30	0.1133446	0.3443058

4.5 Appendix

This appendix gives details concerning Anne Olaug Stigum's search for empirically relevant Probit parameters in subsection 4.2.1. The table from which she picks data for her computation program is table 4.6, "Til R, csv." Note that the v_j column is different from the v_j in the text. In the text v_j is the value of the jth pair, (x_1, x_2), in Q; e.g., for $j = 5$, $v_5 =$ (60, 9). In the table v_j_k records the maximum-likelihood estimate of the MPD probability of the triple in the first column and the kth row; e.g., for $k = 1$, v_$j_1 = p_{15}°$, and for $k = 10$, v_$j_{10} = p_{05}°$. Also, for $1 \leq k \leq 9$, the kth row in the p_j column, p_j_k = v_j_k + v_$j_{(k+9)}$; e.g., for $k = 1$, p_$j_1 = p_{15}° + p_{05}°$. And, for $10 \leq k \leq 18$, p_j_k = p_$j_{(k-9)}$.

Anne Olaug reads in v_j and p_j and uses my maximum-likelihood estimates of α and β in table 4.4 and my assignment of v_j in table 4.1 to calculate the normal probabilities required in equation 4.23. She designates the normal probabilities prob.k. She then calculates two factors (columns), v1 and v2, that she defines by the equations

$$v1_i = ((prob.k)_i {}^* p\_j_i) - v\_j_i), \quad i = 1, \dots, 18$$

and

$$v2_i = ((antall)_i / v\_j_i * v\_j_i), \quad i = 1, \ldots, 18$$

where antall designates the column headed "antall." Here antall is short for number of observed triples of the kind marked in the various rows in the column "kombinasjon." The eighteen $v2_i$ constitute the diagonal elements in $H(\varphi^\circ)$. The eighteen $v1_i$ constitute the components of $(\varphi^* - \varphi^\circ)$ in equation 4.24. Finally, she computes the product v1*v1*v2; i.e., the sum, $\sum_{1 \leq i \leq 18} v1_i * v1_i * v2_i$, and finds that it equals 233.2177.

Now the search for empirically relevant values of α and β begins. Roughly speaking, Anne Olaug constructs a discrete structure within a cube of volume 4 by 4 by 4. One side pertains to α, another to β_1, and the third to β_2. She divides each side into 40 intervals of length 0.1 and marks their end points as follows, [-2, -1.9, ... , -0.1, 0, 0.1, ... , 1.9, 2]. The discrete structure within the cube comprises all the triples, (i, j, k), there are in ({-2, -1.9, ... , 0.1, 0, 0.1, ... , 1.9, 2}).[3] With each triple in the given structure she computes new values of the estimates of α and β in table 4.4 in accord with the following equations, where (i, j, k) is taken to equal (0.1, -1.3, 1.8):

$$\alpha^* = \alpha^\circ + std_\alpha * 0.1 = -0.623402 + 0.05436 * 0.1 = -0.617966,$$

$$\beta_1^* = \beta_1^\circ + std_{\beta1}^* - 1.3 = -0.0111428 + 0.00049341^* - 1.3 = -0.011784233,$$

$$\beta_2^* = \beta_2^\circ + std_{\beta2} * 1.8 = 0.119870 + 0.003987 * 1.8 = 0.1270466.$$

With the new values of α and β, α^*, β_1^*, and β_2^* she computes a new prob.k and new values of v1, v2, and v1*v1*v2. The latter value for the chosen triple, (0.1, -1.3, 1.8), equals 322.2739. This value is larger than the critical value of the pertinent χ^2 variable. Thus, the search continues.

The smallest value of the product v1*v1*v2 that Anne Olaug obtained as she varied (i, j, k) over the given set of such triples was 232.974.

The computation program used in the calculations is as follows:

```
alpha  <-  -0.623402

alphaSD  <-  0.05436

beta1  <-  -0.0111428

beta2  <-  0.11987

beta1SD  <-  0.00049341
```

```
beta2SD <- 0.003987

n = 18

data = read.table("To R.csv», header = TRUE, sep =
";»)

prob.norm <- function(alpha, beta1, beta2){

temp <- rep(NA, n)

ret <- rep(NA, n)

for(i in 1:n){

    if(data[i, 4] = = 1){

        temp[[i]] <-
alpha+beta1*data[i, 6]+beta2*data[i, 5]

    }

}

for(i in 1:n){

    if(data[i, 4] = = 1){

        ret[[i]] <- pnorm(temp[i], mean = 0, sd = 1)

    } else {

        ret[[i]] <- 1-pnorm(temp[i-9], mean = 0, sd = 1)

    }

}

return(ret)

}

run <- function(alpha, beta1, beta2) {

    prob.k <- prob.norm(alpha, beta1, beta2)

    v1 = prob.k*data[, 8] - data[, 7]

    v2 = data[, 3]/data[, 7]^2

    return(sum(v1^2*v2))
```

```
}

mesh <- seq(-2, 2, 0.1)

alphaV <- alpha+alphaSD*mesh

beta1V <- beta1+beta1SD*mesh

beta2V <- beta2+beta2SD*mesh

answer = array(0, dim = c(length(mesh),
length(mesh), length(mesh)))

for(i in 1:length(alphaV)){

    for(j in 1:length(beta1V)){

        for(k in 1:length(beta2V)){

                        answer[[i, j, k]] <-
run(alphaV[i], beta1V[j], beta2V[k])

        }

    }

}

min(answer)
```

5 A Cross-Section Analysis of an Economic Theory

Consider the theory-data confrontations in chapters 3 and 4. Neither in the description of the data nor in the theoretical deliberations did the sample population of consumers play a significant role. In many econometric studies such a cavalier attitude toward the sample population cannot be justified. A place for the sample population in the pertinent formal theory-data confrontation must be found.

A theory-data confrontation in which the sample population plays a significant role has five components. The first is the theory universe, (Ω_T, Γ_T), without the probability space. The second is the data universe, $(\Omega_P, \Gamma_P, (\Omega_P, \aleph_P, P_P(\cdot)))$. The third is the bridge between the two universes, $(\Omega, \Gamma_{T,P}, (\Omega, \aleph, P(\cdot)))$. The fourth is the sample population, $(S, \psi(\cdot), (S, \aleph_S, Q(\cdot)))$. The fifth is a sampling scheme, ξ. Here Ω_T and Ω_P are subsets of two disjoint vector spaces. Their members are ordinary vectors with real numbers and real-valued functions as components. Also, the sample space, Ω, is a subset of $\Omega_T \times \Omega_P$, and Γ_T, Γ_P, and $\Gamma_{T,P}$ are finite sets of axioms that the vectors in the pertinent vector spaces must satisfy. Moreover, as before, $(\Omega_P, \aleph_P, P_P(\cdot))$ and $(\Omega, \aleph, P(\cdot))$ are probability spaces, but now $\aleph$ is a σ field of subsets of Ω (and not of $\Omega_T \times \Omega_P$) . Finally, $\psi(\cdot): S \rightarrow \Omega$ is a well-defined function, and $(S, \aleph_S, Q(\cdot))$ is a probability space that satisfies the conditions

range$(\psi) \in \aleph$,

$P(\text{range}(\psi)) > 0$,

$\psi^{-1}(B) \in \aleph_S$ for all $B \in \aleph$,

and

$Q(\psi^{-1}(B)) = P(B \cap \text{range}(\psi))/P(\text{range}(\psi))$.

The sampling scheme may be a purely random sampling scheme or a stratified random sampling scheme in accord with whatever typification of S that is stipulated in the axioms of the given formal theory-data confrontation. In a purely random sampling scheme, Q(A) denotes the probability of picking a sample point in A.

In this case, the researcher in charge has control over P($\cdot$) in the sense that he is responsible for the description of P($\cdot$). The researcher is equally responsible for the bridge principles. The MPD is determined by P($\cdot$) and the bridge principles. In chapters 2–4 I referred to MPD as the marginal distribution of the components of ω_P. Here the MPD is the marginal distribution of ω_P in Ω. The following example provides an illustration of what I have in mind.

E5.1
Consider the following analogue of the example in E2.2.6 for a case in which the sample population plays a dominant role. For simplicity I assume that the researcher has only one observation, and that therefore the sample population does not enter explicitly in the axioms.

The Γ_T axioms
$\Omega_T = \{-2, 2\} \times \{-1, 1\}$. Thus
$\omega_T \in \Omega_T$ only if $\omega_T = (x, u)$ for some $x \in \{-2, 2\}$, $u \in \{-1, 1\}$, and $(x,u) \in \{-2, 2\} \times \{-1, 1\}$.

The Γ_P axioms
$\Omega_P = \{-2, -1, 0, 1, 2\}$. Thus $\omega_P \in \Omega_P$ only if $\omega_P = y$ for some $y \in \{-2, -1, 0, 1, 2\}$. Also, $\aleph_P$ is the field of all subsets of Ω_P, and $P_P(y = j) = 1/3$ for $j \in \{-2, -1\}$, and $1/9$ for $j \in \{0, 1, 2\}$. Consequently,

TPD$(y = j) = 1/3$ for $j \in \{-2, -1\}$ and $1/9$ for $j \in \{0, 1, 2\}$.

The Bridge
$\Omega \subset \Omega_T \times \Omega_P$. Also, $((x, u), y) \in \Omega$ if and only if $(x, u) \in \Omega_T$, $y \in \Omega_P$, and $y = x + u$. Hence,

$\Omega = \{((-2, 1), -1), ((2, -1), 1)\}$.

Let $\aleph$ be the field of subsets of Ω, let $P(\cdot):\aleph \to [0, 1]$ be the probability measure on $(\Omega, \aleph)$, and suppose that

$P((x, u) = (-2, 1)$ and $((x, u), y) \in \Omega$ for some $y \in \Omega_P) = 1/4$

and

$P((x, u) = (2, -1)$ and $((x, u), y) \in \Omega$ for some $y \in \Omega_P) = 3/4$.

Then

$MPD(y = j) = P(y = j$ and $((x, u), j) \in \Omega$ for some $(x, u) \in \Omega_T)$

$$= 1/4 \text{ for } j = -1, 3/4 \text{ for } j = 1, \text{ and } 0 \text{ for } j = -2, 0, 2.$$

In the very simple example above, there is an important thing to notice: I specify the marginal distribution of the theoretical variables in Ω, and I derive the marginal distribution of the data variable. That is a characteristic that is common to all the theory-data confrontations I consider in which the sample population plays an important role. In spirit it is also analogous to the way I derive the MPD from the RPD and the bridge principles in the examples in section 2.2, as well as in the theory-data confrontations that I discuss in chapters 3 and 4.

In this chapter I will develop a cross-section analysis of Friedman's Permanent Income Hypothesis in which the sample population plays an essential role. My intent is to test the empirical relevance of Friedman's theory in the 1963 US population of consumers. At the end, I will contrast my test with a test of the empirical relevance of Friedman's theory that an econometrician working in the spirit of Frisch 1934 and Haavelmo 1944 might have carried out with the same data. My test occurs in the lower data universe of an appropriate analogue of figure 2.1, whereas Frisch and Haavelmo's test happens in the upper data universe.

The two empirical analyses are especially interesting when one compares them with the corresponding analyses in section 3.3. A small change in the axioms of section 3.3 has a dramatic effect on the analysis in this chapter. In section 3.3 the salient parameters, α and β, were not identifiable, and it was not possible to formulate a meaningful alternative hypothesis to Friedman's null hypothesis that $\alpha = 0$. In this chapter, with a minor change in the axioms of section 3.3, I manage to subject Friedman's hypothesis to a stringent statistical test.

5.1 Friedman's Permanent Income Hypothesis[1]

In this section, the theory I put in the theory box in figure 1.2 is the theory of consumer choice under certainty. The theory concerns the undefined terms *commodity bundle*, *price*, *consumer*, and *consumption bundle* and is derived from the following five axioms.

H1

A commodity bundle is a vector $x \in R_+^n$.

H2

A price is a vector $p \in R_{++}^n$.

H3

A consumer is a pair, $(V(\cdot), A)$, where $A \in R_+$ and $V(\cdot): R_+^n \to R_+$.

H4

A consumption bundle is a vector $c \in R_+^n$ that, for some pair $(p, A) \in R_{++}^n \times R_+$, satisfies two conditions: $pc \leq A$ and, for all $x \in R_+^n$ such that $px \leq A$, $V(x) \leq V(c)$.

H5

$V(\cdot)$ is continuous, strictly increasing, and strictly quasi-concave and has differentiable level sets in $(R_+^n - R_{++}^n) - \{0\}$.

The preceding axioms are variants of the axioms of consumer choice under certainty that one encounters in most intermediate textbooks on economic theory. The axioms have many models. In this chapter I shall question the empirical relevance of a subfamily of models that constitutes Friedman's Permanent Income Hypothesis. For the test I will use data collected by researchers at the Federal Reserve Board in Washington (Projector and Weiss 1966; Projector 1968). The data pertain to economic choices made by US consumers during 1962 and 1963. For each consumer in the sample, the data provide information on 1962 end-of-year net worth, on 1963 disposable income, on the change in net worth during 1963, and on the age of the head of the household in 1962.

To describe the family of models of H1–H5 that constitutes Friedman's Permanent Income Hypothesis, I begin by naming the components of x and p:

$x = (C_0, \ldots, C_{n-1})$,

$p = (1, [1/(1 + r)], \ldots, [1/(1 + r)]^{n-1})$ for some $r \in R_{++}$.

Here r and C_i, respectively, denote the rate of interest and the number of units of account that the consumer spends on consumer goods in period i, where $i = 0, \ldots, n - 1$. Next I interpret A so that

$A = A_{-1} + \Sigma_{0 \leq i \leq n-1}[1/(1 + r)]^i y_i$,

where A_{-1} and y_i are, respectively, the consumer's net worth at the beginning of period 0 and his income from physical work in period i, where $i = 0, \ldots, n - 1$. Finally, I insist that the utility function, in addition to H5, satisfies the following condition.

H6
$V(\cdot)$ is homothetic.

The homotheticity of the utility function plays an important role in Friedman's theory. From this property it follows that, for each pair $(V(\cdot), f(\cdot))$ of a utility function $V(\cdot)$ and a demand function $f(\cdot)$, there exists a function $g(\cdot)$: $R_{++}{}^n \to R_+{}^n$ such that, for all $(p, A) \in R_{++}{}^n \times R_{+}$, $f(p, A) = g(p)A$. Thus, if we let

$$C(r) = g_1(1, [1/(1 + r)], \ldots, [1/(1 + r)]^{n-1}), \quad r \in R_{++}$$

and write $C = C(r)A$, $r \in R_{++}$, then C represents the consumer's optimal outlays on consumer goods in period 0 when the interest rate is r.

The function $C(\cdot)(\cdot)$: $R_+{}^2 \to R_+$ which ought to be called the consumption function of the consumer, is not called that in Friedman's theory, because it is a function of the wrong variables. To derive the consumer's consumption function, Friedman observes that the designation of current receipts as "income" in statistical studies is an expedient enforced by the limitation of the data. On a theoretical level, income is generally defined as the amount a consumer unit could consume (or believes it could) while maintaining its wealth (Friedman 1957, p. 10). Consequently, the consumer's true first-period income should be defined not as y_0 but as

$$y_p = [r/(1 + r)]A.$$

Friedman called such income *permanent income* and used it to define his consumption function as

$$C = k(r)y_p, \quad (r, y_p) \in R_{++} \times R_+,$$

where

$$k(r) = [(1 + r)/r]C(r), \quad r > 0.$$

In a given period, a consumer's measured income is ordinarily taken to equal his salary plus any rent, interest, and/or dividends the consumer earns. Friedman called the difference between measured and permanent income *transitory income*. Thus, if y denotes measured income and y_t is transitory income,

$$y = y_p + y_t.$$

Friedman also hypothesized that a consumer's expenditures on goods and services, c, can be decomposed into a permanent component c_p and a transitory component c_t, so that

$$c = c_p + c_t.$$

The permanent component was, supposedly, the variable with which the theory of consumer choice was concerned. Hence, Friedman insisted that $c_p = k(r)y_p$, where $r > 0$ and $y_p \geq 0$.[2]

5.2 A Formal Theory-Data Confrontation of Friedman's Permanent Income Hypothesis

I begin with the universes and the bridge. I then describe characteristics of the MPD and the sampling scheme.

5.2.1 The Two Universes and the Bridge
In the confrontation of Friedman's theory with data, the theory universe is a pair, (Ω_T, Γ_T), where Ω_T is a subset of a vector space and Γ_T is a finite set of axioms that the vectors in Ω_T must satisfy. One of the members of Γ_T describes the conceptual framework of the theory. Specifically:

APIH1
$\Omega_T \subset R_{++}^4 \times R^3 \times \{15, 16, \dots, 100\}$. Thus, $\omega_T \in \Omega_T$ only if $\omega_T = (r, y_p, y_t, c_p, c_t, A, \alpha, u)$ for some $(r, y_p, c_p, A) \in R_{++}^4$, $(y_t, c_t, u) \in R^3$, $\alpha \in \{15, 16, \dots, 100\}$, and $((r, y_p, c_p, A), (y_t, c_t, u), \alpha) \in R_{++}^4 \times R^3 \times \{15, 16, \dots, 100\}$.

All other members of Γ_T describe the law-like properties of the components of ω_T.

APIH2
For all $\omega_T \in \Omega_T$, $y_p = [r/(1 + r)]A$.

APIH3
Let $\Omega_T(a) = \{\omega_T \in \Omega_T: \alpha = a\}$, with $a \in \{15, 16, \dots, 100\}$. There exists a function, $k(\cdot): R_{++} \times \{15, 16, \dots, 100\} \to R_{++}$ such that for all $\omega_T \in \Omega_T(\alpha)$, $c_p = k(r, \alpha)y_p$.

APIH4

Let h(·) be defined by

$$h(\alpha) = \begin{bmatrix} 25 & \text{if } \alpha < 35 \\ 5(i+6)+5 & \text{if } (i+6)5 \leq \alpha < (i+8)5, \ i = 1, 3, 5 \\ 70 & \text{if } 65 \leq \alpha. \end{bmatrix}$$

Then, for all $\alpha \in \{15, 16, \ldots, 100\}$,

$$k[r, h(\alpha)] = k(r, \alpha), \ r > 0.$$

In the intended interpretation of these axioms, the meaning of r, y_p, y_t, c_p, c_t, and A accords with the meaning I gave to these variables in my description of Friedman's theory. Thus, the relation $y_p = [r/(1 + r)]A$ is a definition of y_p that is not at stake in the test I have in mind for the Permanent Income Hypothesis. Moreover, α is the age of the consumer and h(·) is used to partition the consumers into five age groups within which the consumption function does not vary over individuals. Finally, u is an error term. In reading the axioms, note that y_t, c_t, and u, do not appear in APIH2–APIH4. They enter the theory-data confrontation in the bridge principles.

The data universe for the present empirical analysis is a triple, $\{\Omega_P, \Gamma_P, (\Omega_P, \pounds_P, P_P(\cdot))\}$, where Ω_P is a subset of a vector space, Γ_P is a finite set of axioms that the vectors in Ω_P must satisfy, $\pounds_P$ is a σ field of subsets of Ω_P, and $P_P(\cdot):\pounds_P \rightarrow [0, 1]$ is a probability measure . One of the axioms in Γ_P describes conceptual properties of the data-generating process.

DPIH1

$\Omega_P \subset \{15, \ldots, 100\} \times R_+^2 \times R$. Thus,

$\omega_P \in \Omega_P$ only if $\omega_P = (e_2, y_3, c_3, w_2)$ for some $e_2 \in \{15, \ldots, 100\}$, $(y_3, c_3) \in R_+^2$, $w_2 \in R$, and $(e_2, (y_3, c_3), w_2) \in \{15, \ldots, 100\} \times R_+^2 \times R$.

In the intended interpretation of the foregoing axiom, e_2 and y_3 are the consumer's age in 1962 and disposable income in 1963, w_2 is his net worth at the end of 1962, and c_3 is the difference between his 1963 disposable income and the change in his net worth during 1963.

The remaining axiom in Γ_P describes law-like properties of the components of ω_P that are characteristics of the TPD—that is, of the true probability distribution of the components of ω_P. I do not have a firm idea about the TPD for the present case. Therefore, I would like to make my description of the TPD as general as possible. I think that the axiom I have chosen is an axiom that most econometricians will accept.

DPIH2

Let $G = \{25, 40, 50, 60, 70\}$, and let $\Omega_P(g) = \{\omega_P \in \Omega_P: h(e_2) = g\}$, $g \in G$. Then $\Omega_P(g) \in \pounds_P$ and $P_P(\Omega_P(g)) > 0$, $g \in G$. Also, relative to $P_P(\cdot \mid \Omega_P(g))$, the components of (y_3, c_3, w_2) have finite means, variances, and fourth-order moments; the means of y_3 and c_3 are positive; and the variances and covariances of y_3, c_3, and w_2 are positive, $g \in G$.

The bridge is a triple, $(\Omega, \Gamma_{T,P}, (\Omega, \pounds, P(\cdot)))$, where $\Omega \subset \Omega_T \times \Omega_P$, and $\Gamma_{T,P}$ is a finite set of axioms that the vectors in Ω must satisfy. Also, $\pounds$ is a σ field of subsets of Ω, and $P(\cdot): \pounds \to [0, 1]$ is a probability measure. Three of the members of $\Gamma_{T,P}$ describe how the components of ω_T are related to the components of ω_P.

GPIH1

For all $\omega \in \Omega$, $\alpha = e_2$. Also, there exists a function $q(\cdot): \{25, 40, \ldots, 70\} \to R$ such that, for all $\omega \in \Omega$, $w_2 = q[h(\alpha)] + A + u$.

GPIH2

For all $\omega \in \Omega$, $c_3 = c_p + c_t$ and $y_3 = y_p + y_t$.

GPIH3

Let $\Omega(g) = \{\omega \in \Omega: h(\alpha) = g\}$, $g \in G$. There exists a positive constant r_g such that for all $\omega \in \Omega(g)$, $r = r_g$, and $[(1 + r_g)/r_g] = b_3$, where b_3 is a parameter of the joint distribution of c_3, y_3, w_2, and y_p that I specify later in T5.1(ii).

Here GPIH1 claims that I have accurate observations of the age of the consumer, and that the value of his net worth at the end of 1962 is related in an interesting way to the A and u components of ω_T. The way w_2 is related to A and u is of no consequence for Friedman's hypothesis. However, as will be seen, it establishes an interesting possibility of using w_2 as an instrumental variable in a factor-analytic test of the Permanent Income Hypothesis. In doing so, it also illustrates how "outside" information can be introduced and used in the testing of a theory. GPIH2 formulates relations among c_3, c_p, c_t, y_3, y_p, and y_t that accord with the ideas that Friedman expounded in his 1957 treatise. Finally, GPIH3 claims that r is a constant r_g whose value is related to the value of a statistical parameter that is specified later in T5.1(ii). In that way r_g becomes an important element in the search for a family of data universes in which a meaningful test of the empirical relevance of the Permanent Income Hypothesis can be constructed.

The next three axioms of $\Gamma_{T,P}$ concern the properties of $P(\cdot)$. As in the case of $P_P(\cdot)$, I formulate axioms for $P(\cdot)$ that most econometricians will deem reasonable.

GPIH4
For all $g \in G$, $P(\Omega(g)) > 0$. Also for all $g \in G$, relative to $P(\cdot \mid \Omega(g))$, the variances of y_p, y_t, c_p, and c_t are positive and finite, and the covariances of the pairs (y_t, y_p), (c_p, c_t), (c_t, y_t), and (c_p, y_t) are 0.

GPIH5
Relative to $P(\cdot \mid \Omega(g))$, the variance of u is positive and finite, and the covariances of the pairs (u, A), (u, y_t), (u, c_p), and (u, c_t) are 0, $g \in G$.

GPIH6
Relative to $P(\cdot \mid \Omega(g))$, the means of y_t, c_t, and u are 0, the means of y_p, c_p, and $(q[g] + A)$ are positive, and the fourth-order moments of y_p, y_t, c_p, c_t, and u_t are finite, $g \in G$.

Except for the references to u and A, these axioms express ideas on which Friedman insisted in his treatise. Specifically, GPIH2, GPIH4, and the assertion concerning the means of y_t and c_t in GPIH6 formalize Friedman's assumptions 3.3 and 3.4 (1957, pp. 26 and 30) for the present axiom system.[3] Here it is important to observe that neither GPIH2 and GPIH4 nor GPIH6 heed the restrictions on which APIH3 and APIH4 insist. Also, in GPIH6 I have added a fourth-order moment condition on the probability distribution of y_p, y_t, c_p, c_t, and u_t, the validity of which I take for granted.

5.2.2 The MPD
For each $g \in G$, the axioms of $P(\cdot \mid \Omega(g))$ and the axioms APIH1, APIH2, DPIH1, and GPIH1–GPIH3 induce a probability distribution of ω_P that I denote by MPD and read as the marginal probability distribution of the components of ω_P. The MPD may be very different from the TPD. Here is an example that illustrates how different the two probability distributions may be.

E5.1

Consider the following description of Ω_T, Ω_P, Ω, $P_P(\cdot)$, and $P(\cdot)$: First, Ω_T = {0, 1, 2, 3} × {−1, 1}. Thus $\omega_T \in \Omega_T$ if and only if $\omega_T = (x, u)$ for some $x \in$ {0, 1, 2, 3}, $u \in$ {−1, 1}, and $(x,u) \subset$ {0, 1, 2, 3} × {−1, 1} . Next, $\Omega_P =$ {−2, −1, 0, 1, 2, 3, 4}. Thus $\omega_P \in \Omega_P$ if and only if $\omega_P = y$ for some $y \in$ {−2, −1, 0, 1, 2, 3, 4}. Also, $P_P(y = j) = 1/7$, j = −2, −1, ... , 3, 4. Finally, $(\omega_T, \omega_P) \in \Omega$ if and only if $\omega_T \subset \Omega_T$, $\omega_P \in \Omega_P$, and y = x + u. Also, with respect to $P(\cdot)$, x and u are distributed independently with P(x = j) = 1/4 for j $\in$ {0, 1, 2, 3} and P(u = j) = 1/4 for j = 1 and 3/4 for j = −1. Then P((x, u, y) = (i, j, k)) = 1/16 if (i, j, k) = (0, 1, 1), (1, 1, 2) (2, 1, 3), (3, 1, 4); and 3/16 if (i, j, k) = (0, −1, −1), (1, −1, 0), (2, −1, 1) and (3, −1, 2). Hence TPD(y = j) = 1/7 for j = −2, −1, 0, 1, 2, 3, 4, while

$$MPD(y = j) = \Sigma_{\{(x, u):(x, u) \in \Omega T \text{ and } (x, u, j) \in \Omega\}}P((x, u, j))$$

$$= P(y = j) = 0 \text{ for } j = −2; 3/16$$

for j = −1, 0; 1/4 for j = 1, 2; and 1/16 for j = 3, 4.

The axioms of $P(\cdot)$ together with DPIH1 and GPIH1–GPIH3 imply that the mean and covariance structure of MPD has interesting characteristics. First the obvious: For all g $\in$ G, in the MPD the fourth-order moments of c_3, y_3, and w_2 are finite and their variances are positive and finite. Also, the means of c_3, y_3, and w_2 are positive. Finally, the covariances of the pairs (c_3, y_3), (c_3, w_2), and (y_3, w_2) are finite.

To obtain more information about the mean and covariance structure of MPD, I need an auxiliary theorem, T5.1, that exhibits the relation between the means and variances of the components of (c_3, y_3, w_2) and the components of (y_P, c_P).

T5.1

Suppose that APIH1, APIH2, DPIH1, and GPIH1–GPIH6 are valid. Also, for each g $\in$ G, let $E\{\cdot \mid g\}$ and $\sigma^2(\cdot \mid g)$, respectively, denote the expectation and variance of $(\cdot)$ with respect to $P(\cdot \mid \Omega(g))$. Then

(i) $E\{c_3 \mid g\} = E\{c_p \mid g\}$ and $E\{y_3 \mid g\} = E\{y_p \mid g\}$. Also, $\sigma^2(c_3 \mid g)$ $= \sigma^2(c_p \mid g) + \sigma^2(c_t \mid g)$ and $\sigma^2(y_3 \mid g) = \sigma^2(y_p \mid g) + \sigma^2(y_t \mid g)$

and

(ii) there exist pairs of constants (a_i, b_i), i = 1, 2, 3, and a triple of random variables, ξ_1, ξ_2, and ξ_3, that have mean 0 and finite variance, are orthogonal to y_p, and satisfy the equations $c_3 = a_1 + b_1 y_p + \xi_1$, $y_3 = a_2 + b_2 y_p + \xi_2$, $w_2 = a_3 + b_3 y_p + \xi_3$, with $a_2 = 0$, $b_2 = 1$, $\xi_2 = y_t$, $E\{\xi_1\xi_2 \mid g\} = E\{\xi_2\xi_3 \mid g\} = E\{\xi_3\xi_1 \mid g\} = 0$, and $\xi_3 = u$.

Simple algebra, the relation, $y_p = [r/(1 + r)]A$, GPIH1–GPIH6, and an appeal to a standard theorem in mathematical statistics suffice to establish the theorem, so there is no need to give a detailed proof here. I consider that the most interesting aspect of the theorem is the role r_g plays in T5.1(ii). The relation $b_3 = [(1 + r_g)/r_g]$ that I postulated in the bridge principles, relates a constant in the theory universe to a statistical parameter whose value can be estimated with observations of variables in the data universe. I use this bridge principle to establish the relations, $E\{\xi_3\xi_1 \mid g\} = 0$, and $\xi_3 = u$ in T4.1(ii). As a consequence, it becomes an essential element in my description of the family of models of the data universe within which I am to try the empirical relevance of the Permanent Income Hypothesis.

With T5.1 in hand, I can give a complete characterization of MPD's mean and covariance structure in T5.2. In reading the theorem it is worth noting that its validity depends on the validity of APIH1, APIH2, the axioms of $P(\cdot)$, and GPIH1–GPIH3. I derived the conditions of T5.2 without making use of APIH3 and APIH4.

T5.2
Let $a = (a_1, a_2, a_3)'$, $b = (b_1, b_2, b_3)'$, and $\xi = (\xi_1, \xi_2, \xi_3)'$ be as in T5.1. Let $x = (c_3, y_3, w_2)'$, $M_x^g = E\{xx' \mid g\}$, $\Sigma^g = E\{(x - E\{x \mid g\})(x' - E\{x' \mid g\}) \mid g\}$, and $\Psi^g = E\{\xi\xi' \mid g\}$. Finally, recall that a, b, and ξ vary with g, and suppose that APIH1, APIH2, DPIH1, and GPIH1–GPIH6 are valid. Then, for each $g \in G$,

(i) $a = (a_1, 0, a_3)'$, $b = (b_1, 1, b_3)'$, and Ψ^g is diagonal,
(ii) $E\{x \mid g\} = a + bE\{y_p \mid g\}$,
(iii) $M_x^g = aa' + (ba' + ab')E\{y_p \mid g\} + bb'E\{y_p^2 \mid g\} + \Psi^g$,
(iv) $\Sigma^g = bb' \sigma^2(y_p \mid g) + \Psi^g$.

In my test of the empirical relevance of Friedman's theory I make use of the mean and covariance structure of the MPD together with the assumption that the MPD distribution of c_3, y_3, and w_2 has finite fourth-order moments. The MPD may have many other characteristics, but they are of no relevance in the present deliberations.

5.2.3 An Adequate Sampling Scheme

To complete the present formal data confrontation of the Permanent Income Hypothesis, I must add axioms that characterize the Federal Reserve Board (FRB) sampling scheme.

SPIH1

Let ϑ_i be one of the numbers, $3,000, $5,000, $7,500, $10,000, $15,000, $25,000, $50,000, and $100,000, with $\vartheta_1 < \vartheta_2 < \ldots < \vartheta_8$. Let I_i be defined by the following equations:

$I_1 = \{(\omega_T, \omega_P) \in \Omega : y_3 < \vartheta_1\}$,

$I_i = \{(\omega_T, \omega_P) \in \Omega : \vartheta_{i-1} \leq y_3 < \vartheta_i\}, \quad i = 2, \ldots , 8$

$I_9 = \{(\omega_T, \omega_P) \in \Omega, y_3 \geq \vartheta_8\}$.

Then $I_i \in £$, and $P(I_i) > 0$, $i = 1, \ldots , 9$. Also, $P(I_i \cap \Omega(g)) > 0$ for all $(i, g) \in \{1, \ldots , 9\} \times G$.

SPIH2

There are observations of N consumers with n_i observations from I_i, $i = 1, \ldots , 9$. The probability distribution of the sample is given, in short-hand (!), by $\prod_{1 \leq i \leq 9}[P(\cdot \mid I_i)]^{n_i}$, where $P(\cdot \mid I_i)$ denotes the conditional probability measure on Ω given I_i.

SPIH1 and SPIH2 describe characteristics of the FRB sampling scheme on which my test of Friedman's hypothesis is based. The researchers at the FRB intended the n_i, $i = 1, \ldots , 9$, in SPIH2 to equal 400. Instead they obtained sample sizes ranging from 385 for $i = 3$ to 453 for $i = 5$. I ignore this feature of the actual sampling scheme and assume that the FRB scheme was part of a larger one in which for all $g = 25, 40, \ldots , 70$, and $i = 1, \ldots , 9$, axiom SPIH3 holds.

SPIH3

As the number N of observations tends to ∞, for $i = 1, \ldots , 9$, and $g \in G$,

$\lim_{n \to \infty} n(I_i \cap \Omega(g))/n = P[I_i \mid \Omega(g)]$.

Here n and $n(I_i \cap \Omega(g))$ are, respectively, the number of individuals in age group g and the number who belong to both age group g and income group i. The assumption ensures that the standard estimates of the means, variances, and covariances of MPD are consistent. When estimates of these moments satisfy the strictures on which T5.2 insists, SPIH3 also ensures that my estimates of the T5.2 parameters of a data-admissible MPD are consistent.

If SPIH1 and SPIH2 provide an adequate description of the FRB sampling scheme, SPIH3 ensures that the parameter estimates in my empirical analysis of PIH have adequate asymptotic properties. The adequacy of SPIH1 and SPIH2 is not obvious. I have formulated SPIH1 in terms of the 1963 incomes of the sample consumers. The FRB researchers stratified their sample according to the 1960 incomes of their sample consumers. Moreover, SPIH2 describes characteristics of a stratified random sampling scheme. The FRB researchers sampled their population without replacement. As long as my data satisfy the two axioms as stated, the noted inaccuracies make no difference as far as the data admissibility of my estimates is concerned. My data satisfy SPIH1 and the first of the two strictures of SPIH2 by construction. Further, in the intended interpretation of the axioms, my data satisfy the second stricture of SPIH2 to any degree of approximation. In the interpretation of the axioms that I intend, S is a population of actual and hypothetical consumers in 1962 United States. The actual consumers are those on whom I have data and the other US consumers alive in 1962. The hypothetical consumers are the consumers that the actual consumers could have been if the conditions under which they lived had been different. But if that is so, the number of members of S is so large that the FRB sampling scheme can be likened to a stratified random sampling scheme in accord with SPIH2.

5.3 The Empirical Analysis

My empirical deliberations center on three fundamental ideas that describe the prescriptions underlying the statistical analysis, delineate the salient characteristics of a data-admissible mathematical model of MPD, and describe what it means for a theory to be empirically relevant. In the present context, *the prescriptions that underlie the statistical analysis* detail the way I am to obtain a consistent estimate of a mathematical model of the MPD. Also, a mathematical model of MPD is data admissible if (1) the estimated mathematical model of MPD satisfies the strictures on which DPIH1 and the prescriptions that underlie the statistical analysis insist, (2) the values that the given model assigns to the parameters of MPD satisfy the strictures on which APIH1, APIH2,

DPIH1, and GPIH1–GPIH6 insist, and (3) the model parameters lie within Wald's 95-percent-confidence limits of the parameters of the estimated model of MPD.[6] A family of mathematical models of the axioms, APIH1–APIH4, is *empirically relevant* if and only if there is at least one member of the family that—together with a model of DPIH1 and GPIH1–GPIH6—determines a data-admissible mathematical model of the MPD.

5.3.1 The Prescriptions That Underlie the Statistical Analysis[4]

In the intended interpretation of the axioms APIH1, APIH2, DPIH1, and GPIH1–GPIH6 with a data-admissible MPD, the mean and covariance structure of the MDP, as described in T5.1 and T5.2, is the mean and covariance structure of a restricted factor-analysis model. (See Lawley and Maxwell 1971, pp. 86–104.) The structure of this model is identified exactly, and the values of its parameters can be estimated with standard factor-analytic methods. (See B. Stigum 1990, pp. 689–690.) I used Joereskog and Soerbom's (1978) LISEREL program to estimate the pertinent parameters. Table 5.1 presents a record of some of the results that concern c_3 and y_3. The standard errors in the table are bootstrap estimates that Petter Laake generated for me. The χ^2, μ_c, and μ_y columns, respectively, show the estimated values of the χ^2 variable in LISEREL's factor-analysis program and the sample means of c_3 and y_3 in the same program. Mathematical details concerning Laake's bootstrap estimates and the asymptotic distribution of the LISEREL parameter estimates in tables 5.1 and 5.2 can be found on pages 689–691 and 709–719 of B. Stigum 1990.[5]

5.3.2 Interesting Properties of the Estimates

In a model of APIH1, APIH2, DPIH1, and GPIH1–GPIH6 with a data-admissible model of MPD, the LISEREL estimates of the parameters that concern the distribution of w_2 carry interesting information. For example, from the estimate of b_3 and the equation

$$[(1 + r_g)/r_g] = b_3$$

I obtain an estimate of r_g for all age groups. These estimates of r_g can be interpreted so as to record the mean rate of time preference of the various age groups.

Similarly, from the equations

$$q(g) = a_3$$

Table 5.1
Factor-analytic (FA) estimates with bootstrap standard errors.

Age group	b_1	$\sigma_{yp}^2 10^{-8}$	$\sigma_{yt}^2 10^{-8}$	a_1	$10^{-4}\mu_c$	$10^{-4}\mu_y$	χ^2	d.fr.
< 35	1.6994 (0.568)	0.0955 (0.046)	0.0782 (0.044)	−5402 (260)	0.5547	0.6443	0	362
35–44	7.1114 (4.286)	0.4640 (0.242)	1.2566 (0.452)	−69091 (4070)	1.3735	1.1647	8.4069	408
45–54	2.0647 (1.066)	2.2128 (1.598)	1.8128 (0.457)	−14046 (1800)	1.6443	1.4767	0	426
55–64	1.8760 (0.835)	3.1757 (1.573)	2.5346 (1.364)	−14307 (1890)	1.7867	1.7150	0	403
≥ 65	1.4664 (0.282)	5.5672 (1.408)	0.4727 (0.402)	−4883 (1950)	1.6412	1.4523	0	31
All	2.1221 (0.505)	2.0616 (0.498)	1.5526 (0.354)	−13464 (800)	1.4098	1.2988	0	1912

Table 5.2
The rate of time preference and the human/non-human wealth ratio.

Age group	$10^{-4}\mu_w$	$10^{-4}a_3$	b_3	r_g	$E(A - w_2\,|\,g)/E(w_2\,|\,g)$	d.fr.
< 35	0.8970 (0.2264)	−7.0076 (0.7738)	12.2689 (0.7738)	0.0887	7.8126	362
35–44	10.7684 (4.4029)	−81.4855 (6.4702)	79.2077 (6.4702)	0.0128	7.5671	408
45–54	13.9745 (2.2643)	−34.4984 (1.9000)	32.8252 (1.9000)	0.0314	2.4687	426
55–64	32.3511 (6.9248)	−94.3699 (4.8157)	73.8885 (4.8157)	0.0137	2.9171	403
≥ 65	31.3004 (4.263)	−22.7029 (2.3107)	37.1841 (2.3107)	0.0276	0.7253	313
All	17.5240 (1.8635)	−52.4838 (1.8162)	53.9038 (1.8162)	0.0189	2.9950	1912

and

$$E(w_2 \mid \Omega(g)) = q(g) + [(1 + r_g)/r_g)E(y_p \mid \Omega(g)) = q(g) + E(A \mid \Omega(g))$$

I find that, for all age groups,

$$- a_3/E(w_2 \mid \Omega(g)) = E(A - w_2 \mid \Omega(g))/E(w_2 \mid \Omega(g))$$

$$= E(\text{human wealth} \mid \Omega(g))/E(\text{non-human wealth} \mid \Omega(g)).$$

I obtain an estimate of the right-hand side of the last equation by substituting the sample mean of w_2, μ_w, for $E(w_2 \mid \Omega(g))$ in the respective age groups. This estimate and factor-analytic estimates of some of the other parameters in the distribution of w_2 are shown in table 5.2. There the numbers in parentheses are LISEREL (not bootstrap) estimates of the standard errors of the respective parameter estimates.

Table 5.2 presents estimates of r_g, $q(g)$, and $q(g)/E(w_2 \mid \Omega(g))$ for various age groups in the US population. It is interesting to search for patterns in the observed values of r_g and $q(g)/E(w_2 \mid \Omega(g))$. The latter ought to decrease with age, and it does. As to the former, one may take low (high) values of r_g to indicate that the consumer places a high premium on current (future) consumption. If this is correct, r_g ought to decrease up to a point where the consumer's income stops rising and where the demands of family living level out; it should increase thereafter. This pattern occurs in table 5.2.

5.3.3 A Confidence Region for Data-Admissible Models of the MPD

In reading my explication of a data-admissible MPD and an empirically relevant theory, note that a data-admissible MPD is only required to satisfy the strictures on which APIH1 and APIH2 insist, while an empirically relevant model of the theory must satisfy the strictures on which APIH1–APIH4 insist. This difference allows me to carry out the test of Friedman's theory in two stages. In the first stage I delineate a set of data-admissible MPDs whose parameters lie within a 95-percent-confidence region around the estimated parameters of the MPD, and I show that the set is not empty. In the second stage I try to determine whether there is a member of this set that satisfies the strictures on which APIH3 and APIH4 insist. If such a member exists, Friedman's theory passes the test. Otherwise it does not.

With T5.2 in hand, I can describe the required confidence region of models of the MPD—one for each age group—with which I try the empirical relevance of the permanent Income Hypothesis. Let MPD_g be a factor-analytic estimate of the MPD for the gth age group. Let MPD_g^* be my factor-analytic estimate of the MPD for the gth age group, and denote the corresponding estimates of the parameters in T5.2 by a_{gf}, b_{gf}, M_{gf}, Σ_{gf}, σ_{gf}, Ψ_{gf}, and μ_{gf}, where σ_{gf} and Ψ_{gf} are, respectively, estimates of $\sigma^2(y_p \mid g)$ and Ψ^g, and μ_{gf} denotes the sample mean of x in age group g. Finally, let $MPD_g \in PH$ mean that MPD_g is a data-admissible model of MPD that is determined by a model of APIH1, APIH2, DPIH1, and GPIH1–GPIH6 for the gth age group. The sought-for confidence region of MPDs can then be defined as follows: $R^{PIH}(g) = \{MPD_g: MPD_g \in PH,$ and its values of the components of $(a_g, b_g, M_g, \Sigma_g, \sigma_g, \Psi_g, \mu_g)$ differ from the corresponding values of $(a_{gf}, b_{gf}, M_g, \Sigma_g, \sigma_{gf}, \Psi_{gf}, \mu_{gf})$ by less than two standard deviations}.[6]

My explication of the meaning of a data-admissible MPD does not require that $MPD_g^* \in R^{PIH}(g)$ for any of the g's in G. However, it is the case that for all but one g, $MPD_g^* \in R^{PIH}(g)$, To show why, I use tables 5.1–5.2 to demonstrate that $MPD_g^* \in PH$ for all but one of the g's in G. The means μ_c and μ_y in table 5.1 and μ_w in table 5.2 are finite and positive. Similarly, judging from the factor-analytic estimates of the parameters in T5.2 that are shown in tables 5.1 and 5.2, one sees that the variances of c_3, y_3, and w_2 are finite and positive. Finally, according to T5.1 I may insist that $c_p = a_1 + b_1y_p$ and $c_t = \xi_1$, and according to my discussion of the FRB sampling scheme I may assume that SPIH1 and SPIH2 are valid. If I do, I see from the estimates of T5.2 parameters in tables 5.1 and 5.2 that, with the single possible exception of the 35–44 age group, the MPD_g^*'s of the groups in table 5.1 have the required factor-analytic mean and covariance structure on which APIH1, APIH2, DPIH1, and GPIH1–GPIH6 insist. The possibility that the 35–44 age group constitutes an exception is due to the large value of the χ^2 variable of this group in table 5.1. From this I deduce that it is the case that the MPDg that my data determine for the non-exceptional groups belong to PH, that is, $MPD_g^* \in PH$ for all non-exceptional groups.

5.3.4 A Search for an Empirically Relevant Model of APIH1–APIH4

Next, I will use $R^{PIH}(g)$ to delineate the contours of a set of parameters within which the parameters of an empirically relevant mathematical model of APIH1–APIH4 must lie. The contours of such a set can be described by specifying the allowable values of a_{1g}, r_g, and $k(r_g, \alpha)$. I begin with r_g. The estimates of b_3 and their standard errors that are

Table 5.3
The range of r_g.

Age group	< 35	35–44	45–54	55–64	≥ 65	All
Min r_g	0.0830	0.0118	0.0297	0.0129	0.0260	0.0183
r_g estimate	0.0887	0.0128	0.0314	0.0137	0.0276	0.0189
Max r_g	0.0953	0.0139	0.0334	0.0147	0.0295	0.0196

found in table 5.2 impose limits on the empirically relevant values of r_g that I show in table 5.3. In reading the table, note that in each age group $r_g = [1/(b_{3g} - 1)]$. Hence, the difference between max r_g and min r_g is not to be identified with four standard errors in the distribution of r_g.

Next I look at the sought-for range of values of $k(r, \alpha)$. Let k_g be the value of $k(r_g, \alpha)$ in age group g, g = 25, 40, ... , 70. According to APIH1–APIH4, DPIH1, GPIH2, GPIH4, and GPIH6,

$$c_3 = k_g y_p + c_t; \ E(c_3 \mid \Omega(g)) = k_g E(y_p \mid \Omega(g))$$

and, hence,

$$k_g = E(c_3 \mid \Omega(g))/E(y_p \mid \Omega(g))$$

and

$$k_g = E\{[c_3 - E(c_3 \mid \Omega(g))][y_p - E(y_p \mid \Omega(g))] \mid \Omega(g)\}/\sigma^2(y_p \mid g).$$

Similarly, it follows from T5.1 and T5.2 that

$$E(c_3 \mid \Omega(g)) = a_1 + b_1 E(y_p \mid \Omega(g))$$

and

$$b_1 = E\{[c_3 - E(c_3 \mid \Omega(g))] \ [y_p - E(y_p \mid \Omega(g))] \mid \Omega(g)\}/\sigma^2(y_p \mid g).$$

From these equations I deduce that in an empirically relevant interpretation of APIH3 and APIH4 it must be the case that

$$k_g \in (b_{1f} - 2SD, b_{1f} + 2SD)$$

and

$$0 \in (a_{1f} - 2SD, a_{1f} + 2SD).$$

And since $E(y_p \mid \Omega(g)) = E(y_3 \mid \Omega(g))$, it must be the case that

$$k_g \in (\mu_{cf}/\mu_{yf} - 2\ SD, \mu_{cf}/\mu_{yf} + 2\ SD).$$

I do not have an estimate of the standard deviation of the distribution of μ_{cf}/μ_{yf}, so I rephrase the last relation as

$$(\mu_{cf}/\mu_{yf}) \in (b_{1f} - 2SD, b_{1f} + 2SD),$$

where SD refers to the standard deviation of the distribution of b_{1f} in MPD_g^*. Tables 5.4–5.6 describe the three relations for each age group.

The import of the relations illustrated in tables 5.3–5.6 requires comment. In an economic theory-data confrontation, an econometrician confronts a family of models of the theory with data. In the present case, the relevant family of models can be described entirely in terms of regions in R^3 to which the triples (r_g, a_{1g}, k_g) belong. For a given population, APIH1–APIH4 are empirically relevant if there is at least one empirically relevant value of (r_g, a_{1g}, k_g) for each $g \in G$. I do not know what the empirically relevant values of these parameters are in the 1962 US population. Tables 5.3–5.6 show estimates of the values of the parameters and describe the regions to which their values must belong in order that they be the parameters of a data-admissible mathematical model of the MPD.

The parameters of a data-admissible mathematical model of the MPD need not satisfy all the strictures on which A1–A4 insist. Normally it can be an arduous task to sift out the ones in tables 5.3–5.6 that do. However, in this case the search is easy. The fact that 0 does not belong to any of the intervals in table 5.5 in which a_1 resides

Table 5.4
The range of k_g.

Age group	< 35	35–44	45–54	55–64	≥ 65	All
Min kg	0.5634	0	0	0.206	0.9024	1.1121
kg estimates	1.6994	7.1114	2.0647	1.8760	1.4664	2.1221
Max kg	2.8354	15.6834	4.1967	3.546	2.0304	3.132

Table 5.5
The range of a_1.

Age groups	< 35	35–44	45–54	55–64	≥ 65	All
Min a_1	−5922	−77231	−17646	−18087	−8783	−15064
a_1 estimates	−5402	−69091	−14046	−14307	−4883	−13464
Max a_1	−4882	−60951	−10446	−10527	−983	−11864

Table 5.6
The range of b_{1f}.

Age groups	< 35	35–44	45–54	55–64	≥ 65	All
Min b_{1f}	0.5634	0	0	0.206	0.9024	1.1121
(μ_{cf}/μ_{yf}) estimates	0.8609	1.1793	1.1135	1.0418	1.1301	1.0855
Max b_{1f}	2.8354	15.6834	4.1967	3.546	2.0304	3.1321

suffices to conclude that APIH3 and APIH4 are not relevant in the empirical context that $MPD_g{}^*$ determines in the non-exceptional groups.

5.4 Friedman's Hypothesis in the Upper Data Universe

I described two scenarios for a theory-data confrontation in economics in subsection 2.2.1. In one scenario, the researcher in charge believes that that there is a definite divide between his model world and the world of observations, and that his data may provide inaccurate measurements of the undefined terms of his theory. He formulates his theory in a theory universe and uses bridge principles to describe how his theoretical variables are related to his data variables. The data confrontation of Friedman's hypothesis that I have carried out in sections 5.2 and 5.3 is an example of such a scenario. In the other scenario, the researcher in charge identifies his theory variables with true variables in the real world or believes that he has accurate observations of all the relevant theoretical variables. He formulates his theory, describes his data, and carries out the empirical analysis in the data universe. I take this data universe to be the upper data universe in figure 2.1.

In this section I will use my observations of e_2, y_3, c_3, and w_2 to carry out a test of Friedman's Permanent Income Hypothesis in accord with the second scenario that I described above. This scenario allows me to formulate two different data confrontations of the hypothesis that have interesting relations to the analysis I carried out in the lower data universe. Together the two new data confrontations demonstrate that errors in equations and errors in variables can play an important role in empirical analyses in the upper data universe in figure 2.1. They also demonstrate why errors in variables and inaccuracies in the measurement of theoretical variables are treated so differently in applied econometrics.

5.4.1 The Empirical Relevance of Friedman's Hypothesis with Accurate Observations

To begin with, I presume that I have accurate observations of c_p and y_p; i.e., that $c_3 = c_p$ and $y_3 = y_p$. Then the upper data universe in figure 2.1 is a triple, $\{\Omega_P, \Gamma_P, (\Omega_P, \pounds_P, P_P(\cdot))\}$, where Ω_P is a subset of a vector space, Γ_P is a finite set of axioms that the vectors in Ω_P must satisfy, $\pounds_P$ is a σ-field of subsets of Ω_P, and $P_P(\cdot): \pounds_P \to [0, 1]$ is a probability measure.

For the present analysis, I accept the Γ_P axioms, DPIH1 and DPIH2, as stated above. For ease of reference, I repeat them here.

DPIH1

$\Omega_P \subset \{15, \dots, 100\} \times R_+^2 \times R$. Thus, $\omega_P \in \Omega_P$ only if $\omega_P = (e_2, y_3, c_3, w_2)$ for some $e_2 \in \{15, \dots, 100\}$, $(y_3, c_3) \in R_+^2$, $w_2 \in R$, and $(e_2, (y_3, c_3), w_2) \in \{15, \dots, 100\} \times R_+^2 \times R$.

DPIH2

Let $G = \{25, 40, 50, 60, 70\}$, let $h(\cdot):\{15, \dots, 100\} \to G$ be as defined in APIH4, and let $\Omega_P(g) = \{\omega_P \in \Omega_P: h(e_2) = g\}$, $g \in G$. Then, $\Omega_P(g) \in \pounds_P$ and $P_P(\Omega_P(g)) > 0$, $g \in G$. Also, relative to $P_P(\cdot \,|\, \Omega_P(g))$, the components of (y_3, c_3, w_2) have finite means, variances, and fourth-order moments; the means of y_3 and c_3 are positive; and the variances and covariances of y_3, c_3, and w_2 are positive, for all $g \in G$.

From these axioms and a standard theorem in mathematical statistics I deduce the validity of the following theorem.

T5.3

For each $g \in G$, there are four constants, $\alpha_g \in R$, $\gamma_g \in R$, $\beta_g \in R_{++}$, and $\varphi_g \in R_{++}$, and two random variables, η_g and δ_g, such that, with $P_P(\cdot \,|\, \Omega_P(g))$ probability 1,

$$c_3 = \alpha_g + \beta_g y_3 + \eta_g \tag{5.1}$$

and

$$w_2 = \gamma_g + \varphi_g y_3 + \delta_g. \tag{5.2}$$

Also, relative to $P_P(\cdot \,|\, \Omega_P(g))$, η_g and δ_g have mean 0, finite positive variances, and 0 covariance with y_3.

To the two axioms I add an axiom, DPIH3, concerning α_g and the distribution of η_g and δ_g. The assumption concerning α_g expresses the ideas of APIH3 and APIH4 in an empirical context where c_3 and y_3 are understood to be accurate observations of a consumer's permanent consumption and permanent income.

DPIH3

For each $g \in G$, $\alpha_g = 0$. Also, relative to $P_P(\cdot \mid \Omega_P(g))$, $E(\eta_g \delta_g \mid \Omega_P(g)) = 0$.

I then add versions of the first three axioms concerning the FRB sampling scheme in which Ω_P and $\Omega_P(g)$ take the place of Ω and $\Omega(g)$, respectively.

With these axioms in mind, a simple test of Friedman's theory presents itself. DPIH1–DPIH3 and the three sampling axioms are empirically relevant if and only if, for each $g \in G$, $\alpha_g = 0$, $\beta_g > 0$, and $\varphi_g > 0$. To check whether the three parameters satisfy the given conditions, I obtain ordinary least-squares (OLS) estimates of the parameters in equations 5.1 and 5.2. The results are displayed in table 5.7. The estimates of β and φ are positive and significantly different from 0, and the estimates of α are negative and significantly different from 0.[7] The latter fact demonstrates that DPIH1–DPIH3 and Friedman's hypothesis are not empirically relevant in the empirical context that I have formulated for the upper data universe in figure 2.1.

Table 5.7
FA and least-squares estimates of TPD and MPD parameters.

Age group	b_{1f}	b_{3f}	Φ	β	φ	μ_c/μ_y	$\alpha \ (= a_1)$
< 35	1.6994 (0.568)	12.2689 (0.7738)	0.5497	0.9342 (0.050)	6.7442	0.8609	−5402 (267)
35–44	7.1114 (4.286)	79.2077 (6.4702)	0.2697	1.6015 (0.209)	"21.3623"	1.1793	−69091 (4297)
45–54	2.0647 (1.066)	32.8252 (1.9000)	0.5497	1.1351 (0.075)	18.0440	1.1135	−14046 (1748)
55–64	1.8760 (0.835)	73.8885 (4.8157)	0.5561	1.0433 (0.069)	41.0893	1.0418	−14307 (1926)
≥ 65	1.4664 (0.282)	37.1841 (2.3107)	0.9217	1.3516 (0.076)	34.2726	1.1301	−4883 (1950)
All	2.1221 (0.505)	53.9032 (1.8162)	0.5704	1.2105 (0.043)	30.7464	1.0855	−13464 (912)

5.4.2 The Empirical Relevance of Friedman's Hypothesis When the Data Contain Measurement Errors

In his 1934 book *Statistical Confluence Analysis by Means of Complete Regression Systems*, Ragnar Frisch discusses errors in equations and errors in variables without relating them to his model world. These errors are fundamentally different from the inaccurate measurements of theoretical variables I discussed in section 5.2. Frisch carries out his analysis in his own data universe, and his errors are errors that pertain to the measurement of data variables and not to the measurement of theory variables. The difference is important for the purposes of this book, so a few remarks are required.

When I insist that I have accurate observations of c_p and y_p for the analysis of Friedman's hypothesis in the upper data universe in figure 2.1, I mean to claim (1) that the two concepts have well defined points of reference in the economists' world of ideas, (2) that their values can be computed for each and every consumer in the sample population in one and only one way, and (3) that my sample observations are accurate. Even though the first condition may be satisfied in the present case study, there are good reasons why the second and third conditions are not met. For example, disposable income is taken to be a measure of permanent income. Also, the difference between disposable income and a year's change in net worth is taken to be a measure of permanent consumption. In order that my observations of disposable income be accurate and comparable across my sample consumers, the recorded earnings and taxable value of fixed assets in family tax statements must be accurate and comparable. Also, in order that my observations of permanent consumption be accurate and comparable across my sample consumers, the consumers must share the same understanding of terms such as "disposable income," "liquid and fixed assets," and "debt." Interesting articles by Robert Ferber (1965, 1966) and John Lansing et al. (1961) attest to how demanding the second and third requirements are. The upshot of this discussion is, therefore, that it is unreasonable to believe that my observations of c_P and y_P are accurate and comparable across my sample of consumers. If they are not, my observations are marred by measurement errors.

With that much said about the possibility of errors of measurement in the present upper data universe, I can conclude the chapter by proposing a second test of Friedman's hypothesis in which both errors in equations and measurement errors are decisive. To describe the new test, I begin by adding six components to ω_P: $(\hat{c}_3, \check{c}_3)$, $(\acute{y}_3, \ddot{y}_3)$, and $(\hat{w}_2,$ v), where $(\hat{c}_3, \acute{y}_3) \in R_+^2$ and $(\check{c}_3, \ddot{y}_3, \hat{w}_2, v) \in R^4$. With the new variates, I name the new data universe $(\Omega^*_P, \Gamma^*_P, (\Omega^*_P, \pounds^*_P, P^*_P(\cdot)))$ and rephrase DPIH1 and DPIH2 as follows, the F standing for Frisch.

FDPIH1

$\Omega^*_P \subset \{15, \ldots, 100\} \times R_+^5 \times R^4$. Thus, $\omega_P \in \Omega^*_P$ only if $\omega_P = (e_2, c_3, \hat{c}_3, \check{c}_3, y_3,$ $\acute{y}_3, \ddot{y}_3, w_2, \hat{w}_2, v)$ for some $e_2 \in \{15, \ldots, 100\}$, $(c_3, \hat{c}_3, y_3, \acute{y}_3, w_2) \in R_+^5$, $(\check{c}_3,$ $\ddot{y}_3, \hat{w}_2, v) \in R^4$, and $(e_2, (c_3, \hat{c}_3, y_3, \acute{y}_3, w_2), (\check{c}_3, \ddot{y}_3, \hat{w}_2, v)) \in \{15, \ldots, 100\} \times R_+^5 \times R^4$.

FDPIH2

Let $G = \{25, 40, 50, 60, 70\}$, let $h(\cdot):\{15, \ldots, 100\} \to G$ be as defined in APIH4, and let $\Omega^*_P(g) = \{\omega_P \in \Omega^*_P : h(e_2) = g\}$, $g \in G$. Then, $\Omega^*_P(g) \in \pounds^*_P$ and $P^*_P(\Omega^*_P(g)) > 0$, $g \in G$. Also, relative to $P^*_P(\cdot \mid \Omega^*_P(g))$, the components of (y_3, c_3, w_2) have finite means, variances, and fourth-order moments; the means of y_3 and c_3 are positive; and the variances and covariances of y_3, c_3, and w_2 are positive, for all $g \in G$.

Next, I suppose that my observations of c_3, y_3, and w_2 contain errors and introduce a third axiom to that effect.

FDPIH3

For all $\omega_P \in \Omega_P$, $c_3 = \hat{c}_3 + \check{c}_3$, $y_3 = \acute{y}_3 + \ddot{y}_3$, and $w_2 = \hat{w}_2 + v$.

The equations in FDPIH3 correspond to equation 7.8 on page 51 of Frisch 1934, where Frisch takes $\hat{c}_3$, $\acute{y}_3$, and $\hat{w}_2$ to measure the systematic parts of c_3, y_3, and w_2—that is, the parts that are "systematically connected with the other variates considered" [in the pertinent economic system]. He refers to $\check{c}_3$, $\ddot{y}_3$, v as the "accidental" parts of c_3, y_3, and w_2.

The terms *systematically connected*, *accidental*, and *pertinent economic system* have interesting meanings in this context. The economic system may be identified with the values that observations of e_2, c_3, y_3, and w_2 and observations of variables representing education, tenure, and employment assume in the FRB re-interview survey of consumer finances in the United States. Frisch assumes that there exist a finite number of unobservable basic variates, $z_1, \ldots, z_h$, that have been present and have determined the observed values of the system variables in accord with his equation 7.1 on p. 48; for example, for the observed values of c_3, y_3, and w_2,

$$c_3 = \Sigma_{1 \le j \le h}\, p_{1j}z_j, \quad y_3 = \Sigma_{1 \le j \le h}\, p_{2j}z_j, \quad \text{and} \quad w_2 = \Sigma_{1 \le j \le h}\, p_{3j}z_j, \qquad (5.3)$$

where the p_{ij} are constants.

In the present system, equations 5.3 reduce to the equations in FDPIH3, with $h = 6$ and the six z_j variates denoted by $\check{c}_3$, $\acute{y}_3$, $\hat{w}_2$, $\check{c}_3$, $\ddot{y}_3$, and v. Each of the first three basic variates is systematically connected with other basic variates in the system. To wit:

FDPIH4

For all $\omega_P \in \Omega_P$ and each $g \in G$, there are four constants, α_g, β_g, γ_g, and φ_g, such that

$$\check{c}_3 = \alpha_g + \beta_g \acute{y}_3 \text{ and } \hat{w}_2 = \gamma_g + \varphi_g \acute{y}_3. \qquad (5.4)$$

Also, $\alpha_g = 0$, $\beta_g > 0$, and $\varphi_g > 0$.

In Frisch's semi-absolute sense, the three variates in equation 5.4 exert a systematic effect on the system. In contrast, each of the other three basic variates in FDPIH3 is said to exert an accidental disturbance on the system.

Frisch proposes three assumptions about the means and covariances of the new variables. I will adopt them. In addition, I will insist that the fourth-order moments of $\check{c}_3$ and $\ddot{y}_3$ are finite.

FDPIH5

For each $g \in G$, relative to $P^*_P(\cdot \mid \Omega^*(g))$, $\check{c}_3$ and $\ddot{y}_3$ have means 0, finite positive variances, and finite fourth-order moments; $\check{c}_3$ and $\ddot{y}_3$ are orthogonal, $\check{c}_3$ is orthogonal to $\acute{y}_3$, $\ddot{y}_3$ is orthogonal to $\acute{y}_3$, and the covariance matrix of $\check{c}_3$, $\ddot{y}_3$, and v is diagonal.

With these assumptions in mind, I can reformulate equations 5.1 and 5.2 as a system of three equations:

$$c_3 = \alpha + \beta \acute{y}_3 + \check{c}_3, \qquad (5.5)$$

$$y_3 = \acute{y}_3 + \ddot{y}_3, \qquad (5.6)$$

$$w_2 = \gamma + \varphi \acute{y}_3 + v. \qquad (5.7)$$

These equations constitute a restricted factor-analysis model like the one I analyzed in subsection 5.2.2. According to the axioms, $\alpha = 0$, $\beta > 0$, and $\varphi > 0$. Factor-analytic estimates of the model's parameters are, with the obvious translation, given in table 5.7. As the estimates demonstrate, Friedman's hypothesis is not empirically relevant in the empirical context of the second test. The culprits are the estimates of α, since they are negative and significantly different from 0.

Now, the conclusion at which I arrive with Frisch's ideas looks like the conclusion in section 5.3. Yet there is a fundamental difference. There is only one true TDP in the upper data universe. In the lower data universe there are many MPDs. Therefore, the search for empirically relevant models differs in the two empirical contexts. In the upper data universe it is important that the estimate of α does not reject the idea that $\alpha = 0$ and that the estimates of β, and φ have the right signs and are significantly different from 0. In 95 percent of all samples, the 95-percent-confidence intervals around the estimates of the given parameters will contain the true values of these parameters. If the confidence band contains parameter values with α always negative and with β and φ having the wrong signs, the true parameter value of α need not equal 0 and the true parameter values of β and φ may have wrong signs. This aspect of the empirical analysis plays no role in the lower data universe in section 5.3. There, I am looking for a mathematical model of MPD that is data admissible and satisfies the constraints on which APIH3 and APIH4 insist. If I find one such MPD, it is irrelevant whether the confidence band around the estimated MPD contains data-admissible MPDs whose parameters do not head the restrictions imposed by APIH3 and APIH4.

5.4.3 A Concluding Remark

Frisch developed his analysis of measurement errors with unobservable basic variates to set the stage for his "bunch map" analysis of economic data. (See Frisch 1934, p. 48.) Since Frisch's account of measurement errors is different from mine, it is interesting to record Haavelmo's understanding of Frisch's systematic and accidental variables. According to Haavelmo (1950, pp. 262–263), "the real reason for splitting the variables into 'systematic parts' and 'disturbances' would seem to be, first, the idea that the systematic parts of the variables observed are the would-be 'true economic variables' which according to economic theory would fit exactly [theoretical relations such as those in equation 5.4 above], second, that [these relations] would be autonomous in the sense that [they] would hold regardless of whether or not other economic relations were fulfilled, and, third, that there might be some hope of eventually being able to experience and observe the 'true' variables so that the exact [relations] between them would have value for prediction purposes."[8]

Haavelmo's understanding of Frisch's systematic and accidental variables is interesting in the present context. According to Haavelmo, the systematic parts of Frisch's variables play the role in Frisch's system that Haavelmo's true economic variables play in Haavelmo's treatise. Since Haavelmo's true variables live and function in his data universe, it must also be the case that Frisch's systematic variables live and function in Frisch's data universe. This supports my contention that Frisch's account of errors in variables is very different from my idea of inaccurate measurements of theoretical variables in Frisch's model world. Hence, even though the statistical analysis of the TPD equations 5.5–5.7 is like the statistical analysis of the MPD distribution of (c_3, y_3, w_2) in section 5.3, the two analyses differ greatly in theoretical import.

6 Theory-Data Confrontations with Time-Series Data

In chapters 3–5 I discussed formal theory-data confrontations in which the theory was confronted with cross-section data—that is, with data that were obtained in a random or stratified random sampling scheme and pertained to one fixed period of time. In chapters 7–9 I will present case studies of theory-data confrontations in which the data are time-series observations of a vector-valued random process. When the pertinent vector-valued random variables are independently and identically distributed over time, the empirical analysis of time-series data is, formally, like the analyses I discussed in chapters 3 and 4. In other cases the theory-data confrontation with time-series data becomes much more involved. The vectors in the two universes in chapters 3 and 4 become vector-valued sequences of variables in chapters 7 and 8, and the vector-valued random variables in chapters 3 and 4 become vector-valued random processes in chapters 7 and 8. The present chapter is intended to serve as an introduction to the intricacies of theory-data confrontations with time-series data.

6.1 A Formal Theory-Data Confrontation with Any Number of Observations

The underlying ideas of the present theory-data confrontation are those depicted in figure 1.2. As in section 2.2, I take the confrontation of the theory to happen in the top three boxes of figure 1.2. Also, I distinguish between two possible scenarios. In one of them the researcher in charge identifies his theory variables with true variables in the real world (see Haavelmo 1944, p. 7) and may or may not assume that he has accurate observations of all the relevant theoretical variables. He formulates his theory, describes his data, and carries out the empirical analysis in the data universe. The theory-data confrontation then reduces to the data universe alone. In the other scenario the researcher in charge believes that there is a definite divide between his model world and the world of observations. He may, but need not, assume that his data provide inaccurate measurements of the undefined terms of his theory. Regardless of what he assumes, he formulates his theory in a theory universe and uses bridge principles to describe how his theoretical variables are related to his data variables. Then the theory-data confrontation becomes a triple of two disjoint universes—one for theory and one for data—and a bridge between them.

The first scenario of a theory-data confrontation depicts an abstract view of the way most applied and theoretical econometrics function today. There is a true but unknown local data-generating process (LDGP). The values of the observed variables need not equal the values of the corresponding true variables, and the differences are accounted for in the theory by allowing for errors in variables and errors in equations. Also, the empirical analysis can be likened to a search for a data-admissible econometric model that parsimoniously encompasses the LDGP (Bontemps and Mizon 2003, pp. 356, 359, and 366; Hendry and Krolzig 2003, pp. 380 and 386–391). Most important, the whole theory-data confrontation takes place in a data universe. This data universe is the upper data universe in figure 2.1 and the LDGP is the TPD in the same figure, where TPD is short for the true probability distribution of the data variables.

The second scenario of a theory-data confrontation pictures the way I believe that applied and theoretical econometrics ought to function in a world in which the undefined terms of an economic theory have uncertain relations to observable variables in social reality. There is an LDGP in this theory-data confrontation too. However, it does not play the all-important role that it plays in present-day econometric analysis. Specifically, the empirical analysis is not a search for a data-admissible mathematical model that parsimoniously encompasses the LDGP. Instead, it is a search for a data-admissible mathematical model of a probability distribution, the MPD, whose parameters determine an empirically relevant model of the pertinent economic theory. This difference leads to interesting novel views on the meaning of both congruence and empirical relevance.

Next I will describe the formal details of an empirical analysis in which there are two disjoint universes—a theory universe and a data universe—and a bridge between the two universes. My description differs from the one I gave in section 2.2 to the extent that the axioms allow for any number of observations. These observations may be the result of a random sampling scheme that was carried out at a given point in time or a sequence of observations of the values that a vector-valued function has assumed over a given period of time. The formalism is a bit involved, so I will give simple examples to illustrate the underlying ideas. I begin with the data universe.

6.1.1 The Data Universe

Formally, the data universe in an axiomatized theory-data confrontation is a triple, $(\Omega_P, \Gamma_p, (\Omega_P, \aleph_P, P_P(\cdot)))$, where Ω_P is a subset of a vector space, Γ_p is a finite set of axioms that vectors in Ω_P must satisfy, and $(\Omega_P, \aleph_P, P_P(\cdot))$ is a probability space, where $\aleph_P$ is a σ field of subsets of Ω_P and $P_P(\cdot):\aleph_P \to [0, 1]$ is a probability measure. In the applications that I have in mind for this book, two of the members of Γ_P describe characteristic features of the conceptual framework of the data-generating process. One insists that Ω_P is a space of sequences; i.e., $\Omega_P \subset (R^k)^N$. Thus, $\omega_P \in \Omega_P$ only if $\omega_P = y$ for some vector-valued sequence, $y \in (R^k)^N$ where $N = \{0, 1, \ldots \}$. The other insists that the family of finite-dimensional probability distributions of the components of ω_P induced by $P_P(\cdot)$ is the true family of probability distributions of the components of ω_P. To see how, for each $t \in N$, let the vector-valued function, $y(t, \cdot)$: $\Omega_P \to R^k$, be defined by the equations $y(t, \omega_P) = \omega_{Pt}$, and $\omega_P \in \Omega_P$, where ω_{Pt} is the tth component of ω_P. Then $y(t, \cdot)$, is measurable with respect to $\aleph_P$. Also, subject to the conditions on which Γ_p insists, the family, $Y = \{y(t, \omega_P); t \in N\}$, has a well-defined family of finite-dimensional probability distributions relative to $P_P(\cdot)$. This probability distribution is the true family of probability distributions of Y. I denote it by TPD, where T stands for true, P for probability, and D for distribution.

The remaining assertions in Γ_P delineate properties of TPD that are characteristics of the pertinent data-generating process. Specifically, they will delineate properties of the sampling distribution and describe the way components of ω_P are related to one another. How extensive these axioms are, depends on the researcher in charge and his data.

In reading my description of the data universe there are several characteristics to notice. The Ω_P that appears in two places is one and the same subset of a vector space. Also, $\aleph_P$ is a family of subsets of the given vector space, and $P_P(\cdot)$ assigns numbers to these subsets. Moreover, $y(t,\cdot): \Omega_P \to R^k$ is a vector-valued function means that at any ω_P in its domain $y(t, \omega_P) = (y_1(t, \omega_P),\ldots,y_k(t, \omega_P))$. Also, the equation $y(t, \omega_{Pt}) = \omega_{Pt}$ is short for $(y_1(t, \omega_P),\ldots,y_k(t, \omega_P)) = \omega_{Pt}$. In the present theory-data confrontation y plays two roles—one as a sequence of vectors in Ω_P and

another as a vector-valued random process on $(\Omega_P, \aleph_P)$. The components of y can be observed, and the values that $P_P(\cdot)$ assigns to the
members of $\aleph_P$ can, some times, be calculated. Here is an example.

E6.1.1
Consider the city, called OS, that we met in E2.2.1. The researcher has
obtained a random sample of the disposable incomes of three consum-
ers in OS. So let $\omega_P \in \Omega_P$ if and only if $\omega_P = y$ for some $y \in A^3$, where
$A = \{1, 3, 5, 7\}$. Then Ω_P is a set of sequences that have three components
all of which belong to A. Also, $\aleph_P$ is the field of all subsets of Ω_P.
Examples of members of $\aleph_P$ are $B_1 = \{\omega_P \in \Omega_P: y_1 \in A, y_2 = 3, \text{ and } y_3 \in A\}$ and $B_2 = \{\omega_P \in \Omega_P: y_1 = 7, y_2 \in A, \text{ and } y_3 = 1\}$. Evidently, B_1 is the set
of all sequences in Ω_P whose second component equals 3; and B_2 is the
set of all sequences in Ω_P whose first component equals 7 and whose
third component equals 1.

If for each $t \in \{1, 2, 3\}$ I let $y(t, \cdot): \Omega_P \to A$ be defined by the equations
$y(t, \omega_P) = \omega_{Pt}$ and $\omega_P \in \Omega_P$, where ω_{Pt} is the tth component of ω_P, I can
redefine the sets B_1 and B_2 as follows: $B_1 = \{\omega_P \in \Omega_P: y(2, \omega_P) = 3\}$ and
$B_2 = \{\omega_P \in \Omega_P: y(1, \omega_P) = 7 \text{ and } y(3, \omega_P) = 1\}$.

According to the information I gave in E2.2.1, the probability of
observing the number j in A in the first draw of the sample is $1/4, 1/2$,
$1/5$, or $1/20$ according as $\{j\} = \{1\}, \{3\}, \{5\}$, or $\{7\}$. Consequently, the
probabilities of the two sets are $P_P(B_1) = 1/2$, and $P_P(B_2) = 1/80$. Thus,
the probability of the second draw in the sample being a disposable
income equal to 3 is $1/2$. The probability of the first and the third draw
in the sample being disposable incomes equal to 7 and 1 is $1/80$.

6.1.2 The Theory Universe
Formally, the theory universe in an axiomatized theory-data confronta-
tion is a triple, $(\Omega_T, \Gamma_T, (\Omega_T, \aleph_T, P_T(\cdot)))$, where Ω_T is a subset of a vector
space, Γ_T is a finite set of assertions that the vectors in Ω_T must satisfy,
$\aleph_T$ is a σ field of subsets of Ω_T and $P_T(\cdot):\aleph_T \to [0, 1]$ is a probability
measure. In the applications that I have in mind for this book, two of
the assertions in Γ_T delineate characteristic features of the conceptual
framework of the pertinent theory. The other assertions describe law-
like properties of the elements that play essential roles in the theory.

The features of the conceptual framework of the pertinent theory
reside in the mind of the researcher in charge. They are of two kinds.
One insists that Ω_T is a space of sequences; i.e., $\Omega_T \subset (R^h \times R^k)^N$. Thus,
$\omega_T \in \Omega_T$ only if ω_T is a sequence of pairs of vectors, (x_t, u_t), all of which

belong to $(R^h \times R^k)$. In short, $\omega_T = (x, u)$ for some $(x, u) \in (R^h \times R^k)^N$, where $N = \{0, 1, \ldots\}$. The other insists that the components of ω_T are random processes relative to $P_T(\cdot)$. Specifically, for each $t \in N$, let the vector-valued function, $(x, u)(t, \cdot): \Omega_T \to R_+^{h+k}$, be defined by the equations $(x, u)(t, \omega_T) = \omega_{Tt}$, and $\omega_T \in \Omega_T$, where ω_{Tt} is the tth component of ω_T. Then $(x, u)(t, \cdot)$ is measurable with respect to $\aleph_T$. Also, relative to the conditions on which Γ_T insists, the family, $(X, U) = \{(x, u)(t, \omega_T); t \in N\}$, has a well-defined family of finite-dimensional probability distributions relative to $P_T(\cdot)$. I denote this probability distribution by RPD, where R stands for researcher, P for probability, and D for distribution. I assume that the researcher is its originator.

The law-like properties of the components of ω_T that the remaining assertions in Γ_T describe, delineate salient characteristics of the RPD that are at stake in the theory-data confrontation. For example, in chapters 7 and 8 these characteristics depict distinguishing features of the dynamics of foreign exchange. Specifically, they give a symbolic rendition of the belief that a frictionless foreign-exchange market in equilibrium will function efficiently if the agents in the market, in an aggregate sense, are risk neutral and endowed with rational expectations about the level of future exchange rates.

In reading my description of the theory universe there are several characteristics to notice. The Ω_T that appears in two places is one and the same subset of a vector space. Also, $\aleph_T$ is a family of subsets of the given vector space, and $P_T(\cdot)$ assigns numbers to these subsets. Moreover, for the vector-valued function $(x,u)(t,\cdot)$ the equation $(x,u)(t,\omega_T) = \omega_{Tt}$ is short for $(x_1(t, \omega_T),\ldots, x_h(t, \omega_T), u_1(t, \omega_T),\ldots, u_k(t, \omega_T)) = \omega_{Tt}$. In the present theory-data confrontation (x, u) plays two roles—one as a sequence of vectors in Ω_P and one as a vector-valued random process on $(\Omega_T, \aleph_T)$. The components of (x, u) are theoretical variables whose values cannot be observed. Also, the values that $P_T(\cdot)$ assigns to the members of $\aleph_T$ reside in the mind of the researcher and cannot be calculated by an outsider. Here is an example.

E6.1.2
Consider the City of OS introduced in E6.1.1, and recall that the researcher has obtained a random sample of the disposable incomes of three consumers in OS. As in E2.2.2, the researcher insists that a consumer's disposable income has two components, permanent income, y_p, and transitory income, y_t, and that y_p and y_t are independently distributed. Hence, with each observed y I can associate an

unobservable triple of pairs (y_p, y_t) that I take to be the denotation of (x, u) in a theory universe where $h = 1$, $k = 1$, and $N = \{1,2,3\}$. So, for the present example, $\omega_T = (y_p, y_t)$ for some $(y_p, y_t) \in (A_x \times A_u)^3$, where $A_x = \{2, 4, 6\}$ and $A_u = \{-1, 1\}$. Thus Ω_T is a set of sequences of pairs that have three components all of which belong to $A_x \times A_u$. Also, $\aleph_T$ is the field of all subsets of Ω_T. Examples of members of $\aleph_T$ are $C_1 = \{\omega_T \in \Omega_T$: $(y_{p1}, y_{t1}) \in A_x \times A_u, (y_{p2}, y_{t2}) = (4, -1)$ and $(y_{p3}, y_{t3}) \in A_x \times A_u\}$ and $C_2 = \{\omega_T \in \Omega_T$: $(y_{p1}, y_{t1}) = (6, 1), (y_{p2}, y_{t2}) \in A_x \times A_u,$ and $(y_{p3}, y_{t3}) = (2, -1)\}$. Evidently, C_1 is the set of all sequences of pairs in Ω_T whose second component equals $(4, -1)$; and C_2 is the set of all sequences of pairs in Ω_T whose first component equals $(6, 1)$ and whose third component equals $(2, -1)$.

If, for each $t \in \{1, 2, 3\}$, I let the vector-valued function $(y_p, y_t)(t, \cdot)$: $\Omega_T \rightarrow A_x \times A_u$ be defined by the equations $(y_p, y_t)(t, \omega_T) = \omega_{Tt}$, and $\omega_T \in \Omega_T$, where ω_{Tt} is the tth component of ω_T, I can redefine the two sets, C_1 and C_2, as follows:

$C_1 = \{\omega_T \in \Omega_T$: $(y_p, y_t)(2, \omega_T) = (4, -1)\}$,

$C_2 = \{\omega_T \in \Omega_T$: $(y_p, y_t)(1, \omega_T) = (6, 1)$ and $(y_p, y_t)(3, \omega_T) = (2, -1)\}$.

Since the sample of disposable incomes in OS was random, and since the researcher insists that y_p and y_t are independently distributed, I can use the probabilities in table 2.1 of E2.2.2 to compute the researcher's assignment of probabilities to C_1 and C_2. For ease of reference I restate the table here as table 6.1.

Evidently, $P(C_1) = 1/4$ and $P(C_2) = (1/8)(1/8) = (1/64)$. Consequently, the researcher claims that the probability of obtaining the pair $(4, -1)$ in the second draw of the sample is $1/4$, which differs from the probability the researcher would have assigned to the event "a disposable income equal 3" in the second draw of the sample, $3/8$. Also, the researcher claims that the probability of obtaining the pair $(6, 1)$ in the first draw and the pair $(2, -1)$ in the third draw is $(1/64)$, which I take to be the probability he would have assigned to observing the

Table 6.1

	y_p			
y_t	2	4	6	mp_{yt}
-1	1/8	1/4	1/8	1/2
1	1/8	1/4	1/8	1/2
mp_{yp}	1/4	1/2	1/4	1

disposable incomes 7 and 1, respectively, in the first and last draws of the sample. The researcher's assignment of probabilities need not equal the true probabilities.[1]

6.1.3 The Bridge

In an axiomatized theory-data confrontation, Ω_P is disjoint from Ω_T. I assume that the researcher's sample of observations consists of pairs of vectors, $(\omega_{Tt}, \omega_{Pt})$, where ω_{Tt} and ω_{Pt} are, respectively, the tth component of $\omega_T \in \Omega_T$, and $\omega_P \in \Omega_P$. The observations of the components of ω_T are unobservable, while the observations of the components of ω_P can be seen and recorded. For example, in a cross-section study of the efficiency of firms' choice of input–output variables (see chapters 12 and 14 of Stigum 2003), components of ω_{Tt} may record "observations" of a given firm's efficient choices, while the corresponding components of ω_{Pt} will record the same firm's actual choices. I assume that all the "observations" that the researcher has, belong to a subset of $\Omega_T \times \Omega_P$ that I denote by Ω and call *sample space*. For the present theory-data confrontation, this assumption insists that observation are sequences of pairs of vectors, $((x, u), y)$, that belong to a subset, Ω, of $(R^{h+k} \times R^k)^N$. Thus $(\omega_T, \omega_P) \in \Omega$ only if (ω_T, ω_P) is a sequence of pairs of vectors, $((x_t, u_t), y_t)$, all of which belong to $(R^{h+k} \times R^k)$.

In an axiomatized theory-data confrontation, the σ fields $\aleph_T$ and $\aleph_P$ are taken to be stochastically independent. When $\aleph_T$ and $\aleph_P$ are stochastically independent, the probability spaces in the theory universe and the data universe induce a uniquely determined probability measure on $\Omega_T \times \Omega_P$. I showed how in chapter 2. For ease of reference, I repeat the description here. Let $\varkappa$ denote the family of all sets in $\Omega_T \times \Omega_P$ of the form $E_T \times E_P$ with $E_T \in \aleph_T$ and $E_P \in \aleph_P$, and let $\aleph$ denote the smallest σ field in $\Omega_T \times \Omega_P$ containing $\varkappa$. There is a uniquely determined probability measure, $P(\cdot):\aleph \to [0, 1]$, such that for all $E \in \varkappa$

$$P(E) = P_T(E_T)P_P(E_P).$$

(See Dunford and Schwartz 1957, pp. 183–189.) The probability space $(\Omega_T \times \Omega_P, \aleph, P(\cdot))$ plays a pivotal role in the axioms of the bridge.

Formally the bridge is a pair, $(\Omega, \Gamma_{T,P})$, where Ω is a subset of $\Omega_T \times \Omega_P$, and $\Gamma_{T,P}$ is a finite number of assertions that the elements in Ω must satisfy. The first three of the axioms in $\Gamma_{T,P}$ describe conceptual properties of the relationship between theoretical and observational variables. The other assertions describe law-like properties of this relationship. For the present theory-data confrontation, the first two assertions concerning the conceptual properties of the bridge between theory and data insist that observations are sequences of pairs, of vectors $((x, u), y)$, all of which belong to Ω, and that $\Omega \subset (R^{h+k} \times R^k)^N$. The third assertion refers to the given product probability space on $\Omega_T \times \Omega_P$ and insists that $\Omega \in \aleph$ and that $P(\Omega) > 0$. In chapters 7–9 I will also insist that

$\Omega_T \subset \{\omega_T \in \Omega_T$ for which there is an $\omega_P \in \Omega_P$ with $(\omega_T, \omega_P) \in \Omega\}$.

The remaining assertions in $\Gamma_{T,P}$ describe how the components of ω_T and ω_P in Ω are related to one another. In the present context there is only one such assertion. It claims that there exists a $k \times h$ dimensional matrix, H, such that for all $(\omega_T, \omega_P) \in \Omega$, and $t \in N$, $y(t, \omega_P) = Hx(t, \omega_T) + u(t, \omega_T)$.

In reading my description of the bridge, it is important to observe that Ω is taken to be a subset of $(R^{h+k} \times R^k)^N$ and that Ω, therefore, is a set of sequences each component of which belongs to $(R^{h+k} \times R^k)$. Consequently, if I adopt the definitions of $(x, u)(t, \cdot)$ and $y(t, \cdot)$ that I gave in my description of the theory universe and the data universe, I can think of the vectors in Ω as the values of a family of random vectors, $\{((x, u)(t, \omega_T), y(t, \omega_P)), t \in N\}$, on $(\Omega_T \times \Omega_P, \aleph)$ that satisfy the conditions listed in $\Gamma_{T,P}$. The underlying mathematical details of all this are not easy to grasp; chapter 7 of Halmos 1950 is helpful. The following example will help to fix ideas.

E6.1.3

Consider the City of OS that we discussed in E6.1.1 and E6.1.2. There $y \in A^3$, where $A = \{1, 3, 5, 7\}$, and $(x, u) \in (A_x \times A_u)^3$, where $A_x = \{2, 4, 6\}$ and $A_u = \{-1, 1\}$. Hence, in OS, Ω is a subset of vectors in $((A_x \times A_u) \times A)^3$; i.e., $((x, u), y) \in \Omega$ only if $((x, u), y)$ is a sequence of triples each member of which belongs to $((A_x \times A_u) \times A)$. In fact, in OS, $((x, u), y) \in \Omega$ if and only if $((x, u), y)$ is a sequence of triples the ith member of which belongs to $((A_x \times A_u) \times A)$ and satisfies the equation $x_i + u_i = y_i$, $i = 1, 2, 3$. Also, if I adopt the definitions of $y(t, \cdot)$ and $(x, u)(t, \cdot)$ that I gave in describing the data universe and the theory universe, I find that I can identify vectors in Ω with values of a family of random vectors, $\{((x, u)(t, \omega_T), y(t, \omega_P)); t \in \{1, 2, 3\}\}$ on $((A_x \times A_u) \times A)^3, \aleph)$. which in OS belong to Ω if and only if they satisfy the condition

$y(t, \omega_P) = x(t, \omega_T) + u(t, \omega_T)$, $t = 1, 2, 3$.

In other words,

$\Omega = \{(\omega_T, \omega_P): \omega_T \in \Omega_T, \omega_P \in \Omega_P$

and

$y(t, \omega_P) = x(t, \omega_T) + u(t, \omega_T)$, t = 1, 2, 3}.

A few numerical examples might be helpful. Consider the two sequences (((2, –1), 3), ((4, 1), 5), ((2, 1), 7)) and (((2, –1, 1), ((4, 1), 5), ((2, 1), 3)). The second belongs to Ω; the first does not. Note, also, that in this example

$\Omega_T \subset \{\omega_T \in \Omega_T$ for which there is an $\omega_P \in \Omega_P$ with $(\omega_T, \omega_P) \in \Omega\}$.

To wit: For each of the pairs, (2, –1), (2, 1), (4, –1), (4, 1), (6, –1), (6, 1) I can find a member of {1, 3, 5, 7} to obtain a triple that may be a component of a sequence in Ω. For example, for a sequence of pairs such as ((2, –1), (4, 1), (6, 1)), there is a triple of members of {1, 3, 5, 7} such that the corresponding sequence of triples belong to Ω. In the given case, 1, 5, and 7 will do, since (((2, –1), 1), ((4, 1), 5), ((6, 1), 7)) ∈ Ω.

6.1.4 The MPD

The RPD distribution of $\{(x, u)(t, \omega_T); t \in N\}$ and the bridge principles $\Gamma_{t,p}$ induce a family of finite-dimensional probability distributions of $\{y(t, \omega_P); t \in N\}$ that I denote by MPD and read as the marginal probability distribution of the components of ω_P.

To provide a definition of the MPD, it suffices to describe the salient characteristics of its finite-dimensional probability distributions. In the present case, I may depict a member of the MPD as follows: Let M be a finite positive integer, let $\{t_i, i= 1, \dots , M\}$ be a finite subset of N, where $t_i \neq t_j$ if $i \neq j$, and suppose that $A \subset (R^k)^M$. Also, let $\Omega_T(\Omega) = \{\omega_T \in \Omega_T$ for which there is an $\omega_P \in \Omega_P$ with $(\omega_T, \omega_P) \in \Omega\}$, and assume that $P_T(\Omega_T(\Omega)) > 0$. Then

$MPD((y(t_1,\omega_P), \dots, y(t_M,\omega_P)) \in A)$

$$= \frac{P_T(\{\omega_T \in \Omega_T : (Hx(t_1,\omega_T)+u(t_1,\omega_T), \dots, Hx(t_M,\omega_T)+u(t_M,\omega_T)) \in A\} \cap \Omega_T(\Omega))}{P_T(\Omega_T(\Omega))}.$$

Strictly speaking, the characteristics of MPD are unknown, since I have little factual information about salient features of $P_T(\cdot)$. In a theory-data confrontation, the researcher will deduce properties of MPD from assumptions about $P_T(\cdot)$ that are in accord with the ideas of the theory that confronts his data. For example, in the case studies in chapters 7 and 8 of this book I formulate axioms about $P_T(\cdot)$ that ensure that the dynamics of foreign exchange in the theory universe are as envisioned in the simple efficient-markets hypothesis.

The MPD may be very different from the TPD. How different the two families of probability distributions may be isn't easy to intuit, so an example is in order.

E6.1.4

In the city of OS, $y \in A^3$, where $A = \{1, 3, 5, 7\}$, and $(x, u) \in (A_x \times A_u)^3$, where $A_x = \{2, 4, 6\}$ and $A_u = \{-1, 1\}$. Also, Ω is a subset of vectors in $((A_x \times A_u) \times A)^3$. Specifically, $((x, u), y) \in \Omega$ if and only if $((x, u), y)$ is a sequence of triples each member of which belongs to $((A_x \times A_u) \times A)$ and satisfies the equations $y_i = x_i + u_i$, $i = 1, 2, 3$. In other words,

$$\Omega = \{(\omega_T, \omega_P): \omega_T \in \Omega_T, \omega_P \in \Omega_P, \text{ and } y(t, \omega_P) = x(t, \omega_T) + u(t, \omega_T), t = 1, 2, 3\},$$

where $\Omega_T = (A_x \times A_u)^3$, $\Omega_P = A^3$, and $y(t, \cdot)$, $x(t, \cdot)$, and $u(t, \cdot)$ are as defined in my description of the data universe and theory universe.

According to the definition of MPD,

$\text{MPD}(\{y = (1, 5, 3)\})$

$$= \frac{P_T(\{(x, u) \in (A_x \times A_u)^3 \text{ and } x + u = (1, 5, 3)\} \cap \{(x, u) \in (A_x \times A_u)^3, y \in A^3, ((x, u), y) \in \Omega\})}{P_T(\{(x, u) \in (A_x \times A_u)^3 \text{ with a } y \in A^3 \text{ and } ((x, u), y) \in \Omega\})}.$$

In the present case,

$$\Omega_T \subset \{(x, u) \in (A_x \times A_u)^3 \text{ with a } y \in A^3 \text{ and } ((x, u), y) \in \Omega\}.$$

Consequently,

$$P_T(\{(x, u) \in (A_x \times A_u)^3 \text{ with a } y \in A^3 \text{ and } ((x, u), y) \in \Omega\}) = 1,$$

$$\text{MPD}(\{y = (1, 5, 3)\}) = P_T(\{(x, u) \in (A_x \times A_u)^3,$$

and

$$x + u = (1, 5, 3)\}) = (1/8)(3/8)(3/8) = 9/64$$

in accord with table 6.1. The corresponding value of TPD—that is, $\text{TPD}(\{y = (1, 5, 3)\})$—equals $1/40$.

The equation for MPD can also be expressed in terms of $(x, u)(\cdot)$ and $y(\cdot)$. Here are two examples to fix ideas:

$$\text{MPD}(\{y_1 \in A, y_2 = 3, y_3 \in A\}) = P_T(\{\omega_T \in \Omega_T: x(2, \omega_T) + u(2, \omega_T) = 3\}) = 3/8$$

MPD($\{y_1 = 7, y_2 \in A, y_3 = 1\}$)

$= P_T(\{\omega_T \in \Omega_T: x(1, \omega_T) + u(1, \omega_T) = 7 \text{ and } x(3, \omega_T) + u(3, \omega_T) = 1\}) = 1/64.$

The values of TPD—that is, TPD($\{y_1 \in A, y_2 = 3, y_3 \in A\}$) and TPD($\{y_1 = 7, y_2 \in A, y_3 = 1\}$)—were computed in E6.1 to be, respectively, $1/2$ and $1/80$.

Regardless of how much the MPD differs from the TPD, in a theory-data confrontation with two universes and a bridge between them it is in terms of the MPD and not in terms of the TPD that the researcher is to carry out his empirical analysis. To bring the significance of this fact home, I must describe the actual data universe within which the researcher, in a given theory-data confrontation, is to carry out his empirical analysis. The properties of the MPD and Kolmogorov's Consistency Theorem (see T 15.23 on page 347 of my 1990 book) imply that there exists a probability measure, $P_M(\cdot): \aleph_P \to [0, 1]$, relative to which the family of finite-dimensional probability distributions of the $y(t, \cdot)$ equals the MPD. Consequently, one can think of the empirical analysis as being carried out in a data universe, $(\Omega_P, \Gamma_P{}^*, (\Omega_P, \aleph_P, P_M(\cdot)))$, that differs from the original universe in characteristic ways. In the latter triple, the Ω_P and $\aleph_P$ components are identical with the Ω_p and $\aleph_P$ components of the original data universe. The $\Gamma_P{}^*$ component differs from Γ_P in two ways: $P_M(\cdot)$ is substituted for $P_P(\cdot)$ and MPD is substituted for TPD. Evidently, the probability measure, $P_M(\cdot)$, that determines the family of finite-dimensional probability distributions of $\{y(t, \omega_P) ; t \in N\}$ in the new universe may be very different from $P_P(\cdot)$.

The ideas that I have presented in this subsection are pictured in figure 6.1. In the figure there is one theory universe, two data universes, and one bridge. The data universes have the same pair, $\{\Omega_P, \aleph_P\}$, and share the family of functions, $\{y(t, \cdot); t \in N\}$. The family of finite-dimensional probability distributions of the $y(t, \cdot)$ is TPD in the upper data universe and MPD in the lower data universe. The bridge connects the theory universe with the lower data universe.

Figure 6.1 depicts the import of RPD and the bridge in the unitary methodological basis for applied econometrics that I outline in subsection 6.1.1 The two probability measures on $(\Omega_P, \aleph_P)$, $P_M(\cdot)$ and $P_P(\cdot)$, differ, and so do, also, the families of finite-dimensional probability distributions of $\{y(t, \omega_P) ; t \in N\}$ that constitute MPD and TPD. Consequently, in an empirical analysis in which some of the data variables provide measurements of theoretical variables in a Frischian model

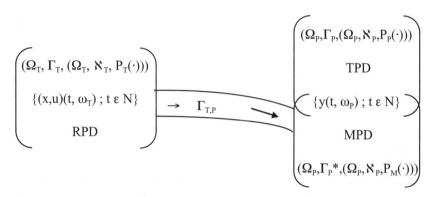

Figure 6.1
Theory-data confrontation with inaccurate observations.

world, one must expect that the observed characteristics of the MPD may be very different from the observed characteristics of the TPD.

The TPD and the MPD in figure 6.1 are not just different families of finite-dimensional probability distributions of the components of ω_P. TPD and MPD are fundamentally different in another way as well. There is one and only one true TPD. In contrast, there are as many MPDs as there are members of the intended families of models of Γ_T and $\Gamma_{T,P}$. Each pair of models of Γ_T and $\Gamma_{T,P}$ determines a mathematical model of MPD, and different pairs of models of Γ_T and $\Gamma_{T,P}$ determine different mathematical models of MPD. This difference between the TPD and the MPD in figure 6.1 causes the empirical analyses in the lower data universe to be fundamentally different from the empirical analyses that present-day econometric theory prescribes for the upper data universe. In particular, concepts such as empirical relevance and congruence receive different meanings in the two universes. My explication of the meaning of empirical relevance in chapter 3, and my discussion of the status of the bridge principles in chapter 10 bear witness to that.

6.2 Discrete-Time Second-Order Random Processes

Let $(\Omega, \aleph, P(\cdot))$ be a probability space, and let $N = \{0, 1, \ldots \}$ be the set of non-negative integers. A discrete-time *second-order random process* on the given probability space is a family of random variables, $X = \{x(t, \omega); t \in N\}$, whose members have finite means and variances. Such processes are a varied lot, and in this and the next three chapters we will encounter several of them with distinctive names; e.g., purely random processes, orthogonal processes, wide-sense stationary processes, and ARIMA processes. Here, a *purely random process* is a second-order random process whose members are independently and identically distributed. An *orthogonal process* is a second-order random process any two members of which have covariance 0. A *wide-sense stationary process* is a second-order random process whose members have the same mean and variance and have covariances that vary only with the difference between the t values of the variables in question. And an ARIMA process is a second-order random process that satisfies a difference equation of the form

$$\Sigma_{0 \le i \le n} a_i x(t - i, \omega) = y(t, \omega), \quad t \ge 1. \tag{6.1}$$

Here $a_0 = 1$ and the the roots of the characteristic polynomial, $\Sigma_{0 \le i \le n} a_i z^{n-i}$, have absolute values less than or equal to 1. Moreover,

$$y(t, \omega) = \Sigma_{0 \le s \le \infty} b_s \xi(t - s, \omega), \quad t \ge 1$$

where $\{\xi(t, \omega); t \in (\dots, -1, 0, 1, \dots)\}$ is a purely random process with mean 0 and finite variance, and where $\Sigma_{0 \le s < \infty} b_s^2 < \infty$. Finally, the initial condition for the process comprises n constants, $x^*_0, x^*_{-1}, \dots, x^*_{-n+1}$, that satisfy the equation $x(1, \omega) = -\Sigma_{1 \le i \le n} a_i x^*_{1-i} + y(1, \omega)$ with probability 1.[2]

6.2.1 Univariate ARIMA Processes

ARIMA stands for *an integrated autoregressive moving average* process. When $n > 0$ in equation 6.1 and the roots of the associated characteristic polynomial of such a process have absolute values less than 1, X is said to be integrated of order 0. When $n = 0$ and $\Sigma_{0 \le s \le \infty} b_s \ne 0$, X is still integrated of order 0.[3] An ARIMA process that is integrated of order 0 is in the vernacular of econometricians called an I(0) process. When k (1 $\le k \le n$) of the roots of the characteristic polynomial have values equal to 1, and the other roots have absolute values less than 1, X is said to be integrated of order k. It is called an I(k) process if its kth difference series, $\Delta^k X$, is an I(0) process.

ARIMA processes have many interesting properties. Two of them have an important bearing on the analysis of positively valued economic time series. E6.2.1 illustrates what I have in mind.

E6.2.1

Let $N = \{0, 1, \dots\}$ be the set of non-negative integers; let $(\Omega, \aleph, P(\cdot))$ be a probability space; and let $Y = \{y(t, \omega); t \in N\}$ and $\eta = \{\eta(t, \omega); t \in N - \{0\}\}$ be two families of random variables on $(\Omega, \aleph)$. Also, suppose that, relative to $P(\cdot)$, Y and η satisfy the following four conditions: (1) The members of η are independently and identically distributed with a continuous probability distribution that has mean 0, finite variance, σ_η^2, and is symmetric around 0; (2) for all $\omega \in \Omega$, $y(0, \omega) = 0$; (3) for all $t \in N - \{0\}$ and all $\omega \in \Omega$, $y(t, \omega) = y(t - 1, \omega) + \eta(t, \omega)$; and (4) for all $t \in N - \{0\}$ and all values of $y(0), \ldots, y(t - 1)$, $E(\eta(t, \omega) \mid y(0), \ldots, y(t - 1)) = 0$. Then Y is a random walk that has two characteristics of particular interest here. For one thing, the number of changes of signs of the $y(t, \omega)$ grows with t (very roughly speaking) at some constant multiple of $\sqrt{t}$. Also, if Π_n is the number of strictly positive terms among $y(1, \omega), \ldots, y(n, \omega)$, then (see theorems 1 and 2 in Feller 1966, pp. 398–399)

$$P(\Pi_n = k) = \binom{2k}{k}\binom{2n-2k}{n-k}^{\frac{1}{2^{2n}}}$$

and, for a fixed $\alpha \in (0, 1)$,

$$\lim_{n \to \infty} P(\Pi_n < n\alpha) \to 2(1/\pi) \text{ arc } \sin\sqrt{\alpha}. \tag{6.2}$$

The given limit distribution has density $(\pi(\alpha(1 - \alpha)^{\frac{1}{2}})^{-1}$, which is unbounded at 0 and 1 and has a minimum at ½. Consequently, for large n, Π_n/n is much more likely to be close to 0 or 1 than to ½.

The properties of Π_n and the fact that the number of crossings of $y(t, \omega)$ grows with t roughly at the rate of $\sqrt{t}$ imply that one should expect to observe long sequences of positive values of $y(t, \omega)$. In Feller 1957, Feller studied a random walk where $P(\eta(t, \omega) = 1) = P(\eta(t, \omega) = -1) = \frac{1}{2}$. He found that in such a process the chances are 1 in 10 that $y(t, \omega)$ will be positive more than 97.6 percent of the time, and that the chances are 1 in 5 that $y(t, \omega)$ will be positive 90.5 percent of the time.

The properties of random walks that I described in E6.2.1 are properties of all the ARIMA processes that I will be discussing in this book. Specifically: Let $\Psi(x) = 1$ or 0 according as $x > 0$ or not. Then it is a fact (see theorem 3 in Stigum 1975) that, if an I(1) ARIMA process $X = \{x(t, \omega); t \in N\}$ satisfies the three conditions

$$0 < \left| \sum_{0 \le s < \infty} b_s \right| < \infty,$$

the function $f(\lambda) = \left| \sum_{0 \le s < \infty} b_s e^{-is\lambda} \right|^2 \sigma_\eta^2$, where $\lambda \in [-\pi, \pi)$, is piecewise continuous and continuous in a neighborhood of 0,

and

the $\eta(t, \cdot)$ have finite fourth-order moments,

it is the case that

$$\lim_{T \to \infty} P(\omega \in \Omega: T^{-1}\Sigma_{1 \leq t \leq T}\Psi(x(t, \omega)) < \alpha) = 2(1/\pi) \text{ arc } \sin\sqrt{\alpha}. \qquad (6.3)$$

This and the fact that the crossings of an I(1) ARIMA process tends to grow with t as a multiple of $\sqrt{t}$ ensure that one is likely to observe long periods of positive values of I(1) ARIMA processes. Later I will show how this property of ARIMA processes can be used in statistical analyses of positively valued time series.[4]

Univariate ARIMA processes and their continuous analogues have been used to study such varied matters as the behavior of prices in the stock market (Cootner 1964) and the use of feedforward-feedback control systems in chemical engineering (Box and Jenkins 1970, chapter 12). The study of multivariate ARIMA processes and their use in econometrics took off in 1981with Clive Granger's discovery of cointegrated time series and with the development of new statistical methods by Peter Phillips (1991), James Stock and Mark Watson (1993), Søren Johansen (1995), and many others. In the next subsection I will discuss properties of multivariate ARIMA processes that are of particular interest in the present context.

6.2.2 Multivariate ARIMA Processes and Cointegrated Time Series
In chapters 7–9 of this book, the pertinent ARIMA processes are families of pairs or triples of random variables that have finite means and covariance matrices and may be integrated of various orders. Suppose that X = {x(t, ω); t $\in$ N} is a p-dimensional ARIMA process. Then there exist p × p matrices, A_i, i = 1, 2, ... , n, a p-dimensional, purely random vector-valued process, $\eta = \{\eta(t, \omega); t \in (\ldots, -1, 0, 1, \ldots)\}$, with mean 0 and finite covariance matrix, C, and a sequence of p × p matrices, B_s, s $\in$ N, such that, for t $\geq$ 1, (1) $A_0 = I_p$ (the p-dimensional identity matrix) and

$$\Sigma_{0 \leq i \leq n}A_i x(t - i, \omega) = y(t, \omega), \qquad (6.4)$$

(2) $y(t, \omega) = \Sigma_{0 \leq s < \infty}B_s\eta(t - s, \omega)$ and $\Sigma_{0 \leq s < \infty}B_sCB_s' < \infty$, and (3) the initial condition of the process comprises n vectors, x^*_j, j = 0, 1, ... , $-n + 1$, that satisfy the equation $x(1, \omega) = -\Sigma_{1 \leq i \leq n}A_i x^*_{1-i} + y(1, \omega)$ with probability 1. Such a process is an I(0) process if $\Sigma_{0 \leq s < \infty}B_s \neq 0$ and if the roots of $|A(z)|$—the determinant of the matrix polynomial, $A(z) = \Sigma_{0 \leq i \leq n} A_iz^{n-i}$—have absolute values less than 1. It is an I(k) process if $\Sigma_{0 \leq s < \infty} B_s \neq 0$ and if k, 1 $\leq$ k $\leq$ n, of the roots of $|A(z)|$ equal 1, and the other

roots have absolute values less than 1. Also, as in the univariate case, if X is a p-dimensional I(k) ARIMA process, then $\Delta^k X$ is an I(0) process.

For the purposes of this chapter it is an interesting fact that an ARIMA process can be formulated in different ways without changing its family of probability distributions. E6.2.2 illustrates what I have in mind.[5]

E6.2.2

Suppose that $X = \{x(t, \omega); t \in N\}$ is a two-dimensional ARIMA process on a probability space, $(\Omega, \aleph, P(\cdot))$. Also suppose that X satisfies the stochastic difference equation

$$x(t, \omega) + Ax(t - 1, \omega) = \eta(t, \omega), \qquad t \in N - \{0\} \tag{6.5}$$

where the $\eta(t)$ constitute a purely random process with mean 0 and finite covariance matrix, C, where $E(\eta(t, \omega) \,|\, x(0), \ldots, x(t-1)) = 0$ a.e., and where $A = (a_{ij})$ with $a_{11} = -0.6$, $a_{12} = -0.8$, $a_{21} = -0.1$, and $a_{22} = -0.8$. Then $|(A(z))| = (1 - 0.4z)(1 - z)$. Hence, with $a' = (-0.4, 0.1)$ and $b' = (1, -2)$, I can reformulate equation 6.5 as

$$\Delta x(t, \omega) = (ab')x(t - 1, \omega) + \eta(t, \omega), \qquad t \in N - \{0\}. \tag{6.6}$$

I can also write the same equation as

$$(x_1(t, \omega) - 2x_2(t, \omega))$$
$$= 0.4(x_1(t - 1, \omega) - 2x_2(t - 1, \omega)) + (\eta_1(t, \omega) - 2\eta_2(t, \omega)) \tag{6.7}$$

and as

$$\Delta x(t, \omega) = a(x_1(t - 1, \omega) - 2x_2(t - 1, \omega)) + \eta(t, \omega), \qquad t \in N - \{0\}. \tag{6.8}$$

Now, X is a solution to equation 6.5, and equations 6.6–6.8 describe some of the characteristics of this solution. For example, equation 6.6 suggests that ΔX is wide-sense stationary if the $b'x(t - 1, \omega)$ constitute a wide-sense stationary process. Equation 6.7 claims that one can chose the $b'x(t - 1, \omega)$ so that they constitute a wide-sense stationary solution to a stochastic difference equation. Finally, equation 6.8—the error-correction formulation of equation 6.5—suggests that the equation $x_1(t, \omega) = 2x_2(t, \omega)$ depicts an equilibrium configuration of the sample paths of X.

For present purposes it is important that any p-dimensional ARIMA process can be formulated as an error-correction model. Let

$\Pi = -I_p - \Sigma_{1 \leq i \leq n} A_i$, and let $\Gamma_i = A_{i+1} + \cdots + A_n, i = 1, \ldots, n - 1$. Then the ARIMA process in equation 6.4 can be written as

$$\Delta x(t, \omega) = \Pi x(t - 1, \omega) + \Sigma_{1 \leq i \leq n-1} \Gamma_i \, \Delta x(t - i, \omega) + y(t, \omega). \tag{6.9}$$

With such an error-correction description of an ARIMA process, I can formulate a characterization of cointegrated I(1) ARIMA processes that is suitable for this book. In my formulation, a p-dimensional I(1) ARIMA process is taken to be cointegrated of order C(1, 1) if there exists a non-null p-dimensional vector, β, such that $\beta'x(t)$ is wide-sense stationary. If it exists, β is termed a cointegrating vector.

Consider the ARIMA process in equation 6.9, and assume that X is an I(1) process whose family of error terms, $\{y(t, \omega); t \in N\}$, constitutes a purely random vector-valued process with mean 0 and finite covariance matrix with positive diagonal elements. Suppose also that the rank of Π is r, and that $0 < r < p$. Then there exist $p \times r$ matrices, α and β, of rank r such that $\Pi = \alpha\beta'$ and such that $\beta'x(t - 1, \omega)$ is wide-sense stationary. Hence, X is C(1, 1) cointegrated, and the rows of β' are cointegrating vectors. There may be many pairs, (α, β) that satisfy the equation $\Pi = \alpha\beta'$. Whatever pair of matrices, α and β, one chooses, the rows of β' are linearly independent cointegrating vectors that form an r-dimensional space that Johansen (1995, p. 37) calls the cointegrating space of X.

Thus, it seems to be the case that an I(1) ARIMA process is cointegrated if and only if the Π matrix in its error-correction formulation has positive but not full rank. That is very interesting. However, it is not always easy to fathom that a given ARIMA process can be formulated as an error-correction model. Also, some times an error-correction model may seem to be an imaginary error-correction model in the sense of not being anchored in economic theory. Here is a relevant example.

E6.2.3
Consider a two-dimensional I(1) ARIMA process that satisfies the stochastic difference equations

$$\Delta x_1(t, \omega) = \eta_1(t, \omega)$$

and

$$x_2(t, \omega) - x_1(t - 1, \omega) = \eta_2(t, \omega), \qquad t \in N - \{0\} \tag{6.10}$$

where the $\eta(t, \omega)$ constitute a purely random process with mean 0 and finite covariance matrix C. These two equations do not look like an error-correction model. Yet they can be rewritten as

$$\Delta x(t, \omega) = (0,1)'(1,-1)x(t-1, \omega) + \eta(t, \omega), \quad t \in N - \{0\} \tag{6.11}$$

which looks like an ordinary error-correction model with $\Pi = (0, 1)'(1, -1)$. Looking back at equation 6.10, I cannot help but think that equation 6.11 is an imaginary error-correction model. It has been obtained by manipulating equations without reference to economic theory. Thus, equation 6.11 depicts a relation among the variables in equation 6.10 that Haavelmo would have characterized as confluent (see Haavelmo 1944, p. 29).

The example may look trivial, but it is not. The model in equation 6.10 is a theoretical model of the dynamics of spot and forward rates in the Swiss franc–US dollar market that Harald Goldstein analyzes in chapter 7. (See figure 7.2.1 and equation 7.48.) It is also Johansen's model with $\alpha = -1$ in example 4.1 on p. 46 of Johansen 1995. Johansen insists that his variables, X_{1t} and X_{2t}, are cointegrated with cointegrating vector, $(1, -1)$. My imaginary error-correction model, equation 6.11, provides no objection to that. Yet I wonder why, in equation 6.10, $x_1(t)$ and $x_2(t)$ are cointegrated and $x_2(t)$ and $x_1(t-1)$ are not.[6] The answer is important, and figure 6.2 shows why. The figure is based on the weekly observations I have on spot and forward dollar–franc exchange rates during the period 2001w19–2005w3. For purposes of this discussion, DSpot = $\Delta x_1(t)$, DisequilibriumBFS = $x_2(t) - x_1(t-1)$, and DisequilibriumNPF = $x_1(t) - x_2(t)$.

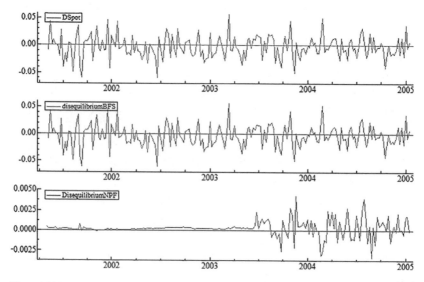

Figure 6.2
Time series of $\Delta x_1(t)$, $x_2(t)-x_1(t-1)$ and $x_1(t)-x_2(t)$ in E6.2.3.

Table 6.2
Normality test for the series in figure 6.2.

DSpot	Asymptotic test	Chi^2(2) = 1.3180 [0.5174]
DisequilibriumBFS	Asymptotic test	Chi^2(2) = 1.5978 [0.4498]
	Normality test	Chi^2(2) = 2.3803 [0.3042]
DisequilibriumNPF	Asymptotic test	Chi^2(2) = 159.08 [0.0000]**
	Normality test	Chi^2(2) = 82.469 [0.0000]**

With 193 observations, all three series failed the ADF tests. The corresponding normality tests ended as shown in table 6.2.

The series for $(x_1(t) - x_2(t))$ exhibits a definite break at 2003(26); the series for $\Delta x_1(t)$ and $(x_2(t) - x_1(t-1))$ do not. Figure 6.2 and tables 6.2–6.4 suggest that in fact it is only the series for $(x_1(t) - x_2(t))$ that suffers from a break. We see that the variance of the series, $(x_1(t) - x_2(t))$, after the break is roughly 41.46 times larger than the variance of the same series before the break. In contrast, the variances of the two series, $\Delta x_1(t)$ and $(x_2(t) - x_1(t-1))$, are, after the break, respectively 0.76 and 0.75 times smaller than the variances of these two series before the break.

The preceding observations may not suffice to establish that the econometric model in equation 6.11 is an imaginary error-correction model. They may also not convince the reader that it is useful to look for other cointegration relationships than the one on which the error-correction model in equation 6.9 insists. Be that as it may, I believe that E6.2.3 with figure 6.2 and table 6.2–6.4 can serve as a good point of departure for a serious discussion of the case studies in chapter 7 and in the appendix to chapter 7.[7]

6.3 ARIMA Processes and the Analysis of Positively Valued Time Series

Hall, Anderson, and Granger, in their 1992 study of the behavior of US Treasury Bills, discovered that yields to maturity on Treasury Bills behave as cointegrated I(1) processes. Also, during periods in which the Federal Reserve specifically targets short-term interest rates, the spread between yields at different maturity define the cointegrating vectors. Yet Hall et al. observe in a note that yields to maturity on Treasury Bills cannot be integrated processes in the strict sense, because nominal yields are bounded below at 0 whereas integrated processes are unbounded (ibid., pp. 116–118, 123).

Table 6.3
Means and correlations of the series in figure 6.2 before the break.

Means		
DSpot	DisequilibriumBFS	DisequilibriumNPF
−0.0035161	−0.0037436	0.00022756

Standard deviations (using T − 1)		
DSpot	DisequilibriumBFS	DisequilibriumNPF
0.021622	0.021602	0.00023037

Correlation matrix			
	DSpot	DisequilibriumBFS	DisequilibriumNPF
DSpot	1.0000	0.99994	0.092287
DisequilibriumBFS	0.99994	1.0000	0.081709
DisequilibriumNPF	0.092287	0.081709	1.0000

Table 6.4
Means and correlations of the series in figure 6.2 after the break.

Means		
DSpot	DisequilibriumBFS	DisequilibriumNPF
−0.0021691	−0.0025116	0.00034251

Standard deviations (using T − 1)		
DSpot	DisequilibriumBFS	DisequilibriumNPF
0.018883	0.018706	0.0014833

Correlation matrix			
	DSpot	DisequilibriumBFS	DisequilibriumNPF
DSpot	1.0000	0.99693	0.15832
DisequilibriumBFS	0.99693	1.0000	0.080531
DisequilibriumNPF	0.15832	0.080531	1.0000

In chapter 7 below, Harald Goldstein's and André Anundsen's empirical analyses demonstrate that spot and forward dollar–franc exchange rates behave as two cointegrated I(1) processes. In chapter 8 below, Goldstein's and Anundsen's empirical analyses demonstrate that the franc–euro, euro–dollar, and franc–dollar exchange rates behave as a triple of I(2) second-order random processes that are non-linearly cointegrated. Obviously, Goldstein's and Anundsen's empirical analyses in chapters 7 and 8 are subject to the same caveat that Hall et al. revealed in a note: Spot and forward exchange rates cannot be integrated processes in the strict sense, since their values are bounded below at 0.

Hall et al. do not claim that yields on Treasury Bills are cointegrated I(1) ARIMA processes. As I understand them, they insist that their theory about the behavior of yields on Treasury Bills is valid only if there exists an I(1) cointegrated ARIMA process of which their data are observations. Similarly, in chapter 7 below I claim that my theory about the dynamics of spot and forward rates is empirically relevant if there exists a cointegrated I(1) ARIMA process of which my data of spot and forward rates are observations. Goldstein's and Anundsen's empirical analyses can be seen as a search for such a cointegrated pair of ARIMA processes. Finally, in chapter 8 below I claim that my theory about the dynamics of three related exchange rates is empirically relevant if there exists a non-linearly cointegrated I(2) ARIMA process of which my data are observations. Again, Goldstein's and Anundsen's empirical analyses can be seen as a search for such an ARIMA process.

The data of Treasury Bill yields presented by Hall et al., like Goldstein's and Anundsen's data of foreign-exchange rates, are from consecutive observations over long periods of time. Such data can be observations of an ARIMA process only if the pertinent ARIMA process experiences long periods in which its variables assume positive values. Here is a case in point.

Figure 6.3 displays a time series of an I(1) ARIMA process that satisfies the stochastic difference equations

$$X(t) = 1.5X(t-1) - 0.5X(t-2) + \eta(t), \qquad t > 0$$

with initial values, $X(0) = X(-1) = 0 = \eta(0)$, and with error terms, the $\eta(t)$s, that are independently and identically distributed normal variables with mean 0 and variance 1.

It is one thing to interpret the claim of Hall et al. and the results of Goldstein and Anundsen in chapters 7 and 8. It is another thing to

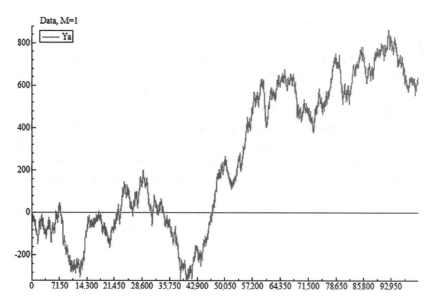

Figure 6.3
A PcGive Monte Carlo simulation of an I(1) ARIMA process.

express the interpretation in the axioms of a formal theory-data confrontation. The following example shows how that is done in a relevant situation with the help of auxiliary variables.

E6.3.1

Consider the market for spot and one-week-forward dollar–franc exchange rates, and let $x_1(t)$ and $x_2(t)$, respectively denote the spot and one-week-forward rate at time t, where $t \in N$. Let $\eta(t)$, $t \in N$, be a sequence of independently and identically distributed random variables with mean 0 and variance σ_η^2. I believe that the agents in the market in an aggregate sense entertain unbiased expectations about the next week's value of the dollar–franc exchange rate. In symbols, I believe that for all $t \in N - \{0\}$ that

$$x_1(t + 1) = x_2(t) + \eta(t + 1), \tag{6.12}$$

and that $\eta(t + 1)$ is orthogonal to $x(s)$ for $s = 0, 1, \dots , t$. I also believe that the way the agents in the market—again in an aggregate sense— form their expectations is as described in the equation

$$x_2(t) = x_2(t - 1) + \alpha(x_1(t) - x_2(t - 1)), \ t \in N - \{0\} \tag{6.13}$$

where $\alpha \in (0, 1)$. In short, I believe that the franc–dollar spot and forward exchange rates behave as if they were generated by the following pair of equations for a two-dimensional I(1) ARIMA process:

$$x_1(t) - x_2(t - 1) = \eta(t), \qquad t > 0 \tag{6.14}$$

$$x_2(t) - x_2(t - 1) = \alpha\eta(t), \qquad t > 0. \tag{6.15}$$

It is important to observe here that the deliberations which I describe above pinpoint arguments that run through my head before I start writing down axioms for a formal theory-data confrontation. Thus, equations 6.12–6.15 reside in my head. They are not part of the formal theory-data confrontation that follows.

To make the example short, I presume that I have accurate observations of both the spot rates and the forward rates. Also, I insist that in the present theory-data confrontation I need only formulate axioms for a single universe—the data universe. Let $(\Omega_P, \Gamma_P, (\Omega_P, \aleph_P, P_P(\cdot))$ be the data universe In this data universe two of the axioms describe conceptual properties of the system. The first insists that Ω_P is a space of sequences.

D1

$\Omega_P \subset (R_+^2 \times R^3)^N$. Thus, $\omega_P \in \Omega_P$ only if ω_P is a sequence of vectors, $(x_{1t}, x_{2t}, y_{1t}, y_{2t}, \eta_t)$, all of which belong to $(R_+^2 \times R^3)$. In short, $\omega_P = (x_1, x_2, y_1, y_2, \eta)$ for some $(x_1, x_2, y_1, y_2, \eta) \in (R_+^2 \times R^3)^N$, where $N = \{0, 1, \ldots \}$.

In this axiom, x_1 and x_2 represent the sequences of spot and one-week-forward rates. The η sequence is a sequence of error terms. The two y sequences are to play auxiliary variables for the x sequences. I will show how in the third axiom.

D2

For each $t \in N$, let the vector-valued function, $(x_1, x_2, y_1, y_2, \eta)(t, \cdot): \Omega_P \to (R_+^2 \times R^3)$ be defined by the equations $(x_1, x_2, y_1, y_2, \eta)(t, \omega_P) = \omega_{Pt}$, and $\omega_P \in \Omega_P$, where ω_{Pt} is the tth component of ω_P. For all $t \in N$, $(x_1, x_2, y_1, y_2, \eta)(t, \cdot)$ is measurable with respect to $\aleph_P$. Also, relative to $P_P(\cdot)$ and subject to the conditions on which Γ_P insists, the family of finite-dimensional probability distributions of the variables in $\{(x_1, x_2, y_1, y_2, \eta)(t, \omega_P); t \in N\}$ is the true family of finite-dimensional probability distributions of the given variables. I denote it by TPD.

The third axiom describes how y_1 and y_2 serve as auxiliary variables for x_1 and x_2. In this axiom I claim that positive observations of x_1 and x_2 are observations of the corresponding y_1 and y_2 as well.

D3
For all $t \in N$ and $\omega_P \in \Omega_P$, $(x_1, x_2)(t, \omega_P) = \max[(y_1, y_2)(t, \omega_P), 0]$.

Next I will formulate two axioms that express my beliefs about the behavior of spot and one-week-forward rates. In reading the axioms, note that they concern y_1 and y_2 and not x_1 and x_2.

D4
For all $t \in N$ and $\omega_P \in \Omega_P$, $y_1(t + 1, \omega_P) = y_2(t, \omega_P) + \eta(t + 1, \omega_P)$.

D5
For all $t \in N-\{0\}$ and $\omega_P \in \Omega_P$,

$$y_2(t, \omega_P) = y_2(t - 1, \omega_P) + \alpha(y_1(t, \omega_P) - y_2(t - 1, \omega_P)).$$

D4 insists that the forward rate at t is an unbiased predictor of the spot rate at $t + 1$. D5 claims that the agents in the market form their expectations in accord with Cagan's (1956) adaptive expectations hypothesis.

The last two axioms concern the probability distributions of the $\eta(t)$.

D6
Relative to $P_P(\cdot)$, the family of random variables, $\{\eta(t, \omega_P); t \in N\}$ are independently and identically distributed with mean 0 and finite variance, σ_η^2.

D7
Relative to $P_P(\cdot)$ and for all $t \in N - \{0\}$, $E(\eta(t, \omega_P) \mid y(0), \dots, y(t - 1)) = 0$.

From these axioms I can deduce several interesting observations.
First,

$$y_1(t, \omega_P) - y_2(t - 1, \omega_P) = \eta(t, \omega_P), \quad t > 0 \tag{6.16}$$

and

$$y_2(t, \omega_P) - y_2(t - 1, \omega_P) = \alpha\eta(t, \omega_P), \quad t > 0. \tag{6.17}$$

Second, by deducting equation 6.17 from equation 6.16, I find that

$$y_1(t, \omega_P) - y_2(t, \omega_P) = (1 - \alpha)\eta(t, \omega_P), \ t > 0. \tag{6.18}$$

Hence, the $y_1(t)$ and $y_2(t)$ constitute a cointegrated I(1) ARIMA process with cointegrating vector (1, –1).

Third, equations 6.16 and 6.17 present a model of an error-correction equation,

$$(\Delta y_1(t, \omega_P), \Delta y_2(t, \omega_P))'$$
$$= -\Pi \ (y_1(t-1, \omega_P), y_2(t-1, \omega_P))' + (\eta(t, \omega_P, \alpha\eta(t, \omega_P))', \tag{6.19}$$

in which $\Pi = (1, 0)'(1, -1)$. Equation 6.19 is an analogue of the error-correction model that Anundsen estimates in chapter 7.

Fourth, an analysis of the time series of observations of spot and forward dollar–franc exchange rates that I have reveals that the series for $y_1(t) - y_2(t-1)$ and $\Delta y_2(t)$ are wide-sense stationary and do not suffer from the break that the series for $y_1(t) - y_2(t)$ displays.

Fifth, and most important, axiom D3 and the fact that I have positive observations of $x_1(t)$ and $x_2(t)$ imply that the latter variables share the characteristics of $y_1(t)$ and $y_2(t)$ in the observation period. In other words, my observations of the spot and one-week-forward dollar–franc exchange rates seem to have been observations of a cointegrated I(1) ARIMA process with cointegrating vector (1, –1).

I have observations of about 200 consecutive pairs of spot and one-week-forward dollar–franc exchange rates. They are positive, and in E6.3.1 I take them to be observations of y_1 and y_2 in a long stretch of positive y pairs. For the statistical analysis, it is not necessary to know the value of t for which the pertinent positive stretch of y's begins. I am free to choose that value myself. In fact, I can analyze my data as if they are observations of the associated auxiliary process during any one of the latter's positive stretches. There is no need to specify which positive stretch.

7 Analysis of Positively Valued Economic Time Series

A long time ago, in 1938, John Maynard Keynes insisted that economics was "a science of thinking in terms of models joined to the art of choosing models which are relevant to the contemporary world" (Keynes 1973, p. 297). In the context of this book, what Keynes called "the art of choosing models which are relevant to the contemporary world" becomes the art of choosing variables and axioms for a pertinent theory-data confrontation. The right variables may be variables of the theory at stake, log transforms of such variables, and all sorts of auxiliary variables. The right axioms may be basic axioms and theorems of the theory joined to assertions that describe the role of the chosen auxiliary variables. The best choice of variables and axioms is determined by the data on hand and by the salient characteristics of available statistical programs.

In this chapter the theory is about behavior characteristics of spot and forward exchange rates—two positively valued random variables. The statistical programs on hand are designed for the analysis of time series of variables that assume both positive and negative values. This causes a serious problem for the empirical analysis of spot and forward exchange rates. The pertinent researcher can solve the problem in one of two ways. The standard way is to formulate axioms for a data confrontation of log transforms of the actual theory variables with log transforms of the data variables. A different way is to formulate axioms for the theory-data confrontation in which actual and auxiliary theory and data variables interact in such a way that the problem disappears. I will choose the second way, and in section 7.1 I show why. Specifically, I delineate rough contours of a pertinent theory and explain why I choose not to use the standard way to solve the given problem. The theoretical underpinnings I need to justify my solution to the problem were presented in sections 6.2 and 6.3.

This chapter has two purposes. One is to study the methodological problems that arise in analyzing positively valued time series in foreign exchange. The other is to contrast the statistical analysis of time series that a formal theory-data confrontation prescribes with the statistical analysis of time series that present-day econometric theory prescribes. In section 7.2, in order to illustrate the striking dissimilarity between the two ways of analyzing time series, I formulate an axiomatic data confrontation of a theory of the dynamics of spot and forward rates in foreign exchange. The data I have consist of observations of spot and forward rates in the market for Swiss francs and US dollars. In section 7.3, Harald Goldstein carries out the analysis of the data that my theory-data confrontation prescribes, and in section 7.4 André Anundsen analyzes the same data with David Hendry's and Søren Johansen's methods. Goldstein's and Anundsen's results differ in ways that have a very interesting bearing on the problem of how best to incorporate economic theory in empirical analyses.

7.1 Spot and Forward Rates in Foreign Exchange

In this chapter I will study the dynamics of a market in which two currencies are traded. One of them is the domestic currency and the other is some foreign currency. The agents engage in both spot and forward transactions. I let S denote the spot exchange rate (that is, the domestic price of the foreign currency), and I let F denote the corresponding forward rate (i.e., the rate agreed now for the domestic price of the foreign currency a given number of periods ahead). I assume that the market is frictionless in the sense that there are no transaction costs and no barriers to arbitrage.

A frictionless foreign-exchange market is efficient if a trader by speculation alone cannot earn excess returns. A frictionless foreign-exchange market is efficient only if both the Uncovered Interest Parity Condition and the Covered Interest Parity Condition are satisfied. The Uncovered Interest Parity Condition insists that in equilibrium a trader's expected gain from acquiring units of the foreign currency must equal the opportunity cost of holding funds in the domestic currency rather than the other. In symbols,

$$S_{t+k}^{e}/S_t = (1 + i_t)/(1 + i^*_t), \tag{7.1}$$

where S_t and S_{t+k} denote, respectively, the spot exchange rate at time t and $t + k$, where i_t and i^*_t are the nominal k-period interest rates available, respectively, on similar domestic and foreign securities, and where e denotes the market expectation based on information at time t. The Covered Interest Parity Condition insists that, if there are no barriers to arbitrage across international financial markets, a frictionless efficient foreign-exchange market in equilibrium must satisfy the condition

$$F^{(k)}_t/S_t = (1 + i_t)/(1 + i^*_t), \tag{7.2}$$

where $F^{(k)}_t$ is the k-period-forward exchange rate, S_t is the spot exchange rate, and i_t and i^*_t are the interest rates I discussed above.[1]

By combining equations 7.1 and 7.2, I find that in equilibrium the exchange market I consider is efficient only if

$$S_{t+k}^e = F^{(k)}_t . \tag{7.3}$$

Theorists believe that a frictionless foreign-exchange market will function efficiently if the market participants, in an aggregate sense, are risk neutral and are endowed with rational expectations. The claim that the agents in a market are risk neutral and endowed with rational expectations is called the Simple Efficient-Markets Hypothesis. (See Sarno and Taylor 2002, p. 10.) I will use it and equation 7.3 with k = 1 to formulate a theory of the dynamics of the currency market I discussed above.

My theory of the salient characteristics of efficient exchange in two foreign spot and forward markets contains five basic assertions with six undefined terms: a week, S, F, Ω, $\aleph$, and $P(\cdot)$. The first four assertions delineate characteristic features of the conceptual framework of the theory:

1. A period is a week, and, beginning at some arbitrary time in the past, the weeks are numbered consecutively with integers from the set $N = \{0, 1, \ldots\}$.
2. For all t in N, the spot exchange rate, S, is a non-negative real number; i.e., $S_t \in R_+$, $t \in N$.
3. For all t in N, the one-week-forward rate, F, is a non-negative real number; i.e., $F_t \in R_+$, $t \in N$.
4. The families $\{S_t; t \in N\}$ and $\{F_t; t \in N\}$ constitute two second-order random processes on some probability space, $(\Omega, \aleph, P(\cdot))$, where Ω is a subset of a vector space, $\aleph$ is a σ field of subsets of Ω, and $P(\cdot): \aleph \rightarrow [0, 1]$ is a probability measure.

The fifth and last assertion aims to determine law-like properties of S_t and F_t. When interpreting S_{t+1}^e to be the rationally expected value of

S_{t+1}, given the past values of S and F, this assertion ends up specifying how the Simple Efficient-Markets Hypothesis functions in the present setting.

5. Let S_{t+1}^{e} denote the expected value of S_{t+1} with respect to $P(\cdot)$, given the observed values of S_s and F_s for $s = 0, 1, \ldots, t$. For all $t \in N$, $F_t = S_{t+1}^{e}$.

The family of models of the five assertions above constitutes a theory of foreign exchange that delineates characteristic features of the families of finite-dimensional probability distributions that determine the behavior over time of spot and one-week-forward rates in a given currency market. From the point of view of a test of the empirical relevance of the Simple Efficient-Markets Hypothesis, the preceding five assertions possess a family of models that is much too large. In section 7.2, I add to the five assertions above several axioms concerning law-like properties of S_t and F_t. In sections 7.3 and 7.4, Harald Goldstein and André Anundsen use the enlarged theory to carry out meaningful tests of the empirical relevance of the hypothesis in the two data universes illustrated in figure 6.1.

7.1.1 Positive Theory Variables and Log-Transformed Data Variables

Many of the most advanced methods in time-series analysis presume that the data variables assume both negative and positive values. Since spot and forward exchange rates assume only positive values, applied econometricians often choose to analyze logarithmic transforms of these variables rather than the variables themselves. Such a choice of data variables may affect the results of the empirical analysis in unintended ways.

Consider the Uncovered and the Covered Interest Parity conditions and their symbolic renditions in equations 7.1 and 7.2. Let lower-case letters denote logarithmic transforms of the given variables; e.g., $s_t = \log S_t$ and $f^{(k)}_t = \log F^{(k)}_t$. Then the assertions in equations 7.1 and 7.2 can be replaced with the assertions in the following two equations:

$$\log S_{t+k}^{e} - s_t \approx i_t - i^*_t, \tag{7.4}$$

$$f^{(k)}_t - s_t \approx i_t - i^*_t. \tag{7.5}$$

These equations raise two questions: How good are the approximations in equations 7.4 and 7.5? May one substitute $(\log S_{t+k})^e$ for $\log S_{t+k}^e$ in equation 7.4?

Applied econometricians seem to believe that the right-hand sides of equations 7.4 and 7.5 provide very good approximations to the right-hand sides of equations 7.1 and 7.2. If they are correct, one may deduce from these equations that

$$f^{(k)}_t = \log S_{t+k}^e. \tag{7.6}$$

Whether one can substitute s_{t+k}^e for $\log S_{t+k}^e$ in equations 7.4 and 7.6 is, however, not certain, since s_{t+k}^e need not, even approximately, be equal to $\log S_{t+k}^e$. For example, if S_{t+k} is log normally distributed given the information available at t, then

$$\log S_{t+k}^e = s_{t+k}^e + \tfrac{1}{2}E[(s_{t+k} - s_{t+k}^e)^2 \mid \text{given information at t].} \tag{7.7}$$

Thus, if in my five assertions above I were to substitute s_{t+1} for $\log S_{t+1}$, f_t for $\log F_t$, and s_{t+1}^e for $\log S_{t+1}^e$, and insist that $f_t = s_{t+1}^e$, I would end up with a theory whose family of models would have characteristics that differed significantly from the characteristics of the family of models of the original theory.[2] Consequently, a time-series analysis of log transforms of the observed values of the spot and forward rates may establish behavior characteristics of the transformed data variables that need not be characteristic properties of the behavior of spot and forward rates in the original theory. For example, a statistical analysis of the transformed data might reject the empirical relevance of the Simple Efficient Markets Hypothesis, whereas a statistical analysis of the original data might accept its empirical relevance.

7.2 A Formal Time-Series Analysis of an Economic Theory

In this section I will develop a formal theory-data confrontation of an enlarged version of the theory of spot and forward exchange that I presented in section 7.1. As in chapter 6, the theory universe, the data universe, and the bridge are represented by $(\Omega_T, \Gamma_T, (\Omega_T, \aleph_T, P_T(\cdot)))$, $(\Omega_P, \Gamma_P, (\Omega_P, \aleph_P, P_P(\cdot)))$, and $(\Omega, \Gamma_{T,P})$. Also, sequences of vectors in the theory universe function as vector-valued sequences in Ω_T and as vector-valued random processes on $(\Omega_T, \aleph_T)$. Similarly, sequences of vectors in the data universe function as vector-valued sequences in Ω_P and as vector-valued random processes on $(\Omega_P, \aleph_P)$. I assume throughout that Ω_T and Ω_P are disjoint, that $\aleph_T$ and $\aleph_P$ are stochastically independent, and that the probability space, $(\Omega_T \times \Omega_P, \aleph, P(\cdot))$, is as I described it in chapter 2.

7.2.1 The Theory Universe

Consider the foreign-exchange market in section 7.1. Let S and F denote a sequence of spot exchange rates and the corresponding sequence of one-period-forward rates. Let y and λ denote two sequences of auxiliary variables, and let η and u denote two sequences of error terms. They are sequences that I use to delineate salient characteristics of the finite-dimensional probability distributions of the components of S and F. The components of the sextuple $(S, F, y, \lambda, \eta, u)$ are the vector-valued variables that roam around in the theory universe. Their values are values that the given sextuple might realize at different points in time— e.g., in the sixth week of the year 2000 or the twenty-fourth week of the year 2006.

Two of the members of Γ_T describe the conceptual framework of the dynamics of spot and forward rates in the theory universe.

A1

$\Omega_T \subset (R_+^2 \times R^4)^N$. Thus, $\omega_T \in \Omega_T$ only if ω_T is a sequence of vectors, $(S_t, F_t, y_t, \lambda_t, \eta_t, u_t)$, all of which belong to $(R_+^2 \times R^4)$. In short, $\omega_T = (S, F, y, \lambda, \eta, u)$ for some $(S, F, y, \lambda, \eta, u) \in (R_+^2 \times R^4)^N$, where $N = \{0, 1, \dots \}$.

A2

For each $t \in N$, let the vector valued function $(S,F,y, \lambda, \eta, u)(t, \cdot): \Omega_T \to R_+^2 \times R^4$ be defined by the equations $(S(t, \omega_T),F(t, \omega_T),y(t, \omega_T), \lambda(t, \omega_T),$ $\eta(t, \omega_T), u(t, \omega_T)) = \omega_{Tt}$ and $\omega_T \in \Omega_T$, where ω_{Tt} is the tth component of ω_T. The functions $(S, F, y, \lambda, \eta, u)(t, \cdot): \Omega_T \to R_+^2 \times R^4$, $t \in N$, are measurable with respect to $\aleph_T$. Also, the family of finite-dimensional probability distributions of the random vectors, $\{(S, F, y, \lambda, \eta, u)(t, \omega_T); t \in N\}$, that $P_T(\cdot)$ determines is the family of probability distributions that the researcher in charge, subject to the conditions on which Γ_T insists, assigns to the given functions. I designate it RPD.

The law-like properties of the given spot and forward markets are expressed in A3–A7. The first three of them describe the roles that the auxiliary theoretical variables play in the present theory-data confrontation. Specifically, A3 describes the way the $y(t, \cdot)$ and the $\lambda(t, \cdot)$, respectively, function as auxiliary variables for the $S(t, \cdot)$ and the $F(t, \cdot)$.

A3

For all $\omega_T \in \Omega_T$, and for all $t \in N$,

$S(t, \omega_T) = \max(y(t, \omega_T), 0)$ and $F(t, \omega_T) = \max(\lambda(t, \omega_T), 0)$.   (7.8)

If we substitute $S(t + 1, \cdot)$ for $y(t + 1, \cdot)$ and $F(t, \cdot)$ for $\lambda(t, \cdot)$ in equation 7.9 below, we see from equation 7.11 that A4 postulates a relationship between the $y(t + 1, \cdot)$ and the $\lambda(t, \cdot)$ that is an analogue of assertion 7.3 in section 7.1.

A4

Let $\acute{y} \in R_{++}$ be a constant. For each $\omega_T \in \Omega_T$ and $t \in N$,

$$\eta(0, \omega_T) = 0;\ y(0, \omega_T) = \acute{y} \text{ and } y(t + 1, \omega_T) = \lambda(t, \omega_T) + \eta(t + 1, \omega_T). \quad (7.9)$$

With $F(t, \cdot)$ substituted for $\lambda(t, \cdot)$ and $S(t, \cdot)$ substituted for $y(t, \cdot)$, A5 describes how the current and past spot rates determine the current forward rate.

A5

Let $\varphi \in (0, 1)$ be a constant. For each $\omega_T \in \Omega_T$ and $t \in N - \{0\}$,

$$\lambda(0, \omega_T) = \varphi y(0, \omega_T)$$

and

$$\lambda(t, \omega_T) = \lambda(t - 1, \omega_T) + \varphi(y(t, \omega_T) - \lambda(t - 1, \omega_T)). \quad (7.10)$$

In economic thought, the relation between $\lambda(t, \cdot)$ and $y(t, \cdot)$ in equation 7.10 is called the *adaptive expectations hypothesis*. Usually attributed to Phillip Cagan (1956, p. 37), it has appeared in various guises throughout the development of the rational-expectations hypothesis. For example, in Cagan's study of the monetary dynamics of hyperinflation, $y(t, \cdot)$ and $\lambda(t, \cdot)$ are interpreted, respectively, as the actual and the expected rate of change of prices. In Marc Nerlove's study of adaptive expectations and cobweb phenomena (1958, p. 231), $y(t, \cdot)$ and $\lambda(t, \cdot)$ are taken to be, respectively, the actual price and the expected normal price of an agricultural commodity.

The last two members of Γ_T describe characteristics of the probability distributions in RPD. They impose conditions on the auxiliary variables, y and λ, and on η, and u, the error components of $(S, F, y, \lambda, \eta, u)(\cdot)$. I can derive the remaining conditions on $(S, F)(\cdot)$ from those conditions and A3.

A6

Relative to $P_T(\cdot)$, the families of functions $\{\eta(t, \omega_T); t \geq 1\}$ and $\{u(t, \omega_T); t \geq 1\}$ constitute independently distributed, purely random processes with means 0 and finite positive variances σ_η^2 and σ_u^2.

A7

Relative to $P_T(\cdot)$, the η, u, λ, and y components of the family of random functions $\{(S, F, y, \lambda, \eta, u)(t, \omega_T); t \in N\}$ satisfy the following conditions: For each $t \in N - \{0\}$,

$$E\{\eta(t, \omega_T) \,|\, (y, \lambda)(0), \ldots, (y, \lambda)(t-1)\} = 0 \text{ a.e.} \tag{7.11}$$

and

$$E\{u(t, \omega_T) \,|\, (y, \lambda)(0), \ldots, (y, \lambda)(t-1), y(t)\} = 0 \text{ a.e.} \tag{7.12}$$

Axioms A1–A7 delineate all the positive analogies of the given markets that are at stake in the present theory-data confrontation and nothing else. They can be read to insist that in equilibrium a frictionless currency market is efficient if the agents' rational expectations about future spot rates in the aggregate are unbiased. This hypothesis has several interesting consequences that I list in T7.5.

T7.5

Suppose that axioms A1–A7 are valid, and let φ be the constant in A5. Then the following assertions are valid:

(1) For all $t \in N$ and relative to $P_T(\cdot)$,

$$\lambda(t, \omega_T) = E\{y(t+1) \,|\, y(0), \ldots, y(t)\} \text{ a.e.} \tag{7.13}$$

(2) For each $\omega_T \in \Omega_T$ and $t \in N - \{0\}$, $y(t, \omega_T)$ satisfies the conditions

$$y(1, \omega_T) = \varphi y(0) + \eta(1, \omega_T)$$

and   (7.14)

$$y(t+1, \omega_T) = y(t, \omega_T) + \eta(t+1, \omega_T) - (1-\varphi)\eta(t, \omega_T).$$

(3) For each $\omega_T \in \Omega_T$ and $t \in N - \{0\}$, $\lambda(t, \omega_T)$ satisfies the conditions

$$\lambda(0) = \varphi y(0)$$

and   (7.15)

$$\lambda(t, \omega_T) = \lambda(t-1, \omega_T) + \varphi\eta(t, \omega_T).$$

(4) Relative to $P_T(\cdot)$, the families of random variables, $\{y(t, \omega_T); t \in N\}$ and $\{\lambda(t, \omega_T); t \in N\}$, are cointegrated second-order random

processes with cointegrating vector, $(1, -1)$, and common trend, $(1 - \varphi)$ $[\acute{y} + \sum_{0 \leq s \leq (t-1)} \eta(t - 1 - s, \omega_T)]$.

By combining equations 7.9 and 7.10, I can formulate the ideas in T7.5(4) with the help of a model of Søren Johansen's fundamental error-correction formula for the characterization of cointegrated second-order random processes (1995, p. 45).

T7.6
Suppose that axioms A1–A7 are valid, and let φ be the constant in A5. Then it is the case that, for all $\omega_T \in \Omega_T$ and $t \in N - \{0\}$, the components of $\{(y, \lambda)(t, \omega_T); t \in N\}$ satisfy equation 7.11 and the following conditions:

$$\begin{pmatrix} \Delta y(t,\omega_T) \\ \Delta \lambda(t,\omega_T) \end{pmatrix} = - \begin{pmatrix} 1 & -1 \\ 0 & 0 \end{pmatrix} \begin{pmatrix} y(t-1,\omega_T) \\ \lambda(t-1,\omega_T) \end{pmatrix} + \begin{pmatrix} \eta(t,\omega_T) \\ \varphi\eta(t,\omega_T) \end{pmatrix}. \tag{7.16}$$

The Data Universe
The data I have are series of weekly quotes on the values of the US dollar–Swiss franc spot and one-week-forward exchange rates. Taken from EcoWin's Database, they pertain to spot and forward rates at the end of Wednesday each week beginning May 9, 2001 and ending January 19, 2005.[3] Here the data are taken to constitute partial realizations of two sequences of variables in the data universe: one for spot rates, $\acute{K}_1$, and one for forward rates, $\acute{K}_2$. Besides $\acute{K}_1$ and $\acute{K}_2$ there are two sequences of variables in the data universe, $\hat{y}_1$ and $\hat{y}_2$, that function as auxiliary variables for $\acute{K}_1$ and $\acute{K}_2$. The components of $\acute{K}_1$ and $\acute{K}_2$ are understood to be observations of the values of the corresponding components of S and F. Similarly, the components of $\hat{y}_1$ and $\hat{y}_2$ are taken to be, respectively, observations of the corresponding components of y and λ.

Two of the members of Γ_P describe the conceptual framework of the data universe.

D1
$\Omega_P \subset (R_+^2 \times R^2)^N$. Thus, $\omega_P \in \Omega_P$ only if ω_P is a sequence of vectors, $(\acute{K}_{1t}, \acute{K}_{2t}, \hat{y}_{1t}, \hat{y}_{2t})$, all of which belong to $(R_+^2 \times R^2)$. In short, $\omega_P = (\acute{K}_1, \acute{K}_2, \hat{y}_1, \hat{y}_2)$ for some $(\acute{K}_1, \acute{K}_2, \hat{y}_1, \hat{y}_2) \in (R_+^2 \times R^2)^N$, $N = \{0, 1, 2, \dots \}$.

D2
Let $\acute{K} = (\acute{K}_1, \acute{K}_2)$ and $\hat{y} = (\hat{y}_1, \hat{y}_2)$ and, for each $t \in N$, let the vector-valued function $(\acute{K}, \hat{y})(t, \cdot): \Omega_P \to R_+^2 \times R^2$ be defined by the equations $(\acute{K}(t, \omega_P),$

$\hat{y}(t, \omega_P)) = \omega_{Pt}$ and $\omega_P \in \Omega_P$, where ω_{Pt} is the tth component of ω_P. The functions $(\acute{K}, \hat{y})(t, \cdot): \Omega_P \to R_+^2 \times R^2$ are measurable with respect to $\aleph_P$. Also, subject to the conditions on which Γ_P insists, the family of finite-dimensional probability distributions of the random vectors $\{(\acute{K}, \hat{y})(t, \omega_P); t \in N\}$ that $P_P(\cdot)$ determines is the true probability distribution of the process that generates the individuals in Ω_P. I designate it TPD.

The assertions that describe law-like properties of the data-generating process are stated in D3 and D4. Here D3 specifies the way $\hat{y}_1$ and $\hat{y}_2$ function as auxiliary variables for $\acute{K}_1$ and $\acute{K}_2$. From this axiom it follows that positive observations of $\acute{K}_1$ and $\acute{K}_2$ are observations of $\hat{y}_1$ and $\hat{y}_2$.

D3
For all $\omega_P \in \Omega_P$, and for all $t \in N$, the components of $\{(\acute{K}, \hat{y})(t, \omega_P); t \in N\}$ satisfy the following conditions:

$\acute{K}_1(t, \omega_P) = max(\hat{y}_1(t, \omega_P), 0)$

$\acute{K}_2(t, \omega_P) = max(\hat{y}_2(t, \omega_P), 0).$
(7.17)

D4
Relative to $P_P(\cdot)$, the family of random vectors, $\{\hat{y}(t, \omega_P); t \in N\}$, constitutes a random process with finite means and finite positive variances.

The Bridge
Four of the members of $\Gamma_{T,P}$, G1–G4, describe the conceptual frame work of the bridge.

G1
Observations are sequences of pairs of vectors, $(\omega_{Tt}, \omega_{Pt})$, that are components of some pair, (ω_T, ω_P), that belongs to the sample space.

G2
The sample space, Ω, is a subset of $\Omega_T \times \Omega_P$; i.e., $\Omega \subset \Omega_T \times \Omega_P$.

G3
$\Omega_T \subset \{\omega_T \in \Omega_T$ for which there is an $\omega_P \in \Omega_P$ with $(\omega_T, \omega_P) \in \Omega\}$.

G4
In $(\Omega_T \times \Omega_P, \aleph, P(\cdot))$ it is the case that $\Omega \in \aleph$ and $P(\Omega) > 0$.

The members of $\Gamma_{T,P}$ that describe how the theory and data variables are related to one another are expressed in G5 and G6. Those two axioms account for inaccurate observations and for the structural differences between how trading takes place in the theory universe and the real world. The components of ω_T are continuous variables, whereas our observations come in discrete units. The market for the spot and forward rates in the theory universe is frictionless, whereas all sorts of frictions permeate the corresponding real-world currency market.

G5
There exists a constant ψ, with $0 < \psi < 1$, such that, for each $(\omega_T, \omega_P) \in \Omega$,

$\hat{y}_1(0, \omega_P) = y(0, \omega_T)$,

$$\hat{y}_1(t, \omega_P) = \hat{y}_1(t - 1, \omega_P) + \psi(y(t, \omega_T) - \hat{y}_1(t - 1, \omega_P)), \quad t \geq 1 \tag{7.18}$$

and

$$\hat{y}_2(t, \omega_P) = \lambda(t - 1, \omega_T) + u(t, \omega_T), \quad t \geq 1. \tag{7.19}$$

G6
For each $(\omega_T, \omega_P) \in \Omega$,

$$\hat{y}_1(t - 1, \omega_P) = \lambda(t - 1, \omega_T), \quad t \geq 1. \tag{7.20}$$

In reading the axioms of the bridge, note that $\Omega \subset \Omega_T \times \Omega_P$ and that $\Omega_T \times \Omega_P \subset ((R_+^2 \times R^4) \times (R_+^2 \times R^2))^N$. Hence, a pair (ω_T, ω_P) is a sequence of pairs of sixtuples and quadruples, and G5, G6, A3, and D3 delineate how the components of these sequences are related to one another. I insist on G3 to exclude uninteresting models of the axioms.

The MPD
I have observed that the vector-valued sequences $(S, F, y, \lambda, \eta, u)$ roam around in a model world, and that their probability distribution, the RPD, resides in the mind of the researcher in charge. I have also observed that the vector-valued sequences $(\acute{K}, \hat{y})$ roam around in a data universe, and that their probability distribution, the TPD, is a true rendition of the data-generating process. Now I want to use the RPD and the bridge principles to derive a probability distribution of the $(\acute{K}, \hat{y})$, the MPD, on which I can base a meaningful empirical analysis of my theory—that is, of the axioms A1–A7.

In the present case, the MPD is the family of finite-dimensional probability distributions of the $(\acute{K}, \hat{y})(t, \cdot)$ that satisfies D1 and D3 and is induced by G1–G6 and the probability distribution of ω_T that A1–A5 and $P_T(\cdot)$ determine. The properties of the MPD and Kolmogorov's Consistency Theorem (B. Stigum 1990, theorem T 15.23, p. 347) imply that there exists a probability measure, $P_M(\cdot){:}\aleph_P \rightarrow [0, 1]$, relative to which the family of finite-dimensional probability distributions of the $\{(\acute{K}, \hat{y})(t, \omega_P); t \in N\}$ equals the MPD. Consequently, one can think of the empirical analysis with the MPD as being carried out in a data universe, $(\Omega_P, \Gamma_P{}^*, (\Omega_P, \aleph_P, P_M(\cdot)))$, that differs from the original universe in characteristic ways. In the latter triple, the Ω_P and $\aleph_P$ components are identical with the Ω_p and $\aleph_P$ components of the original data universe. The $\Gamma_P{}^*$ component differs from Γ_P in two ways: $P_M(\cdot)$ is substituted for $P_P(\cdot)$ and MPD is substituted for TPD. Finally, in the last component of the triple, $P_M(\cdot)$ is substituted for $P_P(\cdot)$.

The preceding ideas are illustrated in figure 7.1 with three universes—one for theory and two for data. The original data universe is taken to be the upper data universe in the figure, and the new data universe is taken to be the lower data universe in the same figure. The two data universes share the functions $(\acute{K}, \hat{y})(t, \cdot)$ and the pair $(\Omega_P, \aleph_P)$. The family of probability distributions of the $(\acute{K}, \hat{y})(t, \cdot)$ is the TPD in the upper data universe and the MPD in the lower data universe.

To provide a complete characterization of the MPD distribution of the family of random quadruples, $\{(\acute{K}, \hat{y})(t, \omega_P); t \in N\}$, I will proceed in two steps. I will begin by studying characteristics of the sample paths of $\hat{y}_1$ and $\hat{y}_2$. Their characteristics are described in T7.7 and T7.8. In reading those two theorems, note that the sequences on the right-hand sides of equations 7.21–7.25 belong to Ω_T, whereas the sequences on the left-hand sides belong to Ω_P. Note, also, that T7.7 appeals to G1–G5,

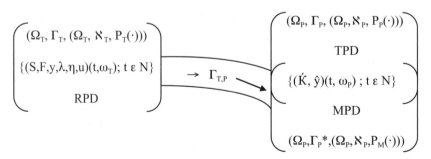

Figure 7.1
Theory-data confrontation in foreign exchange.

that T7.8 appeals to G1–G6, and that the two theorems cannot both be valid unless $\varphi = \psi$.

T7.7

Suppose that A1, A2, A4, A5, D1, and G1–G5 are valid. Then the following equations express salient characteristics of the sample paths of $\hat{y}_1$ and $\hat{y}_2$: For all $(\omega_T, \omega_P) \in \Omega$,

$$\Delta\hat{y}_1(t, \omega_P) - (1 - \psi)\Delta\hat{y}_1(t - 1, \omega_P) = \psi\eta(t, \omega_T) - (1 - \varphi)\psi\eta(t - 1, \omega_T), \ t > 0 \tag{7.21}$$

$$\Delta\hat{y}_2(t, \omega_P) = \varphi\eta(t - 1, \omega_T) + \Delta u(t, \omega_T), \qquad t > 0. \tag{7.22}$$

T7.8

Suppose that A1, A2, A4, A5, D1, and G1–G6 are valid. Then the following equations express salient characteristics of the sample paths of $\hat{y}_1$ and $\hat{y}_2$: For all $(\omega_T, \omega_P) \in \Omega$,

$$\Delta\hat{y}_1(t, \omega_P) = \psi\eta(t, \omega_T), \qquad t > 0 \tag{7.23}$$

$$\Delta\hat{y}_2(t, \omega_P) = \psi\eta(t - 1, \omega_T) + \Delta u(t, \omega_T), \qquad t > 0 \tag{7.24}$$

$$\hat{y}_1(t, \omega_P) - \hat{y}_2(t, \omega_P) = \psi\eta(t, \omega_T) - u(t, \omega_T), \qquad t > 0. \tag{7.25}$$

With T7.7 and T7.8 in mind, I can describe the characteristic properties of the MPD of $\{(\acute{K}, \hat{y})(t, \omega_P); t \in N\}$ as I do in T7.9–T7.11 with the D axioms in $\Gamma_P{}^*$. In T7.9–T7.11 the family $\{(\varsigma, v)(t, \omega_P); t \in N\}$ has replaced the family $\{(\eta, u)(t, \omega_T); t \in N\}$ in equations 7.25–7.29. The new variables are defined by the following equation:

For all $(\omega_T, \omega_P) \in \Omega$, and $t \in N$, $(\varsigma, v)(t, \omega_P) = (\eta, u)(t, \omega_T)$.

From this equation and from G5 and G6 it follows that

$$\hat{y}_1(t, \omega_P) - \hat{y}_1(t - 1, \omega_P) = \psi\varsigma(t, \omega_P), \quad t \geq 1$$

and

$$\hat{y}_2(t, \omega_P) - \hat{y}_1(t - 1, \omega_P) = v(t, \omega_P), \quad t \geq 1.$$

Hence the $(\varsigma, v)(t, \omega_P)$ are well defined and measurable with respect to $\aleph_P$. From this, from G3 and G6, and from the definition of MPD in chapter 6, I conclude that I can describe the characteristics of the finite-dimensional probability distributions in MPD of $(\hat{y}_1, \varsigma, v)(t, \omega_P)$ as follows: Let M be a finite positive integer, let A be an arbitrary subset of $(R^3)^M$, and observe that in this case $\Omega_T(\Omega) = \Omega_T$. For any finite subset of N, $\{t_i, i = 1, \ldots , M\}$, where $t_i \neq t_j$ if $i \neq j$, it is the case that

$$MPD(((\hat{y}_{1,\varsigma}, v)(t_1, \omega_P), \ldots , (\hat{y}_1, \varsigma, v)(t_M, \omega_P)) \in A)$$

$$= P_T(\{\omega_T \in \Omega_T: ((\lambda, \eta, u)(t_1, \omega_T), \ldots , (\lambda, \eta, u)(t_M, \omega_T)) \in A)\}.$$

Hence, the MPD distribution of the $(\hat{y}_1, \varsigma, v)(t, \omega_P)$ is the same as the RPD distribution of the $(\lambda, \eta, u)(t, \omega_T)$. From this and equation 7.23 it follows by an easy argument that, for all $t \in N - \{0\}$, in the MPD distribution $(\varsigma, v)(t, \omega_P)$ is orthogonal to $((\hat{y}_1, \hat{y}_2)(t - s, \omega_P), s = 1, \ldots , t$, with $P_M(\cdot)$ probability 1.

T7.9
Suppose that axioms A1–A7, D1, and G1–G5 are valid. Then, relative to an MPD-determined $P_M(\cdot)$, the family of finite-dimensional probability distributions of $\{\hat{y}(t, \omega_P); t \in N\}$ are the probability distributions of a pair of second-order random processes that constitutes a solution to the following two stochastic difference equations:

$$\Delta\hat{y}_1(t, \omega_P) - (1 - \psi)\Delta\hat{y}_1(t - 1, \omega_P) = \psi\varsigma(t, \omega_P) - (1 - \varphi)\psi\varsigma(t - 1, \omega_P), t \geq 1 \tag{7.26}$$

$$\Delta\hat{y}_2(t, \omega_P) = \varphi\varsigma(t - 1, \omega_P) + \Delta v(t, \omega_P), \qquad t > 0 \tag{7.27}$$

where the $(\varsigma, v)(t, \omega_P)$ are measurable with respect to $\aleph_P$, independently and identically distributed with means 0 and the same covariance matrix as (η_t, u_t), and a.e. satisfy the following equations:

$$(\varsigma, v)(0, \omega_P) = 0$$
$$\tag{7.28}$$
$$E\{(\varsigma, v)(t, \omega_P) \,|\, \hat{y}(0), \ldots , \hat{y}(t - 1)\} = 0, \qquad t > 0.$$

T7.10
Suppose that axioms A1–A7, D1, and G1–G6 are valid. Then, relative to $P_M(\cdot)$, the family of finite-dimensional probability distributions of $\{\hat{y}(t, \omega_P); t \in N\}$ are the probability distributions of a pair of second-order random processes that constitutes a solution to the following stochastic difference equations:

$$\Delta\hat{y}_1(t, \omega_P) = \psi\varsigma(t, \omega_P), \qquad t > 0 \tag{7.29}$$

$$\Delta\hat{y}_2(t, \omega_P) = \psi\varsigma(t - 1, \omega_P) + \Delta v(t, \omega_P), \qquad t > 0. \tag{7.30}$$

Also, the members of $\{\hat{y}(t, \omega_P); t \in N\}$ are cointegrated with cointegrating vector $(1, -1)$; that is,

$$\hat{y}_1(t, \omega_P) - \hat{y}_2(t, \omega_P) = \psi\varsigma(t, \omega_P) - v(t, \omega_P), \qquad t > 0. \tag{7.31}$$

T7.11
Suppose that A1–A7, D1, D3, and G1–G5 are valid. Then, for all $t \in N$, $\acute{K}(t, \omega_P) = \max(\hat{y}(t, \omega_P), 0)$ a.e. in P_M measure.

With regard to the import of figure 7.1, a remark concerning the meaning of a random sample of observations of the $(\acute{K}, \hat{y})(t, \cdot)$ in the two data universes is in order. Suppose that I have observed the values of $(\acute{K}, \hat{y})(t, \omega_P)$, $t = 0, 1, \ldots, M$, for some finite integer M and some point ω_P in Ω_P. The given sequence constitutes a time series. As such, it is to be taken as one observation of the values of the first M + 1 members of the family $\{(\acute{K}, \hat{y})(t, \omega_P); t \in N\}$. In the upper universe, to say that this one-observation sample constitutes a random sample is a short way of saying that the values that the time series comprises were sampled in accordance with the prescriptions of the probability measure $P_P(\cdot)$. In the lower data universe, it is a short way of saying that the time series was sampled in accordance with any one of the MPD determined probability measures $P_M(\cdot)$.

For the purposes of the empirical analyses that Harald Goldstein and André Anundsen carry out in the next two sections, I assume, without saying, that my data constitute a random sample in the respective universes.

7.3 Harald Goldstein's Empirical Analysis[4]

In this section I shall sketch how Harald Goldstein went about estimating the parameters of the MPD and what his results mean for the empirical relevance of axioms A1–A7. Note that Goldstein's analysis is carried out in the lower data universe in figure 7.1 and centers on three fundamental ideas. The first describes the prescriptions underlying the statistical analysis; the second outlines the salient characteristics of a data-admissible mathematical model of MPD; the third defines what it means for a theory to be empirically relevant.

7.3.1 The Prescriptions That Underlie the Statistical Analysis
The data are series of weekly observations of the values of the US dollar–Swiss franc spot and one-week-forward exchange rates. I take these data to be the observed values of $(\acute{K}_1, \acute{K}_2)(t)$, $t = 1, 2, \ldots, 196$. According to D3, $\acute{K}_1(t) > 0 \rightarrow \acute{K}_1(t) = \hat{y}_1(t)$ and $\acute{K}_2(t) > 0 \rightarrow \acute{K}_2(t) = \hat{y}_2(t)$

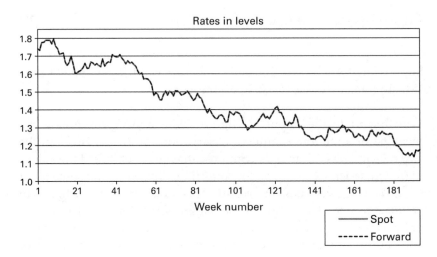

Figure 7.2
Observed series of spot and forward rates.

for all t. Since the observed series of the $(\acute{K}_1, \acute{K}_2)(t)$ is larger than 0 in the observation period, the pertinent members of the two partially observable series, $(\hat{y}_1(t), \hat{y}_2(t))$, are observed in the observation period. The observed series and their first differences are shown in figures 7.2 and 7.3.

Because the two series in figure 7.2 differ only in the fourth decimal place, they appear almost identical in the graph. The first differences are shown in figure 7.3. The two first differenced series appear quite similar, as is confirmed by a contemporaneous correlation of 0.9978.

For the present empirical analysis, the MPD is the probability distribution of the $\hat{y}$ components of ω_P that A1–A7, D1, D3, and G1–G6 determine. With T6.9–T 6.10 in mind, Goldstein began by estimating the parameters of a mathematical model of MPD that has the characteristics of a family of finite-dimensional probability distributions of a second-order stochastic process, $\{(\hat{y}_1(t), \hat{y}_2(t)); t \in N\}$, that constitutes a solution to the following difference equations:

$$\Delta\hat{y}_1(t) = (1 - \psi)\Delta\,\hat{y}_1(t-1) + \psi\varsigma(t) - (1 - \varphi)\,\psi\varsigma\,(t-1), \qquad t \geq 1 \qquad (7.32)$$

$$\hat{y}_2(t) - \hat{y}_1(t-1) = v(t). \tag{7.33}$$

Equation 7.32 is a rewrite of equation 7.26 in T7.9, and equation 7.33 follows from equations 7.29 and 7.31 in T7.10. According to T7.9, $\varsigma(t)$ and $v(t)$ are independent purely random innovation processes with

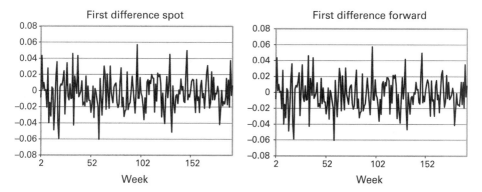

Figure 7.3
First differences of observed spot and forward rates.

means 0 and positive variances σ_η^2 and σ_u^2. In the statistical analysis, we assume, in addition, that $\varsigma(t)$ and $v(t)$ are Gaussian white noise, and we hope to establish that $0 < \varphi < 1$ and $0 < \psi < 1$, as A5 and G5 require.

Equation 7.32 is equivalent to an ARMA(1, 1) model, written in standard form as follows:

$$X_{1t} = \alpha X_{1t-1} + \varepsilon_t + \theta \varepsilon_{t-1}, \tag{7.34}$$

where $X_{1t} := \Delta \hat{y}_1(t)$, $\varepsilon_t = \psi\varsigma(t)$, $\alpha = 1 - \psi$, and $\theta = -(1 - \varphi)$. (ARMA stands for autoregressive moving average.) Standard Box-Jenkins analyses of the observations we have of the $\hat{y}_1(t)$ (i.e., the $\acute{K}_1(t)$) do not provide evidence against a causal and invertible ARMA(1, 1) model for $\{X_{1t}\}$ with $\{\varepsilon_t\}$ as Gaussian white noise, thus justifying restricting α and θ to $-1 < \alpha < 1$ and $-1 < \theta < 1$. The further restrictions $0 < \alpha < 1$ and $-1 < \theta < 0$, implied by the correspondences $\alpha = 1 - \psi$ and $\theta = -(1 - \varphi)$, are also not contradicted by the data. In addition, there appears to be no evidence of heteroscedasticity or ARCH effects in $\{\varepsilon_t\}$. Hence, we can choose equation 7.34, with $0 < \alpha < 1$, $-1 < \theta < 0$, and the ε_t being independent and identically distributed (i.i.d.) $N(0, \sigma^2)$ variables, as a basis for the construction of the family of data-admissible mathematical models of MPD that we need for our test of the empirical relevance of A1–A7. Here $\mathrm{Var}(\varepsilon_t) = \sigma^2$ corresponds to $\psi^2\sigma_\eta^2$ of the MPD, and the $X_1(t) := \Delta \hat{y}_1(t)$ are assumed to be mean adjusted in the usual manner.

The prescriptions underlying Goldstein's statistical analysis insist that he obtain maximum-likelihood estimates of α, θ, and σ^2 and determine the corresponding values of σ_u^2 and σ_η^2. According to Brockwell and Davis' 1987 book *Time Series: Theory and Methods* (referred to below as BD), one may write the log likelihood as

$$l(\alpha,\theta,\sigma^2) = -\frac{n}{2}\ln(2\pi\sigma^2) - \frac{1}{2}\sum_{t=1}^{n}\ln(r_{t-1}) - \frac{1}{2\sigma^2}\sum_{t=1}^{n}\left(X_{1t} - \hat{X}_{1t}\right)^2 \Big/ r_{t-1}$$

where $r_t = r_t(\alpha,\theta) \to 1$ as $t \to \infty$. We have

$$r_0 = \frac{1 + 2\alpha\theta + \theta^2}{1 - \alpha^2}$$

and

$$r_t = 1 + \frac{(r_0 - 1)\theta^{2t}(1 - \theta^2)}{r_0(1 - \theta^2) + (r_0 - 1)(\theta^2 - \theta^{2t})}, \quad t \geq 1.$$

The predicted X_t's are

$$\hat{X}_1 = 0$$

and

$$\hat{X}_{1t+1} = aX_{1t} + \frac{\theta}{r_{t-1}}(X_{1t} - \hat{X}_{1t}), \quad t \geq 1.$$

Write, for short,

$$\beta = (\alpha,\theta)$$

and

$$S(\beta) = \frac{1}{n}\sum_{t=1}^{n}\left(X_{1t} - \hat{X}_{1t}\right)^2 \Big/ r_{t-1}.$$

Concentrating out σ^2, we obtain the maximum-likelihood (ML) estimates

$$\hat{\sigma}^2 = \frac{1}{n}S(\hat{\beta})$$

and the concentrated log likelihood

$$l(\beta) = -\frac{n}{2}\ln(2\pi) + \frac{n}{2} - \frac{n}{2}\kappa(\beta), \tag{7.35}$$

where

$$\kappa(\beta) = \ln\left(\frac{1}{n}S(\beta)\right) + \frac{1}{n}\sum_{t=1}^{n}\ln(r_{t-1}) \tag{7.36}$$

is the objective function to be minimized.

The global minimum of the objective function is found to be

$$\kappa(\hat{\alpha}, \hat{\theta}) = -7.809188$$

with the ML estimates $\alpha^\circ = 0.929370$, $\theta^\circ = -0.999574$, $\varphi^\circ = 0.000426023$, $\psi^\circ = 0.0706301$, $\sigma^2 = 0.0004017888$, and $\sigma_\eta^2 = 0.08054109$. The estimate of σ_u^2 that we obtain directly from equation 7.33 is $\sigma_u^2 = 0.000415953$.

Tests of auxiliary hypotheses

In calculating the preceding estimates, we assumed that the ς and v processes in equations 7.32 and 7.33 are independently distributed Gaussian white-noise innovation processes with means 0 and with unrestricted positive variances. We will now see that this assumption is justified.

The autocorrelation plots and QQ plots for normality for X_{1t} and X_{2t} in figures 7.4–7.7 suggest that there is little evidence in the data against the assumption that $X_{1t} := \Delta\hat{y}_1(t)$ and $X_{2t} = \hat{y}_2(t) - \hat{y}_1(t-1)$ are both Gaussian white noise. Also, the Shapiro-Wilk test for normality gave p values of 0.634 and 0.681 for X_{1t} and X_{2t} respectively.

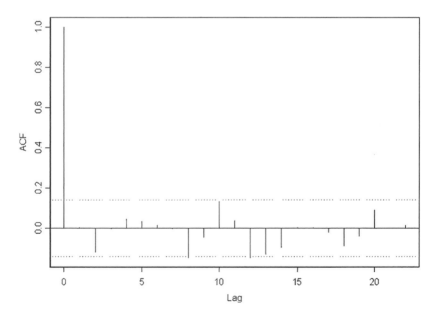

Figure 7.4
ACF plot for X_{1t} (series: ACF for $\Delta y(t)$ (spot)).

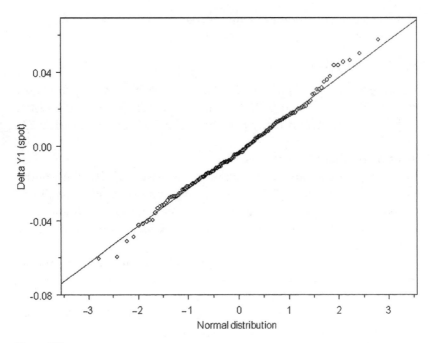

Figure 7.5
QQ plot for X_{1t}.

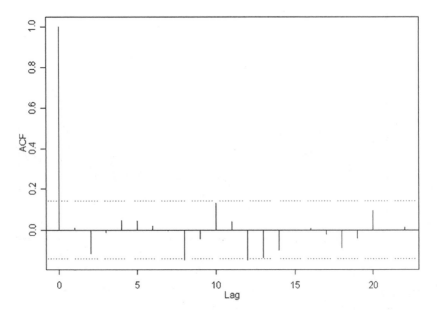

Figure 7.6
ACF plot for X_{2t} (series: $y_2(t) - y_1(t - 1)$).

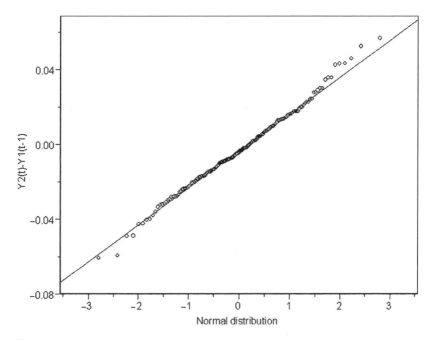

Figure 7.7
QQ plot for X_{2t}.

Two tests for randomness were also tried. The *sequence test*, based on the number of sequences above and below 0 for the mean adjusted series, gave p values of 0.718 and 0.942 for X_{1t} and X_{2t} respectively (with the null hypothesis, H_0, insisting that the two series are white noise). The *turns test*, based on the number of turns in the series (see BD), gave p values of 0.562 and 0.819 for X_{1t} and X_{2t} respectively (with the null hypothesis, H_0, insisting that the two series are white noise).

7.3.2 A Family of Data-Admissible Mathematical Models of MPD

A mathematical model of MPD is data admissible if (1) the estimated mathematical model of MPD satisfies the strictures on which D1, D3, and the prescriptions that underlie the statistical analysis insist, (2) the values that the model assigns to the parameters of MPD satisfy the strictures on which the A axioms, D1, D3, and the six G axioms insist, and (3) the model lies within a 95-percent-confidence region of the estimated mathematical model of MPD. We denote the family of data-admissible mathematical models of MPD by IM_{MPD}.

The results of the preceding likelihood analysis demonstrate that the estimated values of the parameters of the MPD satisfy the strictures on which D1, D3, and the conditions underlying the statistical analysis insist. Next, we shall delineate a 95-percent-confidence region around the maximum-likelihood estimates of the pair (θ, α) and use it and the equations $\theta = -(1 - \varphi)$ and $\alpha = (1 - \psi)$ to search for estimates of φ and ψ that are values of parameters of data-admissible mathematical models of MPD. The region we use is a bootstrap-corrected 95-percent-confidence region that is depicted in figure 7.3.[5] It is the result of a bootstrap experiment that Goldstein carried out by generating 2,000 samples of observations based on equation 7.34 and the assumption that

$$-2l(\beta) - \left(-2l\left(\hat{\beta}\right)\right) = n\left(\kappa(\beta) - \kappa\left(\hat{\beta}\right)\right) \sim \chi_2^2 . \tag{7.37}$$

i.e. that $n(\kappa(\beta) - \kappa(\beta))$ is approximately χ^2 distributed with 2 degrees of freedom, the upper 5% point of which is $\chi^2_{0.05} = 5.99$. The bootstrap-corrected confidence region comprises all the values of β that satisfy the inequality $\kappa(\beta) \leq \kappa(\beta) + 40.32/n = -7.600$ with 40.32 and -7.600 instead of 5.99 and -7.778.

We may think of a member of IM_{MPD} as a quadruple, $\{\varphi, \psi, \varsigma, v\}$. The φ and ψ are parameters that, for some pair (θ, α) in the bootstrap-corrected 95-percent-confidence region, satisfy the equations $\theta = -(1 - \varphi)$ and $\alpha = (1 - \psi)$, with $-1 < \theta < 0$ and $0 < \alpha < 1$. Also, the ς and v are mathematical models of the ς and v processes in equations 7.32 and 7.33 that are independently distributed Gaussian white-noise innovation processes with means 0 and unrestricted positive variances.

Not all the mathematical models of MPD that are determined by the bootstrap-corrected confidence region are data admissible. To be data admissible, the model's parameters must satisfy the restrictions on which the A axioms, D1, D3, and all six G axioms insist. In particular a model of the MPD is data admissible only if $\varphi = \psi$. Hence, we shall identify IM_{MPD} with the mathematical models of MPD whose parameters, for some pair (θ, α) in the bootstrap-corrected 95-percent-confidence region, satisfy the equations

$$\theta = -(1 - \varphi), \ \alpha = (1 - \psi), \ \theta = -\alpha, \ \text{and} \ 0 < \alpha < 1, \tag{7.38}$$

and whose ς and v processes are independently distributed Gaussian white-noise innovation processes with means 0 and unrestricted positive variances.

The pertinent characteristics of the members of IM_{MPD} are described in T7.12.

T7.12

Suppose that A1–A7, D1, D3, and G1–G6 are valid. Let (θ, α) belong to the bootstrap-corrected 95-percent-confidence region, and suppose that $\theta = -\alpha$. Let $\varphi = 1 + \theta$ and $\psi = (1 - \alpha)$, and suppose that there are mathematical models of the ς and v processes in equations 7.32 and 7.33 that, with the given values of φ and ψ, determine a mathematical model of MPD. This mathematical model of MPD is the family of finite-dimensional probability distributions of a mathematical model of a second-order stochastic processes, $\{(\hat{y}_1(t), \hat{y}_2(t)), t \geq 0\}$, that constitutes a solution to the difference equations

$$\Delta\hat{y}_1(t) = \psi\varsigma(t), \; t \geq 1 \tag{7.39}$$

and

$$\Delta\hat{y}_2(t) = \psi\varsigma(t - 1) + \Delta v(t), \quad t \geq 2 \tag{7.40}$$

and satisfies the equation

$$\hat{y}_1(t) - \hat{y}_2(t) = \psi\varsigma(t) - v(t), \quad t \geq 1. \tag{7.41}$$

To see why T7.12 is valid, note that when $\theta = -\alpha$ equation 7.34 reduces to $(1 - \alpha L)X_{1t} = (1 - \alpha L)\varepsilon_t$, where L is the lag operator. This equation is, in the vernacular of statisticians, a common-factor model, and it is well known that in the causal and invertible case the set of stationary solutions are those obtained from the equation after canceling the common factor. Thus, when $\theta = -\alpha$ equation 7.34 reduces to $X_{1t} = \varepsilon_t$; that is, to equation 7.31, $\Delta\hat{y}_1(t) = \psi\varsigma(t)$. To conclude the proof of T7.12, note that equation 7.40 follows from equation 7.33 and the equality $\varphi = \psi$, and that equation 7.41 follows from equations 7.39 and 7.33.

In the case of T7.12 it is important to ascertain that there are pairs (θ, α) in the bootstrap-corrected confidence region that satisfy the equation $\theta = -\alpha$. To see why there are such pairs, note that almost all pairs (θ, α) along the bottom of the objective function satisfy the inequality restrictions on which we insisted when we constructed the bootstrap-corrected confidence region. Also, the restriction $\theta = -\alpha \; (\Leftrightarrow \varphi = \psi)$ satisfies these criteria, since the objective function $K(\alpha, -\alpha)$ is completely flat at the value -7.782.

It is also interesting that in the case of T7.12, $\varphi = \psi$ is not identified. What is identified is only $\sigma^2 = \varphi^2\sigma_\eta^2 = \psi^2\sigma_\eta^2$ with the estimate

$$\hat{\sigma}^2 = 0.00041713255 . \tag{7.42}$$

Since there are no restrictions on the value of σ_η^2, all pairs $(\varphi, \psi) \in (0, 1) \times (0, 1)$ with $\varphi = \psi$ may be parameters of a data-admissible mathematical model of MPD.

7.3.3 The Empirical Relevance of A1–A7

In the present theory-data confrontation, the theory axioms A1–A7 are empirically relevant if and only if there is a member of the intended family of models of the axioms that—together with a model of the non-stochastic axioms of the data universe and the bridge principles—determines a mathematical model of the MPD that belongs to IM_{MPD}.

A mathematical model of the MPD that satisfies the conditions of T7.12 is the MPD of an empirically relevant mathematical model of A1–A7. To see why, pick an MPD in IM_{MPD} that satisfies the conditions of T7.12. In this distribution the family of vector-valued random variables, $\{(\hat{y}_1, \hat{y}_2, \varsigma, v)(t, \omega_P), t \in N\}$, must satisfy the equations

$$\hat{y}_1(t, \omega_P) = \hat{y}_1(t - 1, \omega_P) + \psi\varsigma(t, \omega_P),$$

$$\hat{y}_2(t, \omega_P) = \hat{y}_1(t - 1, \omega_P) + v(t, \omega_P),$$

and, with $P_M(\cdot)$ probability 1,

$$(\varsigma, v)(0, \omega_P) = 0, \text{ and } E\{(\varsigma, v)(t, \omega_P)\{\hat{y}(0), \dots , \hat{y}(t - 1)\} = 0.$$

From these equations and from G1–G6 it follows that if I let ω_P be a vector in the support of the given MPD and define $(y,\lambda,\eta,u)(t)$ by the equations

$$u(t) = v(t, \omega_P),$$

$$\psi\eta(t) = \psi\varsigma(t, \omega_P),$$

$$\varphi = \psi,$$

$$\lambda(t) = \hat{y}_1(t, \omega_P),$$

and

$$y(t) = \hat{y}_1(t - 1, \omega_P) + (\psi)^{-1}(\hat{y}_1(t, \omega_P) - \hat{y}_1(t - 1, \omega_P)).$$

I can use the MPD distribution of the right-hand variables of the latter equations to calculate the RPD distribution of (y, λ, η, u) that the given MPD distribution of $(\hat{y}_1, \hat{y}_2, \varsigma, v)$ determines. This RPD distribution of the theory variables, $y(t)$, $\lambda(t)$, $\eta(t)$, and $u(t)$, satisfies the last four axioms in Γ_T, A4–A7. That goes to show that an MPD in IM_{MPD} that

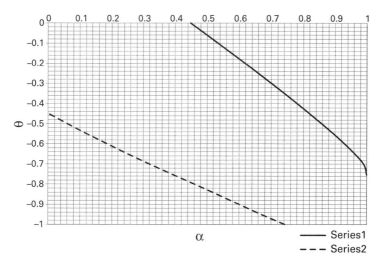

Figure 7.8
Bootstrap-corrected confidence region, 95-percent level (contour objective function = –7.60).

satisfies the conditions of T7.12 determines an empirically relevant model of A1–A7.

We have shown that there are values of θ and α in the bootstrap-corrected confidence region that satisfies the conditions of equation 7.38. We have also shown that the ς and v processes in equations 7.32 and 7.33 are independently distributed Gaussian white noise innovation processes with zero means and unrestricted positive variances. Hence there is a data-admissible mathematical model of MPD that satisfies the conditions of T7.12. That concludes the proof that there is an empirically relevant model of A1–A7.

The researcher in charge ought to search for the largest possible family of mathematical models of A1–A7 that are empirically relevant. He can do that by choosing an appropriate model for D1 and D3 and a family of mathematical models of the $\{(\varsigma, v)(t, \omega_P); t \geq 1\}$ and by identifying the remaining parameters of an admissible mathematical model of MPD with φ and ψ values that satisfy equation 7.38 for pairs of values of θ and α that belong to the 95-percent-confidence region around the ML estimates of θ and α.

7.3.4 Concluding Remarks
Goldstein's maximum-likelihood estimates of φ and ψ are not a pair of parameters of a data-admissible mathematical model of the MPD. This

is so because $\varphi^{\circ} \neq \psi^{\circ}$. Furthermore, the dynamics of foreign exchange in the theory universe are very different from the dynamics of foreign exchange in the data universe. In the theory universe, the dynamics of foreign exchange in P_T measure are depicted in the behavior characteristics of a second-order random process, $\{(y(t, \omega_T), \lambda(t, \omega_T)); t \in N\}$, that constitutes a solution of the difference equations

$$\begin{pmatrix} \Delta y(t) \\ \Delta \lambda(t) \end{pmatrix} = \begin{pmatrix} -1 \\ 0 \end{pmatrix}(1,-1)\begin{pmatrix} y(t-1) \\ \lambda(t-1) \end{pmatrix} + \begin{pmatrix} n(t) \\ \varphi n(t) \end{pmatrix} \tag{7.43}$$

and satisfies equations 7.11 and 7.12.

In contrast, the dynamics of foreign exchange in the lower data universe are in an MPD-determined P_M measure depicted in the behavior characteristics of a second-order stochastic process, $\{\hat{y}(t, \omega_P); t \in N\}$, that constitutes a solution of the difference equations

$$\begin{pmatrix} \Delta \hat{y}_1(t) \\ \Delta \hat{y}_2(t) \end{pmatrix} = \begin{pmatrix} 0 \\ 1 \end{pmatrix}(1,-1)\begin{pmatrix} \hat{y}_1(t) \\ \hat{y}_2(t) \end{pmatrix} + \begin{pmatrix} \psi \varsigma(t) \\ v(t) \end{pmatrix} \tag{7.44}$$

with

$(\varsigma, v)(0, \omega_P) = 0$

and

$E(\varsigma, v)(t, \omega_P) \mid \hat{y}(0), \ldots, \hat{y}(t-1)\} = 0, \quad t > 0.$

7.4 André Anundsen's Empirical Analysis

Harald Goldstein's analysis established the empirical relevance in the lower data universe in figure 7.1 of the theory I presented in section 7.2. In this section I assume that I have accurate observations of the pair $(y, \lambda)(t)$, $t \geq 0$, and I ask whether the given theory has empirical relevance in the upper data universe in figure 7.1. Specifically, I ask whether there exists in P_P measure a pair of i.i.d. random processes, $\{\delta_1, \delta_2\}(t, \omega_P); t \in N\}$, with means 0 and finite covariance matrix, such that

$E\{\delta(t, \omega_P) \mid \hat{y}(0), \ldots, \hat{y}(t-1)\} = 0$ for all $t > 0$ \hfill (7.45)

and such that $\{\hat{y}(t, \omega_P); t \in N\}$ with large probability constitutes a solution to the difference equations

$$\begin{pmatrix} \Delta \hat{y}_1(t) \\ \Delta \hat{y}_2(t) \end{pmatrix} = -\begin{pmatrix} 1 & -1 \\ 0 & 0 \end{pmatrix}\begin{pmatrix} \hat{y}_1(t-1) \\ \hat{y}_2(t-1) \end{pmatrix} + \begin{pmatrix} \delta_1(t) \\ \delta_2(t) \end{pmatrix}, \tag{7.46}$$

where, according to theory, $\delta_2(t) = \varphi\delta_1(t)$ with P_P probability 1.

Since I do not know $P_P(\cdot)$, my question amounts to asking whether my theory with accurate observations is relevant in the empirical context established by André Anundsen's analysis. I believe that this is the way Trygve Haavelmo would have determined the empirical relevance of my theory.

Anundsen uses ideas developed by David Hendry and Søren Johansen to carry out an empirical analysis of the TPD distribution of $\{\hat{y}(t, \omega_P); t \in N\}$ illustrated here in figure 7.1. He adopts D1–D4 as stated, adds the assumption that $\{\hat{y}(t, \omega_P); t \in N\}$ is an ARIMA process with no more than two unit roots, and begins his empirical analysis by establishing the number of unit roots. He then conducts a general-to-specific search for a data-admissible econometric model that parsimoniously encompasses the TPD. In the end, Anundsen's analysis answers my question.

7.4.1 Data Properties

We will begin by examining the orders of integration of the data series using the Augmented Dickey-Fuller (ADF) test (Dickey and Fuller 1979). The hypothesis we seek to test is whether the spot and the forward rates cointegrate with cointegrating vector (1, –1). Initially, we allow for a maximum lag length of 8 in the ADF regressions. We then test down the lag length by choosing the optimal lag truncation to be the lag length consistent with the lowest value of the Akaike information criterion (AIC). The results are presented in table 7.1. The ADF tests show that both the spot and one-week-forward rates are integrated of order 1. It should be noted that for any lag length between 0

Table 7.1
Augmented Dickey-Fuller test for order of integration.

Variable	t-ADF	5%-critical value	Lags	Trend
Levels				
Spot	–2.854	–3.44	0	Yes
Forward	–2.825	–3.44	0	Yes
First differences				
ΔSpot	–10.890	–2.88	1	No
ΔForward	–10.830	–2.88	1	No

Sample: T = 184 (2001w28–2005w3)

and 8 the ADF tests indicate the same order of integration for the two data series considered here.[6]

7.4.2 Cointegrated Vector Autoregression (CVAR) Analysis of Spot and One-Week-Forward Rates

Next we shall use Johansen's (1988b) multivariate approach to cointegration to determine whether the dollar–franc spot and forward rates are linearly cointegrated. As a first step, let us formulate a bivariate VAR model of order 5:

$$\hat{y}(t) = \Sigma_{1 \leq i \leq 5} \Pi_i \, \hat{y}(t - i) + \Psi D(t) + \varepsilon(t), \tag{7.47}$$

where $\hat{y}(t)$ is the 2×1 vector comprising the spot and forward rates and $D(t)$ contains deterministic terms such as a constant and a linear trend. Let us assume that $\varepsilon(t)$ is $IIN(0, \Omega)$.

Diagnostics indicate that the given linear bivariate VAR suffers from severe misspecification. More precisely, although there is no evidence of autocorrelation, the assumptions of normality and homoscedasticity are violated. This means that a key assumption for conducting formal inference using the Johansen procedure is violated. The absence of residual autocorrelation is, however, important in itself, since autocorrelation is often regarded as the most damaging type of misspecification in a time-series model. With these caveats in mind, table 7.2 shows the successive tests for lag reduction.[7]

Though the F-tests favor a lag length of 5 (marginally), both the AIC and the Schwartz criterion (SC) favor a lag length of 1, which is the lag length we have decided to retain for the cointegration analysis. When testing for cointegration, it is convenient to express the VAR model in a vector error-correction form as in equation 7.48, where we have restricted the deterministic trend to enter the cointegrating space.

Table 7.2
Tests on the significance of all lags up to 5.

	F-test	Value [Prob]	AIC	SC	Log.lik
5			−15.9014	−15.4898	1526.6860
4	$F\,(4, 352)$	2.4849[0.0434]	−15.8881	−15.5450	1521.4230
3	$F\,(8, 352)$	1.7177[0.0930]	−15.9095	−15.6351	1519.4482
2	$F\,(12, 352)$	1.3864[0.1700]	−15.9361	−15.7302	1517.9578
1	$F\,(16, 352)$	1.1875[0.2754]	−15.9656	−15.8284	1516.7497
0	$F\,(20, 352)$	31.229[0.0000]	−14.0722	−14.0036	1333.8270

Table 7.3
Trace test for cointegration.[a]

Eigenvalue: λ_i	H_0	H_A	$p[\lambda_{trace}]$	$p[\text{small sample } \lambda_{trace}]$
0.4906	r = 0	r≥1	0.000	0.000
0.0435	r ≤ 1	r ≥ 2	0.226	0.233

Diagnostics[b]	Test statistic	Value [p value]
Vector AR 1–7 test	$F_{(28, 340)}$ =	0.6925[0.3982]
Vector Normality test	$\chi^2(4)$ =	2.5628[0.0000]**
Vector Hetero test	$F_{(18, 509)}$ =	0.8491[0.0000]**
Estimation period	2001w23–2005w3 (T = 189)	

a. Endogenous variables: dollar–franc spot and one-week-forward rates. Restricted variables: A deterministic trend. Unrestricted variables: Constant.
b. See Doornik and Hendry 2009.

$$\Delta \hat{y}(t) = \Pi^* y^*(t - 1) + \Psi D^*(t) + \epsilon(t). \tag{7.48}$$

Hence, $y^*(t - 1) = (\hat{y}(t - 1)', \text{trend})'$, whereas $D^*(t)$ now contains only a constant. Testing for cointegration amounts to testing the rank of the matrix Π^*, which can be done using the trace test. The results from the trace test for cointegration are displayed in table 7.3. In addition to reporting the eigenvalues, the table reports the p values of the asymptotic and small-sample-adjusted trace tests.[8]

The trace test gives clear evidence for a single cointegrating relationship between the two variables. The evidence for one cointegrating vector is rather compelling (p = 0.000), so using the "correct" distribution probably would lead to the same conclusion. This could be investigated more explicitly by considering a bootstrap, but here we will continue the analysis under the assumption that the rank of Π^* is equal to 1, keeping in mind the problems with residual misspecification.

To identify the cointegrating vector exactly, we impose a normalization on the spot exchange rate ($\beta_{Spot} = 1$). (See the results at step 1 in table 7.4.) Having exactly identified the cointegrating vector, we test whether the deterministic trend that the stochastic trend is shown to have cancels when we consider a linear combination of the dollar–franc spot and one-week-forward rates; i.e., $\beta_{Trend} = 0$. These results are reported at step 2 in table 7.4. Then, at step 3, we find supporting evidence for the hypothesis that the one-week-forward rate is weakly exogenous with

Table 7.4
Test for over-identifying restrictions using the full sample, 2001w23–2005w3.

Step 1: The just-identified cointegrating vector normalized with respect to the spot
exchange rate: $\beta_{Spot} = 1$
Spot − 0.9989 Forward + 0.000002 Trend
        0.0014   0.000005
$\alpha_{Spot} = -2.9664$. $\alpha_{Forward} = -1.9872$
       1.5070   1.5015
Log likelihood = 1512.545

Step 2: Testing whether the Trend can be excluded: $\beta_{Trend} = 0$
Spot − 0.9995 Forward
        0.0004
$\alpha_{Spot} = -2.8505$, $\alpha_{Forward} = -1.8709$
       1.5051   1.4993
Log likelihood = 1512.4624

Step 3: Imposing weak exogeneity on the forward exchange rate: $\alpha_{Forward} = 0$
Spot − 0.9995 Forward
        0.0004
$\alpha_{Spot} = -0.9746$
        0.0730
Log likelihood = 1511.6884
LR test of restrictions: $\chi^2(2) = 1.739$ [0.4245]
Partial LR test: Step 2 to Step 3: $\chi^2(1) = [0.2134]$

Step 4: Testing whether $\beta_{Forward} = -1$
Spot − Forward
$\alpha_{Spot} = -0.9663$
        0.0728
Log likelihood = 1511.022
LR test restrictions: $\chi^2(3) = 3.0467$ [0.3845]
Partial LR test: Step 3 to step 4: $\chi^2(1) = [0.2483]$

respect to the cointegrating vector ($\alpha_{Forward} = 0$). Finally, at step 4 we test the hypothesis that $\beta_{Forward} = -1$, and we find good support for that—both partially and jointly with the other restrictions.[9]

The results in table 7.4 indicate that the hypothesis that the dollar–franc spot and one-week-forward exchange rates are linearly cointegrated with coefficient equal to 1 cannot be rejected. In matrix form, the vector error-correction model (VECM) takes the following form, where $\hat{y}_1$ represents the spot rate and $\hat{y}_2$ the forward rate:

$$\begin{pmatrix} \Delta \hat{y}_{1t} \\ \Delta \hat{y}_{2t} \end{pmatrix} = \begin{pmatrix} -0.0030 \\ -0.0033 \end{pmatrix} + \begin{pmatrix} -0.9663 \\ 0 \end{pmatrix} (1,-1) \begin{pmatrix} \hat{y}_{1t-1} \\ \hat{y}_{2t-1} \end{pmatrix} + \begin{pmatrix} \chi_{1(t)} \\ \chi_{2(t)} \end{pmatrix} \tag{7.49}$$

with

$(\chi_1, \chi_2)(0) = 0$, and $E\{(\chi_1, \chi_2)(t) \mid (\hat{y}_1, \hat{y}_2)(0), \dots , (\hat{y}_1, \hat{y}_2)(t-1)\} = 0$, $t > 0$.[10]

7.5 The Dynamics of Foreign Exchange in Figure 7.1

André Anundsen's results are interesting in the context of this book because they establish that the TPD distribution of the members of $\{\hat{y}(t, \omega_P); t \in N\}$ is very different from their MPD distribution. They are also interesting for several other reasons. Under the assumption that I have accurate observations of $(y, \lambda)(t)$, $t \geq 0$, they demonstrate that the theory I developed in section 7.2 is empirically relevant in the upper data universe in figure 7.1. Harald Goldstein's analysis demonstrates that my theory is also empirically relevant in the lower data universe in figure 7.1. Thus, my theory has empirical relevance in both data universes in figure 7.1. Yet the dynamics of foreign exchange in the two universes are very different. I will attend to that puzzle in chapter 10.

7.6 Appendix

In section 6.2 and in E6.2.3 I discussed the implications of Søren Johansen's error-correction formula for the present study of spot and forward exchange in US dollars and Swiss francs. In this appendix, André Anundsen and I will discuss the import of his results for my view that the error-correction formula leaves out of contention many interesting cointegrating relations.

Anundsen recalls that the (not recorded) diagnostics of the VAR model in equation 7.47 indicated that the model suffers from severe misspecification. The final model in equation 7.49 might also be misspecified. To see if it is, he runs a test of the joint distribution of the error terms, VDSpot and VDForward. The results are presented here in table 7.5. These results, and figure 6.2 in chapter 6, suggest to Anundsen that we must take a closer look at the cointegration properties of spot and forward rates in the subsamples that are determined by 2003w26.[11]

Anundsen begins by checking whether the spot and forward rates are cointegrated in the subsamples. His results are presented here in

Table 7.5
A test of the characteristics of the joint distribution of VDSpot and VDForward.

Vector SEM-AR 1–7 test	$F(28, 346) = 0.96211$	[0.5235]
Vector Normality test	$Chi^2(4) = 37.336$	[0.0000]**
Vector Hetero test	$F(6, 368) = 4.1575$	[0.0005]**

Table 7.6
Trace test for cointegration for the first subsample, 2001w23–2003w25.

Eigenvalue: λ_1	H_0	H_1	$p[\lambda_{trace}]$	$p[\lambda_{trace}$ small sample]
0.1531	$r = 0$	$r \geq 1$	0.104	0.131
0.0493	$r \leq 1$	$r \geq 2$	0.548	0.575
Diagnostics	**Test Statistic**	**Value**	**p value**	
Vector AR 1-7 test	$F(28, 142)$	0.6247	[0.9289]	
Vector Normality Test	$\chi^2(4)$	57.121	[0.0000]	
Vector Hetero Test	$F(30, 232)$	0.5753	[0.0326]	

Table 7.7
Trace test for cointegration for the second subsample, 2003w26-20005w5.

Eigenvalue: λ_1	H_0	H_1	$p[\lambda_{trace}]$	$p[\lambda_{trace}$ small sample]
0.4936	$r = 0$	$r \geq 1$	0.000	0.000
0.0741	$r \leq 1$	$r \geq 2$	0.432	0.451
Diagnostics	**Test Statistic**	**Value**	**p value**	
Vector AR 1-7 test	$F(20, 134)$	0.1180	[0.3387]	
Vector Normality Test	$\chi^2(4)$	5.5063	[0.2392]	
Vector Hetero Test	$F(18, 206)$	1.1548	[0.3022]	

tables 7.6 and 7.7. The p value of the small-sample trace test in table 7.6, 0.131, suggests that the dollar–franc spot and forward exchange rates are not cointegrated in the first subsample. In addition, there are clear signs of non-Gaussianity. In contrast, the numbers in table 7.7 provide strong evidence that there is one and only one cointegrating relationship in the second subsample. Also, the diagnostics show no evidence of autocorrelation, non-normality, or heteroscedasticity. Anundsen found corroborating evidence when he used an ADF test to explore whether the difference between the two series is stationary. Although he found the difference to be I(0) for the second sub-sample,

it is I(1) for the first subsample. These results provide strong evidence for a structural break in the data.

To shed more light on the structural break in the full sample, and to test for structural breaks within the two subsamples, Anundsen makes use of the impulse indicator saturation (IIS) algorithm. The algorithm is an integrated part of the Autometrics routine implemented within PcGive (Doornik 2009; Hendry and Doornik 2009). The algorithm includes an impulse dummy for every single observation in the information set, and the model is estimated in blocks to determine which indicators are significant (Hendry et al. 2008; Johansen and Nielsen 2009). On average, approximately αT indicators will be retained by chance, where α denotes a pre-specified significance level and T the number of time-series observations. This is indeed a small price to pay for making a model robust to intermittent structural breaks and data contamination. Castle et al. (2012) show that the IIS algorithm is capable of detecting multiple breaks in the data. It may also be used to test for non-constant parameters (Ericsson and Reisman 2012).

Using a significance level of 1 percent, and re-estimating the VAR(5) for the full sample and the two subsamples, Anundsen finds that 16 dummies are picked up in the first subsample whereas only two are retained for the second subsample. For the full sample analysis, 69 dummies are retained, which clearly suggests huge non-constancies for the full sample. Also, for the first subsample there is evidence of non-constancy, which may explain why results are so different in the first subsample analysis than in the second.

Picking up a large number of dummies may indicate that an important economic variable (perhaps an interest rate) has been omitted, and that the dummies are proxying that variable. The diagnostics for the two subsamples with the dummies included in the models are reported in table 7.8. Including those dummies in the models removes the non-normality problems that were present earlier.

Conditional on the information set, the following conclusions may be drawn:

1. There is a clear structural break in the time-series relationship between the dollar–franc spot rate and one-week-forward exchange rate in 2003w26.
2. For the subsample running from 2001w23 to 2003w25, there is no evidence for cointegration between the spot rate and the one-week-forward exchange rate.

Table 7.8
Diagnostics for VAR(5) for the subsamples with dummies from IIS.

Diagnostics	Test statistic	Value	p value
First subsample			
Vector AR 1–7 test	$F(28, 130)$	0.7576	[0.8014]
Vector Normality Test	$\chi^2(4)$	4.2354	[0.3751]
Vector Hetero Test	$F(66, 200)$	0.7549	[0.9082]
Second subsample			
Vector AR Test	$F(20, 114)$	0.6309	0.8820]
Vector Normality Test	$\chi^2(4)$	0.6885	[0.9527]
Vector Hetero Test	$F(66, 165)$	1.0604	[0.3675]

3. For the subsample 2003w26–2005w3, there is strong evidence for one cointegrating relationship between the two variables.

   a. The spot and one-week-forward rate are co-trending.

   b. The one-week-forward rate is weakly exogenous with respect to the cointegrating vector.

   c. The cointegration coefficients are $(1, -1)$

4. Though there is little evidence of parameter non-constancies for the second subsample, there is much evidence of parameter non-constancies for both the first subsample and the full sample.[12]

Anundsen's interesting analysis does not lend much credibility to my view of the import of figure 6.2 and to my deliberations in E6.2.3 about the error-correction formula and the domain of cointegrating relations. However, since I am given the last word on the matter, I will give my ideas a second try.

Consider the theory I presented in section 7.2. If my observations of the spot and forward exchange rates in the US dollar–Swiss franc currency market are accurate, I can test the empirical relevance of my theory in the empirical context that Anundsen's analysis creates. As table 7.4 and equation 7.49 demonstrate, Anundsen's results do not reject the empirical relevance of my theory in the upper data universe in figure 7.1. That means that there may be a true model of the axioms that is empirically relevant. I do not know what this model looks like, but I can use Anundsen's results to come up with good guesses. The parameters of interest are the value of φ and the probability distribution of the components of $\eta(t)$.

I begin with the probability distribution of the components of $\eta(t)$, and I decide to check whether the errors in equation 7.49 are normally distributed, not heteroscedastic, and not autocorrelated. The answers I obtained from OxMetrix 7, presented in tables 7.9 and 7.10, suggest that I cannot reject the hypothesis that in the true model of my theory the components of the η(t) are normally distributed. (In tables 7.9–7.12 the Portmanteau test is designed to test the goodness-of-fit in a stationary ARMA model. The number in parenthesis records the number of squared residual autocorrelations that are involved in the calculations. The test statistic is asymptotically χ^2 distributed.)

In light of Anundsen's analysis, it is important that I face the error terms in equation 7.49 with the same single-equation tests using the two subsets of the data that the 2003w26 break determines. The results of these tests are displayed in tables 7.11–7.14. They show that the hypothesis that the two error terms are normally distributed is not rejected in the subsamples.

According to my theory, the components of η(t) are multiples of each other. Hence they do not have an ordinary joint two-dimensional

Table 7.9
Single-equation diagnostics using reduced-form residuals: VDSpot Observations 189.

Diagnostics	Test Statistic	Value	p value
Portmanteau(12)[a]	Chi^2(11)	13.977	[0.2343]
AR 1–7 test	F(7, 178)	0.65671	[0.7084]
Normality test	Chi^2(2)	0.7519	[0.6866]
ARCH 1–7 test	F(7, 175)	1.1535	[0.3321]
Hetero test	F(6, 182)	1.9831	[0.0702]
Hetero-X test	F(9, 179)	1.6022	[0.1176]

a. The Portmanteau test is designed to test the goodness of fit in a stationary ARMA model. The number in parentheses is the number of squared residual autocorrelations involved in the calculations. The test statistic is asymptotically χ^2 distributed.

Table 7.10
Single-equation diagnostics using reduced-form residuals: VDForward Observations 189.

Diagnostics	Test Statistic	Value	p Value
p Portmanteau(12)	Chi^2(11)	14.501	[0.2065]
AR 1–7 test:	F(7, 178)	0.71848	[0.6564]
Normality test:	Chi^2(2)	0.76972	[0.6805]
ARCH 1–7 test:	F(7, 175)	1.0769	[0.3802]
Hetero test:	F(6, 182)	2.1408	[0.0508]
Hetero-X test:	F(9, 179)	1.7388	[0.0832]

Table 7.11
Single-equation diagnostics using reduced-form residuals: VDSpot, first subsample.

Diagnostics	Test Statistic	Value	p value
Portmanteau(12)	Chi^2(10)	9.2521	[0.5084]
AR 1-7 test	F(7,94)	0.58605	[0.7657]
ARCH 1-7 test	F(7,93)	0.43410	[0.8785]
Normality test	Chi^2(2)	0.42878	[0.8070]
Hetero test	F(10, 96)	0.70282	[0.7197]
Hetero-X test	F(20, 86)	1.2012	[0.2736]

Table 7.12
Single-equation diagnostics using reduced-form residuals: VDForward, first subsample.

Diagnostics	Test statistic	Value	p value
Portmanteau(12)	Chi^2(10)	9.2919	[0.5046]
AR 1-7 test	F(7,94)	0.58021	[0.7704]
ARCH 1-7 test	F(7,93)	0.42358	[0.8853]
Normality test	Chi^2(2)	0.44266	[0.8015]
Hetero test	F(10, 96)	0.70373	[0.7188]
Hetero-X test	F(20, 86)	1.2017	[0.2732]

Table 7.13
Single-equation diagnostics using reduced-form residuals VDSpot, second subsample.

Diagnostics	Test statistic	Value	p value
Portmanteau(9)	Chi^2(8)	5.1275	[0.7439]
AR 1-5 test	F(5,73)	0.88919	[0.4929]
ARCH 1-5 test	F(5,72)	1.3196	[0.2655]
Normality test	Chi^2(2)	0.34851	[0.8401]
Hetero test	F(6,75)	1.4452	[0.2089]
Hetero-X test	F(9,72)	1.3555	[0.2246]

Table 7.14
Single-equation diagnostics using reduced-form residuals: VDForward, second subsample.

Diagnostics	Test statistic	Value	p value
Portmanteau(9)	Chi^2(8)	5.4286	[0.7109]
AR 1-5 test	F(5,73)	0.93777	[0.4618]
ARCH 1-5 test	F(5,72)	1.1085	[0.3635]
Normality test	Chi^2(2)	0.65505	[0.7207]
Hetero test	F(6,75)	1.6649	[0.1414]
Hetero-X test	F(9,72)	1.5547	[0.1457]

normal distribution. Their joint distribution is singular (T. Anderson 2003, p. 30). The vector normality test of OxMetrics 7 is designed to test whether two variables are jointly normally distributed. Consequently, I cannot use the vector normality test to test whether the *true* model of my theory has two normally distributed components of $\delta(t)$ that are multiples of each other. A rejection by the vector normality test of the probability distribution of the error terms in equation 7.49 has no bearing on the hypothesis that the components of $\delta(t)$ are multiples of each other. The results in table 7.5, therefore, leaves open the possibility that the components of $\delta(t)$ are multiples of each other.

If my interpretation of the numbers in table 7.5 is correct, I can obtain an estimate of φ from the equation

φ = (estimated SD of VDforward)/(estimated SD of VDspot),

which equals 0.9956—a value that accords with my assumption about φ in A5.[13]

I will have more to say about this in chapter 10.

8 Non-Linear Cointegration in Foreign Exchange

It is a fact that the study of three-dimensional random walks is much more involved than the study of two-dimensional and one-dimensional random walks. It is also a fact that time series of many spot exchange rates have characteristics that they share with generalized random walks. Finally, it is the case that many triples of exchange rates are non-linearly cointegrated in obvious ways.[1] These facts have motivated me to write a chapter on non-linearly cointegrated second-order random processes and their relevance to the behavior of spot prices in foreign exchange.

I begin by explaining why the accepted characterization of integrated second-order random processes is inadequate for the analysis of non-linearly cointegrated economic systems. I then propose alternative characterizations of integrated processes, present novel typifications of linearly and non-linearly cointegrated second-order random processes, and check whether the new mathematical concepts have empirical relevance in the markets for Swiss francs, euros, and US dollars.

There are two ways to check whether a mathematically formulated idea of non-linear cointegration has empirical relevance in a foreign-exchange market . One is to develop test statistics for the properties of second-order random processes that the mathematical concept entails, then apply those statistics to pertinent foreign-exchange data.[2] The other is to develop an economic theory of the dynamics of foreign exchange whose variables share the behavior characteristics of the random processes in the mathematical theory, confront the economic theory with data, and check whether the economic theory has empirical relevance.

Each of these methods has pros and cons. With the first method, one can ascertain whether the behavior characteristics of the random processes in the mathematical theory are salient characteristics of a given data-generating process. However, one learns little about the underlying dynamics of foreign exchange. When the data-generating process is shown to have the required properties, an important task remains: to develop an economic theory for a scientific explanation of the observed characteristics of the data-generating process.[3] With the second method, one can realize Ragnar Frisch's vision of a unified theoretical-quantitative and empirical-quantitative approach to economic problems, and one can learn about interesting aspects of the economics of a particular foreign-exchange market. However, one can learn little about inferential procedures that can be used to determine whether the data-generating process in a different setting has the properties that the present chapter's definitions of non-linear cointegration advance. In this chapter I choose the second method.

In section 8.1, I discuss linearly and non-linearly cointegrated second-order random processes. In section 8.2, for the purpose of checking the empirical relevance of my mathematical concepts of linear and non-linear cointegration, I develop an economic theory of foreign exchange whose variables have behavior characteristics like the random processes in the mathematical theory. In sections 8.3 and 8.4, I confront this economic theory with data from the market for Swiss francs, euros, and US dollars. Harald Goldstein carries out the empirical analysis in section 8.3. His estimates of the MPD distribution of my data demonstrate that my economic theory has empirical relevance in the given currency market. His analysis establishes the empirical relevance of my mathematical concepts of linear and non-linear cointegration. In section 8.4, André Anundsen, in the spirit of Haavelmo's Treatise and with David Hendry and Søren Johansen's methods, analyzes the same data to establish characteristics of their TPD distribution. These characteristics are different from the characteristics of the MPD distribution that Goldstein established. Anundsen's results have interesting bearings on the empirical relevance of my mathematical theory of non-linear cointegration.

My mathematical theory of non-linearly cointegrated second-order random processes provides non-linear extensions of Clive Granger and Robert Engle's pioneering work on cointegrated economic time series, suggests an interesting non-linear generalization of Byung Sam Yoo's and Stéphane Gregoir and Guy Laroque's idea of polynomially cointegrated time series, and throws new light on Johansen's characterization of integrated random processes. The references that I have in mind are

Granger 1981, Engle and Granger 1987, Granger 1991, Granger 1995, Yoo 1986, Gregoir and Laroque 1993, Johansen 1992, and chapters 3 and 4 of Johansen 1995. More recent references are Phillips and Park 2001, Aparicio Acosta et al. 2002, Myklebust et al. 2002, Dufrênot and Mignon 2002, and Escanciano and Escribano 2009. I first submitted my theory for publication in the fall of 2007.

8.1 Linearly and Non-Linearly Cointegrated Second-Order Random Processes

According to the theory I develop in section 8.2 and the empirical analyses I present in sections 8.3 and 8.4, spot prices in foreign exchange behave as non-linearly cointegrated second-order random processes that may be both linearly and non-linearly polynomially cointegrated. Before discussing such properties of the dynamics of foreign exchange, I must obtain a reformulation of the standard definition of integrated random processes.

8.1.1 A Reformulation of I(k), k = 0, 1, 2, for Second-Order Random Processes

Granger (1991, pp. 284–286) suggests that the ideas of I(0) and I(k) processes for k > 0 that I describe in section 6.2 have to be reformulated for the purpose of non-linear cointegration analysis. Here is an example that, for the purposes of this chapter, demonstrates why a reformulation is required.

E8.1
Consider a family of random triples, $Y = \{(y_1(t), y_2(t), y_3(t)); t \in N\}$, where $N = \{0, 1, 2, \ldots\}$. Let $\eta = \{(\eta_1(t), \eta_2(t))'; t \in N\}$ be a pair of independently distributed purely random processes, let φ be a 2-by-2 matrix, let $\varphi_i = (\varphi_{i1}, \varphi_{i2})$, with $i = 1, 2$, be the ith row of φ, and assume that the components of Y, for t > 0, satisfy the following equations:

$$y_1(t) = y_1(t-1) + \eta_1(t) + \eta_1(t-1) + \varphi_1(\eta_1(t-1), \eta_2(t-1|))', \qquad (8.1)$$

$$y_2(t) = y_2(t-1) + \eta_2(t) + \eta_2(t-1) + \varphi_2(\eta_1(t-1), \eta_2(t-1))', \qquad (8.2)$$

$$y_3(t) = y_1(t)y_2(t). \qquad (8.3)$$

Assume that $y_i(0)$ and $\eta_i(0) = 0$, $i = 1, 2$, that $\eta_1(t) \in \{1, -1\}$ and $\eta_2(t) \in \{1, -1\}$ for t > 0, and that $\eta_1(t)$ and $\eta_2(t)$ can assume the values 1 and –1 with probability ½ independently of the values assumed by $y_1(t-s)$

and $y_2(t - s)$, $0 < s \leq t$. Assume that $\varphi_{ii} \neq 0$, $i = 1, 2$, and that the eigenvalues of $(I - \varphi)$ in absolute value are less than or equal to 1.

The Y process satisfies a system of stochastic difference equations for which the definition of $I(k)$ processes that I gave in subsections 6.2.1 and 6.2.2 is of limited use. The first two members of Y are $I(1)$ processes. The third member looks like an $I(2)$ process but is not, inasmuch as $\{\Delta^2 y_3(t); t \in N\}$ does not constitute an $I(0)$ process. Hence, Y is not an $I(2)$ process.

Clive Granger has provided many interesting ideas for how best to define $I(0)$ and $I(1)$ processes for non-linear cointegration theory. He began, in Granger 1991, with an idea that I paraphrase in the following example.

E8.2
Consider two real-valued second-order random processes, $X = \{x(t); t \in T\}$ and $Y = \{y(t); t \in T\}$. Let $g(\cdot): R \rightarrow R$ be a continuous function. Suppose that X and Y share a dominant property (say, long memory in mean), and that the process $Z = \{x(t) - g(y(t)); t \in T\}$ does not have this property. Then one can let $I(0)$ comprise all second-order processes that do not have the dominant property, let $I(1)$ contain all other second-order processes, and insist that X and Y are non-linearly cointegrated $I(1)$ processes. (See Granger 1991, p. 285.)

If one defines $I(0)$ and $I(1)$ as in E8.2, one may find a $W \in I(1)$ whose difference series, ΔW, also belongs to $I(1)$. For example, if W is a long memory in mean process, ΔW may be a long memory in mean process too. (See Granger 1995, p. 272.) Such a possibility suggests that, when defining $I(1)$ processes, one should include only those $I(1)$ processes whose difference series belong to $I(0)$. There are many examples of such $(I(0), I(1))$ pairs. They differ in their characterizations of $I(0)$ processes, but they agree in their insistence that the difference of an $I(1)$ process must be an $I(0)$ process.[4]

Here is an example that has played an important role in the development of non-linear cointegration theory.

E8.3
Let $Y = \{Y(t); t \in T\}$ be a second-order random process with constant unconditional mean, $EY(t) = m$. Then Y is a short memory in mean process (SMM) if and only if

$E[\,|\,E\{Y(t+h)\,|\,Y(t), Y(t-1), \ldots\} - m\,|^2] < c_h,$

where c_h is a sequence of constants that converges to 0 as h tends to ∞. I(0) contains all SMM processes and nothing else. If Y is not an SMM process, it is an extended memory in mean process (EMM). Also, Y is an extended I(1) process if and only if it is an EMM process with an SMM difference series. (See Granger 1995, p. 272.)

Granger's profound arguments notwithstanding, I shall not define I(0) and I(1) processes in terms of dominant properties, and I shall not insist that the difference series of an I(1) process be an I(0) process. Instead, I adopt Søren Johansen's definition of I(k) processes (as in section 6.2 above), refer to them as *standard I(k) processes*, and propose a new typification of second-order processes that I denote by J(k), where k = 0, 1, 2.

DEF8.1
Let Y = {y(t) ; t $\in$ N} be a second-order random process, and let $E(y(t))$ denote the mean of y(t). Then Y is a degenerate process if there is a sequence of constants, c_t, t $\in$ N, such that, for all t $\in$ N, $y(t) = c_t$, a.e. If Y is not a degenerate process, then Y is a J(0) process if there exists a constant c such that

$$0 < \liminf_t E(y(t) - c)^2 \text{ and } \limsup_t E(y(t) - c)^2 < \infty, \tag{8.4}$$

Y is a J(1) process if there exists a constant c such that

$$0 < \liminf_t E(y(t) - c)^2/t \text{ and } \limsup_t E(y(t) - c)^2/t < \infty, \tag{8.5}$$

and Y is a J(2) process if there exists a constant c such that

$$0 < \liminf_t E(y(t) - c)^2/t^2 \text{ and } \limsup_t E(y(t) - c)^2/t^2 < \infty. \tag{8.6}$$

When the members of Y have the same mean, c can be taken to equal $E(y(t))$. If X is a triple of second-order processes, X is said to be a J(k) process if its component processes are J(j) processes with all j $\leq$ k and with at least one j = k.[5]

According to DEF8.1, standard I(0) processes are J(0) processes. In fact, all wide-sense stationary processes are J(0) processes. Also, standard I(1) processes are J(1) processes. In particular, the families of $y_1(t)$'s and $y_2(t)$'s in E8.1 are J(1) processes. But so are the families of $\Delta y_3(t)$'s and

$\Delta^2 y_3(t)$'s in E8.1. Finally, standard I(2) processes are J(2) processes. But so are the families of $y_3(t)$'s in E8.1.

It is interesting to see how Granger's definition of SMM and EMM processes in E8.3 and the definition of the same processes in note 4 of Aparicio Acosta et al. 2002 are related to my characterization of integrated processes in DEF8.1. The next two examples attend to that problem.[6]

E8.4

Let U be a normally distributed random variable with mean 0 and variance 1, and let $Y(t) = U$ for all $t=0, 1, 2, \dots$. Then $Y = \{Y(t) ; t \in N\}$ is a second-order process with Granger's $m = 0$ and $E\{Y(t + h) \mid Y(0), \dots , Y(t)\} = U$ for $h > 0$. Consequently, Y is an EMM process according to Granger's definition. It is also easy to see that Y is an EMM process according to the definition of Aparicio Acosta et al., since

$$\text{Lim}_{T \to \infty} \Sigma_{0 \le h \le T} EY(t + h)Y(t) = \text{Lim}_{T \to \infty} \Sigma_{0 \le h \le T} EY(t)Y(t) = \infty.$$

Finally, ΔY is a degenerate process. If a degenerate process is taken to be an SMM process, then Y is an extended I(1) process according to Granger's E8.3 definition of such processes. In contrast, Y is a J(0) process according to DEF8.1, and ΔY is a degenerate process.

E8.5

Let $\{U(t); t \in N\}$ be a Gaussian white noise process with mean 0 and variance 1. Also let $Y(t) = tU(t)$, $t = 0, 1, 2, \dots$. Then $Y = \{Y(t) ; t \in N\}$ is a second-order process with mean 0 and variance t^2. Also, for $h > 0$, $E\{Y(t + h) \mid Y(0), \dots , Y(t)\} = 0$ and $E\{Y(t + h)Y(t)\} = (t + h)tEU(t + h)U(t)$ $= 0$. Hence, Y is an SMM process according to both Granger's definition and that of Aparicio Acosta et al. It is a J(2) process according to DEF8.1. Also, ΔY is an SMM process according to the definitions of Granger and Aparicio Acosta et al., whereas according to DEF8.1 it is a J(2) process.

From E8.4 and E8.5 it follows that an SMM process need not be a J(0) process according to DEF8.1, and a process that is J(0) according to DEF8.1 need not be an SMM process. Also, an extended I(1) process need not be a J(1) process according to DEF8.1, and a process that is J(1) according to DEF8.1 need not be an extended I(1) process on Granger's understanding of the term.

8.1.2 Linear and Non-Linear Cointegration in Triples of Second-Order Random Processes

In this subsection, I present definitions for linearly and non-linearly cointegrated triples of second-order random processes that have no deterministic trends, and I exemplify the definitions with the help of the random process in E8.1. In sections 8.2–8.4, Harald Goldstein, André Anundsen, and I shall use these definitions in our quest to establish salient characteristics of the dynamics of foreign exchange.

Linear cointegration

I begin with linear cointegration. In reading the definition, note that β takes a J(2) process Y into a degenerate process or a J(0) process. That is why I use C(2, 2) instead of Johansen's C(1, 1).

DEF8.2
A J(2) family of second-order random triples, $Y = \{(y_1(t), y_2(t), y_3(t)); t \in N\}$, is linearly cointegrated of order C(2, 2) if there exists a vector, $\beta \in R^3$, with at least two non-zero components such that the members of the family of random variables $\{\beta y(t); t \in N - \{0\}\}$ constitute either a J(0) process or a degenerate process. The vector β is termed a cointegrating vector for Y.

I have given a definition of a three-dimensional J(2) process that is linearly cointegrated of order C(2, 2). The definition generalizes in the obvious way to characterize three-dimensional J(2) processes that are linearly cointegrated of order C(2, 1). In fact, a J(2) family of second-order random triples, $Y = \{(y_1(t), y_2(t), y_3(t)); t \in N\}$, is linearly cointegrated of order C(2, 1) if there exists a linear function, $\beta(\cdot): R^3 \to R$ such that the family of random variables $[\beta(y_1(t), y_2(t), y_3(t)); t \in N]$ is a J(1) process. An example is a transform of the Y process in E8.1, $X = \{(x_1, x_2, x_3)(t); t \in N - \{0\}\}$, where $x_1(t) = y_1(t)$, $x_2(t) = by_1(t) + y_2(t)$, and $x_3(t) = x_1(t)x_2(t)$, and where the φ satisfies the equation $(a_1\varphi_1 + a_2\varphi_2) = 0$ for some pair $a = (a_1, a_2)$. In this case the X process is a J(2) process, and

$$(a,0) \cdot (x_1, x_2, x_3)(t)' = a_2 by_1(t) + a \cdot (\eta_1(t), \eta_2(t))'$$

is a J(1) process.

DEF8.2 also generalizes to characterize three-dimensional J(1) processes that are cointegrated of order C(1, 1). In fact, a J(1) family of second-order random triples, $Y = \{(y_1(t), y_2(t), y_3(t)); t \in N\}$, is linearly cointegrated of order C(1, 1) if there exists a linear function, $\beta(\cdot): R^3 \to$

R such that the family of random variables $[\beta(y_1(t), y_2(t), y_3(t)); t \in N]$ constitutes either a $J(0)$ process or a degenerate process. An example is a second-order random process that satisfies the conditions I specify in E8.1 with equation 8.3 changed to $y_3(t) = y_1(t) + y_2(t)$. In this case the Y process is a $J(1)$ process, the cointegrating vector is $\beta = (1, 1, -1)$, and $\{\beta y(t) ; t \in N - \{0\}\}$ is a degenerate process.

Non-linear cointegration

DEF8.3
A $J(2)$ family of second-order random triples, $Y = \{(y_1(t), y_2(t), y_3(t)); t \in N\}$, is non-linearly cointegrated of order $NC(2, 2)$ if there exists a non-linear function, $f(\cdot): R^3 \rightarrow R$, such that the members of the family of random variables $\{f(y(t)); t \in N - \{0\}\}$ constitute either a $J(0)$ process or a degenerate process. The function $f(\cdot)$ is termed a non-linear cointegrating function for Y.

A $J(2)$ process that is non-linearly cointegrated of order $NC(2, 2)$ with the cointegrating function $f(\cdot)$ may also be non-linearly cointegrated of order $NC(2, 2)$ with an entirely different cointegrating function, $g(\cdot)$. Here is an example.

E8.8
Consider the family of second-order random triples in E8.1,

$$Y = \{(y_1(t), y_2(t), y_3(t)); t \in N\}.$$

The given Y process is non-linearly cointegrated of order $NC(2, 2)$ with the non-linear cointegrating function $f(x, y, z) = z - xy$. Now suppose that there exists a pair of non-zero constants a_1 and a_2 such that $(a_1\varphi_1 + a_2\varphi_2) = 0$. Then Y is linearly cointegrated of order $C(2, 2)$ with the cointegrating vector $(a, 0)$, where $a = (a_1, a_2)$, and non-linearly cointegrated of order $NC(2, 2)$ with the cointegrating function $g(x, y, z) = z - (x - a_2)(y - a_1) + b$, where b is a finite constant. The given linearly cointegrated Y is, also, non-linearly cointegrated of order $NC(2, 2)$ with the non-linear cointegrating function $h(x, y, z) = a_1x + a_2(z/x)$, $x > 0$, and non-linearly cointegrated of order $NC(2, 2)$ with the non-linear cointegrating function $k(x, y, z) = a_1(z/y) + a_2y$, where $y > 0$.[7]

I have defined and given examples of triples of $J(2)$ processes that are non-linearly cointegrated of order $NC(2.2)$. DEF8.3 generalizes in the obvious way to characterize three-dimensional $J(2)$ processes that are non-linearly cointegrated of order NC(2, 1). In fact, a J(2) family of second-order random triples, $Y = \{(y_1(t), y_2(t), y_3(t)); t \in N\}$, is non-linearly cointegrated of order NC(2, 1) if there exists a non-linear function $f(\cdot):R^3 \to R$ such that the family of random variables $\{f(y_1(t), y_2(t), y_3(t)); t \in N\}$ is a J(1) process. An example of such a process is the following variant of the Y process in E8.1: Let Y be a three-dimensional process that satisfies the conditions in E8.1 with equation 8.3 changed to $y_3(t) = (y_1(t))(b + y_2(t))$, where b is a non-zero constant. Let $f(x, y, z) = z - xy$, and observe that the given Y is now a J(2) second-order random process that is non-linearly cointegrated of order NC(2, 1) with the cointegrating function $f(\cdot)$.

DEF8.3 also generalizes to characterize three-dimensional J(1) processes that are non-linearly cointegrated of order NC(1, 1). In fact, a J(1) family of second-order random triples, $Y = \{(y_1(t), y_2(t), y_3(t)); t \in N\}$, is non-linearly cointegrated of order NC(1, 1) if there exists a non-linear function $f(\cdot):R^3 \to R$ such that the family of random variables $\{f(y_1(t), y_2(t), y_3(t)); t \in N\}$ is a J(0) process or a degenerate process. For example, the J(1) version of the family of second-order random triples $Y = \{(y_1(t), y_2(t), y_3(t)); t \in N\}$ in E8.1 in which equation 8.3 is changed to $y_3(t) = y_1(t)^\beta y_2(t)^{1-\beta}$, with $\beta = \frac{1}{2}$, is non-linearly cointegrated of order NC(1, 1) with the cointegrating function $f(x, y, z) = z - x^{1/2}y^{1/2}$. This version of the Y process in E8.1 constitutes a family of mathematical models of Escanciano and Escribano's (2009) general non-linear parametric cointegration model.

Non-linear polynomial cointegration

To state the last definition, I must paraphrase the standard definition of a linearly polynomially integrated random process and introduce a new bit of notation: Dif.Op.F(x, y, z). First linear polynomial cointegration: A three-dimensional second-order random process, X, that is an I(2) process is linearly polynomially cointegrated if there exist two non-zero vectors in R^3, β_0 and β_1, such that $\beta_0 X + \beta_1 \Delta X$ is an I(0) process.[8] Next, Dif. Op.F(x, y, z): Let $F(\cdot): R^3 \to R$ be a non-linear differentiable function. Then

$$\text{Dif.Op.}F(x, y, z) = \partial F(x, y, z)/\partial x \cdot \Delta x + \partial F(x, y, z)/\partial y \cdot \Delta y + \partial F(x, y, z)/\partial z \cdot \Delta z.$$

DEF8.4

A J(2) family of second-order random triples, $Y = \{(y_1(t), y_2(t), y_3(t)); t \in N\}$, is non-linearly polynomially cointegrated if there exist a vector $\beta \in R^3$, a non-linear differentiable function $F(\cdot): R^3 \to R$, and a

differential operator Dif.Op.F(x, y, z) such that the members of the
family of random variables{$\beta y(t)$ + Dif.Op.F(y(t)); $t \in N - \{0\}$} constitute
either a J(0) process or a degenerate process.

My definition of non-linear polynomial cointegration is a natural extension of the original definition of (linearly) polynomially cointegrated
second-order random processes. The following two theorems will bear
witness to this fact. The proofs are easy and therefore are left to the
reader.

T8.1
Consider the family of J(2) second-order random triples in E8.1, Y =
{$(y_1(t), y_2(t), y_3(t))$; $t \in N$}. Y is non-linearly polynomially cointegrated
with $\beta = 0$, and F(x, y, z) = xy − z.

T8.2
Consider the family of J(2) second-order random triples in E8.1, Y =
{$(y_1(t), y_2(t), y_3(t))$; $t \in N$}, and suppose that Y is linearly cointegrated
with the cointegrating vector $(a_1, a_2, 0)$. Let F(x, y, z) = xy − z, and choose
β to be the cointegrating vector. Then the members of the family of
random variables {$\beta y(t)$ + Dif.Op.F(y(t)) ; $t \in N - \{0\}$} constitute a J(0)
process. Hence Y is, also, non-linearly polynomially cointegrated.

8.2 A Formal Theory-Data Confrontation in Foreign Exchange

In this section I develop a formal data confrontation of a theory of non-
linearly cointegrated foreign-exchange rates. As in chapter 6, the theory
universe, the data universe, and the bridge are represented by (Ω_T, Γ_T,
(Ω_T, $\aleph_T$, $P_T(\cdot)$)), (Ω_P, Γ_P, (Ω_P. $\aleph_P$, $P_P(\cdot)$)), and (Ω, $\Gamma_{T,P}$). Also, sequences of
vectors in the theory universe function as vector-valued sequences in
Ω_T and as vector-valued random processes on (Ω_T, $\aleph_T$). Similarly,
sequences of vectors in the data universe function as vector-valued
sequences in Ω_P and as vector-valued random processes on (Ω_P, $\aleph_P$). I
assume throughout that Ω_T and Ω_P are disjoint, that $\aleph_T$ and $\aleph_P$ are stochastically independent, and that the probability space, ($\Omega_T \times \Omega_P$, $\aleph$,
$P(\cdot)$), is as I described it in chapter 2.

8.2.1 The Theory Universe
In this subsection I address the functioning of a foreign-exchange
market in which three currencies—the Swiss franc, the US dollar, and

the euro—are traded. For this market there are six possible exchange rates. I pick three of them—the franc–euro rate, the euro–dollar rate, and the franc–dollar rate—and assign them one significant property: The value of one of the three equals the product of the values of the other two. I assume that the market is frictionless.

Two of the members of Γ_T describe conceptual characteristics of the currency market. In these axioms, S denotes a sequence of triples of the chosen three exchange rates, and x and λ denote two sequences of triples of auxiliary variables. ξ denotes a sequence of triples of error terms, N denotes the set of all periods beginning at some arbitrary time in the past, and a period is taken to be a week.

A1

$\Omega_T \subset (R_+^3 \times R^9)^N$. Thus, $\omega_T \in \Omega_T$ only if ω_T is a sequence of vectors, $(S_t, x_t, \lambda_t, \xi_t)$, all of which belong to $R_+^3 \times R^3 \times R^3 \times R^3$. In short, $\omega_T = (S, x, \lambda, \xi)$ for some $(S, x, \lambda, \xi) \in (R_+^3 \times R^9)^N$, where N = {0, 1, ... }.

A2

For each $t \in N$, let the vector-valued function $(S, x, \lambda, \xi)(t, \cdot): \Omega_T \to (R_+^3 \times R^3 \times R^3 \times R^3)$ be defined by the equations $(S(t, \omega_T), x(t, \omega_T), \lambda(t, \omega_T), \xi(t, \omega_T)) = \omega_{Tt}$ and $\omega_T \in \Omega_T$, where ω_{Tt} is the tth component of ω_T. The functions $(S, x, \lambda, \xi)(t, \cdot): \Omega_T \to (R_+^3 \times R^3 \times R^3 \times R^3)$, $t \in N$, are measurable with respect to $\aleph_T$. Moreover, the family of finite-dimensional probability distributions of the $(S, x, \lambda, \xi)(t, \cdot)$ that $P_T(\cdot)$ determines is the family of probability distributions that the researcher in charge, subject to the conditions on which Γ_T insists, assigns to the given functions. I denote it by RPD.

The next members of Γ_T describe law-like properties of the elements that play essential roles in the theory that the researcher is confronting with data. Of them, the first four, A3–A6, delineate the way the auxiliary variables x and λ function in the theory. The last two, A7 and A8, depict characteristics of the RPD distribution of $(S, x, \lambda, \xi)(t, \cdot)$.

In the theory, x is to play the role of S. In A3 I describe how it does so.

A3

For all $\omega_T \in \Omega_T$, and for all $t \in N$, $S_3(t, \omega_T) = S_1(t, \omega_T) S_2(t, \omega_T)$. Also,

$$S_i(t, \omega_T) = \max(x_i(t, \omega_T), 0), \quad i = 1, 2$$

and   (8.7)

$S_3(t, \omega_T) = \max(x_3(t, \omega_T), 0)$ if $x_1(t, \omega_T) \geq 0$ or $x_2(t, \omega_T) \geq 0$; otherwise, $S_3(t, \omega_T) = 0$.

Thus, for $i = 1, 2$ the sample path of $S_i(\cdot, \omega_T)$ coincides with the sample path of $x_i(\cdot, \omega_T)$ over any stretches of time in which the $x_i(t, \omega_T)$ assume positive values. Similarly, the sample path of $S_3(\cdot, \omega_T)$ coincides with the sample path of $x_3(\cdot, \omega_T)$ over any stretches of time in which both $x_1(t, \omega_T)$ and $x_2(t, \omega_T)$ are positive.

In the theory, λ is to play the role of the rationally expected value of x while x is playing the role of S. I describe how in the following axioms. A4 describes how the market participants' expectations are formed; A5 and A6 delineate the conditions that a market in equilibrium must satisfy.

A4

Let φ be a 2×2 matrix. Assume that $\varphi_{ii} \neq 0$, $i = 1, 2$, and that the eigenvalues of $(I - \varphi)$ have absolute values that are less than or equal to 1. Let α_t, $t \geq 0$, be a sequence of constants. For all $\omega_T \in \Omega_T$, and for all $t \in N$,

$$\begin{pmatrix} \lambda_1 (0,\omega_T) \\ \lambda_2 (0,\omega_T) \end{pmatrix} = \varphi \begin{pmatrix} x_1 (0,\omega_T) \\ x_2 (0,\omega_T) \end{pmatrix}, \tag{8.8}$$

$$\lambda_3 (0, \omega_T) = \lambda_1 (0, \omega_T) \lambda_2 (0, \omega_T) + \alpha_0,$$

$$\begin{pmatrix} \lambda_1 (t,\omega_T) \\ \lambda_2 (t,\omega_T) \end{pmatrix} = \begin{pmatrix} \lambda_1 (t-1,\omega_T) \\ \lambda_2 (t-1,\omega_T) \end{pmatrix} + \varphi \begin{pmatrix} x_1 (t,\omega_T) - \lambda_1 (t-1,\omega_T) \\ x_2 (t,\omega_T) - \lambda_2 (t-1,\omega_T) \end{pmatrix}, \quad t \geq 1 \tag{8.9}$$

and

$$\lambda_3(t, \omega_T) = \lambda_1(t, \omega_T)\lambda_2(t, \omega_T) + \alpha_t, \quad t > 0. \tag{8.10}$$

A5

Let $\acute{y} \in R_+^3$ be a constant vector with $\acute{y}_3 = \acute{y}_1 \cdot \acute{y}_2$. For all $\omega_T \in \Omega_T$, and for all $t \in N$,

$$\xi_i(0, \omega_T) = 0, \quad i = 1, 2$$
$$x(0, \omega_T) = \acute{y}, \tag{8.11}$$

$$x_i(t + 1, \omega_T) = \lambda_i(t, \omega_T) + \xi_i(t + 1, \omega_T), \quad i = 1, 2 \tag{8.12}$$

and

$$x_3(t + 1, \omega_T) = x_1(t + 1, \omega_T)x_2(t + 1, \omega_T). \tag{8.13}$$

A6

For all $\omega_T \in \Omega_T$, and for all $t \in N$,

$$\xi_3(t + 1, \omega_T) = \lambda_1(t, \omega_T)\xi_2(t + 1, \omega_T) + \lambda_2(t, \omega_T)\xi_1(t + 1, \omega_T)$$

$$+ [\xi_1(t + 1, \omega_T)\xi_2(t + 1, \omega_T) - \alpha_t] \qquad (8.14)$$

and

$$x_3(t + 1, \omega_T) = \lambda_3(t, \omega_T) + \xi_3(t + 1, \omega_T). \qquad (8.15)$$

When we look back at equations 8.9, 8.12, and 8.15 and take axioms A7 and A8 below into account, it should not be too difficult to intuit that the three equations depict an equilibrium state of a frictionless foreign-exchange market in which the agents in the market, in an aggregate sense, are risk neutral and are endowed with rational expectations about future exchange rates.

A7

Relative to $P_T(\cdot)$, the family of functions $\{\xi(t, \omega_T); t \geq 1\}$ constitutes a vector-valued second-order stochastic process whose first two components form a two-dimensional orthogonal J(0) process with means 0 and with the covariance matrix

$$\Sigma_\xi(t) = \begin{pmatrix} \sigma_{\xi 1}(t)^2 & \sigma_{12}(t) \\ \sigma_{12}(t) & \sigma_{\xi 2}(t)^2 \end{pmatrix}$$

with positive diagonal elements.

A8

Relative to $P_T(\cdot)$, for each $t \in N - \{0\}$, the first two components of ξ and the three x components of the family of functions $\{(S, x, \lambda, \xi)(t, \omega_T); t \in N\}$ satisfy the following conditions:

(i) $E\{\xi_i(t, \omega_T) \mid x(0), \dots, x(t - 1)\} = 0$ a.e., $i = 1, 2$.
(ii) There exists a sequence of positive constants, M_t, such that $E\{\xi_i(t, \omega_T)^4 \mid x(0), \dots, x(t - 1)\} < M_t$ a.e., $i = 1, 2$.
(iii) $E\{\xi_1(t, \omega_T) \xi_2(t, \omega_T) \mid x(0), \dots, x(t - 1)\} = \alpha_{t-1}$ a.e.

Again it is important to note that axioms A1–A8 delineate all the positive analogies of behavior in the markets under consideration that are at stake in the present theory-data confrontation and nothing else. These axioms have interesting logical consequences, which I record in the following theorem.

T8.3
Suppose that A1–A8 are valid, and let φ be the matrix in A5. Let I be the 2×2 identity matrix. Let $\varphi_1 = (\varphi_{11}, \varphi_{12})$ and $\varphi_2 = (\varphi_{21}, \varphi_{22})$. Let $x^*(t) = (x_1, x_2)(t)'$. Let $\xi^*(t) = (\xi_1, \xi_2)(t)'$. Then, for all $t \in N$,

a. with $P_T(\cdot)$ probability 1,
1. $\lambda(t, \omega_T) = E\{x(t+1) \mid x(0), \dots, x(t)\}$.
2. for all s>0, $E\{\xi_i(t+s, \omega_T)\xi_i(t, \omega_T) \mid x(0), \dots, x(t-1)\} = 0, i = 1, 2;$
b. for all $\omega_T \in \Omega_T$,
1. $x^*(t+1, \omega_T)' = x^*(t, \omega_T)' + \xi^*(t+1, \omega_T) - (I - \varphi)\xi^*(t, \omega_T),$
2. $x_3(t, \omega_T) = x_1(t, \omega_T) \cdot x_2(t, \omega_T),$
3. $x^*(t+1, \omega_T)' = \varphi \cdot x^*(0) + \varphi\Sigma_{0 \leq s \leq t} \xi^*(t-s, \omega_T) + \xi^*(t+1, \omega_T),$ and
4. $x_3(t+1, \omega_T) = [\varphi_1 \cdot x^*(0) + \varphi_1\Sigma_{0 \leq s \leq t} \xi^*(t-s, \omega_T) + \xi_1(t+1, \omega_T)]$
   $\cdot [\varphi_2 \cdot x^*(0) + \varphi_2\Sigma_{0 \leq s \leq t} \xi^*(t-s, \omega_T) + \xi_2(t+1, \omega_T)].$

8.2.2 Linear and Non-Linear Cointegration in the Theory Universe
The characteristic features of the families of finite-dimensional probability distributions of the first two components of x in T8.3 are characteristics that they share with the probability distributions of all generalized random walks. The third component of x is a product of such processes. The components of x may assume both negative and positive values, but the components of S can assume only non-negative values. In the intended interpretation of the axioms, the pertinent characteristics of the probability distributions of the components of x are also characteristics of the probability distributions of S in long stretches of positive values of the components of x. This fact is important for our empirical analysis. I observe the values of empirical counterparts of the components of S. Since these values are positive, they are also observations of empirical counterparts of the components of x.

The foreign-exchange market that I study in this section has many interesting characteristics. To wit: Let $\ddot{X} = \{(x_1(t), x_2(t), x_3(t); t \in N\}$ be the x process in T8.3 and assume that A1–A8 are valid. Then the first two components of $\ddot{X}$ are J(1) processes, the third component is a J(2) process, and $\ddot{X}$ itself is a J(2) process. Moreover, the three components of $\ddot{X}$ are non-linearly cointegrated of order NC(2, 2) with the cointegrating function $f(x, y, z) = z - xy$, and when the M_t in A8(ii) are uniformly bounded the three components of $\ddot{X}$ are non-linearly polynomially cointegrated with the non-linear cointegrating differential operator

$$\text{Dif.Op.}F(x(t)) = \partial F(x, y, z)/\partial x \cdot \Delta x + \partial F(x, y, z)/\partial y \cdot \Delta y$$
$$+ \partial F(x, y, z)/\partial z \cdot \Delta z,$$

where $F(x, y, z) = xy - z$. Finally, the three components of $\ddot{X}$ may be linearly cointegrated; if they are, they are also non-linearly cointegrated with several new non-linear cointegrating functions. They are linearly cointegrated of order $C(2, 2)$ if and only if there is a pair of constants a_1 and a_2 such that $a_1\varphi_1 + a_2\varphi_2 = 0$. Moreover, if $\ddot{X}$ is linearly cointegrated of order $C(2, 2)$, it is non-linearly cointegrated of order $NC(2, 2)$ with three new non-linear cointegrating functions:

$$g(x, y, z) = z - (x - a_2)(y - a_1) + b, \text{ where b is a constant,} \tag{8.16}$$

$$h(x, y, z) = a_1x + a_2(z/x), \qquad x > 0 \tag{8.17}$$

and

$$k(x, y, z) = a_1(z/y) + a_2y, \qquad y > 0. \tag{8.18}$$

When the M_t in A8(ii) are uniformly bounded, the linearly cointegrated $\ddot{X}$ is polynomially cointegrated with $\beta = (a_1, a_2, 0)$ and Dif.Op.$F(x(t))$, with $F(x, y, z) = xy - z$.

Equations 8.17 and 8.18 might give the impression that my insistence in A1–A8 that the third component of $\ddot{X}$ be a product of the first two components—i.e., that $x_3(t) = x_1(t)x_2(t)$ for all t in N—was arbitrary, and that I could just as well have assumed that $x_3(t) = x_1(t)/x_2(t)$ for all t in N. For purposes of this chapter, it is important to note that my choice was well motivated. In this section I set out to develop a theory of the dynamics of foreign exchange within the framework of second-order random processes. When A1–A8 are valid, all the mathematical models of the $\ddot{X}$ process in T8.3 are second-order processes. In contrast, a vector-valued random process $\ddot{X}^*$ that satisfies the conditions of A1–A8 and T8.3 with equation 8.10 changed to $x_3(t + 1) = x_1(t + 1)/x_2(t + 1)$ has any number of mathematical models that are not second-order processes.

8.2.3 The Data Universe

Two of the members of Γ_P describe the conceptual framework of the data universe. In these axioms, the components of K, K_i, $i = 1, 2, 3$, denote sequences of weekly quotes on three spot exchange rates. These sequences are understood to be observational counterparts of the three components of S in Ω_T. Also, the components of $\hat{y}$, $\hat{y}_i$, i= 1, 2, 3, are auxiliary series that I need to delineate the stochastic properties of the observed values of the components of K. They are understood to be observational counterparts of the components of the x in Ω_T. Finally, the numbers in N denote consecutive "weeks" beginning at some arbitrary time.

D1

$\Omega_P \subset (R_+^3 \times R^3)^N$. Thus, $\omega_P \in \Omega_P$ only if ω_P is a sequence of vectors, $(K_t, \hat{y}_t)$, all of which belong to $R_+^3 \times R^3$. In short, $\omega_P = (K, \hat{y})$ for some $(K, \hat{y}) \in (R_+^3 \times R^3)^N$, where $N = \{0, 1, 2, \dots \}$.

D2

For each $t \in N$, let the vector-valued function, $(K, \hat{y})(t, \cdot): \Omega_P \to R_+^3 \times R^3$, be defined by the equations $(K(t, \omega_P), \hat{y}(t, \omega_P)) = \omega_{Pt}$ and $\omega_P \in \Omega_P$, where ω_{Pt} is the tth component of ω_P. The functions $(K, \hat{y})(t, \cdot)$ are measurable with respect to $\aleph_P$. Moreover, subject to the conditions on which Γ_P insists, the family of finite-dimensional probability distributions of the members of $\{(K(t, \omega_P), \hat{y}(t, \omega_P)); t \in N\}$ that $P_P(\cdot)$ determines is the true family of probability distributions of the given functions. I denote it by TPD.

The assertions that describe law-like properties of the data-generating process are stated in D3 and D 4. D3 describes the way the three components of $\hat{y}$ serve as auxiliary variables for the components of K.

D3

For all $\omega_P \in \Omega_P$, and for all $t \in N$, the components of $\{(K, \hat{y})(t, \omega_P); t \in N\}$ satisfy the following conditions:

$$K_1(t, \omega_P) = \max(\hat{y}_1(t, \omega_P), 0),$$
$$K_2(t, \omega_P) = \max(\hat{y}_2(t, \omega_P), 0),$$

$$\tag{8.19}$$

$$K_3(t, \omega_P) = K_1(t, \omega_P) \cdot K_2(t, \omega_P),$$
$$\hat{y}_3(t, \omega_P) = \hat{y}_1(t, \omega_P) \cdot \hat{y}_2(t, \omega_P).$$

$$\tag{8.20}$$

From these conditions it follows that $K_3(t, \omega_P) = \max(\hat{y}_3(t, \omega_P), 0)$ if $\hat{y}_1(t, \omega_P)$ or $\hat{y}_2(t, \omega_P)$ or both are positive. Otherwise $K_3(t, \omega_P) = 0$. Note, also, that positive observations of the K_i, $i = 1, 2$, are observations of the associated $\hat{y}_i$.

D4

Relative to $P_P(\cdot)$, the family of random vectors, $\{\hat{y}(t, \omega_P); t \in N\}$, constitutes a J(2) family of second-order random triples.

8.2.4 The Bridge

Four of the members of $\Gamma_{T,P}$, G1–G4, describe the conceptual frame work of the bridge.

G1

Observations are sequences of pairs of vectors, $(\omega_{Tt}, \omega_{Pt})$, that are components of some pair, (ω_T, ω_P), that belongs to the sample space.

G2

The sample space, Ω, is a subset of $\Omega_T \times \Omega_P$; that is, $\Omega \subset \Omega_T \times \Omega_P$.

G3

$\Omega_T \subset \{\omega_T \in \Omega_T$ for which there is an $\omega_P \in \Omega_P$ with $(\omega_T, \omega_P) \in \Omega\}$.

G4

In $(\Omega_T \times \Omega_P, \aleph, P(\cdot))$ it is the case that $\Omega \in \aleph$ and $P(\Omega) > 0$.

The remaining axiom in $\Gamma_{t,p}$ describes how the x components of ω_T are related to the y components of ω_P in the sample space. This description is taken to account for inaccurate observations and for the structural differences under which trading takes place in the theory universe and the real world.

G5

Let $\acute{y} \in R^3$ be the vector of constants in A4, let ψ be a 2×2 matrix, and suppose that the eigenvalues of $(I - \psi)$ have absolute values less than 1 and that $|\psi| \neq 0$. For each $(\omega_T, \omega_P) \in \Omega$,

$$\hat{y}_i(0, \omega_P) = \acute{y}_i, \; i = 1, 2, 3$$

$$(\hat{y}_1, \hat{y}_2)(t, \omega_P)'$$

$$= (\hat{y}_1, \hat{y}_2)(t - 1, \omega_P)' + \psi(x_1(t, \omega_T) - \hat{y}_1(t - 1, \omega_P), x_2(t, \omega_T) - \hat{y}_2(t - 1, \omega_P))', \; t \geq 1 \tag{8.21}$$

and

$$\hat{y}_3(t, \omega_P) = \hat{y}_1(t, \omega_P) \, \hat{y}_2(t, \omega_P), \; t \geq 1. \tag{8.22}$$

Since $(\hat{y}_1, \hat{y}_2)(t, \omega_P)' = \Sigma_{0 \leq s \leq t}(I - \psi)^s \, \psi(x_1, x_2)(t - s, \omega_T)'$, G3 is included in the axioms to rule out uninteresting models.

8.2.5 The MPD

The RPD of A1–A8 and D1, D3, and G1–G5 induce a family of finite-dimensional probability distributions of ω_P that I denote by MPD and read as the marginal probability distribution of the components of ω_P. The properties of the MPD and Kolmogorov's Consistency Theorem (see B. Stigum 1990, p. 347, theorem T 15.23) imply that there exists a probability measure, $P_M(\cdot){:}\aleph_P \to [0, 1]$, relative to which the family of finite-dimensional probability distributions of the $\{(\check{K}, \hat{y})(t, \omega_P); t \in N\}$ equals the MPD. I shall use the P_M measure to describe the characteristics of the MPD distribution of the family of triples $(\hat{y}_1, \hat{y}_2, \hat{y}_3)(t, \omega_P)$.

The characteristics of the present MPD are as described in the following theorems. Before I state the theorems a few clarifying remarks are necessary. First, the definition of two new error terms: For all $(\omega_T, \omega_P) \in \Omega$ and all $t \in N - \{0\}$, $(\varsigma_1, \varsigma_2)(t, \omega_P) = (\xi_1, \xi_2)(t, \omega_T)$. From this definition, from the fact that $(\xi_1, \xi_2)(0, \omega_T) = 0$, and from

$$\psi(\varsigma_1, \varsigma_2)(t, \omega_P)' + \psi(I - \varphi)(\varsigma_1, \varsigma_2)(t - 1, \omega_P)'$$

$$= (\Delta\hat{y}^*(t, \omega_P) - (I - \psi)\Delta\hat{y}^*(t - 1, \omega_P)), \quad t > 1$$

where $\hat{y}^*(t, \omega_P) = (\hat{y}_1, \hat{y}_2)(t, \omega_P)'$, it follows that the $(\varsigma_1, \varsigma_2)(t, \omega_P)$ are well defined and measurable with respect to $\aleph_P$. But if that is right, I can use the definition of MPD in chapter 6 to show that the $(\varsigma_1, \varsigma_2)(t, \omega_P)$ in the MPD distribution has the same probability distribution as the $(\xi_1, \xi_2)(t, \omega_T)$ have in the RPD distribution. To wit: Let M be a finite positive integer, let A be a subset of $(R^2)^M$, and observe that, according to G 3, $\Omega_T(\Omega) = \Omega_T$. For any finite subset of N, $\{t_i, i = 1, \ldots, M\}$, where $t_i \neq t_j$ if $i \neq j$, it must be the case that

$$\text{MPD}(((\varsigma_1, \varsigma_2)(t_1, \omega_P), \ldots, (\varsigma_1, \varsigma_2)(t_M, \omega_P)) \in A)$$

$$= P_T(\{\omega_T \in \Omega_T: ((\xi_1, \xi_2)(t_1, \omega_T), \ldots, (\xi_1, \xi_2)(t_M, \omega_T)) \in A\}).$$

An equally easy argument shows that, for all $t \in N - \{0\}$, in the MPD distribution $(\varsigma_1, \varsigma_2)(t, \omega_P)$ is orthogonal to $((\hat{y}_1, \hat{y}_2)(t - s, \omega_P), s = 1, \ldots, t$, with P_M measure 1.

Recall that G5 and T8.3.3 imply that, with $\hat{y}^*(t, \omega_P) = (\hat{y}_1, \hat{y}_2)(t, \omega_P)'$, it is the case that, for all $t \in N - \{0\}$ and all $\omega \in \Omega$,

$$\Delta\hat{y}^*(t, \omega_P) - (I - \psi)\Delta\hat{y}^*(t - 1, \omega_P) = \psi\,\xi^*(t, \omega_T) - \psi \cdot (I - \varphi)\,\xi^*(t - 1, \omega_T), t \geq 1.$$

T8.4

Suppose that A1–A8, D1, D3, and G1–G5 are valid, and let $\hat{y}^*(t, \omega_P) = (\hat{y}_1(t, \omega_P), \hat{y}_2(t, \omega_P))'$, $t \in N$. The MPD distribution of $\{(K, \hat{y})(t, \omega_P), t \in N\}$ then has the following characteristics.

(i) Relative to $P_M(\cdot)$, the family of finite-dimensional probability distributions of $\{\hat{y}^*(t, \omega_P); t \in N\}$, are the probability distributions of a pair of second-order random processes that constitutes a solution to the stochastic difference equation

$$\Delta\hat{y}^*(t) - (I - \psi)\Delta\hat{y}^*(t - 1) = \psi\varsigma^*(t) - \psi(I - \varphi)\varsigma^*(t - 1), \quad t \geq 1. \tag{8.23}$$

Also,

$$\hat{y}_3(t) = \hat{y}_1(t)\ \hat{y}_2(t), \qquad t \geq 0. \tag{8.24}$$

The pairs $\varsigma^*(t) = (\varsigma_1, \varsigma_2)(t, \omega_P)$, $t \in N$, in equation 8.21 are measurable with respect to $\aleph_P$ and $\varsigma^*(0) = 0$. Relative to $P_M(\cdot)$, they constitute an orthogonal $J(0)$ second-order random process with means 0, with the same covariance matrix as ξ^*,

$$\Sigma_\varsigma(t) = \begin{pmatrix} \sigma_{\xi 1}(t)^2 & \sigma_{12}(t) \\ \sigma_{12}(t) & \sigma_{\xi 2}(t)^2 \end{pmatrix},$$

and with finite fourth-order moments that are uniformly bounded in all mathematical models of the axioms in which the M_t in A8(ii) are uniformly bounded.

(ii) In a mathematical model of the axioms in which $\psi = \varphi$, relative to $P_M(\cdot)$,

$$\Delta\hat{y}^*(t) = \psi\varsigma^*(t) \text{ for all } t \geq 1 \tag{8.25}$$

and

$$\hat{y}_3(t) = \hat{y}_1(t)\hat{y}_2(t) \text{ for } t \geq 0. \tag{8.26}$$

(iii) Relative to $P_M(\cdot)$, the family of random triples $\hat{y} = \{(\hat{y}_1(t), \hat{y}_2(t), \hat{y}_3(t)); t \in N\}$ is a $J(2)$ second-order random process that is non-linearly cointegrated of order $NC(2, 2)$ with the cointegrating function $f(x, y, z) = z - xy$. In mathematical models of the axioms in which the M_t in A8(ii) are uniformly bounded, $\hat{y}$ is non-linearly polynomially cointegrated with

$$\text{Dif.Op.}F(\hat{y}(t)) = \hat{y}_2(t)\Delta\hat{y}_1(t) + \hat{y}_1(t)\Delta\hat{y}_2(t) - \Delta\hat{y}_3(t), \tag{8.27}$$

where $F(x, y, z) = xy - z$.

(iv) For all $t \in N$ and a.e. in P_M measure, $K(t, \omega_P) = 0$ if both $\hat{y}_1(t, \omega_P) < 0$ and $\hat{y}_2(t, \omega_P) < 0$. Otherwise, $K(t, \omega_P) = \max(\hat{y}(t, \omega_P), 0)$.

T8.5
Let $\ddot{X} = \{(x_1(t), x_2(t), x_3(t)); t \in N\}$ be as in T8.3, let $\hat{y} = \{\hat{y}_1(t), \hat{y}_2(t), \hat{y}_3(t));$ $t \in N\}$, and suppose that A1–A8, D1, D3, and G1–G5 are valid. Then,

relative to $P_M(\cdot)$, $\hat{y}$ is linearly cointegrated of order $C(2, 2)$ with the cointegrating vector $a = (a_1, a_2, 0)$ if and only if $\ddot{X}$, relative to $P_T(\cdot)$, is linearly cointegrated of order $C(2, 2)$ with the cointegrating vector a.

8.3 Harald Goldstein's Econometric Analysis[9]

For the present empirical analysis of the markets for three foreign currencies, the MPD is the family of finite-dimensional probability distributions of the $\hat{y}$ components of ω_P that is determined by A1–A8, D1, D3, and G1–G5. Since the third component of $\hat{y}$, for all $t \geq 0$, satisfies the equation $\hat{y}_3(t) = \hat{y}_1(t)\hat{y}_2(t)$ without an error term, it does not provide statistical information over and above the information one obtains from analyzing the behavior of the first two components of $\hat{y}$. For that reason, we will, to begin with, ignore $\hat{y}_3$ in our statistical analysis. As in the preceding chapters, our statistical deliberations will center on three fundamental ideas that describe the prescriptions that underlie the statistical analysis, outline the salient characteristics of a data-admissible mathematical model of MPD, and define what it means for a theory to be empirically relevant.

8.3.1 The Prescriptions That Underlie the Statistical Analysis

Our data consist of 400 triples of observations of three exchange rates that were taken from the EcoWin database and pertain to weekly spot rates of the Swiss franc relative to the euro, the euro relative to the US dollar, and the Swiss franc relative to the US dollar from January 6, 1999 to August 30, 2006. In the present statistical analysis, the observed triples of spot rates are taken to be, respectively, partial realizations of the first three components of ω_P, K_1, K_2, and K_3. According to D3, $K_j(t) > 0$ for $j = 1, 2, 3$ implies that $K_j(t) = \hat{y}_j(t)$ for $j = 1, 2, 3$. Since the observed series is larger than 0 in the observation period,

$$(K_1(t), K_2(t), K_3(t)) = (\hat{y}_1(t), \hat{y}_2(t), \hat{y}_3(t)) \text{ for } t = 1, 2, \ldots, n,$$

where $n = 400$. Hence, the series of triples $\{(\hat{y}_1(t), \hat{y}_2(t), \hat{y}_3(t)); t \in N\}$ have been observed in the observation period. The observed series and the corresponding $(\Delta\hat{y}_1(t), \Delta\hat{y}_2(t), \Delta\hat{y}_3(t))$ series are shown in figure 8.1.

The prescriptions that underlie our statistical analysis insist that we use our data to estimate parameters of the MPD distribution of $\hat{y}_1$ and $\hat{y}_2$. They are parameters of the family of finite-dimensional probability distributions of a two-dimensional second-order random process that constitutes a solution to the equation

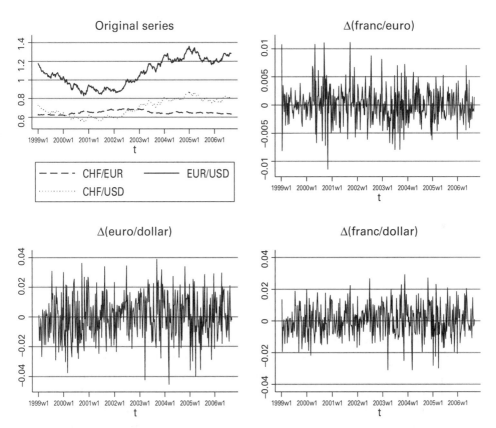

Figure 8.1
Graphs of Swiss franc–euro, euro–dollar, and Swiss franc–dollar exchange rates.

$$\Delta\hat{y}^*(t) - (I - \psi)\Delta\hat{y}^*(t - 1) = \psi\varsigma^*(t) - \psi(I - \varphi)\psi^{-1}\psi\varsigma^*(t - 1), \quad t \geq 1. \quad (8.28)$$

The equation in 8.28 is a simple reformulation of equation 8.23. In the vernacular of econometricians, equation 8.28 constitutes an *econometric model*. This econometric model has many mathematical models. In our statistical deliberations we will introduce assumptions about the finite-dimensional probability distributions of the $\varsigma^*(t)$ that we did not mention in T8.4. At the end of the statistical analysis we will establish the empirical relevance of the additional assumptions.

In the prescriptions underlying the statistical analysis we assume that $\varsigma^*(0) = 0$ and that, relative to $P_M(\cdot)$, the family of random variables, $\{\varsigma^*(t, \omega_P), t \in N\}$ is an orthogonal $J(0)$ second-order random process with means 0 and covariance matrix

$$\Sigma_{\varsigma^*}(t) = \begin{pmatrix} \sigma_{\varsigma^*1}(t) & \sigma_{12}(t) \\ \sigma_{12}(t) & \sigma_{\varsigma^*2}(t) \end{pmatrix}$$

with positive diagonal elements. We set the start values of $\hat{y}^*$ so that $\Delta\hat{y}^*(1)$ equals the observed value of $(\Delta K_1(1), \Delta K_2(1))$.

The equations to be analyzed in the statistical analysis are formulated in terms of a family of random pairs,

$$\{(z_1(t), z_2(t)); t \in N - \{0\}\},$$

where

$$z(t) = Q\Delta\hat{y}^*(t)$$

and where

$$Q = \begin{pmatrix} q_1 & 0 \\ 0 & q_2 \end{pmatrix}$$

is a known scaling matrix. We use Q to ensure that the series we analyze vary within similar intervals—a characteristic that will improve the convergence properties of our estimation algorithm. Choosing $q_1 = 100$ and $q_2 = 25$ makes both series vary in the interval $[-1.14, 1.14]$.

We choose a vector ARMA-GARCH formulation of the equations for $z(t)$ along lines that Ling and McAleer (2003) and Bollerslev (1990) have suggested. (GARCH stands for *generalized autoregressive conditional heteroskedasticity*.) The estimation principle we use is quasi-maximum-likelihood (QML) with Gaussian likelihood function, combined with a constrained inference approach, in particular for the GARCH parameters, as described by Silvapulle and Sen (2005).

Let I_t denote the history of the observed series up to t. We formulate the pair of equations for $z(t)$ as a VARMA(1, 1) as follows, using the notation of Ling and McAleer:

$$\begin{aligned} z(t) &= \Phi z(t - 1) + \zeta(t) + \Psi\zeta(t - 1) \text{ with } \zeta(0) \\ &= 0 \text{ and } z(t) = Q\Delta\hat{y}^*(t). \end{aligned} \tag{8.29}$$

(VARMA stands for *vector autoregressive moving-average*.) Here $\zeta(t) = (\zeta_1(t), \zeta_2(t))' = Q\psi\varsigma^*(t)$. We assume that the $\zeta(t)$ constitute a Martingale difference series with respect to I_t, structured such that $\zeta(t) = D_t\eta(t)$. The conditional heteroscedasticity is given by

$$D_t = \begin{pmatrix} \sqrt{h_{1t}} & 0 \\ 0 & \sqrt{h_{2t}} \end{pmatrix}$$

and $\eta(t)$ is assumed to be independent and identically distributed (i.i.d.) white noise with mean 0 and with the covariance matrix

$$\Gamma = \begin{pmatrix} 1 & s \\ s & 1 \end{pmatrix}.$$

As in Luetkepohl 1993, the specification in equation 8.29 is in echelon form if $\Phi \neq \Psi$, and is hence identified since the AR order is the same as the MA order.

In order to obtain a Gaussian likelihood, we assume that the $\eta(t)$ are normally distributed. The data do not provide evidence against this assumption for the $z_2(t)$ series but do provide evidence against normality for the $z_1(t)$ series, thus motivating the QML approach used here, which, to a certain degree, compensates for non-normality of the error terms. We then have $E\{\zeta(t) \mid I_{t-1}\} = 0$ and $\mathrm{cov}\{\zeta(t) \mid I_{t-1}\} = D_t \Gamma D_t$. For the heteroscedasticity we assume a GARCH(1, 1) structure for $t > 0$,

$$h_t \equiv (h_{1t}, h_{2t})' = w + A(\zeta_1(t-1)^2, \zeta_2(t-1)^2)' + B h_{t-1}, \tag{8.30}$$

where A and B are constant 2×2 matrices, w is a constant 2×1 vector, and h_t and D_t belong to I_{t-1}. In addition we assume that $w > 0$, that all the elements in A and B are non-negative, and that the roots of the polynomials in the lag operator L,

$$\mid I - (A + B)L \mid,$$

$$\mid I - \Phi L \mid,$$

and

$$\mid I + \Psi L \mid,$$

are outside the unit circle.[10] Finally, we assume that $-1 < s < 1$. The assumption that the conditional correlation, $\mathrm{corre}\{\zeta_1(t), \zeta_2(t)) \mid I_{t-1}\}$, equals a constant, s, may appear to be a strong assumption, but it simplifies the analysis. No attempt has been made to test the constancy of the conditional correlation of the components of $\zeta(t)$ here. We are content to refer readers to Tse 2000 for a Lagrange multiplier test that, for a similar data set of exchange rates, did not give evidence against this assumption.[11]

8.3.2 Estimates of the Parameters of the MPD

The likelihood function for this problem, developed by Ling and McAleer (2003), was maximized using the CMLMT (Constrained

Maximum Likelihood MT) module of the GAUSS Mathematical and
Statistical System, which was developed for constrained optimization
with inequality constraints such as we have here. We shall estimate the
parameters in equations 8.29 and 8.30, then use them to obtain estimates of the parameters in equation 8.28. To manage that, we must first
delineate the relation between the parameters in equations 8.28 and
8.29. We multiply both sides of equation 8.28 by Q and reformulate
equation 8.29 as

$$Q\Delta\hat{y}^*(t) = Q(I - \psi)Q^{-1}Q\Delta\hat{y}^*(t - 1)$$
$$+ Q\psi\varsigma^*(t) - Q\psi(I - \varphi)\psi^{-1}Q^{-1}Q\psi\varsigma^*(t - 1). \qquad (8.31)$$

By comparing the parameters in equations 8.28 and 8.31, we deduce
that

$$\Phi = Q(I - \psi)Q^{-1} \leftrightarrow \psi = I - Q^{-1}\Phi Q,$$

$$\Psi = -Q\psi(I - \varphi)\psi^{-1}Q^{-1} \leftrightarrow \varphi = I + \psi^{-1}Q^{-1}\Psi Q\psi,$$

and   (8.32)

$$\zeta(t) = Q\psi\varsigma^*(t) \leftrightarrow \varsigma^*(t) = \psi^{-1}Q^{-1}\zeta(t).$$

Hence, conditional heteroscedasticity of $\zeta(t)$ implies the same for $\varsigma^*(t)$.
   The invertibility and stationarity condition that the eigenvalues of
Ψ and of Φ should be smaller than 1 in absolute value translates to the
condition $|v - 1| < 1$ for any eigenvalue, v, of φ or ψ. This follows from

$$|\varphi - vI| = |I + \psi^{-1}Q^{-1}\Psi Q\psi - vI| = |\Psi - (v - 1)I|$$

and

$$|\psi - vI| = |I - Q^{-1}\Phi Q - vI| = |\Phi - (1 - v)I|.$$

   Using equations 8.32, we obtain the corresponding estimates for φ
and ψ from estimates of the parameters in equations 8.28 and 8.29.
These estimates and their Wald 95-percent-confidence limits are
recorded in table 8.1. The estimates have interesting characteristics. For
example, φ_{11} and φ_{22} differ from 0; the eigenvalues of $I_2 - \varphi$ are -0.21592
and -0.95905; and the eigenvalues of $I_2 - \psi$ are -0.22220 and -0.90421.
These values are in accord with the stipulations concerning φ and the
eigenvalues of $(I - \varphi)$ and $(I - \psi)$ in A5 and G5. It is also the case that
the estimated values of s, w, A, and B satisfy the required conditions,
$-1 < s < 1$, $w > 0$, $0 \leq A$, and $0 \leq B$.[12]
   Moreover, $|I - (A + B)L| = 1 - (A_{11} + B_{11})L = 0$ has one root ($L = [1/
(A_{11} + B_{11})] = 1.264$), $|I + \Psi L|$ has two roots (-4.631 and -1.043), and $|I$

Table 8.1
Estimates of the parameters of equations 8.29 and 8.30.

| | Estimate | Standard error | 95% Wald confidence limits | |
			Lower	Upper
φ_{11}	1.2225	0.4395	0.3611	2.0840
φ_{12}	0.0185	0.1245	−0.2255	0.2624
φ_{21}	0.2640	0.3982	−0.5164	1.0445
φ_{22}	1.9524	0.0481	1.8582	2.0467
ψ_{11}	1.2226	0.3886	0.4609	1.9842
ψ_{12}	0.0018	0.1214	−0.2363	0.2398
ψ_{21}	0.1395	0.3830	−0.6113	0.8902
ψ_{22}	1.9038	0.0517	1.8026	2.0051
w_1	0.0060	0.0053	−0.0044	0.0164
w_2	0.1345	0.0095	0.1158	0.1533
A_{11}	0.0827	0.0482	−0.0120	0.1774
A_{12}	0.1006	0.0472	0.0077	0.1934
A_{21}	0	—	—	—
A_{22}	0	—	—	—
B_{11}	0.7084	0.0728	0.5654	0.8515
B_{1s}	0	—	—	—
B_{21}	0	—	—	—
B_{22}	0	—	—	—
S	−0.0581	0.0511	−0.1586	0.0424

$-\Phi L| = 0$ has two roots (−4.501 and −1.106). The values of these roots are in accord with our assumption that the roots of the given polynomials in L should lie outside the unit circle.

The estimates of the determinants of φ and ψ recorded in table 8.2 imply that φ and ψ are of full rank. Full rank of φ and G4 implies that there is no pair a = (a_1, a_2) such that $\{a\Delta\hat{y}^*(t) ; t \in N - \{0\}\}$ constitutes a degenerate second-order process. Also, full rank of φ and T8.5 shows that the components of $\{\hat{y}^*(t); t \in N\}$ are not linearly cointegrated in the estimated mathematical model of the MPD distribution of $\hat{y}_1$ and $\hat{y}_2$.

8.3.3 Remarks Concerning the Statistical Assumptions Underlying the Empirical Analysis

In our empirical analysis, we made several assumptions concerning the finite-dimensional probability distributions of the error variables, $\eta(t)$, $\varsigma^*(t)$, and $\zeta(t)$. Some of these assumptions correspond to the

Table 8.2
Estimates of determinants and trace of φ and ψ.

Determinant	Estimate	Standard error	95% Wald confidence limits	
			Lower	Upper
$\lvert\varphi\rvert$	2.3820	0.9101	0.5982	4.1659
$\lvert\psi\rvert$	2.3273	0.7676	0.8228	3.8318
$tr(\varphi)$	3.1750	0.4636	2.2663	4.0836
$tr(\psi)$	3.1264	0.4056	2.3800	3.9699

characteristics we ascribed to the $\varsigma(t)$ in equation 8.29. Others were added for the purposes of the empirical analysis. A few remarks concerning the validity of these assumptions are called for.

The residuals corresponding to $\eta(t) = D_t^{-1}\varsigma(t)$ should behave as i.i.d. (0, I) white noise. Some simple diagnostics for the residuals (not reported here) show that the $\eta_1(t)$ series seems to behave as i.i.d. white noise. It does not seem to contain remaining volatility effects, but it shows evidence against being Gaussian, thus justifying the choice of a pseudo-maximum-likelihood approach for estimating the parameters of the MPD. There was, also, no evidence against the white-noise hypothesis for the $\eta_2(t)$ series, and no evidence that $\eta_2(t)$ isn't Gaussian.

We see from equation 8.32 and from A7, A8, and T8.4(i) that $\varsigma^*(t)$ and $\zeta(t)$ are both taken to be orthogonal J(0) second-order processes. Also, as equation 8.32 shows, we need only show that the $\zeta(t)$ constitute an orthogonal second-order J(0) process. Equations 8.28 and 8.32 imply that the $\zeta(t)$ constitute an orthogonal second-order process. This follows directly from the Martingale structure of the $\zeta(t)$. To wit: If $v \neq 0$, then $E\{\zeta(t)\cdot\zeta(t+v)'\,|\,I_{t-1}\} = 0$. That is obvious when $v < 0$. Suppose that $v > 0$. Then, since $\zeta(t) \in I_{t+v-1}$,

$$E\{\zeta(t)\cdot\zeta(t+v)'\,|\,I_{t-1}\} = E\{[E\{\zeta(t)\zeta(t+v)'\,|\,I_{t+v-1}\}\,|\,I_{t-1}\} = 0.$$

By taking the marginal expectation, we see that $E\zeta(t)\zeta(t+v)' = 0$ for $v \neq 0$. (The marginal expectation is, in fact, conditional on the given initial values I_0, $E(\cdot) = E\{\cdot\,|\,I_0\}$.)

On the other hand, the $\zeta(t)$ need not constitute a wide-sense stationary process. If $s = cov(\eta_1(t), \eta_2(t)) = 0$, it follows that the $\zeta(t)$, conditional on their starting values, are asymptotically wide-sense stationary. However, if $s \neq 0$, the $\zeta(t)$, conditional on their starting values, may fail to be asymptotically wide-sense stationary. To see why, let $\zeta(t)^{2\prime} = (\zeta_1(t)^2,$ $\zeta_2(t)^2)\prime$. Then $E\{\zeta(t)^{2\prime} \mid I_{t-1}\} = h_t$. If we let $u_t = \zeta(t)^{2\prime} - h_t$, u_t will be a Martingale difference series. That will allow us to rewrite equation 8.30 as

$$\zeta(t)^{2\prime} = w + (A + B)\,\zeta(t-1)^{2\prime} + u_t - Bu_{t-1}.$$

By taking expectation, conditionally on I_0 on both sides, we can deduce that that $E\zeta(t)^{2\prime} = w + (A + B)E\zeta(t-1)^{2\prime}$. The condition $\zeta(0) = 0$ implies that

$$E\zeta(1)^{2\prime} = w,$$

$$E\zeta(2)^{2\prime} = (I + A + B)w, \ldots ,$$

and

$$E\zeta(t)^{2\prime} = (I + (A + B) + \cdots + (A + B)^{t-1})w,$$

from which we deduce that $E\zeta\,(t)^{2\prime} = (I - A - B)^{-1}(I - (A + B)^t)$, which approaches a constant as $(A + B)^t$ becomes negligible. Thus, if $s = 0$, $\Gamma = I$, and $\zeta(t)$ becomes wide-sense stationary in the limit. If $s \neq 0$, $E[\zeta(t) \zeta(t)\prime] = E(D_t\Gamma D_t)$ with $sE(h_{1t}h_{2t})^{1/2}$ outside the main diagonal, which according to the preceding results and Schwartz inequality is uniformly bounded. Hence, the $\zeta(t)$ constitute a $J(0)$ process, as was to be shown.

8.3.4 Data-Admissible Models of the Data Universe and the MPD
In the present context, a mathematical model of the MPD distribution of the components of $\hat{y}$ is data admissible if (1) its finite-dimensional probability distributions have the characteristics on which the A axioms, D1, D3, and the G axioms insist, (2) the values of its φ and ψ parameters lie within a 95-percent-confidence region of the estimated values of these parameters, and (3) the estimated mathematical model of the MPD distribution of $\hat{y}_1$ and $\hat{y}_2$ satisfies the strictures on which D1, D3, and the prescriptions underlying the statistical analysis insist.[13]

Our deliberations in subsections 8.3.1–8.3.3 show that the estimated values of φ, ψ, and the covariance of $\varsigma^*(t)$ satisfy the prescriptions underlying the statistical analysis and determine a family of mathematical models of the MPD distribution of the components of $\hat{y}$ that satisfy the strictures on which A1–A7, A8(i), A8(iii), D1, D3, and G insist. Whether the members of this family of mathematical models of the MPD satisfy the fourth-order moment assumption in A8(ii) is uncertain and is of much concern.

The possibility that A8(ii) is not empirically relevant is unsettling. We need the assumption that the $\varsigma^*(t)$ have finite fourth-order moments to show that $\hat{y} = \{(\hat{y}_1(t), \hat{y}_2(t), \hat{y}_3(t)); t \in N\}$ is a J(2) second-order random process, and we need the assumption that these fourth-order moments are uniformly bounded to show that $\hat{y}$ is non-linearly polynomially cointegrated. Finally, we know of no general statistical test by which we could establish the existence of the required moments.

The preceding three facts leave us with two options. We can introduce and test new ad hoc hypotheses concerning the probability distributions of the $\varsigma^*(t)$ that ensure the existence of the finite fourth-order moments of $\varsigma^*(t)$—e.g., that they are independently and identically distributed, and that their components are either distributed independently of each other, normally distributed, or t-distributed with more than four degrees of freedom. We can also simply assume that our data do not contradict the assumption that the members of the family of random variables $\{\varsigma^*(t); t \in N\}$ have finite fourth-order moments. For the purposes of this chapter, it seems reasonable to choose the second option. We adopt as a fundamental assumption that there is a mathematical model of the family of estimated residuals in equation 8.29 that, in P_M measure, has finite fourth-order moments. These moments may, but need not, be uniformly bounded. Together, this assumption and our deliberations in subsections 8.3.1–8.3.3 imply that the estimated values of φ and ψ and the covariance of $\varsigma^*(t)$ are parameters of a data-admissible mathematical model of the MPD distribution of the components of $\hat{y}$.[14] We shall use this insight to delineate the contours of a non-empty 95-percent-confidence region for the parameters of data-admissible mathematical models of the MPD distribution of the components of $\hat{y}$. In constructing this confidence region, we treat the ARCH and GARCH parameters as known constants whose values equal their estimated values.

A 95-percent-confidence region for data-admissible models of the MPD

To delineate a 95-percent-confidence region for the parameters of interest, φ and ψ, we begin by assuming that the estimates of (φ, ψ), the pair we presented in table 8.1, are consistent in P_M measure and asymptotically normally distributed.[15] We then let

$$\theta = \begin{pmatrix} \text{vec}(\psi') \\ \text{vec}(\varphi') \end{pmatrix}$$

and let C be the estimated asymptotic covariance matrix of θ^*, the given estimate of θ. We let $\chi^2_{.95,\,8}$ be the 95th-percentile critical value of the χ^2 distribution with 8 degrees of freedom, and we let

$$D' = \{\theta: (\theta^* - \theta)C^{-1}(\theta^* - \theta) \le \chi^2_{95.8}\}.$$

The region D' constitutes an approximate 95-percent-confidence region for the parameters of interest and therefore delineates the contours of a set of parameters of data-admissible mathematical models of the MPD distribution of the components of $\hat{y}$. A particular value, θ_0, is the parameter of a data-admissible mathematical model of the MPD distribution of the components of $\hat{y}$ if $\theta_0 \in D'$ and if the salient characteristics of the associated mathematical model of MPD satisfy the strictures on which the A axioms, D1, D3, and the G axioms insist.

For example, we may ask whether the MPD of a joint COMFAC solution to equation 8.29 in which $\varphi = \psi$ might be data admissible. By equation 8.32, the equality $\varphi = \psi$ is equivalent to the equality vec(Φ + Ψ) = 0. Let ρ = vec($\Phi + \Psi$), and let Cρ denote the asymptotic covariance matrix of ρ. The Wald-test statistic for $\rho = 0$ is $\rho'C_\rho^{-1}\rho = 8.391$, which leads to the (asymptotic) p value 0.078. This implies that the value $\rho = 0$ is contained in the joint 95-percent-confidence region for ρ. Hence, an MPD of a joint COMFAC solution to equation 8.29 belongs to D'. Note also that if $\varphi = \psi$ then φ and ψ are not identified, since the matrix factor, $I - (I - \psi)L$, can be cancelled from equation 8.29, reducing the equation to $\Delta\hat{y}^*(t) = \psi\xi^*(t)$.[16] Hence, all the θ's with $\varphi = \psi$ can be added to D' to obtain a new set, D, of vectors whose values might be the parameters of a data-admissible mathematical model of MPD of the components of $\hat{y}$. The set D is given by

$$D = \{\theta: (\theta^* - \theta)C^{-1}(\theta^* - \theta) \le \chi_{9\,5.8}\}\cup\{\theta: \varphi = \psi\}.$$

The confidence-region limits that D determines are given in table 8.3.

Interesting Ideas about the Structure of D
It is well known that a confidence region of the ellipsoid type, like D', satisfies the following useful property: Let G be the set of all real-valued functions, one-dimensional or not, defined on the range space of (φ,ψ), a subset of R^8 that contains D. Then

$$P(\lambda \in D') = P\{\cap_{g \in G} (g(\lambda) \in g(D'))\} \approx 0.95. \tag{8.33}$$

The proof of this is simple—see, e.g., Scheffé 1959, appendix III.

Table 8.3
95-percent-confidence region for estimates of φ and ψ.

	Estimate	Standard error	95% Wald confidence limits		95%-confidence-region limits	
			Lower	Upper	Lower	Upper
φ_{11}	1.2225	0.4395	0.3611	2.0840	−0.5083	2.9533
φ_{12}	0.0185	0.1245	−0.2255	0.2624	−0.4717	0.5086
φ_{21}	0.2640	0.3982	−0.5164	1.0445	−1.3040	1.8311
φ_{22}	1.9524	0.0481	1.8582	2.0467	1.7630	2.1418
ψ_{11}	1.2226	0.3886	0.4609	1.9842	−0.3078	2.7529
ψ_{12}	0.0018	0.1214	−0.2363	0.2398	−0.4765	0.4801
ψ_{21}	0.1395	0.3830	−0.6113	0.8902	−1.3690	1.6479
ψ_{22}	1.9038	0.0517	1.8026	2.0051	1.7004	2.1073

Scheffé (1959) implies that, in particular, for a one-dimensional linear case, $g(\lambda) = a'\lambda$, the image 95-percent-confidence interval takes the form

$$a'\lambda' \pm \sqrt{\chi^2_{95.8}} \sqrt{a'Ca} = a'\lambda' \pm 3.938\sqrt{a'Ca} \,,$$

where $\sqrt{a'Ca}$ is the estimated standard error of $a'\hat{\lambda}$. The rightmost two columns in table 8.3 give the image confidence intervals for the parameters of interest. It is seen that 0 seems to be a data-admissible value for some of them except φ_{22} and ψ_{22}. Note, therefore, that a value of 0 for φ_{11} is not data admissible according to A4.

In the case of a non-linear g, an advantage with equation 8.33 is that we do not need further linearization of g. On the other hand, of course, there is no guarantee that $g(D')$ is an interval. That must be checked in each case.

As a second example, we may wish to check whether a φ and a ψ with rank less than 2 are parameters of a data-admissible mathematical model of the MPD distribution of the components of $\hat{y}$. If they are, then 0 must belong to the image confidence intervals of the determinants, $g_1(\lambda) = |\varphi|$ and of $g_2(\lambda) = |\psi|$. To find the image, $g_1(D')$, we need to find the max and the min of $|\varphi|$ constrained by the condition in D'. It is clear that the max and the min can occur only on the boundary, since, for any inner point in D', it is always possible to find directions along which the determinants increase and directions along which they decrease, and because of convexity all directions are permissible. It is also clear from the mean-value theorem, the convexity of D', and the continuity of g_1 that the image $g_1(D')$ is connected, and hence an interval. We use the Lagrange method to find the interval for $|\varphi|$ given by $g_1(D') = [-1.335, 5.889]$, and for $|\psi|$, $g_2(D') = [-0.846, 5.338]$. Hence, it seems that values of φ and ψ with rank less than 2 might be parameters of a data-admissible model of the MPD distribution of the components of $\hat{y}$.

The last observation is interesting because it provides a second demonstration that not all vectors in D' need be parameters of a data-admissible mathematical model of the MPD distribution of the components of $\hat{y}$. To wit: The confidence interval for $|\psi|$ includes the value $|\psi| = 0$, which is ruled out by G5. The confidence interval for $|\varphi|$ gives us a different kind of example. By A4, $|\varphi| = 0$ is not ruled out of contention. Hence, there may be linearly cointegrated data-admissible mathematical models of the MPD in D. Section 10.3 presents an example.

8.3.5 The Empirical Relevance of A1–A8
In the present theory-data confrontation, axioms A1–A8 are empirically relevant if and only if there is a member of the intended family of models of the axioms that, together with a model of the non-stochastic axioms of the data universe and the bridge principles, determines a mathematical model of the MPD that belongs to D.

For the empirical analysis it is important to demonstrate that a data-admissible model of the MPD determines a model of A1–A8 that is empirically relevant. To establish that we proceed as follows: In the lower data universe in figure 2.1 the dynamics of the three markets that a given data-admissible MPD determines have the characteristics of a random process, $\hat{y} = \{(\hat{y}_1, \hat{y}_2, \hat{y}_3)(t, \omega_P)) ; t \in N\}$, that in $P_M(\cdot)$ measure is a solution to the difference equations

$$\Delta\hat{y}^*(t, \omega_P) - (I - \psi^0)\Delta\hat{y}^*(t - 1, \omega_P)' = \psi^0\eta^*(t, \omega_P)' - \psi^0(I - \varphi^0)\eta^*(t - 1, \omega_P)',$$
$$t > 0$$

and

$$\hat{y}_3(t) = \hat{y}_1(t) \cdot \hat{y}_2(t), \quad t \geq 0$$

where ψ^0, φ^0, and η are the two ψ and φ matrices and the error terms of the given MPD and where $\eta^* = (\eta_1, \eta_2)'$ and $\hat{y}^* = (\hat{y}_1, \hat{y}_2)'$. If we let ω_P be a vector in the support of the given MPD and let $x^* = (x_1, x_2)'$, we can appeal to G5 and define the components of $x^*(t)$, $\xi^*(t)$, and $\lambda(t-1)$, for all $t > 0$, by the equations

$\xi^*(t) = \eta^*(t, \omega_P)$,

$x^*(t) = \hat{y}^*(t-1, \omega_P) + (\psi^0)^{-1}\Delta\hat{y}^*(t, \omega_P)$

and

$\lambda(t-1) = \hat{y}^*(t-1, \omega_P) + (\psi^0)^{-1}\Delta\hat{y}^*(t, \omega_P) - \eta^*(t, \omega_P)$.

Then $x^*(t)$, $\lambda(t-1)$, and $\xi^*(t)$ are well defined for all $t > 0$, and the MPD distribution of the right-hand variables in the three defining equations determine an RPD distribution of the left-hand variables. In this RPD distribution the $x^*(t)$, $\lambda(t-1)$, and $\xi^*(t)$ for $t > 0$ satisfy the equations

$\xi^*(0, \omega_T) = 0$,

$x^*(t) = \lambda(t-1) + \xi^*(t)$,

$\Delta x^*(t) = \xi^*(t) - (I - \varphi^0)\,\xi^*(t-1)$,

and

$\lambda(t-1) = \lambda(t-2) + \varphi^0\xi^*(t-1)$.

These equations demonstrate that in the given RPD distribution the $x^*(t)$, $\lambda(t-1)$, and $\xi^*(t)$ satisfy the conditions in axioms A4 and A5 in subsection 8.2.2 that concern them. But if that is so, we can use equation 8.13 to obtain the values of the $x_3(t)$, apply A7 and A8(iii) to reconstruct a sequence of α_t and use equations 8.10 and 8.14 to determine the values of $\lambda_3(t)$ and $\xi_3(t)$. In the given RPD distribution the values of $x_3(t)$, $\lambda_3(t)$, and $\xi_3(t)$ satisfy the equation

$x_3(t+1) = \lambda_3(t) + \xi_3(t+1)$.

With that we have shown that the given MPD and the pertinent bridge principles determine one empirically relevant model of Γ_T.

In subsections 8.3.2–8.3.4 we saw that our QML estimates of parameters of the MPD distribution of $\hat{y}_1$ and $\hat{y}_2$ satisfy the strictures on which D1, D3, and the prescriptions underlying the statistical analysis insist. We also saw that the estimated mathematical model of the MPD distribution of the components of $\hat{y}$ that result from the MPD distribution of $\hat{y}_1$ and $\hat{y}_2$ and the equation $\hat{y}_3 = \hat{y}_1\hat{y}_2$ satisfies all the restrictions on which A1–A7, A8(i), A8(iii), D1, D3, and the G axioms insist. From this and from the fundamental assumption that there is a mathematical model of the family of estimated residuals in equation 8.29 that in P_M measure has finite fourth-order moments, we infer that the estimated mathematical model of the MPD distribution of $\hat{y}_1$ and $\hat{y}_2$ and the equation $\hat{y}_3 = \hat{y}_1 \hat{y}_2$ determine a data-admissible mathematical model of the MPD distribution of the components of $\hat{y}$. From this and the proof that a data-admissible MPD and the bridge principles determine an empirically relevant model of Γ_T, we can conclude that there are empirically relevant models of A1–A8.

8.3.6 Spot Prices in Foreign Exchange

With the MPD distribution of $(\hat{y}_1, \hat{y}_2)$ that Goldstein's empirical analysis determined, and with the equation $\hat{y}_3 = \hat{y}_1 \hat{y}_2$, we can show that the family of triples $\hat{y} = \{(\hat{y}_1(t), \hat{y}_2(t), \hat{y}_3(t)); \, t \in N\}$ in P_M measure is a $J(2)$ second-order random process that is non-linearly cointegrated of order $NC(2, 2)$ with the cointegrating function $f(x, y, z) = z - xy$. When the fourth-order moments of the given mathematical model of the family of estimated residuals in equation 8.29 are uniformly bounded, $\hat{y}$ is, also, non-linearly polynomially cointegrated with the differential operator

$$\text{Dif.Op.}F(\hat{y}(t)) = \hat{y}_2(t)\Delta\hat{y}_1(t) + \hat{y}_1(t)\Delta\hat{y}_2(t) - \Delta\hat{y}_3(t),$$

where $F(x, y, z) = xy - z$.

We have established the existence of one data-admissible mathematical model of the MPD distribution of the components of $\hat{y}$. There may be many more. To find them, we must pick pairs (φ, ψ) in D and look for mathematical models of the $\varsigma^*(t)$ with finite fourth-order moments and with ARCH and GARCH parameters equal to the ones we have estimated that we can pair with the chosen D parameters to produce data-admissible models of the MPD distribution of the components of $\hat{y}$. Each successful search will reveal interesting new information about the characteristics of data-admissible mathematical models of the family of triples $\hat{y} = \{(\hat{y}_1(t), \hat{y}_2(t), \hat{y}_3(t)); \, t \in N\}$.

As we saw in section 8.3, the (φ, ψ) pairs in D have interesting characteristics. No ψ is of reduced rank, some φ's may be of reduced rank, and there may be φ's that have the same value as a ψ. From this, T8.4, and T8.5 it follows that in P_M measure (1) there is no non-zero vector $a \in R^2$ such that $\{(a, 0)\Delta\hat{y}(t); \, t \in N - \{0\}\}$ is degenerate; (2) the family of random variables $\{\hat{y}(t); \, t \in N\}$ may be linearly cointegrated of order $C(2, 2)$, and hence there may exist linearly cointegrated efficient foreign-exchange markets in the real world; and (3) there are pairs (φ, ψ) in D that are parameters of a data-admissible mathematical model of the MPD distribution of the components of $\hat{y}$ and for which the solutions to equations 8.23 and 8.24 may satisfy equations 8.25 and 8.26.

Finally, solutions to equations 8.23 and 8.24 or equations 8.25 and 8.26 with a data-admissible mathematical model of the MPD distribution of the components of $\hat{y}$ ensure that the family of random variables $\{\hat{y}(t);\ t \in N\}$ in P_M measure is non-linearly cointegrated of order NC(2, 2) with the cointegrating function $f(x, y, z) = z - xy$ and may be non-linearly polynomially cointegrated with the differential operator

$$\text{Dif.Op.}F(\hat{y}(t)) = \hat{y}_2(t)\Delta\hat{y}_1(t) + \hat{y}_1(t)\Delta\hat{y}_2(t) - \Delta\hat{y}_3(t),$$

where $F(x, y, z) = xy - z$.

The existence of mathematical models of A1–A8 that are empirically relevant in the markets for Swiss franc, euros, and US dollars goes to show that the mathematical concepts of linear and non-linear cointegration that I presented in section 8.1 have relevance for a study of the behavior characteristics of spot prices in foreign-exchange markets.

8.3.7 Concluding Remarks

For the purposes of this chapter, it is important to observe that the dynamics of the foreign-exchange markets in the theory universe differ from the dynamics of the same markets in the data universe. Specifically, in the theory universe the dynamics of the three markets have the characteristics of a random process, $\ddot{X} = \{(x_1, x_2, x_3)(t, \omega_T);\ t \in N\}$, that in P_T measure is a solution to the difference equations

$$\Delta(x_1, x_2)(t)' = (\varphi^0\xi_1,\ \xi_2)(t)' - (I - \varphi)(\xi_1,\ \xi_2)(t - 1)', \qquad t > 0 \tag{8.34}$$

and

$$x_3(t) = x_1(t)x_2(t), \quad t \geq 0. \tag{8.35}$$

In the lower data universe in figure 2.1, the dynamics of the three markets have the characteristics of a random process, $\hat{y} = \{(\hat{y}_1, \hat{y}_2, \hat{y}_3)(t, \omega_P))\ ;\ t \in N\}$, that in $P_M(\cdot)$ measure is a solution to the difference equations

$$\Delta(\hat{y}_1, \hat{y}_2)(t)' - (I - \Psi^0)\Delta(\hat{y}_1, \hat{y}_2)(t - 1)' = \Psi^0(\varsigma_1,\ \varsigma_2)(t)' - \Psi^0(I - \varphi^0)(\varsigma_1,\ \varsigma_2)(t - 1)', t > 0 \tag{8.36}$$

and

$$\hat{y}_3(t) = \hat{y}_1(t)\hat{y}_2(t), \quad t \geq 0 \tag{8.37}$$

where Ψ^0 and φ^0 denote Goldstein's QML estimates of the two matrices. Also, in the theory universe the $\ddot{X}$ process is linearly cointegrated if and only if there exists a pair of constants, $a = (a_1, a_2)$, such that $a \cdot \varphi =$

0. In the lower data universe in figure 2.1, the $\hat{y}$ process is not linearly cointegrated in the estimated mathematical model of MPD. Both the $\ddot{X}$ process and the $\hat{y}$ process are non-linearly cointegrated with the cointegrating function $f(x, y, z) = z - xy$, and they may be non-linearly polynomially cointegrated.

8.4 André Anundsen's Econometric Analysis

Goldstein's analysis established the empirical relevance in the lower data universe in figure 6.1 of the theory I presented in section 8.2. In this section, I assume that I have accurate observations of the triples $(x_1, x_2, x_3)(t)$, $t \geq 0$, and I ask whether that theory has empirical relevance in the upper data universe in figure 6.1. Specifically, I ask whether there exists in P_P measure an i.i.d. pair of random processes, $\{\delta_1, \delta_2)(t, \omega_P); t \in N\}$, with means 0 and finite covariance matrix, such that

$$E\{\delta(t, \omega_P) \mid \hat{y}(0), \dots, \hat{y}(t-1)\} = 0 \text{ for all } t > 0 \tag{8.38}$$

and such that $\{\hat{y}(t, \omega_P); t \in N\}$ with large probability constitutes a solution to the difference equations

$$\begin{pmatrix} \Delta\hat{y}_1(t) \\ \Delta\hat{y}_2(t) \end{pmatrix} = \begin{pmatrix} \delta_1(t) \\ \delta_2(t) \end{pmatrix} - (I-\varphi)\begin{pmatrix} \delta_1(t-1) \\ \delta_2(t-1) \end{pmatrix}, \quad t > 0 \tag{8.39}$$

and

$$\hat{y}_3(t) = \hat{y}_1(t)\hat{y}_2(t), \quad t \geq 0. \tag{8.40}$$

Here φ is taken to satisfy the conditions $\varphi_{11} \neq 0$ and $\varphi_{22} \neq 0$, and the absolute values of the eigenvalues of $(I - \varphi)$ are less than or equal to 1.

As in the case study in chapter 7, I do not know $P_P(\cdot)$, Hence, my question amounts to asking whether a family of models of A1–A8 are relevant in the empirical context that André Anundsen establishes in the upper data universe in figure 6.1. I believe that, on the assumption that I have accurate observations of the $(x_1, x_2, x_3)(t)$, this is the way Trygve Haavelmo would have determined the empirical relevance of my theory.

Anundsen adopts D1–D4 as stated, adds the assumption that $\{(\hat{y}_1, \hat{y}_2)(t, \omega_P); t \in N\}$ is an ARIMA process with no more than two unit roots, and uses ideas of David Hendry and Søren Johansen to carry out an empirical analysis of the TPD distribution of the first two components of $\{\hat{y}(t, \omega_P); t \in N\}$. His results answer my question. Since the difference equations 8.36 are different from the difference equations 8.39,

Anundsen's results, also, throw new light on the question of how to incorporate economic theory in empirical economic analyses. Anundsen's empirical analysis follows.

8.4.1 Vector-Autoregression-Based Results for Exchange-Rate Cointegration

In this subsection we shall use Johansen's (1988a,b, 1995) multivariate approach to cointegration to determine whether there exists a link between the Swiss franc–euro and euro–dollar exchange rates in a long-run perspective. As is evident from figure 8.1, both series display non-stationarities over the entire sample period, from 1999w1 to 2006w36. Judging by a visual inspection of the series, the researcher in charge may believe that the series are integrated of order 1, perhaps with a structural break in the euro–dollar exchange rate early in 2000 and for both series between 2002 and 2003. Though we will not dig into details concerning interpretation of what might have caused these structural changes in this analysis, it is still worth mentioning as a backdrop for the empirical analysis.

With E1 standing for the franc–euro exchange rate and E2 for the euro–dollar rate, the supposed I(1)-ness of the two exchange rates is supported by the ADF tests in table 8.4. In the table, a constant and a trend are included in the test when testing the levels. Consistent with this, only the constant is included when testing the differences. For the lag determination in the ADF regressions, we have chosen to rely on the Akaike information criterion (AIC). Consecutive F-tests reached the same conclusion as the AIC. We started with a generous lag length of eight lags in the first differences (i.e., nine in levels), then reduced the lag lengths in accord with the AIC procedure. We reach the same conclusion regarding the order of integration for all lag lengths from 0 to 8: Both exchange rates are integrated of order 1.[17]

Misspecification tests indicate that the residuals from the ADF regression for the franc–euro exchange rate suffer from heteroscedasticity and non-normality (also in first differences). Thus, the differenced franc–euro series has a non-stationary component that we cannot model by allowing one or more additional unit roots in the characteristic polynomial. This can cause some inference problems in a linear vector autoregression—a matter to which we will return in the next subsection.

Though the franc–euro and euro–dollar exchange-rate series show clear evidence of non-stationarity, it is not clear from figure 8.1 that they share the same underlying stochastic trend (i.e., that they are cointegrated).

Table 8.4
Augmented Dickey-Fuller test for order of integration.

Levels

Variable	t-ADF	5%-critical value	Lags	Trend
E1	−1.690	−3.42	0	Yes
E2	−2.409	−3.42	0	Yes

Sample: T = 391 (1999w10–2006w36)

First differences

Variable	t-ADF	5%-critical value	Lags	Trend
$\Delta E1$	−20.92	−2.87	0	No
$\Delta E2$	−20.03	−2.87	0	No

Sample: T = 390 (1999w11–2006w3)

8.4.2 Cointegration Analysis

To ascertain whether there exists a linear combination of the two exchange rates that is stationary, we use Johansen's (1988b) multivariate approach to cointegration. As a starting point, we formulate a bivariate VAR of order 5,

$$y(t) = \sum_{1 \le i \le 5} \Pi_i y(t - i) + \Phi D(t) + \epsilon(t), \qquad (8.41)$$

where $y(t)$ is a pair whose components denote values of the franc–euro and euro–dollar exchange rates. As was said above, we will refer to the franc–euro and the euro–dollar exchange rates, respectively, as E_1 and E_2. $D(t)$ represents deterministic terms such as a linear trend, a constant, and potentially some impulse dummies. $\epsilon(t)$ is a 2×1 random vector that is taken to be $IIN(0, \Omega)$.

For the purpose of conducting statistical inference, and for the validity of using the Johansen procedure, it is important that the residuals in equation 8.41 are well behaved. The VAR model we have formulated above suffers from both non-normality and heteroscedasticity. Hence, there are non-normality and non-stationarities in the data that are not captured by the linear VAR. It is, therefore relevant that non-normality might be handled by introducing impulse dummies. Also, simulation studies show that statistical inference in a cointegrated VAR model is rather robust to heteroscedasticity. (See Juselius 2006, p. 47.)

In an attempt to move the model closer to satisfying the Gaussian requirements, we use the "large outlier" option in Autometrics (see, e.g., Doornik 2009) with significance level 0.01 to detect significant outliers. Searching for outliers we pick up the following set of impulse dummies: I:2000w18, I:2000w37, I:2000w44, I:2001w38, I:2002w30, I:2002w52, I:2004w10. Some of these dummies can be interpreted in a historical context. For example, 2000w18 is the week in which the legal requirement that the Swiss franc be backed by 40 percent gold reserves was abandoned, and the dummy, I:2000w18, is significant only in the franc–euro equation.

Though the aim of this analysis is not to give a clear interpretation of the dummies, it is clear that they, as table 8.5 shows, move us closer to satisfying the assumption of a Gaussian VAR.[18]

With the dummies included in the model, we cannot reject normality, but there are still signs of heteroscedasticity. In any case, the statistical inference in this model has been shown to be quite robust to residual heteroscedasticity, so we have decided to leave that issue aside.

To explore whether the dimensionality of the VAR can be reduced, we inspect the Akaike information criterion, the Schwarz information criterion, and a series of consecutive F-tests. Results from this exercise are reported in table 8.6.[19]

Whether we choose to rely on the F-tests, on the Akaike information criterion, or on the Schwarz information criterion, we reach the same

Table 8.5
Diagnostics from VAR(5) in E_1 and E_2 with outliers in VAR. Estimation period: 1999w6–2006w36 (T = 395).

Diagnostics	Test statistic	Value [p value]
Vector AR 1–7 test:	F (28, 712)	0.7554 [0.8161]
Vector normality test	$\chi^2(4)$	1.8147 [0.7698]
Vector hetero test	F(66, 1069)	1.4489 [0.0127]

Table 8.6
Tests on the significance of all lags up to 5. Estimation period: 1999w6–2006w36 (T = 395).

Lag length	F-test	Value [Prob]	AIC	SC	Log likelihood
5			−14.4905	−14.1077	2899.8742
4	F (4, 750)	0.7405 [0.5645]	−14.5029	−14.1604	2898.3172
3	F (8, 750)	0.7011 [0.6908]	−14.5161	−14.2139	2896.9312
2	F (12, 750)	0.6363 [0.8120]	−14.5310	−14.2691	2895.8732
1	F (16, 750)	0.8704 [0.6041]	−14.5347	−14.3131	2892.6067
0	F (20, 750)	1182.9 [0.0000]	−7.6267	−7.4454	1524.2658

conclusion: The lag length of the variables in the VAR can be reduced to 1, which is the specification we will retain when, in the next subsection, we use the trace test to determine whether the two exchange rates are linearly cointegrated.

8.4.3 Testing for the Number of Cointegrating Relationships

In the preceding subsection, we showed that the inclusion of a set of dummies implied an almost well-specified VAR and a lag length of 1. Let us now rewrite the VAR in equation 8.41 into the vector error-correction form, imposing a lag length of 1 and including the dummies unrestrictedly. In order to avoid quadratic trends in the data, we restrict the linear trend to enter the cointegration space:

$$\Delta y(t) = \Pi^* y^*(t-1) + \Phi^* D^*(t) + \mathcal{E}(t), \tag{8.42}$$

where $y^*(t-1) = (y(t-1)', \text{trend})'$ and where $D^*(t)$ now includes a constant and the set of dummies that solved our misspecification problem. Also, $\Pi^* = (\Pi, \delta)$ with $\Pi = \Pi_1 - I$, and δ represents the trend coefficients. Johansen's (1988b) trace test amounts to testing the rank of the matrix Π, which coincides with the number of cointegrating relationships among the variables included in $y(t)$ The results from both the asymptotic trace test and the small-sample-adjusted trace test are reported in table 8.7.[20]

Controlling for the outliers, we find, if we accept a 10 percent significance level, that the rank of the Π matrix is 1. This is also the case when we consider the sample-adjusted test statistic. In other words, the test implies that there exists one cointegrating relationship among the variables in our information set—though the evidence is not strong.

Table 8.7
Trace test for cointegration. Endogenous variables: E_1 and E_2. Restricted variables: A deterministic trend. Unrestricted variables: Constant and the set of dummies used to correct for large outliers. Estimation period: 1999w6–2006w36 (T = 395).

Eigenvalue: λ_i	H_0	H_A	p [λ_{trace}]	p [small sample λ_{trace}]
0.0375	r = 0	r ≥ 1	0.103	0.107
0.0204	r ≤ 1	r ≥ 2	0.249	0.252
Diagnostics[a]		Test statistic		Value [p value]
Vector AR 1–7 test:		F (28, 728)		0.7982 [0.7623]
Vector normality test:		$\chi^2(4)$		1.7753 [0.7770]
Vector hetero test:		F (18, 1058)		2.7099 [0.0000]

a. See Doornik and Hendry 2009.

Table 8.8
Tests for over-identifying restrictions.

Step 1: The just-identified cointegrating vector normalized with respect to the
franc–euro exchange rate: $\beta_{E1} = 1$

franc/euro + 0.145euro/dollar – 0/00012Trend

            0.036   0.00005

$\alpha_{franc/euro}$ + –0.039, $\alpha_{euro/dollar}$ = 0.033

       0.010   0.055

Log likelihood = 2888.5448

Step 2: Imposing weak exogeneity on the dollar-euro exchange rate: $\alpha_{82} = 0$

franc/euro + 0.159euro/dollar – 0.00015Trend

            0.036   0.00005

$\alpha_{franc/euro}$ = – 0.039

       0.010

Log likelihood = 2888.4577

LR test of restrictions: $\chi^2(1) = 0.1743$ [0.6763]

To identify the single cointegrating vector, we normalize on E_1 (β_{E1} = 1). The exactly identified vector is given at step 1 in table 8.8. At step 2, we test whether the euro–dollar rate is weakly exogenous with respect to the long-run coefficients. As seen from the likelihood ratio test, weak exogeneity is borderline accepted (p = 0.6763). Also, we do not find evidence of co-trending which could reflect that there are important variables omitted from the information set. We conclude that E_1 and E_2 are cointegrated with a trend and that the cointegrating vector is (1, 0.159) for E1 and E2 and –0.00005 for the trend.[21]

In matrix notation, the VECM takes the form

$$
\begin{pmatrix} \Delta E_1(t) \\ \Delta E_2(t) \end{pmatrix}
= \begin{pmatrix} 0.031 \\ 0.001 \end{pmatrix} - \begin{pmatrix} 0.039 \\ 0 \end{pmatrix} \begin{pmatrix} 1 \\ 0.159 \\ -0.00005 \end{pmatrix}' \begin{pmatrix} E_1(t-1) \\ E_2(t-1) \\ \text{Trend} \end{pmatrix} + \begin{pmatrix} \psi_{E1} \\ \psi_{E2} \end{pmatrix} \text{Dummies} + \begin{pmatrix} \xi_1(t) \\ \xi_2(t) \end{pmatrix}
$$

(8.43)

where Dummies is a 7×1 vector comprising the dummies we have included unrestrictedly, and where ψ_{E1} and ψ_{E2} are the estimated dummy coefficients.

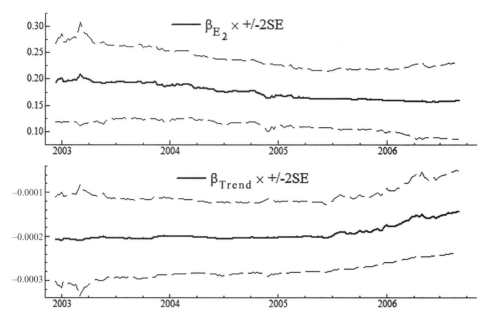

Figure 8.2
Recursively estimated cointegration coefficients for 1999w6–2006w36.

To shed some light on the stability of the cointegrating coefficients in the vector error-correction model, figure 8.2 plots the recursively estimated coefficients (in black) along with recursively estimated 95 percent confidence intervals (dashed lines from 2002w50). The first recursive observation was calculated using a sample of 200. It is clear that the coefficients are relatively stable, which is reassuring.

8.4.4 Cross-Checks
In this subsection, we perform a cross-check of the results derived in the preceding subsection. The reason to do so is that the trace test showed that we could accept cointegration with rank equal 1 only at a 10 percent significance level. Under the assumption of weak exogeneity, we can reformulate the VECM given in equation 8.42 as a conditional model for E_1 and a marginal model for E_2 (see, e.g., Johansen 1994):

$$\Delta E_1(t) = (\mu_{E1} - \omega\mu_{E2}) + (\psi_{E1} - \omega\psi_{E2})\text{Dummies}(t) + \omega\Delta E_2(t)$$
$$+ \alpha_{E1}\beta' y^*(t-1) + (\epsilon_{E1}(t) - \omega\epsilon_{E2}(t)), \tag{8.44}$$

$$\Delta E_2(t) = \mu_{E2} + \psi_{E2}\text{Dummies} + \epsilon_{E2}(t), \tag{8.45}$$

where the composite error term in equation 8.44 is orthogonal to the error term in equation 8.45. Hence, OLS estimation equation by equation is efficient. The notation is the same as earlier with the addition of ω, which is defined by $\omega = \Omega_{E1E2}\Omega^{-1}_{E1E2}$.

We start with a more general formulation for the above equations. From the outset we allow for a more generous lag length. This can also be seen as an additional test of the lag structure we chose for the cointegration analysis. Having shown that the lag length of the variables in the VAR (measured in levels) could be reduced from 5 to 1, we would expect the lag length of the first differences to reduce to 0. Following Ericsson and MacKinnon (2002), we derestrict the variables in the cointegrating vector to estimate them freely. Expressed in mathematical terms, our general unrestricted models (GUMs) for ΔE_1 and ΔE_2 are the following:

$$\Delta E_1(t) = (\mu_{E1} - \omega\mu_{E2}) + (\psi_{E1} - \omega\psi_{E2})\text{Dummies}(t) + \omega\Delta E_2(t) + \alpha_{E1}E_1(t-1)$$

$$+ \beta_{E1E2}E_2(t-1) + \beta_{E1\text{Trend}}\text{Trend}(t-1) + \sum_{1\leq i\leq 4}\gamma_{E1,\,i}\Delta E_1(t-i)$$

$$+ \sum_{1\leq i\leq 4}\gamma_{E1,\,4+i}\Delta E_2(t-i) + (\epsilon_{E1}(t) - \omega\epsilon_{E2}(t)),$$

$$(8.46)$$

$$\Delta E_2(t) = \mu_{E2} + \psi_{E2}\text{ Dummies}$$

$$+ \sum_{1\leq i\leq 4}\gamma_{E2,\,i}\Delta E_1(t-i) + \sum_{1\leq i\leq 4}\gamma_{E2,\,4+i}\Delta E_2(t-i) + \epsilon_{E2}(t). \qquad (8.47)$$

We estimate equation 8.46, using Autometrics to search for a parsimonious specification that is nested in the respective GUM and choosing 0.01 as the significance level. We know from Granger's representation theorem (Engle and Granger 1987) that if we have error correction we also have cointegration. Thus, if the coefficient on the variable $E_1(t-1)$ in equation 8.46 is significant, we have corroborating evidence for our earlier findings. The results of estimating equation 8.46 are reported in table 8.9.[23]

Though an ordinary t-test would reject the hypothesis of no cointegration, we must remember that other critical values must be used under the null of no cointegration. Fortunately, these critical values have been tabulated. On the basis of the critical values tabulated in table 4 of Ericsson and McKinnon 2002 with $k = 2$, we reject the hypothesis of no cointegration at a 5 percent significance level (critical value -3.6873). Furthermore, both the adjustment coefficient, α_{E1}, and the long-run effect on E2, $-\beta_{E1E2}/\alpha_{E1}$, assume values close to those we found using the Johansen approach—specifically, $\alpha_{E1} = -0.039$ and $\beta_{E1E2}/\alpha_{E1} = 0.154$.

Table 8.9
Conditional equilibrium correction model for Swiss franc and US dollar. Dependent variable: $\Delta E_{1,t}$. Estimation period: 1999w6–2006w36 (T = 395).

Variable	Coefficient	t
Constant	0.310	3.76
$E1_{t-1}$	−0.039	3.69
$E2_{t-1}$	−0.006	3.04
$trend_{t-1}$	0.000005	2.26
I : 2000w18	0.010	3.65
I : 2000w37	0.010	3.75
I : 2000w44	−0.012	4.26
I : 2001w38	0.011	4.00
I : 2002w30	0.010	3.53
I : 2002w52	0.009	3.30
σ	0.0027	

Diagnostics	Test statistic	Value [p value]
AR 1–7 test	$F(7, 378)$	1.5262 [0.1568]
Normality test	$\chi^{2(2)}$	1.6044 [0.4483]
Hetero test	$F(6, 382)$	2.5720 [0.0187]

We conclude that both unconditional and conditional VAR analysis show that there is formal (though weak) statistical evidence for cointegration between the two exchange rates.[23]

8.4.5 Concluding Remarks

Anundsen's results are interesting for many reasons. First of all, they demonstrate that the MPD distribution of the components of $\hat{y}$; i.e., of $\{(\hat{y}_1(t, \omega_P), \hat{y}_2(t, \omega_P), \hat{y}_3(t, \omega_P)); t \in N\}$ differs from their TPD distribution. The differences are interesting. In the TPD distribution, $\hat{y}$ is linearly cointegrated of order C(2, 2) with the cointegrating vector $\beta = (1, 0.159, 0)$. This β is a cointegrating vector in the MPD distribution of $\hat{y}$ only if there is a value of the φ parameters of a data-admissible mathematical model of MPD such that $(1, 0.159)\varphi = 0$. Such a value of φ does not belong to Wald's 95-percent-confidence interval of Goldstein's QML estimate of φ, but it may belong to D.

If we assume that the error terms in equation 8.43 have finite fourth-order moments, then in the TPD distribution the components of $\hat{y}$ are non-linearly cointegrated of order NC(2, 2) with four different cointegrating functions:

$f(x, y, z) = z - xy$,

$g(x, y, z) = z - (x - 0.159)(y - 1) + b$, where b is a constant,

$h(x, y, z) = x + 0.159(z/x)$, where $x > 0$,

$k(x, y, z) = (z/y) + 0.159y$, where $y > 0$.

In the estimated mathematical model of the MPD, there is only one cointegrating function, $f(x, y, z) = z - xy$.

If the residuals in equation 8.43 have uniformly bounded fourth-order moments, then in the TPD distribution $\hat{y}$ is non-linearly polynomially cointegrated. In fact, $\{(1, 0.159, 0) \hat{y}(t) + \text{Dif.Op.}F(\hat{y}(t); t \in N\}$ is then a J(0) process with $F(x, y, z) = xy - z$. If there is a mathematical model of the residuals in equation 8.36 with uniformly bounded fourth-order moments, $\hat{y}$ is non-linearly polynomially cointegrated in its estimated MPD distribution.

If we assume that we have accurate observations of $x(t)$, $t \geq 0$, then the theory I developed in section 8.1 is not empirically relevant in the empirical context that Anundsen's analysis establishes in the upper data universe in figure 2.1. In other words, in the TPD distribution of $\hat{y}$, there is a high probability that $\hat{y}$ is not a solution to the difference equations 8.38 and 8.39. The evidence I have for this claim is twofold: Suppose first that the absolute values of the characteristic roots of $(I - \varphi)$ are less than 1, and observe that equation 8.38 can be rewritten in the equivalent form

$$\begin{pmatrix} \Delta\hat{y}_1(t) \\ \Delta\hat{y}_2(t) \end{pmatrix} = -\Sigma_{1 \leq s \leq t-1}(I - \varphi)^s \begin{pmatrix} \Delta\hat{y}_1(t-s) \\ \Delta\hat{y}_2(t-s) \end{pmatrix} + \begin{pmatrix} \delta_1(t) \\ \delta_2(t) \end{pmatrix}. \tag{8.48}$$

For large t, $(I - \varphi)^t$ becomes very small. Anundsen estimated equation 8.48 with 20 lags or less, and found that all lags were insignificant. Hence, if the characteristic roots of $(I - \varphi)$ are less than 1 in absolute value, it is highly probable that $\varphi = I$, and

$$\begin{pmatrix} \Delta\hat{y}_1(t) \\ \Delta\hat{y}_2(t) \end{pmatrix} = \begin{pmatrix} \delta_1(t) \\ \delta_2(t) \end{pmatrix}.$$

That cannot be the case in Anundsen's empirical context.

Suppose next that the absolute value of one of the characteristic roots of $(I - \varphi)$ equals 1. I estimated each of the equations in 8.48 with PcGive's ARFIMA program and found that $(1 - \varphi_{11})$ and $(1 - \varphi_{22})$ were not significantly different from 0. I take that to imply that a family of models of my theory in which the absolute value of one of the roots of $I - \varphi$ equals 1 is not relevant in Anundsen's empirical context.

The rejection of my theory in the upper data universe in figure 6.1 has one interesting consequence: In the TPD distribution, as in the MPD distribution, the characteristics of $\hat{y}$ seem to demonstrate that my mathematical concepts of linear and non-linear cointegration have empirical relevance for foreign-exchange markets. However, there is an important difference. The data admissibility of the estimated mathematical model of MPD implies that axioms A1–A8, have empirical relevance and, hence, that my mathematical concepts have economic as well as empirical relevance. Since Anundsen's results reject the theory I developed in section 8.2, the observed characteristics of the TPD have no bearing on their economic relevance.

9   Scientific Explanation in Economics and Econometrics

I believe that there is a need for a formal account of the meaning of scientific explanation in economics and econometrics. An *explanation* is an answer to a "why" question. It makes clear or intelligible something that is not known or understood by the person asking the question. A *scientific explanation* is one in which the ideas of some scientific theory play an essential role. In economics, that scientific theory is an economic theory. The ideas contained within it are used to provide scientific explanations of regularities that applied economists and econometricians have observed in their data.

There are all sorts of "why" questions, and usually there are many possible answers to a single question. The questions that are of interest here concern the occurrence of certain events (for example, a sudden sharp drop in the price of West Texas Intermediate Crude Oil) or the characteristics of observed phenomena (for example, prolonged periods of severe unemployment in European economies). An answer to a question of the first kind might be a list of the causes of the event or events in question. An answer to a question of the second kind might be a list of reasons why the observed phenomena were to be expected.

The forms in which the causes of events and the reasons for observed phenomena are listed and used in a scientific explanation differ among scientists, even within a discipline. There is, therefore, a need for criteria by which good scientific explanations can be distinguished from bad ones. These criteria must list the necessary elements of a scientific explanation and must explicate the ideas of a logically and an empirically adequate scientific explanation.

In this chapter I give two formal characterizations of logically and empirically adequate scientific explanations—one for economics and one for econometrics. I exemplify them with scientific explanations of interesting observed regularities in experimental economics and in the dynamics of financial markets. In experimental economics the explanation throws new light on stylized facts that Maurice Allais has observed in his many tests of the expected-utility hypothesis. In the economics of finance the explanation explicates an interesting characteristic of the US money market that Hall et al. discovered in 1992: Yields to maturity of US Treasury Bills are cointegrated I(1) ARIMA processes, and the spreads between yields of different maturity define the cointegrating vectors.

Most of the material in sections 9.1–9.4 is based on ideas that I originally published in two articles, "Theory-Data Confrontations in Economics" and "Scientific Explanation in Econometrics." The former appeared in a 1995 issue of *Dialogue: Canadian Philosophical Review*. The latter appeared in the proceedings of the 1998 Ragnar Frisch Centennial Symposium, *Econometrics and Economic Theory in the 20th Century*. The estimates by Geir Storvik in section 9.5 and Heather Anderson in section 9.6 were first published on pages 596–603 of my 2003 book *Econometrics and the Philosophy of Economics*. The formal scientific explanation of HAG's (that is, Hall, Anderson, and Granger's) Dictum in sections 9.4–9.6 is a reformulation of the scientific explanation that Heather Anderson, Geir Storvik, and I gave on pages 586–606 of *Econometrics and the Philosophy of Economics*. The reformulation is designed to go with the ideas underlying the formal unitary methodological basis for the science of economics that I presented in sections 2.2 and 6.1 of the present volume.

My scheme for scientific explanations in economics has, superficially, much in common with Carl Hempel's deductive-nomological scheme for scientific explanations. For motivation and for ease of reference, I begin by discussing relevant aspects of Hempel's fundamental ideas as they appear in chapters 10 and 12 of his 1965 book *Aspects of Scientific Explanation* and in Wesley Salmon's 1989 survey article "Four Decades of Scientific Explanation."

9.1 The Deductive-Nomological Scheme for Scientific Explanations

Hempel's (1965, pp. 245–251) *deductive-nomological scheme* (DNS) is the most influential existing formal characterization of scientific explanations. According to the DNS, a scientific explanation of an event or a phenomenon must have four elements:

a sentence E that describes the event or the phenomenon in question a list of sentences $C_1, C_2, \ldots, C_n$ that describe relevant antecedent conditions

a list of general laws $L_1, L_2, \ldots, L_k$

arguments that demonstrate that E is a logical consequence of the C's and the L's.

The purpose of the following example is to fix these ideas.

E9.1

An explanation is required as to why Glen, a human being, cannot live forever. To provide it, let G denote Glen and let $E(x)$ insist that x is mortal. Then E becomes $E(G)$. Next, let $C(x)$ assert that x is a human being and observe that $C(G)$. Finally, let L denote a law of biology that insists that $(\forall x)[C(x) \supset E(x)]$. In first-order logic, L implies that $[C(G) \supset E(G)]$, and $C(G)$ and $[C(G) \supset E(G)]$ imply that $E(G)$. Consequently, $E(G)$ is a logical consequence of $C(G)$ and L as required by condition 4 of Hempel's scheme.

According to the DNS, a scientific explanation is *adequate* only if it is both logically and empirically adequate. An explanation is *logically adequate* only if at least one L plays an essential part in the demonstration that the *explanandum*, E, is a logical consequence of the *explanans*, the family of C's and L's. Moreover, the explanation is *empirically adequate* only if (i) it is possible, at least in principle, to establish by experiment or observation whether the C's that are used in condition 4 are satisfied and (ii) the L's that are used in condition 4 have been subjected to extensive tests and have passed them all.[1] Evidently the scientific explanation of $E(G)$ in E9.1 is logically adequate, since L plays an essential role in the proof that $E(G)$ is a logical consequence of $C(G)$ and L. The explanation is also empirically adequate, since observation alone suffices to determine whether an x satisfies C, and since history accounts for numerous tests of L, all of which failed to falsify L.

Hempel's DNS has attractive features, and he and others have used it to give interesting scientific explanations of events and phenomena in different sciences. (See, e.g., Hempel 1965, pp. 335–338; Nagel 1961, pp. 30–32.) Even so, influential philosophers of science have criticized it for many failings, and have expressed reservations about applying it in the social sciences. In economics, for example, there are very few laws in Hempel's sense of the term. The assertions that in a scientific explanation play the role of Hempel's L's are theorems of a pertinent economic theory that, for the most part, has limited empirical relevance. Also, the list of C's in a scientific explanation is often empty or, for good reasons, incomplete. Certainly, if one were to use the DNS as a basis for a scientific explanation of the severe unemployment that Americans have experienced during the years 2008–2014, one would be hard put to specify all the relevant C's.[2]

The philosophers' reservations about applying the DNS in the social sciences are not to be taken lightly, so in this chapter I will present two new formal schemes for scientific explanations. I believe that they will enable scientists to distinguish good scientific explanations from bad ones in economics and in econometrics.

9.2 A Formal Characterization of Scientific Explanations in Economics

To me a scientific explanation is a theory-data confrontation in reverse. I have observed interesting aspects of my data, and I am looking for a theory that I can use to explain them. If my view is correct, I must be able to give an adequate formal characterization of scientific explanations in economics and econometrics within the framework of theory-data confrontations that I developed in sections 2.2 and 6.1 of this book.

9.2.1 SE1—A Scientific Explanation in Economics

I have observed certain regularities in a set of data. These regularities are like stylized facts that other researchers have observed in their data, and I am searching for a scientific explanation of them. The regularities in my data and the stylized facts I have in mind pertain to characteristics of vectors in a certain formal data universe. Thus, my search can be described as follows.

SE1

Let (Ω_P, Γ_P) be some given data universe. Assume that the components of the vectors in Ω_P denote some units of objects that have been observed and that Γ_P delineates the salient properties of the data. Let H be a finite family of assertions concerning Ω_P, and let M be a family of models of (Ω_P, Γ_P) in which all the assertions of H are true. M is taken to be the intended interpretation of the data universe, and it is assumed that H delineates the characteristics of the data that are to be explained. Then to give a scientific explanation of H means to find a theory universe (Ω_T, Γ_T) that is disjoint from the data universe, a sample space, $\Omega \subset \Omega_T$

× Ω_P, and a collection of bridge principles, $\Gamma_{T,P}$, that in Ω link Ω_T with Ω_P such that H becomes a logical consequence of a model of Γ_T, Γ_P, and $\Gamma_{T,P}$.

Such an explanation is logically adequate if H is not a logical consequence of the model of Γ_P alone. It is empirically adequate if there is a member of M (say, M_1) with the property that the logical consequences of the assertions in the model of Γ_T, $\Gamma_{T,P}$, and Γ_P that concern components of ω_P are valid in M_1.

In SE1 there are several things to note and to keep in mind for later discussion. First, as in Hempel's DNS, the explanandum is a logical consequence of the explanans, and the explanation is logically adequate if at least one of the components of Γ_T plays an essential role in the proof of H. Second, the empirical adequacy of an SE1 scientific explanation hinges on the empirical relevance of Γ_T. Specifically, my scientific explanation of H is empirically adequate only if Γ_T is relevant in the empirical context that a certain member of M determines. This member is taken to be a model of the data universe in which my own data reside.

With the proper translation, an SE1 explanation can be made to look like a DNS explanation. To wit: Hempel's C's, L's, and E concern individuals in one and the same universe. This universe is, in SE1, my data universe. There the members of Γ_P play the roles of Hempel's C's, the translated versions of the members of Γ_T play the roles of Hempel's L's, and H has taken the place of Hempel's E. Still, there is a fundamental difference. Hempel's criteria for a DNS explanation to be empirically adequate insist that his L's must have been subjected to extensive tests and have passed them all. I insist only that my L's, the members of Γ_T, be relevant in the given empirical context in which the explanation is formulated.

My criteria cannot differ that much from the criteria on which present-day philosophers of science insist. Here are two observations in support of my contention:

A law of nature is not an assertion that has a truth value. It is, rather, a statement that comes with a list of situations in which applying it has proved possible (Toulmin 1953, pp. 86–87).
Theories are applied selectively in scientific explanations. For example, one says that Newton's theory can be used to explain the tides even though it is known that Newton's laws do not satisfy Hempel's criteria for empirical adequacy. Whether a theory explains

some fact or other is independent of whether the real world as a whole fits the theory (van Fraassen 1980, p. 98).

9.2.2 An Example of an SE1 Scientific Explanation in Economics

My explication of a scientific explanation in economics may sound unfamiliar, so here is an example to fix ideas.[3]

E9.3

I believe that individuals rank uncertain prospects according to their expected utilities. To test this hypothesis, I talk one of my students into participating in two experiments. In the first experiment, I present the student with a large number N of uncertain binary prospects in which he can earn \$1,000 with probability q and \$0 with probability $(1 - q)$, where q is one of the members of $\{q_1, \ldots, q_N\}$. For each q_i, I ask the student for his certainty equivalent of the given prospect—that is, the number of dollars, $x_i \in [0, 1000]$, that would make him indifferent between receiving x_i dollars and trying his luck in the prospect. At the end, I construct the student's "utility function," $W(\cdot)$, in accord with the equations $W(0) = 0$, $W(1000) = 1$, and $W(x_i) = q_i$, where $i = 1, \ldots, N$. It turns out that the defined values of $W(x_i)$ are also values of the function

$$W(x) = 0.5\{1 + [(x - 500)/500]^{1/3}\}, \quad x \in [0, 1000]. \tag{9.1}$$

With $W(\cdot)$ in hand, I present the student with a new set of prospects in which all the q's equal ½. I ask for his certainty equivalent to each prospect. I use his answers to construct a function $V(\cdot) : [0, 1000] \to [0, 1]$ as follows: I assign the values 0 and 1, respectively, to $V(0)$ and $V(1,000)$. When $V(\cdot)$ has been defined at x and y, I let $V(C(x, y)) = \frac{1}{2}V(x) + \frac{1}{2}V(y)$, with $C(x, y)$ equal to the student's certainty equivalent of the option x with probability 1/2 and y with probability 1/2. For all $x \in [0, 1,000]$ at which I have defined $V(\cdot)$, I find that $V(\cdot)$ satisfies the relation

$$V(x) = x/1000, \quad x \in [0, 1,000]. \tag{9.2}$$

In 1952 Maurice Allais ran a sequence of similar pairs of experiments. The $W(\cdot)$ and $V(\cdot)$ functions that he observed differed from the respective functions in equations 9.1 and 9.2. However, Allais' functions shared with my functions an interesting characteristic: $V(x)$ tended to be larger than $W(x)$ for low values of x and smaller than $W(x)$

for high values of x. In my experiment, for example, W(500) = V(500), and

$$V(x) > W(x) \text{ if } x \in (0, 500),$$

$$V(x) < W(x) \text{ if } x \in (500, 1{,}000). \tag{9.3}$$

The standard theory of choice under uncertainty insists that a subject in the given kind of experiments chooses among uncertain prospects according to their expected utilities only if, for all observed x, W(x) = V(x). Therefore, on the basis of his experimental results, Allais concluded (in my words) that the expected-utility hypothesis for choice under uncertainty has little empirical relevance. (See Allais and Hagen 1979, pp. 620–627 and 649–654.[4])

Allais' profound arguments and interesting experimental results notwithstanding, I am not willing to draw the conclusion that the expected-utility hypothesis is empirically irrelevant in my experiment. It is true that my $W(\cdot)$ differs from my $V(\cdot)$. It is also true that my V(x) is larger than my W(x) for small x and that my V(x) is smaller than my W(x) for large x. However, these stylized facts may be due to my student's false perception of the values of the q_i with which I presented him in my first experiment. To explore this possibility, I will now present an SE1 scientific explanation of the relations depicted in equations 9.1–9.3 in which the decision maker in the theory universe ranks prospects according to their expected value.

I begin by describing the data universe, (Ω_P, Γ_P), and by formulating the assertion to be explained, H. The data universe is a set of seven-tuples that satisfy the following axioms.

D1
$\omega_P \in \Omega_P$ only if $\omega_P = (q, x, W, y, z, C, V)$ for some $q \in [0, 1]$, x, y, z $\in$ [0, 1,000], $W(\cdot) : [0, 1{,}000] \to [0, 1]$, $y \leq z$, $V(\cdot) : [0, 1000] \to [0, 1]$, V(0) = 0, V(1,000) = 1, and $C(\cdot) : [0, 1{,}000]^2 \to [0, 1{,}000]$.

D2
For all $\omega_P \in \Omega_P$, W(x) = q, and V(C(y, z)) = ½V(y) + ½V(z).

D3
If (q, x, W, y, z, C, V) $\in \Omega_P$, then (q, x, W, 0, 1000, C, V) $\in \Omega_P$, (q, x, W, y, C(y, z), C, V) $\in \Omega_P$, and (q, x, W, C(y, z), z, C, V) $\in \Omega_P$.

The explanandum, H, is as follows.

H

For all $\omega_P \in \Omega_P$: (i) the value of $W(\cdot)$ at x satisfies equation 9.1; (ii) the values of $V(\cdot)$ at y, z, and $C(y, z)$ satisfy equation 9.2; and (iii) the value of $W(\cdot)$ at x and the value of $V(\cdot)$ at $C(y, z)$ satisfy the inequalities in equation 9.3 whenever $x = C(y, z)$.

My experiments demonstrate that H is true in some model of (Ω_P, Γ_P). However, it is not a logical consequence of D1–D3.

Next the theory universe, (Ω_T, Γ_T). The theory universe is a set of sextuples that satisfy the following axioms.

A1

$\omega_T \in \Omega_T$ only if $\omega_T = (p, r, U, s, t, \hat{C})$ for some $p \in [0, 1]$, $r, s, t \in [0, 1000]$, $U(\cdot) : [0, 1{,}000] \rightarrow [0, 1]$, $s \leq t$, and $\hat{C}(\cdot) : [0, 1{,}000]^2 \rightarrow [0, 1{,}000]$.

A2

For all $\omega_T \in \Omega_T$, $U(r) = p$, and $U(\hat{C}(s, t)) = \frac{1}{2}U(s) + \frac{1}{2}U(t)$.

A3

For all $\omega_T \in \Omega_T$, $r = 1{,}000p$.

In these axioms, the triple (p, r, U) plays the same role that the triple (q, x, W) plays in D1–D3, with p taken to be the decision maker's perceived probability. Also, $\hat{C}(s, t)$ is to be interpreted as the certainty equivalent of the random options s and t, both with perceived probability $1/2$. In its intended interpretation, $(\Omega_T, A1–A3)$ is the universe of a theory in which the decision maker orders prospects according to their perceived expected values.

Finally, I must describe how the individuals in Ω_T are related to the individuals in Ω_P. I insist on accurate observations of r, s, t, and $\hat{C}$. I also assume that the student's perceived probabilities appropriately overvalue low probabilities and undervalue high probabilities.

G1

Ω_T and Ω_P are disjoint, and the sample space Ω is a subset of $\Omega_T \times \Omega_P$.

G2

If $(\omega_T, \omega_P) \in \Omega$ and $(\omega_T, \omega_P) = (p, r, U, s, t, \hat{C}, q, x, W, y, z, C, V)$, then $(p, r, U, 0, 1{,}000, \hat{C}, q, x, W, 0, 1{,}000, C, V) \in \Omega$, $(p, r, U, s, \hat{C}(s, t), \hat{C}, q, x,$

W, y, C(y, z), C, V) ∈ Ω, and (p, r, U, Ĉ(s, t), t, Ĉ, q, x, W, C(y, z), z, C, V) ∈ Ω.

G3

For all $(\omega_T, \omega_P) \in \Omega$, r = x, s = y, t = z, and Ĉ(s, t) = C(y, z).

G4

For all $(\omega_T, \omega_P) \in \Omega$, $p = 0.5 + 4(q - 0.5)^3$.

A remark concerning the content of G4 is called for. The phenomenon that individuals tend to overvalue low probabilities and undervalue high ones has been observed in many experimental studies and is discussed at some length in a survey article by R. Duncan Luce and Patrick Suppes (1965, pp. 321–327). By how much perceived and objective probabilities differ and how this difference varies with the characteristics of individuals are less well documented. It is, therefore, interesting that the way in which perceived and quoted probabilities differ in G4 accords with the way in which the psychological probabilities of Frederick Mosteller and Philip Nogee's (1951, p. 397) guardsmen differed from the true probabilities.

To demonstrate that I can use (Ω_T, Γ_T) and $\Gamma_{T,P}$, as described above, to give a scientific explanation of the relations in equations 9.1–9.3, I use M to designate the intended model of the data universe and presume that it is also a model of H. Next I observe that

$$[[[[W(x) = q] \wedge [r = x]] \wedge [p = 0.5 + 4(q - 0.5)^3]] \wedge [r = 1,000p]]$$

$$\supset [W(x) = 0.5 + 0.5((x - 500)/500)^{1/3}]]. \tag{9.4}$$

From equation 9.4 it follows that, for all $(\omega_T, \omega_P) \in \Omega$, the value of W(·) at x must satisfy equation 9.1. Moreover, I deduce from A2 and A3 that Ĉ(s, t) = ½s + ½t, and then, from A2 and G3, that C(y, z) = ½y + ½z. Finally, by an obvious inductive argument, it follows that, for all $(\omega_T, \omega_P) \in \Omega$, the value of V(y) equals the value of U(s). Consequently, V(·) must satisfy equation 9.2. But if that is so, the value of W(·) at x and the value of V(·) at C(y, z) must satisfy the inequalities in equation 9.3 whenever x = C(y, z). Hence, (Ω_T, Γ_T) and $\Gamma_{T,P}$ provide the required scientific explanation of H. My explanation, equations 9.1–9.3 and standard expected-utility theory notwithstanding, suggests that my student may rank uncertain prospects according to their expected utilities.

The explanation of H that I have delineated is obviously logically adequate. In the two experiments that I carried out with my student, it is also empirically adequate. Besides, my explanation suggests that Allais' rejection of the empirical relevance of the expected-utility hypothesis was justified only if his subjects' perceived probabilities were veridical.

9.3 A Formal Characterization of Scientific Explanations in Econometrics

The situation envisaged in SE1 is similar to the experimental tests of physical theories that Pierre Duhem described on pages 144–147 of his 1954 book *The Aim and Structure of Physical Theory*. However, it differs from the situations econometricians usually face when they search for the empirical relevance of economic theories. In SE1, H is a family of sentences each of which has a truth value in every model of (Ω_P, Γ_P) and all of which are true in some model of (Ω_P, Γ_P). In contrast, in econometrics H is often a family of statistical relations. One H might insist that "on the average, families with high incomes save a greater proportion of their incomes than families with low incomes." Another H might claim that "the prices of soybean oil and cottonseed oil vary over time as two cointegrated I(1) ARIMA processes." These assertions are about properties of the data-generating process. They need not have truth values in a model of (Ω_P, Γ_P).

9.3.1 SE2—A Scientific Explanation in Econometrics
When an observed H is a family of statistical relations, a scientific explanation of H must be based on statistical arguments. Such scientific explanations can be characterized as follows.

SE2
Let $(\Omega_P, \Gamma_P, (\Omega_P, \aleph_P, P_p(\cdot)))$ be some given data universe, where Ω_P is a subset of a vector space, Γ_p is a finite set of axioms that the vectors in Ω_P must satisfy, $\aleph_P$ is a σ field of subsets of Ω_P, and $P_p(\cdot) : \aleph_P \to [0, 1]$ is a probability measure. Let TPD denote the family of finite-dimensional probability distributions of the vectors in Ω_P, which, subject to the conditions on which Γ_P insists, is determined by $P_P(\cdot)$. Moreover, let H_1 and H_2 be, respectively, a finite family of assertions concerning the characteristics of the vectors in Ω_P and the TPD, and let I_1 and I_2, respectively, be two families of models of H_1 and (Ω_P, Γ_P) and of H_2 and the

TPD. Finally, suppose that I_1 is the intended interpretation of (Ω_P, Γ_P) and that I_2 is the intended interpretation of the TPD. Then to give a scientific explanation of the pair (H_1, H_2), means to find a theory universe $(\Omega_T, \Gamma_T, (\Omega_T, \aleph_T, P_T(\cdot))$ that is disjoint from the data universe, a sample space $\Omega \subset \Omega_T \times \Omega_P$, a finite set of bridge principles $\Gamma_{T,P}$,that in Ω relates members of Ω_T to members of Ω_P, and a model of Γ_T, Γ_P, and $\Gamma_{T,P}$ with two properties: (1) H_1 is a logical consequence of the given model; and (2) the MPD which the model determines has the characteristics of TPD on which H_2 insists.

Such an explanation is logically adequate if the pair (H_1, H_2) is not a logical consequence of the model of Γ_P and the axioms of $P_P(\cdot)$. The explanation is empirically adequate if the model of Γ_T, $\Gamma_{T,P}$, and Γ_P and the associated mathematical model of the MPD have the following properties: (1) The logical consequences of Γ_T, $\Gamma_{T,P}$, and Γ_P that concern H_1 and characteristics of the vectors in Ω_P are valid in a member of I_1. (2) There is a member of I_2 whose model of TPD shares with the model of MPD the characteristics on which H_2 insists. (3) The given model of MPD is data admissible; i.e., it lies in a 95-percent-confidence region of a meaningful statistical estimate of the MPD.

　My SE2 scientific explanation is not standard and requires several clarifying remarks. One good way to think about H_1 and H_2 is to think of them as stylized facts that researchers have observed in many different empirical analyses. A pair of members of I_1 and I_2 is a pair of models of the data universe and the data-generating process in one of these empirical analyses. For example, in the example of an SE2 scientific explanation that I give below, H_1 and H_2 refer to stylized facts concerning US Treasury Bill yields that Hall et al. (1992), Anderson (1999), and Anderson, Storvik, and I (in Stigum 2003) have observed. The data and the data-generating processes in the three empirical analyses are different and require three different pairs of models of the pertinent data universe and the data-generating process to describe them. In a given empirical analysis, the pair (I_1, I_2) reduces to a pair of models, say (M_1, M_2), and the scientific explanation of the stylized fact in question is empirically adequate if the model of the theory universe, the bridge principles, the data universe, and the MPD satisfies the three conditions listed above with M_1 and M_2 substituted for I_1 and I_2.

　Because it is difficult to give logically and empirically adequate SE2 explanations of regularities in data such as I have in mind for SE2, a detailed example is called for. The following example is a

reformulation of an SE2 explanation that Heather Anderson, Geir
Storvik, and I published on pages 585–608 of Stigum 2003. It gives a
scientific explanation of regularities in the Treasury Bill market that
Hall, Anderson, and Granger discovered in 1992. I refer to it as HAG's
Dictum, and formulate it as follows.

HAG's Dictum
Yields to maturity of US Treasury Bills are cointegrated I(1) processes.
During periods in which the Federal Reserve specifically targets short-
term interest rates, the spreads between yields of different maturity
define the cointegrating vectors.

The present SE2 scientific explanation differs from the one I formulated
in Stigum 2003. My explanation in that work went with the ideas of a
theory-data confrontation that I developed there—which I paraphrased
in the introductory pages of chapter 5 of the present book. The present
formulation goes with the ideas of a theory-data confrontation that I
delineated in sections 2.2 and 6.1 of this book. The explanations differ
in two ways: In 2003 the theory universe was a pair; here it is a triple,
one component of which is a probability space. In 2003 the bridge (that
is the sample space) was a triple, one component of which was a probability space; here the bridge is a pair, $(\Omega, \Gamma_{T,P})$, and the probability
measure on subsets of Ω is the product probability measure on subsets
of $\Omega_T \times \Omega_P$ that is generated by the probability measures in the theory
and data universes.

9.4 A Formal Scientific Explanation of HAG's Dictum

The Treasury Bill market is a part of the money market in the United
States. The yields in the money market are interrelated. Consequently,
when the relevant positive analogies for the functioning of the Treasury
Bill market are delineated, one must take into account how the functioning of the remainder of the money market influences the determination of yields in the Treasury Bill market.

There are many different money-market instruments even when
they are distinguished only by the name of the issuer and the kind of
issue (for example, Treasury versus General Electric, and 3-month bills
versus 6-month bills). There are many more when instruments are also
distinguished by maturity. For the purposes of this chapter it is not
necessary to take this multiplicity of money-market instruments into
account. To keep the arguments clear and simple, I will argue here as

if there were only two bills and only one other money-market instrument. In due course I will show that my arguments' gain in clarity will not come at the expense of loss of insight.

To provide a formal scientific explanation of HAG's Dictum, I begin by putting together the elements of a formal theory-data confrontation that I need for the task. As in chapter 6, the theory universe, the data universe, and the bridge are represented by $(\Omega_T, \Gamma_T, (\Omega_T, \aleph_T, P_T(\cdot)))$, $(\Omega_P, \Gamma_P, (\Omega_P, \aleph_P, P_P(\cdot)))$, and $(\Omega, \Gamma_{T,P})$. Sequences of vectors in the theory universe function as vector-valued sequences in Ω_T and as vector-valued random processes on $(\Omega_T, \aleph_T)$. Similarly, sequences of vectors in the data universe function as vector-valued sequences in Ω_P and as vector-valued random processes on $(\Omega_P, \aleph_P)$. I assume throughout that Ω_T and Ω_P are disjoint, that $\aleph_T$ and $\aleph_P$ are stochastically independent, and that the probability space, $(\Omega_T \times \Omega_P, \aleph, P(\cdot))$, is as I described it in chapter 2.

9.4.1 The Data Universe

I have 150 monthly observations of yields of bills that mature in 1 and 2 months. My sample dates from the period January 1983–June 1995. Each observed yield pertained to the last trading day of the month and was taken from the Fama Twelve-Month Treasury Bill Term Structure File of the Center for Research in Securities Prices at the University of Chicago. $\acute{K}_1$ and $\acute{K}_2$ represent the two yield series.

In addition to my observations of the two Treasury Bill yields, I have a corresponding series of monthly observations of the overnight Federal Funds rate provided by Heather Anderson (2003, chapter 21). Each observation records the weekly effective (annualized) rate of overnight Federal Funds. Data (from 1984 onward) were obtained from the Federal Reserve, and earlier data were obtained from the *Federal Reserve Bulletin*. Further, the weekly data were converted to monthly observations by using the last observation for each month. I denote the series of observations of the Federal Funds rate by ff.

The first two axioms of Γ_P describe the conceptual framework of my scientific explanation. In them $\hat{y}_1$, $\hat{y}_2$, and $\hat{y}_3$ are auxiliary variables that I need to describe the probability distribution of $\acute{K}_1$, $\acute{K}_2$, and ff relative to $P_P(\cdot)$. I delineate the relationship between the six variables in D3.

D1

$\Omega_P \subset (R_+^3 \times R^3)^N$. Thus, $\omega_P \in \Omega_P$ only if ω_P is a sequence of vectors, $(\acute{K}_{1t}, \acute{K}_{2t}, ff_t, \hat{y}_{1t}, \hat{y}_{2t}, \hat{y}_{3t})$, all of which belong to $(R_+^3 \times R^3)$. In short, $\omega_P = (\acute{K}_1, \acute{K}_2, ff, \hat{y}_1, \hat{y}_2, \hat{y}_3)$ for some $(\acute{K}_1, \acute{K}_2, ff, \hat{y}_1, \hat{y}_2, \hat{y}_3) \in (R_+^3 \times R^3)^N$, where $N = \{0, 1, 2, \ldots\}$.

D2

Let Ω_P be as above, let $\acute{K} = (\acute{K}_1, \acute{K}_2)$, let $\hat{y} = (\hat{y}_1, \hat{y}_2, \hat{y}_3)$, and for each $t \in$ N let the vector-valued function

$(\acute{K}, ff, \hat{y})(t, \cdot) : \Omega_P \to R_+^2 \times R_+ \times R^3$

be defined by the equations

$(\acute{K}(t, \omega_P), ff(t, \omega_P), \hat{y}(t, \omega_P)) = \omega_{Pt}$ and $\omega_P \in \Omega_P$,   (9.5)

where ω_{Pt} denotes the tth component of ω_P. For each $t \in$ N, $(\acute{K}, ff, \hat{y})$ $(t, \cdot)$ is measurable with respect to $\aleph_P$. Also, relative to $P_p(\cdot)$ and subject to the conditions on which Γ_P insists, the probability distributions of the family of random vectors $\{(\acute{K}, ff, \hat{y})(t, \omega_P); t \in$ N$\}$ equals the family of finite-dimensional probability distributions of the process that generates the individuals in Ω_P; i.e., the TPD.

The third assertion in Γ_P describes the way in which the $\hat{y}_1$, $\hat{y}_2$, and $\hat{y}_3$ sequences function as auxiliary sequences for the $\acute{K}_1$, $\acute{K}_2$, and ff sequences. For the present analysis it is significant that on stretches of t values where $\hat{y}_i(t, \omega_P)$ assumes positive values its values coincide with the values of the corresponding component of $(\acute{K}, ff)(t, \omega_P)$. The data I have consist of positive values of the components of $(\acute{K}, ff)$. These values are values of the corresponding components of $\hat{y}$.

D3

For each $\omega_P \in \Omega_P$ and all $t \in$ N,

$\acute{K}_1(t, \omega_P) = \max(\hat{y}_1(t, \omega_P), 0)$,

$\acute{K}_2(t, \omega_P) = \max(\hat{y}_2(t, \omega_P), 0)$,

and   (9.6)

$ff(t, \omega_P) = \max(\hat{y}_3(t, \omega_P), 0)$.

With axioms D1–D3 in hand, I can formulate the assertion for which I intend to give a scientific explanation.

H

Let $P_P(\cdot) : \aleph_P \to [0, 1]$ be the probability measure on whose existence I insist in D2. Let the vector-valued function $(\acute{K}, ff, \hat{y})(\cdot) : N \times \Omega_P \to R_+^2 \times R_+ \times R^3$ be as described in equation 9.5. Then, relative to $P_p(\cdot)$, the family of random vectors $\{(\acute{K}, ff, \hat{y})(t, \omega_P); t \in N\}$, satisfies the following conditions:

1. For all $t \in N$, $(\acute{K}, ff)(t, \omega_P) = (\max(\hat{y}_1(t, \omega_P), 0), \max(\hat{y}_2(t, \omega), 0), \max(\hat{y}_3(t, \omega), 0))$ a.e.
2. $\{\hat{y}(t, \omega_P); t \in N\}$ is an I(1) vector-valued ARIMA process.
3. The two first components of $\{\hat{y}(t, \omega_P); t \in N\}$ are cointegrated with cointegrating vector $(-1, 1, 0)$, that is, $\{\hat{y}_2(t, \omega_P) - \hat{y}_1(t, \omega_P); t \in N\}$ is a wide-sense stationary process.

Here a few remarks are called for. They concern H and the two models, M_1 and M_2, that play the roles of I_1 and I_2 in my SE2 explanation of H.

First H: H does not sound quite like HAG's dictum. However, if one interprets HAG's claim with their footnote 5 in mind, one must end up with H as stated. In their note 5, HAG observe that yields to maturity, such as $(\acute{K}, ff)(t, \cdot)$, cannot be integrated processes in the strict sense, because nominal yields are bounded below at 0 while integrated processes are unbounded. From that note and from my deliberations in section 6.3 it follows that formulating HAG's Dictum in terms of the auxiliary $\hat{y}$ sequences is a reasonable way to express HAG's claim.

Next M_1: It is important to observe that H is not an integral part of Γ_P. The axioms of the data universe are D1–D3. Hence the pertinent M_1 in my SE2 explanation of H is a model of $(\Omega_P, D1, D3)$. In its intended interpretation M_1 is a model of Ω_P that satisfies D1 and D3 and that comprises (possibly all the) sequences in Ω_P of which my data are partial realizations.

Then M_2. In D2 I follow in Trygve Haavelmo's footsteps and postulate that my data have "associated with [them] one particular 'true', but unknown probability law" (see Haavelmo 1944, p. 49). This probability law is the TPD in my case. Also, in its intended interpretation, M_2 is the true model of the TPD in my SE2 explanation of H. I do not know M2, but I assume, without say, that it satisfies the conditions on which H insists.

My assumption concerning the properties of M_2 is not far-fetched. To wit: Anderson's empirical analysis of the money market on pages 604–606 of Stigum 2003 demonstrates that there is a model of the present data-generating process in which H is valid. In different words and more precisely, Heather's analysis demonstrates that one cannot reject the hypothesis that the true model of the present TPD has the characteristics on which H insists.

9.4.2 The Theory Universe

In the theory universe the assertions in Γ_T concern twelve sequences of variables. Six of them—K_1, K_2, FF, y_1, y_2, and y_3—are related to the data variables in interesting ways. Specifically, K_j, where j = 1, 2, represents the yield series on a j-month Treasury Bill in the theory universe, FF represents the series of rates on Federal Funds in the theory universe, and y_1, y_2, and y_3 are sequences of auxiliary variables for K_1, K_2, and FF in the same way that $\hat{y}_1$, $\hat{y}_2$, and $\hat{y}_3$ are sequences of auxiliary variables for the $\acute{K}_1$, $\acute{K}_2$, and ff sequences.

I denote the remaining six sequences of variables in the theory universe by G_2, λ_1, λ_2, Λ, η_1, and η_2. Here G_2 represents the equilibrium rate of return from contracting today to buy a one-month Treasury Bill next month. Also, λ_j, where j = 1, 2, represents the next-month expected value of K_j based on current information. Λ, η_1, and η_2 denote series of error terms.

The first two axioms in Γ_T describe the conceptual framework of the theory in my scientific explanation.

A1

$\Omega_T \subset (R_+^4 \times R^8)^N$. Thus, $\omega_T \in \Omega_T$ only if ω_T is a sequence of vectors, $(K_{1t}, K_{2t}, G_{2t}, FF_t, \lambda_{1t}, \lambda_{2t}, \Lambda_t, \eta_{1t}, \eta_{2t}, y_{1t}, y_{2t}, y_{3t})$, all of which belong to $(R_+^4 \times R^8)$. In short, $\omega_T = (K_1, K_2, G_2, FF, \lambda_1, \lambda_2, \Lambda, \eta_1, \eta_2, y_1, y_2, y_3)$ for some $(K_1, K_2, G_2, FF, \lambda_1, \lambda_2, \Lambda, \eta_1, \eta_2, y_1, y_2, y_3) \in (R_+^4 \times R^8)^N$, where N = {0, 1, ...}.

A2

Let Ω_T be as above, let $K = (K_1, K_2)$, $\lambda = (\lambda_1, \lambda_2)$, $\eta = (\eta_1, \eta_2)$, $y = (y_1, y_2, y_3)$, and for each $t \in N$, let the vector-valued function $(K, G_2, FF, \lambda, \Lambda, \eta, y)(t, \cdot) : \Omega_T \to (R_+^4 \times R^8)$ be defined by the equations $(K(t, \omega_T), G_2(t, \omega_T), FF(t, \omega_T), \lambda(t, \omega_T), \Lambda(t, \omega_T), \eta(t, \omega_T), y(t, \omega_T)) = \omega_{Tt}$ and $\omega_T \in \Omega_T$, where ω_{Tt} is the tth component of ω_T. The functions $(K, G_2, FF, \lambda, \Lambda, \eta, y)(t, \cdot) : \Omega_T \to (R_+^4 \times R^8)$, $t \in N$, are measurable with respect to $\aleph_T$. Also, subject to the conditions on which the theory axioms insist, their family of finite-dimensional probability distributions relative to $P_T(\cdot)$ is well defined. I denote it by RPD.

The next members of Γ_T describe law-like properties of the elements that play essential roles in the theory I will use to explain HAG's Dictum. A3–A6 delineate the way the auxiliary variables y and λ function in the theory. A7 and A8 depict characteristics of the RPD distribution of $(K, G_2, FF, \lambda, \Lambda, \eta, y)(t, \cdot)$.

In the theory, y is to play the role of (K, FF). I describe how in A3.

A3

For each $\omega_T \in \Omega_T$ and $t \in N$,

$$K_1(t, \omega_T) = \max(y_1(t, \omega_T), 0),\tag{9.7}$$

$$K_2(t, \omega_T) = \max[y_2(t, \omega_T), G_2(t, \omega_T), 0],\tag{9.8}$$

and

$$FF(t, \omega_T) = \max(y_3(t, \omega_T), 0).\tag{9.9}$$

Thus, for $i = 1, 2$, the sample path of $K_i(\cdot, \omega_T)$ coincides with the sample path of $y_i(\cdot, \omega_T)$ over any stretches of time in which $y_i(t, \omega_T)$ assume positive values. Similarly, the sample path of $FF(t, \omega_T)$ coincides with the sample path of $y_3(\cdot, \omega_T)$ over stretches of time in which $y_3(t, \omega_T)$ assume positive values.

In the theory, λ is to play the role of the rationally expected value of y_1 and y_3 while y is playing the role of (K, FF). I describe how in axioms A4–A6. A4 describes how the market participants' expectations are formed; A5 and A6 delineate conditions that a market in equilibrium must satisfy.

A4

Let φ be a 2×2 matrix. Assume that $\varphi_{ii} > 0$, $i = 1, 2$, and that the eigenvalues of $(I - \varphi)$ have absolute values that are less than or equal to 1. For all $\omega_T \in \Omega_T$, and $t \in N - \{0\}$,

$$\lambda(0, \omega_T)' = \varphi(y_1(0, \omega_T), y_3(0, \omega_T))'$$

and   (9.10)

$$\lambda(t, \omega_T)' - \lambda(t - 1, \omega_T)' = \varphi[(y_1(t, \omega_T), y_3(t, \omega_T))' - \lambda(t - 1, \omega_T)'].$$

A5

For each $\omega_T \in \Omega_T$ and $t \in N$,

$$y_1(t + 1, \omega_T) = \lambda_1(t, \omega_T) + \eta_1(t + 1, \omega_T)\tag{9.11}$$

and

$$y_3(t + 1, \omega_T) = \lambda_2(t, \omega_T) + \eta_2(t + 1, \omega_T).\tag{9.12}$$

Also, $\eta_1(0, \omega_T) = 0$, $\eta_2(0, \omega_T) = 0$; and there exists a positive pair $(\acute{y}_1, \acute{y}_3)$ such that $y_1(0, \omega_T) = \acute{y}_1$, and $y_3(0, \omega_T) = \acute{y}_3$.

A6

For each $\omega_T \in \Omega_T$ and $t \in N$,

$$y_2(t, \omega_T) = \tfrac{1}{2}[y_1(t, \omega_T) + G_2(t, \omega_T)] \tag{9.13}$$

and

$$G_2(t, \omega_T) = \lambda_1(t, \omega_T) + \Lambda(t, \omega_T). \tag{9.14}$$

Also, $\Lambda(0, \omega_T) = 0$.

In my scientific explanation of H, the preceding axioms are taken to delineate important positive analogies of the behavior over time of equilibrium yields in the US money market and nothing else. The equations in these axioms depict relationships between different yields that must hold because of the possibilities for arbitrage in the market, and describe essential features of the dynamics of the money market. In particular, equations 9.10–9.12 and 9.14 above and assertions A7 and A8 below depict an equilibrium state of a frictionless money market in which the agents in the market, in an aggregate sense, are risk neutral and endowed with rational expectations about future bill yields and Federal Funds rates.

The next two assertions in Γ_T concern the finite-dimensional probability distributions of the vectors in Ω_T relative to $P_T(\cdot)$.

A7
Relative to $P_T(\cdot)$, . the family of functions$\{(\Lambda, \eta)(t, \omega_T); t \geq 1\}$is a vector-valued wide-sense stationary process. The family of functions, $\{\eta(t, \omega_T); t \in N\}$ constitutes a purely random processes with mean 0 and covariance matrix, Σ_η. The families $\{\eta(t, \omega_T); t \in N\}$and $\{\Lambda(t, \omega_T); t \in N\}$ are distributed independently of each other.

A8
Let the function $(K, G_2, FF, \lambda, \Lambda, \eta, y)(\cdot) : N \times \Omega \rightarrow (R_+^4 \times R^8)$ be as described in A2. Then, relative to $P_T(\cdot)$, the functions $\{(\Lambda, \eta, y_1, y_3)(t, \omega_T); t \geq 1\}$ satisfy the following conditions: For each $t \in N - \{0\}$,

$E\{\Lambda(t, \omega_T) \,|\, (y_1, y_3)(0), \dots , (y_1, y_3)(t)\} = \Lambda(t, \omega_T)$ a.e.,

$E\{\eta(t, \omega_T) \,|\, (y_1, y_3)(0), \dots , (y_1, y_3)(t-1)\} = 0$ a.e.

9.4.3 The Dynamics of the Money Market in the Theory Universe
Axioms A1–A8 have interesting logical consequences that I record in theorems T9.1–T9.5. For example, according to T9.1 the $\lambda(t, \omega_T)$ of A4 can be interpreted as the theoretical money market's prediction of the

most likely value of $(y_1, y_3)(t + 1, \omega_T)$, conditional upon the observed values of $(y_1, y_3)(s)$, $s = 0, 1, \ldots, t$. Also, according to T9.2–T9.4, in the RPD distribution the family of random variables $\{y(t, \omega_T); t \in N\}$ constitutes a three-dimensional I(1) ARIMA process that is cointegrated with cointgrating vector $(-1, 1, 0)$. T9.5 adds an interesting relationship of K_1, K_2, and G_2 to the relations in D3. The theorems are simple logical consequences of the axioms.

T9.1
Let I_2 be the 2×2 identity matrix, and let φ be the 2×2 matrix in A4. Suppose that A1–A8 are valid. Then, for each $\omega_T \in \Omega_T$ and all $t \in N$,

$$\lambda(t, \omega_T)' = \Sigma_{0 \leq s \leq t}(I_2 - \varphi)^s \varphi \cdot (y_1, y_3)(t - s, \omega_T)'. \tag{9.15}$$

Also, relative to $P_T(\cdot)$,

$$\lambda(t, \omega)))' = E((y_1, y_3)(t + 1, \omega_T)' \mid (y_1, y_3)(0), \ldots, (y_1, y_3)(t)) \text{ a.e.} \tag{9.16}$$

T9.2
Let φ be the 2×2 matrix of A4, and let $\eta = (\eta_1, \eta_2)'$. Also, suppose that A1–A6 are valid. Then, for each $\omega_T \in \Omega_T$,

$$(y_1, y_3)(1, \omega_T)' = \varphi(y_1, y_3)(0, \omega_T)' + \eta(1, \omega_T)$$

and $\tag{9.17}$

$$(y_1, y_3)(t + 1, \omega_T)' = (y_1, y_3)(t, \omega_T)' + \eta(t + 1, \omega_T) - (I - \varphi)\eta(t, \omega_T), \quad t \geq 1.$$

Hence, if A1–A8 are valid, the family $\{(y_1, y_3)(t, \omega_T), t \in N\}$ constitutes, in the RPD distribution, an I(1) ARIMA process.

T9.3
Let φ be the 2×2 matrix of A4. Let η_{1t}, η_{2t}, Λ_t, and ξ_t be short for $\eta_1(t, \omega_T)$, $\eta_2(t, \omega_T)$, $\Lambda(t, \omega_T)$, and $\xi(t, \omega_T)$. Let $\xi \in R^N$ be defined by

$$\xi_0 = 0, \; \xi_1 = \tfrac{1}{2}[(1 + \varphi_{11})\eta_{11} - (1 - \varphi_{11})y_{10} + \varphi_{12}y_{30} + \varphi_{12}\eta_{21} + \Lambda_1]$$

and $\tag{9.18}$

$$\xi_t = \tfrac{1}{2}[(\eta_{1t} - \eta_{1t-1}) + \varphi_{11}(\eta_{1t} + \eta_{1t-1}) + \varphi_{12}(\eta_{2t} + \eta_{2t-1}) + \Lambda_t - \Lambda_{t-1}], \quad t \geq 2.$$

Then, for all $(t, \omega_T) \in N \times \Omega_T$, $\xi(t, \omega_T)$ is well defined by equations 9.18. Suppose that A1–A6 are valid. Then, for each $\omega_T \in \Omega_T$,

$$y_2(0, \omega_T) = \tfrac{1}{2}[(1 + \varphi_{11})y_1(0, \omega_T) + \varphi_{12}y_3(0, \omega_T)]$$

and   (9.19)

$y_2(t, \omega_T) = y_2(t - 1, \omega_T) + \xi(t, \omega_T),$ $t \geq 1.$

Hence, if A1–A8 are valid, the family $\{y_2(t, \omega_T), t \in N\}$ constitutes, in the RPD distribution, an I(1) ARIMA process.

T9.4
Let ϕ be the 2×2 matrix of A4, and suppose that A1–A6 are valid. Then, for each $\omega_T \in \Omega_T$,

$y_2(0, \omega_T) - y_1(0, \omega_T) = \tfrac{1}{2}[\Lambda(0, \omega_T) + (y_1(1, \omega_T) - y_1(0, \omega_T)) - \eta_1(1, \omega_T)]$

and   (9.20)

$y_2(t, \omega_T) - y_1(t, \omega_T) = \tfrac{1}{2}[\Lambda(t, \omega_T) - (1 - \phi_{11})\eta_1(t, \omega_T) + \phi_{12}\eta_2(t, \omega_T)], \quad t \geq 1.$

Hence, if the Axioms A1–A8 are valid, the family of auxiliary variables, $\{(y_1, y_2, y_3)(t, \omega_T), t \in N\}$, constitutes, in the RPD distribution, a cointegrated I(1) ARIMA process with cointegrating vector $(-1, 1, 0)$.

T9.5
Suppose that A1–A6 are valid. Then, for each $\omega_T \in \Omega_T$ and all $t \in N$,

$K_2(t, \omega_T) = \max[\tfrac{1}{2}(K_1(t, \omega_T) + G_2(t, \omega_T)), 0].$ (9.21)

9.4.4 The Bridge
So much for the theory universe. I will now describe the bridge in my scientific explanation of H and present several characteristics of the dynamics of Treasury Bill yields that can be derived from the A axioms and the bridge principles.

Four of the members of $\Gamma_{T,P}$, G1–G4, describe the conceptual framework of the bridge.

G1
Observations are sequences of pairs of vectors, $(\omega_{Tt}, \omega_{Pt})$, that are components of some pair, (ω_T, ω_P), that belongs to the sample space.

G2
The sample space, Ω, is a subset of $\Omega_T \times \Omega_P$; i.e., $\Omega \subset \Omega_T \times \Omega_P$.

G3
$\Omega_T \subset \{\omega_T \in \Omega_T$ for which there is an $\omega_P \in \Omega_P$ such that $(\omega_T, \omega_P) \in \Omega\}$.

G4
In $(\Omega_T \times \Omega_P, \aleph, P(\cdot))$ it is the case that $\Omega \in \aleph$ and $P(\Omega) > 0$.

The fifth member of $\Gamma_{T,P}$ describes how, in Ω, the components of ω_T are related to the components of Ω_P.

G5
There exists an invertible 3×3 matrix, $\psi = (\psi_{ij})$, with strictly positive diagonal elements whose largest absolute eigenvalue is less than 1, such that, for each $(\omega_T, \omega_P) \in \Omega$,

$$\hat{y}(0, \omega_P) = \hat{y}_0$$

and   (9.22)

$$\hat{y}(t, \omega_P) - \hat{y}(t - 1, \omega_P) = \psi(y(t, \omega_T) - \hat{y}(t - 1, \omega_P)), \quad t \geq 1$$

where $\hat{y} = (\hat{y}_1, \hat{y}_2, \hat{y}_3)'$, and $y = (y_1, y_2, y_3)'$.

Since $\hat{y}(t, \omega_P) = \Sigma_{0 \leq s \leq t}(I - \psi)^s \, \psi y(t - s, \omega_T)$, G3 is an assumption I invoke to rule out uninteresting models of the axioms.

9.4.5 The MPD
The finite-dimensional probability distributions of the components of ω_P that (1) satisfy D1 and D3 and (2) are induced by G1–G5 and the probability distribution of ω_T that A1–A8 and $P_T(\cdot)$ determine constitute the marginal probability distribution of the components of ω_P, the MPD. (See section 2.2.) From A1–A8, D1, D3, and G1–G5 I can derive interesting characteristics of the MPD distribution of the family of functions $\{\hat{y}(t, \omega); t \in N\}$. The first two theorems concern sequences in Ω and not the probability distributions of the $\hat{y}(t)$ as such.

T9.6
Let U denote the forward shift operator, let ξ be as described in equation 9.9, and let $\zeta = (\zeta_1, \zeta_2, \zeta_3) \in (R^3)^N$ be defined for arbitrary t by

$$\zeta_{1t} = \psi_{11}[\eta_{1t} - (1 - \varphi_{11})\eta_{1t-1} + \varphi_{12}\eta_{2t-1}] + \psi_{13}[\eta_{2t} - (1 - \varphi_{22})\eta_{2t-1}$$
$$+ \varphi_{21}\eta_{1t-1}] + \psi_{12}\xi_t,$$ (9.23)

$$\zeta_{2t} = \psi_{21}[\eta_{1t} - (1 - \varphi_{11})\eta_{1t-1} + \varphi_{12}\eta_{2t-1}] + \psi_{23}[\eta_{2t} - (1 - \varphi_{22})\eta_{2t-1}$$
$$+ \varphi_{21}\eta_{1t-1}] + \psi_{22}\xi_t,$$ (9.24)

and

$$\zeta_{3t} = \psi_{31}[\eta_{1t} - (1 - \varphi_{11})\eta_{1t-1} + \varphi_{12}\eta_{2t-1}] + \psi_{33}[\eta_{2t} - (1 - \varphi_{22})\eta_{2t-1}$$
$$+ \varphi_{21}\eta_{1t-1}] + \psi_{32}\xi_t. \tag{9.25}$$

Then, for all $(t, \omega_T) \in N \times \Omega_T$, $\zeta(t, \omega_T)$ is well defined by equations 9.23–9.25. Let U designate the shift operator and suppose that A1–A6, D1, D3, and G1–G5 are valid. For each $(\omega_T, \omega_P) \in \Omega$,

$$\hat{y}_0 = \acute{y}_0,$$

$$[I - (I - \psi)U^{-1}]\hat{y}(1, \omega_P) = \psi \begin{pmatrix} \varphi_{11}y_1(0, \omega_T) + \varphi_{12}y_3(0, \omega_T) + \eta_1(1, \omega_T) \\ y_2(0, \omega_T) + \xi(1, \omega_T) \\ \varphi_{21}y_1(0, \omega_T) + \varphi_{22}y_3(0, \omega_T) + \eta_2(1, \omega_T) \end{pmatrix},$$

and $\tag{9.26}$

$$(I - (I - \psi)U^{-1})(I - IU^{-1})\hat{y}(t, \omega_P) = \zeta(t, \omega_T), \quad t \geq 2.$$

T9.7

Suppose that A1–A6, D1, D3, and G1–G5 are valid, and let $\varepsilon(t, \omega_T)$ be defined by (9.27) for all $t \in N - \{0, 1\}$:

$$\varepsilon(t, \omega_T) = [I - (I - \psi)U^{-1}]^{-1} \zeta(t, \omega_T), \tag{9.27}$$

where ζ is as described in equations 9.23–9.25. For each $(\omega_T, \omega_P) \in \Omega$ and all $t \in N - \{0, 1\}$,

$$\hat{y}_2(t - 1, \omega_P) - \hat{y}_1(t - 1, \omega_P)$$

$$= y_2(t, \omega_T) - y_1(t, \omega_T) + (-1, 1, 0)\psi^{-1}(-\varepsilon(t, \omega_T))$$

$$= \tfrac{1}{2}[\Lambda(t, \omega_T) - (1 - \varphi_{11})\eta_1(t, \omega_T) + \varphi_{12}\eta_2(t, \omega_T)] + (-1, 1, 0)\,\psi^{-1}(-\varepsilon(t, \omega_T)). \tag{9.28}$$

Before I derive the MPD distribution of the $\hat{y}(t, \omega_P)$ from T9.6 and T9.7, a few preliminary remarks are called for. First I must introduce several new variables.

For all $(\omega_T, \omega_P) \in \Omega$ and all $t \in N - \{0\}$, let

$$(\acute{\eta}, \chi, \delta, \varsigma, \pi)(t, \omega_P) = (\eta, \xi, \Lambda, \zeta, \varepsilon)(t, \omega_T).$$

Then the equations

$$\psi^{-1}\big(\psi\Delta\hat{y}(t, \omega_P) - (I - \psi)\,\Delta\hat{y}(t - 1, \omega_P)\big)$$

$$= \begin{bmatrix} \acute{\eta}_1(t, \omega_P) - (1 - \varphi_{11})\acute{\eta}_1(t - 1, \omega_P) + \varphi_{12}\acute{\eta}_2(t - 1, \omega_P) \\ \chi(t, \omega_P) \\ \acute{\eta}_2(t, \omega_P) - (1 - \varphi_{22})\acute{\eta}_2(t - 1, \omega_P) + \varphi_{21}\acute{\eta}_2(t - 1, \omega_P) \end{bmatrix}$$

and the fact that $\acute{\eta}(0, \omega_P) = 0$, demonstrate that $\acute{\eta}$ and χ are well defined and measurable with respect to $\aleph_P$. Similarly, equation 9.22 with χ substituted for ξ, with $\acute{\eta}$ substituted for η, and with δ substituted for Λ demonstrates that δ is well defined and measurable with respect to $\aleph_P$. Moreover, equation 9.30 with ς substituted for ζ demonstrates that ς is well defined and measurable with respect to $\aleph_P$. Finally, equation 9.31 with ς substituted for ζ and π substituted for ε demonstrates that π is well defined and measurable with respect to $\aleph_P$. Hence, all the new variables are well defined and measurable with respect to $\aleph_P$. But if that is so, I can use the definition of MPD in chapter 6 to show that the $(\acute{\eta}, \chi, \delta, \varsigma, \pi)(t, \omega_P)$ in the MPD distribution has the same probability distribution as the $(\eta, \xi, \Lambda, \zeta, \varepsilon)(t, \omega_T)$ have in the RPD distribution. To wit: Let M be a finite positive integer, let A be a subset of $(R^5)^M$, and observe that, according to G3, $\Omega_T(\Omega) = \Omega_T$. For any finite subset of N, $\{t_i, i = 1, \dots, M\}$, where $t_i \neq t_j$ if $i \neq j$, it must be the case that

$$\text{MPD}((\acute{\eta}, \chi, \delta, \varsigma, \pi)(t_1, \omega_P), \dots, (\acute{\eta}, \chi, \delta, \varsigma, \pi)(t_M, \omega_P)) \in A)$$

$$= P_T(\{\omega_T \in \Omega_T : ((\eta, \xi, \Lambda, \zeta, \varepsilon)(t_1, \omega_T), \dots, (\eta, \xi, \Lambda, \zeta, \varepsilon)(t_M, \omega_T)) \in A)\}.$$

With the preceding remarks in mind, it follows from T9.6 and T9.7 (with the pertinent new variables on the right-hand sides of equations 9.30–9.32), from A7 and A8, and from T9.2–T9.4 that the family of random vectors $\{\hat{y}(t, \omega_P); t \in N\}$ constitutes a cointegrated three-dimensional I(1) ARIMA process with cointegrating vector $(-1, 1, 0)$. To wit:

T9.8
Suppose that A1–A8, D1, D3 and G1–G5 are valid. In the MPD distribution, the family of functions $\{\hat{y}(t, \omega_P); t \in N\}$ is a cointegrated I(1) ARIMA process with cointegrating vector $(-1, 1, 0)$.

With standard arguments (B. Stigum 1990, pp. 344–347) one can show that the MPD distribution of the family of random vectors $\{(\acute{K}_t, \mathrm{ff}_t, \hat{y}_t); t \in N\}$ determines a probability measure $P_M(\cdot) : \aleph_p \to [0, 1]$ relative to which the family of finite-dimensional probability distributions of the functions $\{(\acute{K}, \mathrm{ff}, \hat{y})(t, \omega_P); t \in N\}$ is the MPD. From this and T9.8 the validity of T9.9 follows.

T9.9
Suppose that A1–A8, D1, D3, and G1–G5 are valid. Then there exists a probability measure, $P_M(\cdot) : \aleph_p \to [0, 1]$, relative to which the family of

finite-dimensional probability distributions of the functions $\{(\acute{K}, ff, \hat{y})(t, \omega_P); t \in N\}$ is the MPD. In P_M 888 measure, the family of functions $\{(\acute{K}, ff, \hat{y})(t, \omega_P); t \in N\}$ satisfies the following two conditions:

(1) The family $\{\hat{y}(t, \omega_P); t \in N\}$ constitutes a cointegrated three-dimensional $I(1)$ ARIMA process with cointegrating vector $(-1, 1, 0)$.

(2) $(\acute{K}(t, \omega_P), ff(t, \omega_P) = (\max(\hat{y}_1(t, \omega_P), 0), \max(\hat{y}_2(t, \omega_P), 0), \max(\hat{y}_3(t, \omega_P), 0))$ a.e.

9.4.6 The Scientific Explanation and Its Logical Adequacy

The probability measure $P_M(\cdot)$ need not be the same as the probability measure $P_p(\cdot)$ on whose existence I insist in D2. However, it follows from T9.9 that the family of finite-dimensional probability distributions of the family $\{(\acute{K}, ff, \hat{y})(t, \omega_P) : t \in N\}$ relative to $P_M(\cdot)$ and $P_p(\cdot)$ share the conditions on which H insists. Specifically, from T9.9 it follows that H—with $P_M(\cdot)$ substituted for $P_p(\cdot)$—is true in all models of D1, D3, A1–A8, and G1–G5. Since H is true in some but not all models of D1 and D3, I conclude that A1–A8 and G1–G5 provide a logically adequate scientific explanation of H.

9.5 The Empirical Adequacy of My Scientific Explanation of HAG's Dictum

Taking stock of the formal scientific explanation of H I have presented so far calls for several remarks. Note first that one can think of H as a pair (H_1, H_2) in which H_1 repeats what is said in D1, D3, and H_2 comprises the assertions in H. Next, note that the theory universe and the bridge principles have many models. The models of the theory universe vary with the values of the pair $(\hat{y}_1, \hat{y}_3)$ in A4, the matrix φ in A4, and the values of σ_Λ and the components of Σ_η in A7–A8. The models of the bridge principles vary with the values of the vector $\hat{y}_0$ and the matrix ψ in G5. In developing my scientific explanation of H, I established its logical adequacy without referring to any of these models. Hence the MPD in my explanation comprises a large family of MPDs that the models of A1–A8, D1, D3, and G1–G5 determine. When, below, I set out to establish the empirical adequacy of my explanation, I shall use statistical analysis of the data to pick out one model of the triple $(\Gamma_T, \Gamma_P, \Gamma_{T,P})$, derive the associated model of the MPD, and check whether the explanation of H that the two models provide is empirically adequate. I will judge the explanation empirically adequate if there is a data-admissible model of the MPD in a 95-percent-confidence region around the estimated MPD whose salient characteristics comprise the characteristics of TPD on which H insists.

My data are series of monthly quotes on the values of one-month and two-month Treasury Bill yields, $\acute{K}(1)$ and $\acute{K}(2)$, and on the values of the Federal Funds rate, ff. I take these quotes to be the observed values of $(\acute{K}_1, \acute{K}_2, ff)(t)$, $t = 1, 2, \ldots, 196$. According to D3, $\acute{K}_1(t) > 0 \rightarrow \acute{K}_1(t) = \hat{y}_1(t)$, $\acute{K}_2(t) > 0 \rightarrow \acute{K}_2(t) = \hat{y}_2(t)$, and $ff(t) > 0 \rightarrow ff(t) = \hat{y}_3(t)$ for all t. Since the observed series of the $(\acute{K}_1, \acute{K}_2, ff)(t)$ is larger than 0 in the observation period, the partially observable series, $(\hat{y}_1(t), \hat{y}_2(t), \hat{y}_3(t))$, are observed in the observation period. The latter series is used in the statistical analysis to estimate a mathematical model of the MPD distribution of the $\hat{y}(t)$.

The empirical analysis is based on two fundamental ideas. One describes the prescriptions underlying the statistical analysis; the second delineates the salient characteristics of a data-admissible mathematical model of MPD. Geir Storvik designed and carried out the statistical analysis. Details of his analysis are given on pages 596–603 of Stigum 2003. Here, for brevity's sake, I will describe only the parts I need for establishing the empirical adequacy of my explanation of HAG's Dictum.

9.5.1 Storvik's Statistical Analysis

A7–A8 do not put stringent conditions on the probability distributions of η and Λ. Thus, we begin by assuming that η_1, η_2, and Λ constitute three independently distributed purely random processes. For the sake of argument, we assume that these processes are Gaussian. We then reformulate the relations in equation 9.25 so that they can be expressed by a state-space model. For that purpose we let $v(t) = (\acute{\eta}_1(t), \acute{\eta}_2(t), \delta(t))'$ and observe that, with $\acute{\eta}_1$, $\acute{\eta}_2$, δ, and ς substituted for η_1, η_2, Λ, and ζ,

$$\varsigma(t) = C_0 v(t) - C_1 v(t-1), \quad t = 1, 2, \ldots \tag{9.29}$$

with

$$C_0 = \begin{pmatrix} \psi_{11} + (1/2)\psi_{12}(1+\varphi_{11}) & \psi_{13} + (1/2)\psi_{12}\varphi_{12} & (1/2)\psi_{12} \\ \psi_{21} + (1/2)\psi_{22}(1+\varphi_{11}) & \psi_{23} + (1/2)\psi_{22}\varphi_{12} & (1/2)\psi_{22} \\ \psi_{31} + (1/2)\psi_{32}(1+\varphi_{11}) & \psi_{33} + (1/2)\psi_{32}\varphi_{12} & (1/2)\psi_{32} \end{pmatrix}$$

and

$$
C_1 = \begin{pmatrix}
[\psi_{11} + (\tfrac{1}{2})\psi_{12}](1-\varphi_{11}) - \psi_{13}\varphi_{21} \\
[\psi_{21} + (\tfrac{1}{2})\psi_{22}](1-\varphi_{11}) - \psi_{23}\varphi_{21} \\
[\psi_{31} + (\tfrac{1}{2})\psi_{32}](1-\varphi_{11}) - \psi_{33}\varphi_{21}
\end{pmatrix}
$$

$$
\begin{array}{cc}
-[\psi_{11} + (\tfrac{1}{2})\psi_{12}]\varphi_{12} + \psi_{13}(1-\varphi_{22}) & (\tfrac{1}{2})\psi_{12} \\
-[\psi_{21} + (\tfrac{1}{2})\psi_{22}]\varphi_{12} + \psi_{23}(1-\varphi_{22}) & (\tfrac{1}{2})\psi_{22} \\
-[\psi_{31} + (\tfrac{1}{2})\psi_{32}]\varphi_{12} + \psi_{33}(1-\varphi_{22}) & (\tfrac{1}{2})\psi_{32}
\end{array}
$$

Also, we let $A = I_3 - \psi$, and write equation 9.25 as

$$
\hat{y}(t) - \hat{y}(t-1) = A[\hat{y}(t-1) - \hat{y}(t-2)] + C_0 v(t) - C_1 v(t-1). \tag{9.30}
$$

Then, with $x(t) = [\hat{y}(t) - \hat{y}(t-1), v(t), v(t+1)]$, the searched-for state-space form of equation 9.25 becomes

$$
x(t) = \begin{pmatrix} A & -C_1 & C_0 \\ 0 & 0 & I_6 \\ 0 & 0 & 0 \end{pmatrix} x(t-1) + \begin{pmatrix} 0 \\ 0 \\ v(t+1) \end{pmatrix}, \tag{9.31}
$$

$$
\hat{y}(t) = \hat{y}(t-1) + \{I_3 \ 0 \ 0\}x(t). \tag{9.32}
$$

Equation 9.31 describes the dynamics of the state vector. Equation 9.32 insists that $\hat{y}(t)$ is observed at each time point and that there are no observation errors.

There are sixteen parameters to be estimated: the nine components of ψ, the four components of φ, and the three variances of the components of v. To estimate the values of these parameters we proceed as follows. We calculate the likelihood of our sample observations with the help of a Kalman filter (Harvey 1989) and use the resulting likelihood and Powell's method of numerical optimization (Press et al. 1992) to search for the parameter values at which the likelihood will attain its maximum height. Powell's method is not fast, but it seems to give reliable optima. To obtain uncertainty measures and confidence intervals for our maximum-likelihood parameter estimates, we use the bootstrapping method (Efron 1982; Davison and Hinkley 1997). The parameter estimates and the results of 1,000 bootstrap simulations are shown in table 9.1.

In our statistical calculations we assumed that the two η processes and the Λ process were independently distributed, purely random Gaussian processes. Our statistical tests of these hypotheses (Stigum 2003, pp. 601–603) indicate that the independence assumption seems to be realistic for η and Λ. However, while independence in time seems

Table 9.1
Estimates of the state-space model parameters.

Parameter	Estimate	Bias	SE	Numbers determining 95% confidence interval	
$\sigma_{\eta,1}$	0.356	−0.179	0.022	0.493	0.577
$\sigma_{\eta,2}$	0.632	−0.446	0.027	1.022	1.128
σ_{Λ}	10.54	−0.779	1.553	8.046	14.119
φ_{11}	0.787	0.003	0.056	0.678	0.899
φ_{12}	0.216	−0.106	0.059	0.208	0.435
φ_{21}	0.68	−0.024	0.076	0.558	0.849
φ_{22}	0.632	−0.049	0.081	0.526	0.837
ψ_{11}	0.604	−0.006	0.016	0.577	0.638
ψ_{12}	0.012	−0.004	0.002	0.012	0.019
ψ_{13}	0.15	0.026	0.01	0.103	0.144
ψ_{21}	0.562	0.005	0.007	0.544	0.57
ψ_{22}	0.064	−0.003	0.002	0.065	0.071
ψ_{23}	0.088	−0.008	0.005	0.087	0.109
ψ_{31}	−0.01	−0.002	0.015	−0.039	0.02
ψ_{32}	0.031	−0.018	0.004	0.042	0.057
ψ_{33}	0.284	−0.016	0.007	0.287	0.313
$\lambda_{1,\varphi}$	0.682	−0.085	0.094	0.607	0.976
$\lambda_{2,\varphi}$	0.101	−0.03	0.054	0.002	0.199
$\lambda_{1,\psi}$	0.825	−0.019	0.02	0.603	0.681
$\lambda_{2,\psi}$	0.265	−0.004	0.009	0.253	0.287
$\lambda_{3,\psi}$	0.062	−0.001	0.002	0.059	0.068

reasonable for η_1 and η_2, our results do not ensure that the Λ process is purely random. Our results also cast doubt on the assumption that the η_2 process is Gaussian. Since we did not insist on these characteristics in the A axioms, we shall ignore this uncertainty here.

A Family of Data-Admissible Mathematical Models of the MPD

A mathematical model of MPD is data admissible if (1) the estimated mathematical model of MPD satisfies the strictures on which D1, D3, and the prescriptions that underlie the statistical analysis insist, (2) the values that the given model assigns to the parameters of MPD satisfy the strictures on which the A axioms, D1, D3, and the five G axioms insist, and (3) the model lies within a 95-percent-confidence region, I_{MPD}, of the estimated mathematical model of MPD.

The results of Storvik's likelihood analysis demonstrate that the estimated values of the parameters of the MPD satisfy the strictures on which D1, D3, and the conditions underlying the statistical analysis insist. The estimates in table 9.1 can be used to construct a data-admissible mathematical model of the MPD distribution of the $\hat{y}$ series. To wit: From the estimates in table 9.1 and equation 9.32 it follows that

$$\hat{y}(t) - 3.048\hat{y}(t-1) + 3.3614\hat{y}(t-2) - 1.5689\hat{y}(t-3) + 0.2555\hat{y}(t-4)$$
$$= B(U)\varsigma(t), \quad t \geq 4 \tag{9.33}$$

$$\Delta\hat{y}(t) - 2.048\Delta\hat{y}(t-1) + 1.3134\Delta\hat{y}(t-2) - 0.2555\Delta\hat{y}(t-3)$$
$$= B(U))\varsigma(t), \quad t \geq 4 \tag{9.34}$$

and

$$\hat{y}_2(t-1) - \hat{y}_1(t-1) = \tfrac{1}{2}[\delta_t(t) - 0.213\acute{\eta}(1,t) + 0.216\acute{\eta}(2,t)] - (-1, 1, 0)\psi^{-1}\pi(t), \tag{9.35}$$

where

$B(U)$

$$= \begin{pmatrix} 1-1.652U^{-1}+0.6675U^{-2} & -0.562U^{-1}+0.4024U^{-2} & 0.0174U^{-2} \\ -0.012U^{-1}+0.0133U^{-2} & 1-1.112U^{-1}+0.2835U^{-2} & -0.031U^{-1}+0.0123U^{-2} \\ -0.012U^{-1}+0.0133U^{-2} & -0.088U^{-1}+0.1191U^{-2} & 1-1.332U^{-1}+0.364U^{-2} \end{pmatrix},$$

$$\psi^{-1} = \begin{pmatrix} 1.527382 & 0.1227996 & -0.8447666 \\ -15.867849 & 0.1227996 & 3.0796806 \\ 1.785835 & -1.8631533 & 3.1552191 \end{pmatrix},$$

and, with $D(U) = \mathrm{Det}(I - AU^{-1}) = 1 - 2.048U^{-1} + 1.3134U^{-2} - 0.2555U^{-3}$,

$\pi(t) = D(U)^{-1}B(U)\zeta(t)$.

The description of the MPD that equations 9.33–9.35 provide implies that the characteristic polynomials of equations 9.33 and 9.34, $P_{\hat{y}}(z)$ and $P_{\Delta\hat{y}}(z)$, are given by the following equations:

$$P_{\hat{y}}(z) = (1 - z)(z - 0.366508)(z - 0.742084)(z - 0.939408), \tag{9.36}$$

$$P_{\Delta\hat{y}}(z) = (z - 0.366508)(z - 0.742084)(z - 0.939408). \tag{9.37}$$

Hence, $\Delta\hat{y}(t)$ satisfies the equation of a wide-sense stationary autoregressive moving average process, that is, of an I(0) ARIMA process.

Also, $\hat{y}(t)$ satisfies the equation of an I(1) ARIMA process. This and equation 9.35 imply that the $\hat{y}(t)$ process has all the characteristics on which H(ii) and H(iii) insist. Since the components of $\acute{K}(1)$, $\acute{K}(2)$, and ff_t are non-negative by construction, we see that the estimated MPD distribution of the vector, $(\acute{K}(t, \cdot), ff(t, \cdot); i.e., \hat{y}(t, \cdot))$, has the characteristics on which H, and hence H_2, insists. Finally, it is clear that the estimated mathematical model of MPD has all the characteristics on which A1–A8, D1, D3, and G1–G5 insist. Hence we have succeeded in constructing a data-admissible mathematical model of the MPD with the characteristics on which HAG's Dictum insists. In doing that, we have established the empirical adequacy of my SE2 explanation of HAG's Dictum.

9.5.2 The Empirical Relevance of A1–A8 and the Empirical Adequacy of the Explanation

The theory in my SE2 explanation of HAG's Dictum is an economic theory. Such a theory cannot be considered a law in Hempel's sense of the term. Hence, for the import of my explanation, it is important to observe that my SE2 explanation is empirically adequate only if my theory is empirically relevant in the empirical context in which the explanation is carried out.

In the empirical context that Storvik's analysis establishes, the intended family of models of A1–A8 is empirically relevant if and only if there is at least one member of the family that—together with a model of D1, D3, and G1–G5—determines a data-admissible model of the MPD. Suppose that I accept the assumptions about the distribution of η and Λ that were made in the prescriptions of the empirical analysis. Then the estimates that appear in table 9.1 and arbitrary values of $(\hat{y}_1, \hat{y}_3)$ and $\hat{y}_0$ provide me with a model of the quadruple $(\Gamma_T, D1, D3, \Gamma_{T,P})$ from which, in subsection 9.5.2, we derived a data-admissible mathematical model of the MPD. Hence I can conclude that A1–A8 have an empirically relevant model, and that the theory in my scientific explanation is empirically relevant in the present empirical context.

9.6 The Cointegration Space in the Two Pertinent Data Universes in Figure 2.1

Hall, Anderson, and Granger (1992) and Anderson (1999) studied the dynamics of Treasury Bill yields in the US money market. HAG based their analysis on 228 monthly observations of eleven yield series—R(1, t), ... , R(11, t)—from the period January 1970–December 1988. Anderson based her analysis on 150 monthly observations of two yield series (R(1, t) and R(2, t)), the Federal Funds Rate (FF(t)), the yield to maturity on 5-year Treasury bonds (B(t)), and the natural logarithm of the total dollar value of federal debt (lnD(t)) from the period January 1983–June 1995. Hall et al. (1992, pp. 116–118 and 123) found (1) that the R(j, t) for j = 2, ... , 11 were cointegrated with R(1, t); (2) that the cointegrating vectors were (–1, 1, 0, ... , 0), (–1, 0, 1, 0, ... , 0), ... , (–1, 0, ... , 1); and (3) that the cointegrating space of the vector-valued process, {(R(1, t), ... , R(11, t)); t ∈ N}, was spanned by the given ten cointegrating vectors. Anderson (2003, p. 552) found (1) that R(2, t), FF(t), and B(t) were cointegrated with R(1, t); (2) that the cointegrating vectors were (–1, 1, 0, 0, 0), (–1, 0, 1, 0.0), and (–1, 0, 0, 1, 0); and (3) that the cointegrating space of the vector-valued process {(R(1, t), R(2, t), FF(t), B(t), LnD(t)); t ∈ N} was spanned by the given three cointegrating vectors.

The results HAG and Anderson obtained are interesting by themselves. They are particularly interesting in the context of this book because they were derived under the implicit assumption that HAG's and Anderson's data represented accurate measurements of the corresponding theoretical variables. Hence, from the point of view of this book, HAG's and Anderson's empirical analyses were carried out in a pertinent upper data universe in figure 2.1. In contrast, Geir Storvik carried out his statistical analysis in the corresponding lower data universe in figure 2.1.

9.6.1 The Cointegration Space in the Lower Data Universe, $(\Omega_P, \Gamma_P, (\Omega_P, \aleph_P, P_M(\cdot)))$, in Figure 2.1

In this section I shall determine the dimension of the cointegration space in the lower data universe in figure 2.1 that pertains to the scientific explanation I presented in section 9.4. I have shown that $(-1, 1, 0)$ is a cointegration vector in both the theory universe and the data universe. With Geir Storvik's estimates I can show that there is no other cointegrating vector in either universe. To wit: Let $y_t, \hat{y}_t, \eta_{1t}, \eta_{2t}, \eta_t, \zeta_t, \varepsilon_t$ be short for $y(t), \hat{y}(t), \eta_1(t), \eta_2(t), \eta(t), \zeta(t), \varepsilon(t)$. It follows from T9.2–T9.4 that

$$y_t = \begin{pmatrix} \varphi_{11} & \varphi_{12} \\ \varphi_{11} & \varphi_{12} \\ \varphi_{21} & \varphi_{22} \end{pmatrix} \left((\hat{y}_1, \hat{y}_3)' + \sum_{0 \le s \le (t-1)} \eta_{t-1-s} \right) + \begin{pmatrix} \eta_{1t} \\ (2t1/2)[\Lambda_{1t} + \eta_{1t} + (\varphi_{11}, \varphi_{12})\eta_t] \\ \eta_{2t} \end{pmatrix}.$$

$$(9.38)$$

From equation 9.38 we see that $(-1, 1, 0)$ is a cointegrating vector no matter what the values of the φ_{ij} are. If I set in the estimated values of the φ_{ij} in the matrix in equation 9.38, I find that there is no other vector $\alpha = (\alpha_1, \alpha_2, \alpha_3)$ such that αy_t is a wide-sense stationary process. Hence, with the estimated values of the φ_{ij}, $(-1, 1, 0)$, or a multiple of it, is the only cointegrating vector in the theory universe.

I derive the same conclusion for the data universe from equations 9.22, 9.26, and 9.27. From equation 9.22 it follows that

$$\hat{y}_t - \hat{y}_{t-1} = \psi(y_t - \hat{y}_{t-1}),$$

from equation 9.26 it follows that

$$(I - (I - \psi)U^{-1})(\hat{y}_t - \hat{y}_{t-1}) = \zeta_t,$$

and from equation 9.27 I conclude that

$$\varepsilon_t = [I - (I - \Psi)U^{-1}]^{-1} \zeta_t.$$

Together these three equations imply that

$$\hat{y}_{t-1} = y_t - \psi^{-1}\varepsilon_t$$

and that, with $\alpha = (\alpha_1, \alpha_2, \alpha_3)$,

$$\alpha \hat{y}_{t-1} = \alpha y_t - \alpha \psi^{-1}\varepsilon_t.$$

With Storvik's estimates I can have only one cointegration vector in the theory universe. The last equation, therefore, implies that in the estimated MPD distribution of the $\hat{y}_t$ there is only one cointegrating vector in the lower data universe as well.

Is there a value of φ in a 95-percent-confidence region around Storvik's estimate of φ, φ°, whose determinant equals 0? To find out, Anne Olaug Stigum chose as the confidence region the region determined by Storvik's bootstrap estimates of the standard deviations of φ_{11}°, φ_{12}°, φ_{21}°, and φ_{22}°. Then she constructed a discrete structure within a cube of volume 4×4 by 4×4. One side pertained to φ_{11}, another to φ_{12}, the third to φ_{21}, and the fourth to φ_{22}. She divided each side into 40 intervals of length 0.1 and marked their end points as follows: $[-2, -1.9, \ldots, -0.1, 0, 0.1, \ldots, 1.9, 2]$. The given structure comprised all the quadruples, $(a_{11}, a_{12}, a_{21}, a_{22})$, in $(\{-2, -1.9, \ldots, 0.1, 0, 0.1, \ldots, 1.9, 2\})^4$. With each quadruple Anne Olaug computed a value of φ in accord with the following equations:

$$\varphi_{11}^* = \varphi_{11}^\circ + std_{\varphi11} \cdot a_{11} = 0.787 + 0.056a_{11},$$

$\varphi_{12}{}^* = \varphi_{12}{}^\circ + \text{std}_{\varphi12} \cdot a_{12} = 0.216 + 0.059a_{12}$,

$\varphi_{21}{}^* = \varphi_{21}{}^\circ + \text{std}_{\varphi21} \cdot a_{21} = 0.68 + 0.076a_{21}$,

$\varphi_{22}{}^* = \varphi_{22}{}^\circ + \text{std}_{\varphi22} \cdot a_{22} = 0.632 + 0.081a_{22}$.

The value of $\text{Det}(\varphi^\circ)$ is 0.350504. The maximum value of the determinant of φ^* that Anne Olaug obtained by varying the a_{ij} over the given substructure was Max $\text{Det}(\varphi^*) = 0.662062$. The minimum value was Min $\text{Det}(\varphi^*) = 0.039362$. Hence I can conclude with 95 percent certainty that there is only one cointegrating vector in the lower data universe.

9.6.2 The Cointegration Space in the Upper Data Universe, $(\Omega_P, \Gamma_P, (\Omega_P, \aleph_P, P_P(\cdot)))$, in Figure 2.1

Heather Anderson, on pages 603–606 of Stigum 2003, analyzed Geir Storvik's data with Søren Johansen's (1995) techniques. She assumed, implicitly, that her observations of the yields of one-month and two-month Treasury Bills and of the Federal Funds rate represented accurate observations of the corresponding theoretical variables. Also, she introduced sufficiently many lags (in differences) in her models to ensure that the residuals were serially uncorrelated. Finally, she added dummy variables to remove the effects of outliers and to ensure that the residuals were normally distributed. Anderson's results are displayed in table 9.2. They suggest that in the TPD distribution the cointegration space of the $\hat{y}$ series is two-dimensional with cointegrating vectors $(1, -1, 0)$ and $(1, 0, -0.8860)$.

All models represented in table 9.2 use four lags of (differenced) endogenous variables and assume no deterministic trend. The residuals in the column 2 models are not normally distributed (at < 0.00001 percent level of significance). The dummies in the column 3 models ensure that residuals are normally distributed.

9.7 Concluding Comments

There are three aspects of my scientific explanation of HAG's Dictum that deserve concluding comments. One aspect concerns the generality of my explanation. If my H is a correct rendition of HAG's Dictum for two Treasury Bills, the generality of my scientific explanation of H stands and falls on whether I sacrificed insight into the workings of the US money market by considering only two bills and one other money-market instrument. However, as axioms A3, A4, and G5 can be easily

Table 9.2

Cointegration analysis of the TPD distribution of $(\hat{y}_{t1}, \hat{y}_{t2}, \hat{y}_{t3})$.

Variables	Model without dummies	Model with dummies
Number of dummies in VAR	0	8
Rank of β (tests use 5% critical Values)	1	2
Estimated β (conditional on rank $\beta = 1$)	$(1, -1.0889, 0.0960)$	$(1, -0.8243, 0.1201)$
P_P value for test of H_0: $\beta = (1, -1, 0)$ (conditional on rank $\beta = 1$)	0.1529	0.1137
P_P value for test of H_0: $\beta = (1, 0, -1)$ (conditional on rank $\beta = 1$)	0.0002	0.0001
Estimated β (conditional on rank $\beta = 2$)	$(1, -0.9812, 0)$ $(1, 0, -0.8743)$	$(1, -0.9921. 0)$ $(1, 0, -0.8860)$
P_P value for test of H_0: $\beta 1 = (1, -1, 0)$ and $\beta 2 = (1, 0, -1)$ (conditional on rank $\beta = 2$)	0.1617	0.0062
P_P value for test of H_0: $\beta 1 = (1, -1, 0)$ (conditional on rank $\beta = 2$)	0.1203	0.4304
P_P value for test of H_0: $\beta 1 = (1, 0, -1)$ (conditional on rank $\beta = 2$)	0.0606	0.0000

generalized to a market with many more securities, it is clear that the gain in clarity has not been at the expense of a loss in generality.

A second aspect concerns the empirical contexts which the empirical analyses in sections 9.4 and 9.5 establish for the two universes in figure 2.1. The empirical context which Heather Anderson establishes for the upper data universe is different from the empirical context that Geir Storvik establishes for the lower data universe. Heather gives a very interesting account of the import of these differences in section 23.5 of Stigum 2003. Here, I will be content to refer the reader to Heather's discussion and to add that the given differences provide a third illustration of the way present-day econometric time-series analysis differs from the time-series analysis that a formal theory-data confrontation prescribes.

The second aspect by itself is sufficient reason for calling for a serious discussion of how best to incorporate economic theory in applied econometrics. In the present case, there is a third aspect that adds an interesting dimension to that discussion. The stylized fact that HAG discovered pertained to vectors in a model of the upper data universe in figure 2.1. My explanation pertains to the same vectors in a model of the corresponding lower data universe. The characteristics of the TPD that the stylized facts describe are shared by the MPD that

I derived from the RPD of the theory and the bridge principles. Yet the TPD and the MPD differ significantly.

My explanation of HAG's Dictum exemplifies the strictures of an SE2 scientific explanation. It also brings to bear my understanding of the essence of an economic theory. The theory delineates certain characteristics of social reality that an economist has found interesting and nothing else. My explanation explains the whys and wherefores of a stylized fact concerning the US money market and nothing else. The fact that the TPD and the MPD differ exemplifies Bas van Fraassen's (1980, p. 98) interesting remark that whether a theory explains some fact or other is independent of whether the real world as a whole fits the theory.[5]

10 Bridge Principles and Theory in Applied Econometrics

I begin this chapter by discussing the status of bridge principles in applied economics. I then show how the ideas of encompassing and congruence can be used to determine the status of bridge principles in formal theory-data confrontations in econometrics. I conclude with a discussion of what the case studies in this book have taught me about econometric methodology and about the use of theory in applied econometrics.

10.1 Bridge Principles in Applied Economics

In this section I will use rudiments of the propositional calculus and modal logic to establish the status of bridge principles in applied economics. I take a theory-data confrontation in applied economics to be an empirical analysis in which both the TPD and the MPD are absent. Good examples are Wassily Leontief's 1953 study of domestic production and foreign trade in the United States, Edward Leamer's 1984 book on sources of international comparative advantage, and my 2004 formal study of the empirical relevance for Norwegian trade flows of the Heckscher-Ohlin conjecture.

10.1.1 The Propositional Calculus
The propositional calculus is a first-order predicate calculus without terms, with just 0-ary predicate symbols, without the logical symbols $\forall$ and $=$, with only simple parentheses, and with no commas.[1] Thus, I can describe its symbols and formulas briefly.

First, there are the members of the non-logical vocabulary. They are given by an infinite list of propositional variables: p, q, r, s, t, p_1, q_1, r_1, s_1, t_1, p_2, q_2, ... In the intended interpretation of the propositional calculus, the propositional variables vary over a set of declarative sentences which are written in some particular language (say English) and have as their range two truth values: truth and falsehood.

Second, there are the members of the logical vocabulary: brackets and the sentence connectives ~ and ⊃, which combine with members of the non-logical vocabulary to form the longer expressions we call formulas. In the intended interpretation of the propositional calculus, ~ is read as "not" and ⊃ is read as "(materially) implies."

Third, there are symbols (such as Γ, Δ, A, B, a, b, S, and T) that one uses to denote so-called syntactical variables. Logical and non-logical symbols belong to the propositional calculus, while symbols denoting syntactical variables do not. The latter variables form part of a poorly delimited language that one uses to study formal aspects of the propositional calculus.

The sentences of the propositional calculus are formulas. They are well formed (wf) if and only if their being well formed follows from the following three formation rules.

FR1
A propositional variable standing alone is a wf formula (wff).

FR2
If A is wf, then ~ A is wf.

FR3
If A and B are wf, then [A ⊃ B] is wf.

Examples of wffs are p, [p ⊃ p], and [~ p ⊃ [p ⊃ q]]. The last two formulas present symbolic renditions of the *law of the excluded middle* and the *law of denial of the antecedent*.

The axioms of the propositional calculus are values of the following axiom schemata.

PLA1
[A ⊃ [B ⊃ A]]

PLA2
[[A ⊃ [B ⊃ C]] ⊃ [[A ⊃ B] ⊃ [A ⊃ C]]]

PLA3
[[~A ⊃ ~ B] ⊃ [B ⊃ A]]

PLA1–PLA3 determine the meaning of the logical symbols of the propositional calculus. Examples of values of these axiom schemata are [p ⊃ [q ⊃ p]], [[p ⊃ [q ⊃ r]] ⊃ [[p ⊃ q] ⊃ [p ⊃ r]]], and [[~ p ⊃ ~ q] ⊃ [q ⊃ p]]. They provide symbolic renditions of the *law of affirmation of the consequent*, the *self-distributive law of (material) implication*, and the *converse law of contraposition*.

The formation rules show how one can produce wffs out of existing wffs. Some of the wffs are theorems. A *theorem* either is an axiom or is derived from the axioms with the help of a rule of inference. For the propositional calculus, the rule of inference is the so-called *modus ponens*.

RI1
Let A and B be wffs. From [A ⊃ B] and A, we infer B.

From the axioms of the propositional calculus and the RI1 one can derive many interesting theorems—for example, [[A ⊃ B] ⊃ [[B ⊃ C] ⊃ [A ⊃ C]]] and [[A ⊃ B] ⊃ [[A ⊃ ~ B] ⊃ ~ A]]. The values of these theorem schemata present symbolic renditions of the *transitive law of (material) implication* and the *law of reductio ad absurdum*. I will make good use of the first law in my endeavor to establish the status of bridge principles in applied economics.

One interprets the propositional calculus by assigning truth values to its wffs. This one does by induction on the length of formulas. Let t denote truth, f falsehood. A wff consisting of a variable a alone has the value t for the value t of a, the value f for the value f of a. For a given assignment of values to the variables of the wff A, the value of ~A is f or t according as the value of A is t or f. Finally, for a given assignment of values to the variables of the wffs A and B, the value of [A ⊃ B] is t if the value of A is f or if the value of B is t. The value of [A ⊃ B] is f if the value of B is f and the value of A is t.

A wff that assumes the value truth no matter what it asserts is a tautology. It is easy to demonstrate that, in the intended interpretation of the propositional calculus, the values of PLA1–PLA3 are tautologies. From this and the fact that modus ponens preserves tautologies it follows that, when interpreted, the theorems of the propositional calculus become tautologies as well. The converse of the preceding observation (i.e., a wff is a tautology only if it is a theorem) is also true. A proof is given on pages 65–67 of B. Stigum 1990. Consequently, one has T10.1, the Tautology Theorem.

T10.1

A wff A is a theorem if and only if it is a tautology in the intended interpretation of the propositional calculus.

T10.1 is interesting for several reasons. I defined the term "theorem" as it applies to an uninterpreted language. T10.1 uses my interpretation of the propositional calculus to give a complete characterization of the language's theorems. In addition, T10.1 provides a foolproof method for checking in a finite number of steps whether a wff in the propositional calculus is a theorem: Compute the wff's truth table.

E10.1

The Tautology Theorem and the following truth table show that [p ⊃ p] and [~ p ⊃ [p ⊃ q]] are theorems in the propositional calculus. They also explicate in what way the assertion "p materially implies q" in the propositional calculus is equivalent to the assertion [p ⊃ q]. Finally, they demonstrate that in the propositional calculus the assertion ~[p ⊃ ~q] is equivalent to the assertion "p and q." I will make good use of the latter observation in my endeavor to establish the status of bridge principles in applied economics. The same theorem and the given truth table also demonstrate that the propositional calculus is consistent in the sense that it does not contain a proposition p such that both p and ~p are theorems. To wit: If both p and ~p are theorems, then [~ p ⊃ [p ⊃q]] and RI1 imply that q, no matter what q asserts, must be a theorem as well. As the second column in table 10.1 shows, that cannot be the case.

10.1.2 Modal Logic on Top

In discussing knowledge of variable hypotheticals (universals) in chapter 2, I mentioned that one can know them when they describe its instances in terms of a finite number of characteristics that are independent of the state of the world. Such a description will prescribe necessary properties of the instances of the universal—for instance, that a human being is a rational animal.

The branch of mathematical logic in which logicians attempt to explicate the idea of necessity is called *modal logic*. Next I will formulate a modal-logical language, ML, that I can use to characterize the wffs in the propositional calculus that are necessarily true.

ML is a symbolic language with the same non-logical vocabulary as the propositional calculus and with a logical vocabulary that consists

Table 10.1
Truth table for [p ⊃ p], [p ⊃ q], [~ p⊃ [p ⊃ q]], and ~[p ⊃ ~q].

p	q	~p	[p ⊃ p]	[p ⊃ q]	[~ p ⊃ [p ⊃q]]	~[p ⊃ ~q]
t	t	f	t	t	t	t
t	f	f	t	f	t	f
f	t	t	t	t	t	f
f	f	t	t	t	t	f

of an operation symbol, □, and all the logical symbols of the propositional calculus. The wffs of ML are determined by four formation rules: the three formation rules of the propositional calculus and FR4.

FR4
If A is wf, then □A is a wff.

In the intended interpretation of ML, □A asserts "necessarily A." Roughly speaking, □A will denote truth if A denotes truth in all possible worlds, and will denote falsehood otherwise.

A possible world can be an undefined term, such as a point of reference in Montague's (1974, pp. 98, 108) pragmatics. It can also be a state description, such as a maximal consistent set of atomic sentences in Rudolf Carnap's (1956, p. 9) theory of meaning and necessity. And it can simply be a way that things could have been, as in David Lewis' (1973, p. 84) theory of counterfactuals. Here a possible world is a model of the propositional calculus.

The theorems of ML are derived from six axiom schemata and two rules of inference. The axioms are values of the three axiom schemata of the propositional calculus and of the following three axiom schemata.

M1
If A is a wff, then [□A ⊃ A].

M2
If A and B are wffs, then [□ [A ⊃ B] ⊃ [□A ⊃ □B]].

M3
If A is a wff, then [□A ⊃ □□ A].

The rules of inference of M are the modus ponens of the propositional calculus and RI2.

RI2
If A is a theorem of the propositional calculus, then □A is a theorem of ML.

In the intended interpretation of ML the values of ~A, [A ⊃ B], and □A are, respectively, read as "not A," " "A materially implies B, " and "necessarily A." Specifically (see Kripke 1971), the intended interpretation of ML is given in the form of a model structure with characteristic features. A model structure for ML is a quadruple, $(X, \hat{R}, \xi, \phi)$, which I denote by η. Here X denotes the set of all possible worlds, ξ belongs to X and denotes the "Real World," and $\hat{R}$ is a binary reflexive and transitive relation in X.[2] Roughly speaking, if H_1 and H_2 belong to X, then the relation $H_1 \hat{R} H_2$ is meant to suggest that the two worlds H_1 and H_2 are not greatly different. For example, it might be the case that $H_1 \hat{R} H_2$ only if the natural laws that are valid in H_1 are valid in H_2 as well. In the vernacular of logicians, $\hat{R}$ is called an *accessibility relation* and a modal structure in which $\hat{R}$ is reflexive and transitive is called an *S_4-structure*. ϕ is a function $\phi(\cdot)$: ML × X → {t, f} which for each H in X is a model of the axioms of ML and assigns truth values to the wffs of ML. In this assignment of truth values, $\phi(\sim A, H) = f$ or t according as $\phi(A, H) = t$ or f; $\phi([A \supset B], H) = f$ if $\phi(A, H) = t$ and $\phi(B, H) = f$. Otherwise $\phi([A \supset B], H) = t$. $\phi(\Box A, H) = t$ if A is valid in all worlds H' that satisfies the relation H $\hat{R}$ H' There are many model structures for ML. For example, for each triple $(X, \hat{R}, \xi)$, there are as many functions $\phi(\cdot, \xi)$: ML → {t, f} as there are different assignments of truth values to the propositional variables of ML. It is, therefore, interesting to record the following completeness theorem for ML.

T10.2
Let $(X, \hat{R}, \xi)$ be fixed, and let A be a wff in ML. Let Φ denote the collection of all functions $\phi(\cdot, \xi)$: ML → {t, f} with the property that $\phi(\cdot, \xi)$ and $(X, \hat{R}, \xi)$ constitute an S_4 model structure for ML. Then A is a theorem in ML if and only if, for all $\phi(\cdot, \xi) \in \Phi$, $\phi(A, \xi) = t$.

A proof of this theorem is given in Kripke 1963.

10.1.3 The Status of Bridge Principles in Applied Economics
My deliberations about the status of bridge principles in applied economics are based on three fundamental assumptions. The first assumption is that the theory in a formal theory-data confrontation is about

imaginary matters. I have no reason to believe that the pertinent imaginary matters do not behave as the theory prescribes, so I will insist that the axioms and all the theorems in the theory universe are valid in all possible worlds that are accessible from the Real World. The second assumption is that the researcher in charge has collected observations and created data for the data universe himself. I have no reason to doubt the researcher's judgment and care, so I will insist that the axioms and the theorems concerning the researcher's data in the data universe are valid in all possible worlds that are accessible from the Real World. Third, I am not so sure about the researcher's bridge principles. The most I am willing to claim is that there is at least one world that is accessible from the Real World in which they are all valid. Whether that world is the Real World is to be determined by the empirical analysis.

If my fundamental assumptions are valid, the next theorem can be interpreted so as to provide an explication of the role of bridge principles in applied economics. Think of A as the conjunction of axioms and theorems in the theory and data universes of a theory-data confrontation in economics. Think of B and φ, respectively, as a finite family of bridge principles and a finite family of assertions concerning the researcher's data in the same theory-data confrontation. Recall that a wff A is valid in the propositional calculus if and only if it is a tautology, and that $\square$A is valid in ML if and only if A assumes the value t in all possible worlds that are accessible from the Real World.

T10.3

Consider three well-formed formulas, A, B, and φ. Suppose that $\square$A is valid in ML, and that $\sim \square\sim$B (i.e., that there is a possible world that is accessible from the Real World in which B is valid). Suppose, also, that A and B materially implies φ in all possible worlds that are accessible from the Real World; i.e., that $\square$ [$\sim$[A$\supset\sim$B] $\supset\varphi$] is valid. Then it is the case that $\sim \square\sim\varphi$; i.e., there is at least one possible world that is accessible from the Real World in which φ is true.

The proof of T10.3 goes as follows: I can assert, by hypothesis, that $\square$A, $\sim \square\sim$B, and $\square$ [$\sim$[A $\supset \sim$B] $\supset \varphi$]. From this and M1 it follows that A and [$\sim$[A $\supset \sim$B] $\supset\varphi$] are valid wffs. But if that is so, PLA3 implies that [[$\sim$[A $\supset \sim$B] $\supset \varphi$] $\supset$ [$\sim\varphi \supset$ [A $\supset \sim$B]]], which, by RI1, implies that [$\sim\varphi \supset$ [A $\supset \sim$B]] is a valid wff. Consequently, by RI2, $\square$ [$\sim\varphi \supset$ [A $\supset \sim$B]] is a valid wff., and by M2, [$\square$ [$\sim\varphi \supset$ [A $\supset \sim$B]] $\supset$ [$\square\sim\varphi \supset \square$ [A $\supset \sim$B]]] is valid as well. Then, by applying RI1, I find that [□~φ ⊃ □ [A ⊃ ~B]], and—since [□ [A ⊃ ~B] ⊃ [□A ⊃ □~B]]—that [□~φ ⊃ [□A ⊃ □~B]] are valid wffs. But if that is so, I can use PLA3 and RI1 to deduce that [[□~φ ⊃ [□A ⊃ □~B]] ⊃ [~ [□ A⊃~~ □~B] ⊃ ~□~φ]] and [~ [□ A ⊃ ~ ~ □~B] ⊃ ~□~φ]] are valid wffs. From the last wff and the first two hypotheses of T10.3 I deduce that ~□~φ—i.e., that there is a possible world that is accessible from the Real World in which φ is true.

Consider the theory-data confrontation that I presented in E1.4.2 in chapter 1. I will use a variant of that example, E10.2, to exemplify the ideas that I have expressed in T10.3. The language in which E10.2 is expressed is much more involved than the language of the propositional calculus. Still, when I argue with care I can use E10.2 and T10.3 to explicate the status of bridge principles in the empirical analysis in E10.2.

E10.2
I believe that students at my university order simple random prospects according to their expected values. I believe, also, that the students have a tendency to overvalue low probabilities and undervalue high probabilities. To test these hypotheses, I have picked at random one of these students and talked him into participating in a simple experiment. In the experiment I face the student with a large number N of uncertain binary prospects in which he can earn $1,000 with probability q and $0 with probability $(1 - q)$, where q is one of the members of $\{q_1, \ldots, q_N\}$. For each q_i, I ask the student for his certainty equivalent of the given prospect—that is, the smallest number of dollars, $x_i \in [0, 1,000]$, such that he would be indifferent between receiving x_i dollars and trying his luck in the prospect. At the end, I construct $N + 2$ values of the student's "empirical utility function," $W(\cdot): [0, 1,000] \rightarrow [0, 1]$, as follows: $W(0) = 0$, $W(1,000) = 1$, and $W(x_i) = q_i$, $i = 1, \ldots, N$.

In accord with the preceding description, I find that I can formulate the axioms for the data universe as follows. In reading the axioms, note that they describe how I obtained my observations of the components of (q, x, W). They say nothing about the values of the respective components that I actually observed.

The Γ_P Axioms
D1
$\omega_P \in \Omega_P$ only if $\omega_P = (q, x, W)$ for some $q \in [0, 1]$, $x \in [0, 1,000]$, and $W(\cdot) : [0, 1,000] \rightarrow [0, 1]$.

D2
For all $\omega_P \in \Omega_P$, $W(0) = 0$, $W(1{,}000) = 1$, and $W(x) = q$.

My hypothesis concerning how students order uncertain prospects is presented in the axioms of the theory universe.

The Γ_T Axioms

A1
$\omega_T \in \Omega_T$ only if $\omega_T = (p, r, U)$ for some $p \in [0, 1]$, $r \in [0, 1{,}000]$, and $U(\cdot)$: $[0, 1{,}000] \to [0, 1]$.

A2
For all $\omega_T \in \Omega_T$, $U(r) = p$, and $r = 1{,}000p$.

My hypothesis concerning students' perception of probabilities is specified in the bridge principles.

The $\Gamma_{T,P}$ Axioms

G1
Ω_T and Ω_P are disjoint, and the sample space Ω is a subset of $\Omega_T \times \Omega_P$.

G2
$(\omega_T, \omega_P) \in \Omega$ only if $(\omega_T, \omega_P) = (p, r, U, q, x, W)$ for some $(p, r, U) \in \Omega_T$ and $(q, x, W) \in \Omega_P$.

G3
For all $(\omega_T, \omega_P) \in \Omega$, $r = x$, and $p = 0.5 + 4(q - 0.5)^3$.

For the purposes of this example, I will, with the specification of ω_P in D1, treat D2 as a closed wff that is valid in all the possible worlds that are accessible from the Real World.[3] In short, I will assume that $\Box\Gamma_P$ is a valid wff. I will also, with the specification of ω_T in A1, treat A2 as a closed wff that is valid in all the possible worlds that are accessible from the Real World. In short, I will assume that $\Box\Gamma_T$ is a valid wff. Finally, I will, with the specification of Ω in G1 and G2, treat G3 as a closed wff that is valid in at least one possible world that can be reached from the Real World. In short, I will assume that $\sim\Box\sim\Gamma_{T,P}$ assumes the value t.

With the given assumptions, I can assert $\Box\Gamma_T$, $\Box\Gamma_P$, and $\sim\Box\sim\Gamma_{T,P}$. From these assertions it follows that Γ_T and Γ_P are valid assertions. It is also a fact that if I let [A ∧ B] be short for ~[A ⊃ ~B] and read the formula as "A and B," I can show that, for any sixtuple (p, r, U, q, x, W) in Ω,

$$[[[\Gamma_T \wedge \Gamma_P] \wedge \Gamma_{T,P}] \supset [W(x) = 0.5 + 0.5((x - 500)/500)^{1/3}]]. \quad (10.1)$$

This follows immediately from the equation

$$[[[[[[U(r) = r/1,000] \wedge [U(r) = p]] \wedge [W(x) = q]] \wedge [r = x]] \wedge [p = 0.5 + 4(q - 0.5)^3]]$$

$$\supset [W(x) = 0.5 + 0.5((x - 500)/500)^{1/3}]]. \quad (10.2)$$

From my assumptions and equation 10.1, I deduce that

$$\sim\Box\sim[W(x) = 0.5 + 0.5((x - 500)/500)^{1/3}]. \quad (10.3)$$

Consequently, I can assert that there is a world that can be reached from the Real World in which the utility function of a student is as described in equation 10.3. That possible world may or may not be the Real World. In the present case, the Real World is the possible world that my student's answers determine. Hence, in the present case I can check whether the bridge principles are valid in the Real World by checking whether the N + 2 values of my students utility function are values of the W(·) in equation 10.1.

The formal-logical details that are required to express and carry out the arguments in E10.2 are given on pages 511–518 of Stigum 2003. There the proper analogue of T10.3 is T 6 on p. 514.

10.2 Congruence and Encompassing in Applied Econometrics

According to David Hendry's account of model evaluation (Hendry 1995, chapter 9), the requirement that an econometric model be congruent and encompassing can substitute for truth as a final decision criterion in empirical modeling. If that is right, it opens up an interesting possibility: Congruence and encompassing may play a role in formal econometrics that is analogous to the roles played by truth and the Real World in my modal-logical explication of the status of bridge principles in applied economics. I will explore this possibility next.

10.2.1 Encompassing in the Two Data Universes in Figure 2.1
Roughly speaking, an econometric model is said to *encompass* another econometric model if it can account for the results obtained by the

latter. (See Mizon 1984; Hendry and Richard 1989.) My discussion of encompassing is designed to show how and why the explications of encompassing differ in the two universes in figure 2.1. Because I am trying to present simple ideas of encompassing that go with the rest of the book, I consider only cases of parametric encompassing. Also, I adopt the simplest version of the many binding functions that appear in articles on encompassing (e.g., Gourieroux et al. 1983; Mizon 1984; Florens et al. 1996). Since I have had little to say about Bayesian econometrics in the book, I do not discuss Bayesian ideas of encompassing here. (For a comprehensive survey of the development of the encompassing principle in econometrics, see Bontemps and Mizon 2008.)

I will be discussing the problem of encompassing within the confines of some given formal theory-data confrontation. As always, I denote the two data universes in figure 2.1 by $(\Omega_P, \Gamma_P, (\Omega_P, \aleph_P, P_P(\cdot)))$ and $(\Omega_P, \Gamma_{P^*}, (\Omega_P, \aleph_P, P_M(\cdot)))$. It is understood that there is only one $P_P(\cdot)$ and that there are many different $P^M(\cdot)$'s. Also, the pair $(\Omega_P, \aleph_P)$ is the same in the two data universes. Hence, I am discussing cases in which there is one measurable space, $(\Omega_P, \aleph_P)$, with many different probability measures. I also presume that I am considering the probability distribution of a random vector, $y(\cdot)$, relative to the given probability measures. The distribution of $y(\cdot)$ relative to $P_P(\cdot)$ is the TPD distribution of $y(\cdot)$. Relative to a particular $P_M(\cdot)$, the distribution of $y(\cdot)$ is the MPD distribution corresponding to $P_M(\cdot)$. I will denote a vector of parameters of the TPD distribution of $y(\cdot)$ by θ_P and any one of the theoretically possible vectors of parameters of the MPD distribution of $y(\cdot)$ by θ_M. Also, I will denote an econometric model of MPD by a pair, $(M1, \theta_M^o(\cdot))$ and an econometric model of TPD by a pair, $(M2, \theta_P^o(\cdot))$, where, M1 and M2, and $\theta_P^o(\cdot)$, and $\theta_M^o(\cdot)$ are two probability distributions and two estimators of θ_P and θ_M, respectively. Finally, I will let s_n denote a finite sample, $y_1, \dots, y_n$, of observations of $y(\cdot)$. The problem I try to resolve is to give necessary and sufficient conditions that an econometric model, $(M1, \theta_M^o(\cdot))$, in which M1 is a data-admissible model of MPD in a 95-percent-confidence band around the estimate, $\theta_M^o(s_n)$, encompasses a given econometric model of TPD.

Throughout my discussion of encompassing, I take for granted that the characteristics of the TPD are as described in the axioms of the data universe in the pertinent theory-data confrontation. Also, whereas there is only one true model of TPD, I presume that there are as many mathematical models of the MPD as there are models of the theory universe and the pertinent bridge principles. This difference has one particularly important implication: The estimator in an econometric model of the TPD is an estimator of the "true" value of a pertinent TPD parameter. In contrast, the estimator in an econometric model of the MPD is an estimator of the value of an MPD parameter of any one of the possible mathematical models of the MPD. In other words: In an econometric model of the TPD, (M, $\theta_P^o(\cdot)$), the parameter of M, θ_P, has a true value. In an econometric model of the MPD, (M, $\theta_M^o(\cdot)$), the parameter of M, θ_M, may assume any one of a number of "true" values.

Encompassing in the Upper Data Universe in Figure 2.1
For the sake of clarity, I will begin by studying encompassing in the upper data universe. In this case I face two econometric models of the TPD, (M1, $\theta_S^o(\cdot)$) and (M2, $\theta_P^o(\cdot)$), and I provide criteria that will ensure that one of them encompasses the other—first exactly and then approximately. I assume throughout, without saying so, that the TPD encompasses both (M1, $\theta_S^o(\cdot)$) and (M2, $\theta_P^o(\cdot)$).

Def1
Suppose that there are two subsets of R^k, Φ_P and Φ_S, such that $\theta_P \in \Phi_P$ and $\theta_S \in \Phi_S$. Suppose, also, that I have obtained n independently and identically distributed observations of y, $y_1, \ldots, y_n$, and let $\theta_P^o(\cdot)$ and $\theta_S^o(\cdot)$, respectively, be estimators of θ_P and θ_S in the given sample. Suppose that (M1, $\theta_S^o(\cdot)$) and (M2, $\theta_P^o(\cdot)$) are two different econometric models of the TPD, and that the two estimators are consistent in their respective models. Then, (M1, $\theta_S^o(\cdot)$) exactly encompasses (M2, $\theta_P^o(\cdot)$) if and only if there is a binding function, $\Gamma(\cdot):\Phi_S \to \Phi_P$, such that in M1 the estimates of θ_P and θ_S satisfy the equation $\theta_P^o(s_n) = \Gamma(\theta_S^o(s_n))$ a.e.

As I understand this definition, the values of θ_S and θ_P are not known, but each parameter has a true value in M1 and M2. Also, the statement that (M1, $\theta_S^o(\cdot)$) is an econometric model of TPD is taken to mean that the characteristics of M1 are characteristics of the TPD. It does not mean that M1 is identical with the TPD.

E10.3
Recall the urn in the experimental-economics example in section 3.3. The urn had 1,000 identical balls. Some of the balls were red. The others were blue. No one knew how many blue balls there were. A blindfolded man was to pull 250 balls at random from the urn. After each draw, the color of the ball was recorded, the drawn ball was returned

to the urn, and the urn was shaken well before the next ball was drawn. Let θ_S and θ_P, respectively, denote the proportion of red balls in the urn in M1 and M2. Let the characteristics of TPD be as described in the Γ_P axioms. Let $\Phi_S = (0, 1)$ and $\Phi_P = (0, 1)$. In the given case, the two maximum-likelihood estimators of θ_S and θ_P satisfy the equation $\theta_S^o(s_n)$ $= \theta_P^o(s_n)$. Hence, (M1, $\theta_S^o(\cdot)$) exactly encompasses (M2, $\theta_P^o(\cdot)$) with binding function $\Gamma(\theta) = \theta$. It is also a fact that (M2, $\theta_P^o(\cdot)$), with $\Gamma^{-1}(\theta) =$ θ, exactly encompasses (M1, $\theta_S^o(\cdot)$), since in M2 $\theta_P^o(s_n) = \theta_S^o(s_n)$ a.e.

Def1 is in accord with Definition 1 (Exact encompassing) on page 6 of Bontemps and Mizon 2008. Bontemps and Mizon attribute the definition to Florens et al. (1996). I have several problems with using Def1 in the lower data universe. First, there need not be a true value of θ_M that I can use to describe the distribution in M1. Second, there is no reference to the limiting distributions of the two estimates. In E10.3 the two limiting distributions are very different. To wit: In M1, $\text{plim}\theta_S^o(s_n) = \theta_S$, and $\text{plim}\theta_P^o(s_n) = \theta_S$. In M2, $\text{plim}\theta_S^o(s_n) = \theta_P$, and $\text{plim}\theta_P^o(s_n) = \theta_P$. In particular, if M2 is the TPD, then in P_P measure $\text{plim}\theta_S^o(s_n) = \theta_{P0}$, where θ_{P0} is the true value of θ_P in the TPD distribution.

There are two versions of the idea that an econometric model approximately encompasses another. Here is the simplest one for the upper data universe in figure 2.1.

Def2
Suppose that there are two subsets of R^k, Φ_P and Φ_S, such that $\theta_P \in \Phi_P$ and $\theta_S \in \Phi_S$. Suppose, also, that I have n independently and identically distributed observations of y, $y_1, \ldots , y_n$, and let $\theta_P^o(\cdot)$ and $\theta_S^o(\cdot)$ be estimators of θ_P and θ_S, respectively. Suppose that (M2, $\theta_P^o(\cdot)$) and (M1, $\theta_S^o(\cdot)$) are econometric models of the TPD, and that the estimators $\theta_P^o(\cdot)$ and $\theta_S^o(\cdot)$ are consistent in their respective models. Then (M1, $\theta_S^o(\cdot)$) approximately encompasses (M2, $\theta_P^o(\cdot)$) if and only if there is a binding function, $\Gamma(\cdot):\Phi_S \rightarrow \Phi_P$, such that, in M1, $\Gamma(\theta_S) = \text{plim}\theta_P^o(s_n))$ and $\theta_P^o(s_n)$ $= \Gamma(\theta_S)^o(s_n)$ a.e., where $\Gamma(\theta_S)^o(\cdot))$ is the estimator of $\Gamma(\theta_S)$.

Def2 makes sense only if there is a true value of θ_S that I can put in $\Gamma(\theta_S)$. That is all right in the upper data universe. It is not all right in the lower data universe in figure 2.1, since there need not be a true value of θ_S as such in that data universe.

Here is an example to fix ideas. I learned of the ideas in this example by reading Hendry and Richard 1989. In the example, the TPD distribution of y can be taken to be the normal distribution with mean μ and variance σ^2.

E10.4
Let y be a random variable that in M1 is normally distributed with mean μ and variance 1. Suppose that y in the M2 distribution has mean 0 and unknown variance σ^2. Also suppose that I have n observations of y, $y_1, \ldots , y_n$ and that these observations are distributed independently with the same probability distribution as y. Then in M2 the maximum-likelihood estimate of σ^2 is $\sigma^{2o}(s_n) = n^{-1}\Sigma_{1 \leq i \leq n}y_i^2$. In M1 the maximum-likelihood estimate of μ is $\mu^o(s_n) = n^{-1}\Sigma_{1 \leq i \leq n}y_i$. Also in M1, $\text{plim}\sigma^{2o}(s_n) = 1 + \mu^2$. Consequently, *(M1, $\mu^o(\cdot)$) approximately encompasses (M2, $\sigma^{2o}(\cdot)$)* if and only if the maximum-likelihood estimate of $1 + \mu^2$ in M1 equals $n^{-1}\Sigma_{1 \leq i.n}y_i^2$ a.e. Since the given estimates, in fact, are equal a.e. in M1, *(M1, $\mu^o(\cdot)$) approximately encompasses (M2, $\sigma^{2o}(\cdot)$)*.

The Def2 version of approximate encompassing is in accord with Bontemps and Mizon's (2008) Definition 4 (Approximate encompassing) with $\Gamma(\cdot)$ as defined in their equation 6 on page 11. It is also in accord with Hendry and Richard's (1989, p. 396) Definition 1 (Sampling) concerning exact parametric encompassing. In E10.4, as in Def2, I assume that there are true values of θ_S and θ_P.

There is a kind of approximate encompassing that, in Def3, I simply call *encompassing*. The definition pertains to a case where M2 in the encompassed model is the TPD. As stated, the definition is a rewording of Bontemps and Mizon's definition of *encompassing* (2003, p. 359).

Def3
Suppose that there are two subsets of R^k, Φ_P and Φ_S, such that $\theta_P \in \Phi_P$ and $\theta_S \in \Phi_S$. Suppose, also, that I have n independently and identically distributed observations of y, $y_1, \ldots , y_n$, and let $\theta_P^o(\cdot)$ and $\theta_S^o(\cdot)$ be estimators of θ_P and θ_S, respectively. Suppose that (M2, $\theta_P^o(\cdot)$) and (M1, $\theta_S^o(\cdot)$) are different econometric models of the TPD, that M2 actually is the TPD, and that the estimators $\theta_P^o(\cdot)$ and $\theta_S^o(\cdot)$ are consistent in their respective models. Then (M1, $\theta_S^o(\cdot)$) encompasses (M2, $\theta_P^o(\cdot)$) if and only if there is a binding function, $\Gamma(\cdot):\Phi_S \to \Phi_P$, such that, in M1, $\Gamma(\theta_{S0}) = \text{plim}\theta_P^o(s_n)$, and, in M2, $\theta_{P0} = \text{plim}\theta_P^o(s_n)$, $\theta_{S0} = \text{plim}\theta_S^o(s_n)$, and $\theta_{P0} = \Gamma(\theta_{S0})$.

Def2 and Def3, are not identical. To see why, recall E10.3, where, in M1, $\theta_S = \text{plim}\theta_P^o(s_n)$, $\Gamma(\theta_S) = \theta_S$, and $\theta_P^o(s_n) = \Gamma((\theta_S)^o(s_n) = \theta_S^o(s_n)$. It follows that (M1, $\theta_S^o(\cdot)$) approximately encompasses (M2, $\theta_P^o(\cdot)$) according to Def2. Suppose, now, that M2 is the TPD. Then, in M2, $\theta_{P0} = \text{plim}\theta_P^o(s_n)$, $\theta_{S0} = \text{plim}\theta_S(s_n)$, and $\theta_{P0} = \theta_{S0}$. But if that is so, (M1, $\theta_S^o(\cdot)$) does not encompass (M2, $\theta_P^o(\cdot)$) in the sense of Def3 unless θ_{S0} equals θ_S.

Encompassing in the Lower Data Universe of Figure 2.1

Now the big question of what to do when there is no true value of θ_S in M1 arises, as is the case in the lower data universe when the probability distribution in (M1, $\theta_M^o(\cdot)$) is a model of the MPD and there are many possible models of the MPD. Here is how I would rephrase Def3 so that it applies to the lower data universe in figure 2.1.

Def4
Suppose that there are two subsets of R^k, Φ_P and Φ_M, such that $\theta_P \in \Phi_P$ and $\theta_M \in \Phi_M$. Suppose, also, that I have n independently and identically distributed observations of y, $y_1, \ldots, y_n$, and let $\theta_P^o(\cdot)$ and $\theta_M^o(\cdot)$ be estimators of θ_P and θ_M, respectively. Suppose that (M2, $\theta_P^o(\cdot)$) and (M1, $\theta_M^o(\cdot)$), respectively, are econometric models of the TPD and the MPD, that M2 actually is the TPD, and that the estimators $\theta_P^o(\cdot)$ and $\theta_M^o(\cdot)$ are consistent in their respective models. Then (M1, $\theta_M^o(\cdot)$) encompasses (M2, $\theta_P^o(\cdot)$) if and only if there is a value of $\theta_M \in \Phi_M$ and a binding function $\Gamma(\cdot):\Phi_M \to \Phi_P$ such that, in M1, $\Gamma(\theta_M) = \text{plim}\theta_P^o(s_n)$, and, in M2, $\theta_{P0} = \text{plim}\theta_P^o(s_n)$, $\theta_{M0} = \text{plim}\theta_M^o(s_n)$, and $\theta_{P0} = \Gamma(\theta_{M0})$.

When reading Def4, note that, in M1 $\text{plim}\theta_M^o(s_n) = \theta_M$. The required θ_M need not satisfy the equation $\theta_M = \theta_{M0}$. However, if $\theta_M = \theta_{M0}$, (M1, $\theta_M^o(\cdot)$) also encompasses (M2, $\theta_P^o(\cdot)$) in the sense of Def3. In that sense, Def4 is the natural extension of Def3 to the lower data universe in figure 2.1.

E10.5
Consider the urn in E10.3. Suppose that θ_M and θ_P denote, respectively, the proportion of red balls in the urn in M1 and M2. Suppose also that (M1, $\theta_M^o(\cdot)$) is an econometric model of an MPD, and that (M2, $\theta_P^o(\cdot)$) is an econometric model of the TPD. Suppose that $\theta_{P0} \in [0.5, 0.6]$, and let $\Phi_M = [0.5, 0.6]$, $\Phi_P = (0, 1)$. In M1 the two maximum-likelihood estimators of the proportion of red balls in the urn satisfy the equation $\theta_M^o(s_n) = \theta_P^o(s_n)$ a.e. Consequently, if I choose a $\theta_M \in [0.5, 0.6]$ and let

$\Gamma(\theta) = \theta$ for all $\theta \in \Phi_M$, I can show that (M1, $\theta_M°(\cdot)$) encompasses (M2, $\theta_P°(\cdot)$) in accord with my Def4. To wit: in M1, $\Gamma(\theta_M) = \theta_M = \text{plim}\theta_P°(s_n)$; in M2, $\theta_{P0} = \text{plim}\theta_P°(s_n)$, $\theta_{M0} = \text{plim}\theta_M°(s_n)$, and $\theta_{P0} = \theta_{M0} = \Gamma(\theta_{M0})$. Here θ_M need not equal θ_{P0}.

10.2.2 Congruence in Figure 2.1

The concept of congruence plays a pivotal role in the LSE methodology. According to Mizon (1995), in the LSE methodology an econometric model is congruent if it is coherent with *a priori* theory, is coherent with observed sample information, coherent with the measurement system, and encompasses all rival models. For present purposes I will insist on the following modified explication of congruence.

Def5

Suppose that there are two subsets of R^k, Φ_P and Φ_S, such that $\theta_P \in \Phi_P$ and $\theta_S \in \Phi_S$. Suppose, also, that I have n independently and identically distributed observations of y, $y_1, \ldots, y_n$, and let $\theta_P°(\cdot)$ and $\theta_S°(\cdot)$ be estimators of θ_P and θ_S, respectively. Suppose that (M2, $\theta_P°(\cdot)$) and (M1, $\theta_S°(\cdot)$) are, respectively, different econometric models of the TPD and the MPD with M2 actually being the TPD, and suppose that the estimators, $\theta_P°(\cdot)$ and $\theta_S°(\cdot)$, are consistent in their respective models. Then, (M1, $\theta_S°(\cdot)$) is congruent if and only if M1 is coherent with the pertinent *a priori* theory and (M1, $\theta_S°(\cdot)$) encompasses (M2, $\theta_P°(\cdot)$) in accord with Def4.

In Def5 the *a priori* theory is a family of models of the axioms of the data universe in a pertinent formal theory-data confrontation. It is, therefore, important to observe that the parameters of a congruent econometric model, (M1, $\theta_S°(\cdot)$), need not satisfy the conditions of a data-admissible mathematical model of the MPD. However, I hope to find conditions that ensure the existence of a congruent econometric model with an M1 that resides in a 95-percent-confidence band around a prescribed estimate of the MPD. Here is an example to fix ideas.

E10.6

Consider the two econometric models in E10.3, (M1, $\theta_M°(\cdot)$) and (M2, $\theta_P°(\cdot)$), and recall that $\theta_{P0} \in [0.5, 0.6]$, $\Phi_M = [0.5, 0.6]$, $\Phi_P = (0, 1)$ and M2 is the TPD. If I choose a $\theta_M \in [0.5, 0.6]$ and let $\Gamma(\theta) = \theta$, then M1 satisfies the *a priori* theory in section 3.3, since $\theta_M \in (0, 1)$. Also, (M1, $\theta_M°(\cdot)$) encompasses (M2, $\theta_P°(\cdot)$) in accordance with Def4. Hence, (M1, $\theta_M°(\cdot)$) is congruent.

It is, also, a fact that with the given choice of θ_M, M1 resides in the 95-percent-confidence band around $\theta_M^o(s_n)$. In fact, with the given choice of θ_M, M1 itself becomes a data-admissible mathematical model of the MPD in the 95-percent-confidence region of the estimate of MPD.

10.2.3 Data-Admissible Confidence Regions in Figure 2.1

In Stigum 2003 I suggested that an interpretation of the MPD (that is, a family of mathematical models of the MPD) is data admissible if it satisfies two criteria: (1) the sampling scheme that generates the data is adequate, and (2) the interpretation of the MPD contains a model of the MPD whose functionals equal the corresponding functionals of the TPD. For present purposes, I can formulate this suggestion as follows.

Def6
Consider a theory-data confrontation in which the sampling scheme that generates the data is adequate. The 95-percent-confidence region around the estimated mathematical model of the MPD is data admissible if it contains both a data-admissible mathematical model of the MPD and a congruent econometric model.

E10.6 shows that the 95-percent-confidence band around the estimated model of the MPD in section 3.3 is data admissible. To wit: The sampling scheme of the blindfolded man is adequate by assumption. Also, with the chosen value of θ_M, the econometric model, (M1, $\theta M^0(\cdot)$) is congruent, and M1 is a data-admissible mathematical model of the MPD that belongs to the given confidence region.

E10.7
Consider the theory-data confrontation in section 3.4, where the Γ_P axioms imply that there exist a pair of constants, a and b, and a random variable, η, such that $c = a + by + \eta$, $b > 0$, and $E\eta = E\eta y = 0$. The true value of (a, b, σ_η^2) in the TPD distribution is (0.5418, 0.4867, 0.5114). The value of the same triple in the one and only MPD distribution is (2/3, 1/3, 0.4167). I denote the two triples, respectively, by θ_P and θ_M, and I let $\theta_P^o(\cdot)$ and $\theta_M^o(\cdot)$ be, respectively, the least-squares estimator of the linear relations depicted in equations 3.15 and 3.16; i.e., $c = \alpha + \beta \cdot y + \eta$. Moreover, I designate ϕ_M and ϕ_P by the same region, $\{x \in [0.5, 0.75] \times [0.25, 0.6] \times [0.3, 0.6]\}$, and I let (M2, $\theta_P^o(\cdot)$) and (M1, $\theta_M^o(\cdot)$), respectively, be econometric models of the TPD and the MPD. Finally, I observe that the sampling scheme is adequate. Then, in M1, $\theta_P^o(s_n) = \theta_M^o(s_n)$ a.e., and

$\text{plim}\theta_P^{\circ}(s_n) = (2/3, 1/3, 0.4167)$. In M2, $\theta_{P0} = \text{plim}\theta_P^{\circ}(sn) = (0.5418, 0.4867, 0.5114) = \text{plim}\theta_M^{\circ}(s_n) = \theta_{M0}$. Hence, (M1, $\theta_M^{\circ}(\cdot)$) exactly encompasses (M2, $\theta_P^{\circ}(\cdot)$). With $\Gamma(\theta) = \theta$ (M1, $\theta_M^{0}(\cdot)$), also, encompasses (M2, $\theta_M^{0}(\cdot)$) in the sense of Def4. Since (M1, $\theta_M^{0}(\cdot)$) is coherent with the pertinent *a priori* theory as well, it follows that, with the given choice of θ_M, (M1, $\theta M^{0}(\cdot)$) is congruent.

In this case, it is interesting that the 95-percent-confidence region around the estimated parameters of the MPD contains the true values of these parameters in the TPD distribution. Even so, the given confidence region is not data admissible, since it does not contain a data-admissible mathematical model of the MPD.

E10.8

Consider the theory-data confrontation in section 3.5, where the Γ_P axioms imply that there exist six constants, a_0, a_1, a_2, b_0, b_1, and b_2, and two random variables, ξ_1 and ξ_2, with means 0 and finite covariance matrix Π, such that, relative to $P_P(\cdot)$,

$$y_1 = a_0 + a_1y_3 + a_2y_4 + \xi_1,$$
$$y_2 = b_0 + b_1y_3 + b_2y_4 + \xi_2, \tag{10.4}$$

and

$$\text{TPD.cov}((\xi_1,\xi_2)'(y_3,y_4)) = 0. \tag{10.5}$$

The true values of the parameters in the TPD distribution are as follows: Π is the 2×2 identity matrix I, and $(a_0, a_1, a_2, b_0, b_1, b_2) = (5.5, 0.5, 0.25, 2.25, 0.25, -0.125)$.

According to the Γ_T and $\Gamma_{T,P}$ axioms, there exist six constants, γ_0, γ_1, γ_2, φ_0, φ_1, and φ_2, and two independently distributed random variables, η_1, and η_2 with means 0 and finite, positive variances, $\sigma_{\eta1}^2$ and $\sigma_{\eta2}^2$, such that, relative to $P_M(\cdot)$,

$$y_1 = \gamma_0 + \gamma_1y_3 + \gamma_2y_4 + \eta_1; \ y_2 = \varphi_0 + \varphi_1y_3 + \varphi_2y_4 + \eta_2 \tag{10.6}$$

and

$$\text{MPD.cov}((\eta_1,\eta_2)'(y_3,y_4)) = 0. \tag{10.7}$$

The values of the constants γ_0, γ_1, γ_2, φ_0, φ_1, and φ_2 are required to satisfy the following equations:

$$(\gamma_1,\gamma_2) = \Sigma_{11}(\text{MPD})\Sigma_{22}(\text{MPD})^{-1},$$
$$(\varphi_1,\varphi_2) = \Sigma_{12}(\text{MPD})\Sigma_{22}(\text{MPD})^{-1}, \tag{10.8}$$

$$\gamma_0 = \delta_1 - a_1\delta_3 - a_2\delta_4,$$

$$\phi_0 = \delta_2 - b_1\delta_3 - b_2\delta_4,$$

(10.9)

where

$$\Sigma_{22}(MPD) = MPD.cov.((y_3,y_4)'(y_3,y_4)),$$

$$\Sigma_{11}(MPD) = MPD.cov((y_1,(y_3,y_4)),$$

$$\Sigma_{12}(MPD) = MPD.cov.(y_2,(y_3,y_4)),$$

and

$$\delta_i = MPD.mean(y_i), \qquad i = 1, 2, 3, 4.$$

Also, the values of the α's and β's that the same constants determine in the equations

$$\alpha_1 = \gamma_2/\phi_2; \ \beta_1 = \gamma_1/\phi_1: \ -\alpha_2 = ((\alpha_1 - \beta_1)/\beta_1)\gamma_1; \ \beta_2 = ((\alpha_1 - \beta_1)/\alpha_1)\gamma_2$$

and

(10.10)

$$\beta_0 = \gamma_0 - \beta_1\phi_0; \ \text{and} \ \alpha_0 = \gamma_0 - \alpha_1\phi_0$$

must satisfy the sign constraints that Γ_T imposes on the α's and β's. There are no other restrictions.

In this case, there are two econometric models to consider, (M1, $\theta_M{}^\circ(\cdot)$) and (M2, $\theta_P{}^\circ(\cdot)$), where M1 is any one of the many MPD distributions, $\theta_M{}^\circ(\cdot)$ is a maximum-likelihood estimator of (γ_0, γ_1, γ_2, ϕ_0, ϕ_1, ϕ_2, $\sigma_{\eta1}{}^2$, $\sigma_{\eta2}{}^2$), M2 is the TPD distribution, and $\theta_P{}^\circ(\cdot)$ is the maximum-likelihood estimator of (a_0, a_1, a_2, b_0, b_1, b_2, $\sigma_{\xi1}{}^2$, $\sigma_{\xi2}{}^2$). The maximum-likelihood estimators are consistent, and in M1 it is a fact that $\theta_M{}^\circ(s_n) = \theta_P{}^\circ(s_n)$ a.e. Hence, (M1, $\theta_M{}^\circ(\cdot)$) exactly encompasses (M2, $\theta_P{}^\circ(\cdot)$). Moreover, no matter which θ_M of the possible MPD parameters one chooses for M1, it is the case that in M1 $plim\theta_P{}^\circ(s_n) = \theta_M$. It is, also, the case that in M2, $plim\theta_P{}^\circ(s_n) = \theta_{P0} = plim\theta_M{}^\circ(s_n)$. Hence, with $\Gamma(\theta) = \theta$ and an appropriate choice of M1, M1 is coherent with the pertinent *a priori* theory, and (M1, $\theta_M{}^\circ(\cdot)$) encompasses (M2, $\theta_P{}^\circ(\cdot)$) in the sense of Def4. Since the sampling system in the present case is adequate, it follows that, with an appropriate choice of θ_M, (M1, $\theta_M{}^\circ(\cdot)$) is congruent. It is also easy to verify from tables 3.4 and 3.5 and from equations 10.8 that the value of $\theta_M{}^\circ(s_n)$ in the given sample determines a data-admissible mathematical model of the MPD that belongs to the confidence region determined by Wald's confidence intervals. Hence, the confidence region determined by Wald's confidence intervals is data admissible.

10.2.4 The Status of Bridge Principles in Figure 2.1

In this subsection I shall contend that the bridge principles in a given theory-data confrontation are valid in the Real World if the 95-percent-confidence region of the estimated MPD is data admissible. Because such a contention cannot be proved, I must be content to present examples and arguments that demonstrate that the contention is reasonable. In reading my demonstration, keep in mind that the Real World in a given example is the world in which the objects of which I have observations reside.

Earlier in this chapter I discussed the data admissibility of interpretations of three different MPDs. Example E10.6 shows that the 95-percent-confidence band around the estimated model of the MPD in section 3.3 is data admissible. In this case I am convinced that I have good reasons to believe that the given bridge principles are valid in the Real World. The bridge principles insist that I have accurate observations of the theory variables. In other words, they insist that I am not color blind and that I am careful when I record the color of an observed ball. I believe that I satisfy those conditions.

In the theory-data confrontation in section 3.4, the 95-percent-confidence region around the estimated parameters of the MPD contains a congruent econometric model. However, the given confidence region is not data admissible, since it does not contain a data-admissible mathematical model of the MPD. The bridge principles play a central role in Friedman's Permanent Income Hypothesis. Since my test rejects the empirical relevance of Friedman's theory in the empirical context of section 3.4, it seems reasonable to claim that the bridge principles in my test are not valid in the Real World I generated.

The confidence region determined by Wald's confidence intervals in section 3.5 is data admissible. In this case, the econometric model in the lower data universe, $(M1, \theta_M^\circ (\cdot))$, is like an errors-in-variables model with a twist: the theoretical variables belong in a theory universe instead of a data universe. I generated the data, and I used PcGive's Autometrics to estimate the parameters. The results that I record in tables 3.4–3.10 give me good reasons to believe that the given bridge principles are valid in the Real World that I generated.

In the preceding examples, I generated the data for the theory-data confrontations. In those cases, the Real World was the world of the pertinent number generators. I will now present an example in which the Real World is the world of US consumers during the years 1962 and 1963.

E10.7
Consider the theory-data confrontation that I discussed in section 3.6, where the Γ_P axioms imply that there exist real-valued constants, a and b, and a random variable, η, such that

$$m^* = a + bA^* + \eta. \tag{10.11}$$

With respect to $P_P(\cdot)$, η has mean 0 and finite positive variance σ_η^2 and is orthogonal to A^*. Also, $\mu^* + m^* = A^*$, where μ^* and m^*, respectively, denote the value of a consumers' investments in safe assets and risky assets at the end of 1963, and A^* is a measure of a consumer's net worth at the end of 1963. Let $\theta_P = (a, b, \sigma_\eta^2)$. This triple is a parameter of the TPD distribution whose value the Γ_P axioms do not reveal. Even the signs of a and b are left unspecified. The only information I have is an estimate of (a, b) that is positive and significantly different from 0. I have no estimate of σ_η^2. For ease of reference, I record the estimate here[4]:

$$\theta_P^\circ(s_n) = (8.542, 0.987, \sigma_\eta^{2\circ}),$$

where $\sigma_\eta^{2\circ}$ is some arbitrary value of σ_η^2.
    Equation 10.11 has an alias in the MPD distribution:

$$m^* = \alpha + \beta A^* + \varsigma.$$

In the MPD distribution, the value of the triple, $(\alpha, \beta, \sigma_\varsigma^2)$ is positive and $\beta < 1$. Let $\theta_M = (\alpha, \beta, \sigma_\varsigma^2)$, and observe that $\theta_M^\circ(s_n) = (8.542, 0.987, \sigma_\eta^{2\circ})$, with $\sigma_\eta^{2\circ}$ the arbitrary estimate of the value of $\sigma_\eta^{2\circ}$. Now let $(M2, \theta_P^\circ(\cdot))$ and $(M1, \theta_M^\circ(\cdot))$, respectively, be econometric models of the TPD and the MPD. Then, by construction, in M1, $\theta_P^\circ(s_n) = \theta_M^\circ(s_n)$ a.e. Hence, $(M1, \theta_M^\circ(\cdot))$ exactly encompasses $(M2, \theta_P^\circ(\cdot))$. I choose θ_M to equal the estimated value of θ_M, $\theta_M^\circ(s_n)$, then, in M1, $\theta_P^\circ(s_n) = \text{plim}\theta_P^\circ(s_n) = \theta_M^\circ(s_n)$. In M2, $\theta_{P0} = \text{plim}\theta_P^\circ(s_n) = \text{plim}\theta_M^\circ(s_n)$. With $\Gamma(\theta) = \theta$ it follows that $(M1, \theta_M^\circ(\cdot))$ encompasses $(M2, \theta_P^\circ(\cdot))$ in the sense of Def4. Thus, if the sampling scheme that generated the data was adequate, $(M1, \theta_M^\circ(\cdot))$ is congruent. M1 with the chosen value of θ_M is a data-admissible model of MPD. It follows that a 95-percent-confidence region around the estimated model of MPD is data admissible and that the bridge principles in section 3.6 are valid in the Real World of US consumers in 1962 and 1963.

10.3 Theory in Applied Econometrics

I have described two scenarios for research in applied econometrics—one for present-day econometrics in the tradition of Trygve Haavelmo and one for the kind of formal theory-data confrontation that I believe Ragnar Frisch envisioned in his formulation of the constitution of the Econometric Society. The book presents case studies of economic phenomena that contrast the empirical analysis that present-day applied econometrics prescribes with the empirical analysis that a formal theory-data confrontation prescribes. My goal has been to develop a basis for meaningful discussions of the best way to incorporate economic theory in empirical analyses.

The role that theory plays in the two scenarios varies with the subject matter and may vary with the researcher in charge of the empirical analysis. It also varies with the understanding of the essence of an economic theory. In present-day econometrics, the researcher seems to identify the undefined terms of the theory with Haavelmo's true variables in social reality. In the vision of econometrics that I ascribe to Frisch, the researcher takes his theory to be about imaginary matters that reside in Frisch's model world—a world that has little in common with social reality.

The difference in the researchers' understanding of the essence of an economic theory is the root cause that the empirical analyses in the two scenarios differ. In either scenario, the theory delineates the positive analogies that the originator of the theory considered sufficient to describe the kind of situation he had in mind. In present-day econometrics, the pertinent positive analogies become characteristics of the data-generating process. There is only one true data-generating process—be it the local data-generation process (LDGP) in the London School of Economics (LSE) methodology, the Haavelmo Distribution in Aris Spanos' error-statistical reformulation of Haavelmo's methodology, or the TPD in the upper data universe in figure 2.1 in the present volume. Therefore, in present-day econometrics the pertinent economic theory has only one true model. Also, estimates of the parameters of the data-generating process become estimates of parameters, each of which has a true value.

In the theory-data confrontation that I believe Frisch envisioned, the situation is different. The theory in Frisch's model world has any number of true models. Also, the bridge principles that link the theory's undefined terms with the researcher's data may have many models. Consequently, the probability distribution of the data that is derived from the probability distribution of the theory variables and the bridge principles—that is, the MPD—has many true models. In the theory-data confrontation that Frisch envisioned, the MPD takes the place that the TPD holds in present-day econometrics. Since there are many models of the MPD, it follows that estimates of the parameters of an MPD become estimates of the parameters of any one of the many true models of the pertinent MPD.

In my discussion of differences above, I have placed present-day econometrics in the upper data universe in figure 2.1, and I have placed the empirical analysis of a formal theory-data confrontation in the lower data universe. The differences that I have described have important consequences for the meaning of empirical relevance, the meaning of encompassing, and the meaning of congruence in the two universes. In the upper data universe, encompassing and congruence assume the meanings those two concepts have in present-day econometrics. Empirical relevance, however, assumes the meaning I gave to the concept in chapter 3. Thus, in the upper data universe, the claim that a theory is empirically relevant is analogous to the claim in mathematical statistics that there is no good reason to reject the theory. In cross-section analyses this is obviously the case. In time-series analyses it is the case too, once it is understood that a theory is empirically relevant if it is empirically relevant in the empirical context that a pertinent congruent econometric model determines.

In the lower data universe, the meanings of the three concepts differ from their meanings in the upper data universe. I described the differences in the meanings of congruence and encompassing in section 10.2, and I have nothing to add here. I described the difference in the meaning of empirical relevance in the two data universes in chapter 3. In that chapter, a theory in a formal theory-data confrontation was taken to be empirically relevant if and only if there is at least one member of the family of mathematical models of the theory axioms that—together with a model of the non-stochastic data axioms and the bridge principles—determines a data-admissible mathematical model of the MPD. A model of the MPD is data admissible if it resides in a 95-percent-confidence region around a statistically meaningful estimate of the MPD and satisfies all the conditions on which the theory axioms, the non-stochastic data axioms, and the bridge principles insist. There may be many data-admissible models of the MPD in the given confidence region, and each data-admissible model of MPD determines an empirically relevant model of the theory.

The fact that empirical relevance has different meanings in the two data universes in figure 2.1 raises interesting questions for the use of theory in empirical analyses. Some of the questions concern behavior characteristics of data variables. The behavior of the variables in the two data universes differs. What is the cause of the differences? Do the differences matter in applied econometrics? Other questions concern the inference about social reality that one may draw from statistical analyses. The statistical analyses in the two data universes differ. Do such differences affect our understanding of pertinent economic aspects of social reality? If they do, who are we to believe: the econometrician in the upper data universe, or his colleague in the lower data universe?

There are many cases to consider. Suppose, first, that the theory, T, is deemed empirically relevant in both data universes. Two examples are the simultaneous-equations model of a perfectly competitive commodity market in chapter 3 and the theory of a perfectly competitive market for spot and forward exchange in chapter 7. I begin with the simultaneous-equations example.

In the simultaneous-equations example, social reality is the world in which the data-generating process resides. I describe this process in chapter 3, where the true parameters of the corresponding TPD are presented in equations 3.33–3.35.

In the upper data universe of figure 2.1, the assumptions I make about the data-generating process ensure that equations 3.34 and 3.35 constitute a statistically adequate econometric model in Aris Spanos' sense of the term (2012, p. 9). The researcher in charge estimates the parameters in the given equations and uses equations 3.36 to obtain estimates of the respective structural TPD parameters in equation 3.33. These estimates heed the sign constraints on which the Γ_T axioms insist. Also, the equations in 3.36 and each member of the 95-percent-confidence region around the estimates of the parameters in equations 3.34 and 3.35 that Wald's confidence intervals determine produce estimates of the structural parameters in equation 3.33 that heed the required sign constraints. Hence the researcher's original estimates of the structural TPD parameters are theoretically meaningful. The given confidence region around the estimates of the parameters in equations 3.34 and 3.35 contains the true parameter vector of the TPD. Moreover, the set of structural parameters that the given confidence region and the equations in 3.36 determine contains the true values of the structural parameters in equation 3.33.

In the lower data universe, the estimated model of the MPD is identical to the estimated model of the TPD. Hence, the variables behave similarly in the two data universes. Moreover, the 95-percent-confidence region around the estimated model of the MPD contains both a congruent econometric model and a data-admissible model of the MPD and therefore is data admissible. Hence the bridge principles are valid in the Real World. Even so, the inferences about social reality yielded by the statistical analysis in the lower data universe differ in interesting ways from the inferences yielded by the statistical analysis in the upper data universe.

In the upper data universe the estimated structural model is theoretically meaningful. This structural model is a model of the data variables that describes how demand for and supply of the given commodity are related to the actual purchases of the commodity and to the observed values of the price of the commodity and the explanatory variables. If the researcher's assumption that he has accurate observations of his theory variables is valid, the values of the observed variables are the values of the corresponding true variables. Then the researcher's structural model becomes an estimate of the true simultaneous-equations model of the given commodity market.

In the lower data universe the estimated model of the MPD and the bridge principles determine a structural model whose import differs considerably from the structural model in the upper data universe. The estimated structural model in the theory universe is a model of the intended demand and supply of a given commodity as linear functions of hypothetical values of the price of the commodity and the explanatory variables. The estimated model of the MPD and the bridge principles, also, determine meaningful values of the given intended demand and supply variables in the theory universe. Finally, the estimated model of the MPD, the 95-percent-confidence region around the estimate, and the bridge principles determine a family of empirically relevant models of the theory of a competitive market for some given commodity.

What have I learned about social reality from the empirical analyses? According to my contention, in applied econometrics one can learn about characteristic features of social reality that are of economic interest. For the empirical analysis in the lower data universe, the interesting characteristics are the positive analogies of a competitive commodity market that the theory depicts—that is, the structural model and the mean and covariance structure of the theory variables $x_1, \ldots, x_5$ in the RPD distribution. For the empirical analysis in the upper data universe, the pertinent characteristics of social reality are the characteristic features of the TPD distribution of the data variables as determined by the true values of the parameters in equations 3.33–3.35.

In comparing the inferences about social reality that the two statistical analyses yield, it is relevant that the parameters of an MPD distribution of the data variables that is induced by the RPD distribution of x_1, ... , x_5 and the bridge principles need not be true parameters of the TPD distribution of the data variables. However, the true values of the parameters of the TPD distribution as expressed in equations 3.33–3.35 are the parameters of a model of the Γ_T axioms. Also, the parameters of a theoretically meaningful structural model in the upper data universe are parameters of an empirically relevant structural model in the Γ_T axioms. Finally, the true vector-valued parameter of the structural model in the upper data universe is an empirically relevant vector-valued parameter in the theory universe.

It appears that the statistical analyses in the two universes provide identical information about interesting characteristics of social reality. However, there is a fundamental difference in the basis on which the information rests. In the upper data universe, the researcher in charge may claim to have good reasons to believe that the true structural parameters belong in the confidence region around the theoretically meaningful vector-valued parameters of the structural model. In the lower data universe, the researcher in charge can claim to know that all the vector-valued parameters in the same confidence region determine empirically relevant models of the theory axioms. It is of little importance to the latter researcher that one of the vectors in the confidence region may constitute the parameters of a true structural model.

In chapter 7 social reality is the market for Swiss francs and US dollars during the period for which I have observations of the spot rates and one-week-forward rates at which the two currencies were exchanged. André Anundsen (in the upper data universe of figure 2.1) and Harald Goldstein (in the lower data universe of figure 2.1) analyzed the same data with different methods.

The dynamics of the market for spot and forward exchange of US dollars for Swiss francs that Anundsen's analysis determines are very different from the dynamics of the same market that Goldstein's statistical analysis determines. By the assumption of accurate observations, in the upper data universe (see equations 7.45 and 7.46), for all $t > 0$,

$$\begin{pmatrix} \Delta \hat{y}_1(t) \\ \Delta \hat{y}_2(t) \end{pmatrix} = - \begin{pmatrix} 1 & -1 \\ 0 & 0 \end{pmatrix} \begin{pmatrix} \hat{y}_1(t-1) \\ \hat{y}_2(t-1) \end{pmatrix} + \begin{pmatrix} \delta_1(t) \\ \delta_2(t) \end{pmatrix} \qquad (10.12)$$

and

$\delta(0, \omega_P) = 0$ and $E\{\delta(t, \omega_P) \mid \hat{y}(0), \ldots, \hat{y}(t-1)\} = 0$, a.e. $P_P(\cdot)$ measure.

$$(10.13)$$

By Goldstein's empirical analysis, in the lower data universe (see equation 7.44), for all $t > 0$,

$$\begin{pmatrix} \Delta\hat{y}_1(t) \\ \Delta\hat{y}_2(t) \end{pmatrix} = \begin{pmatrix} 0 \\ 1 \end{pmatrix}(1, -1)\begin{pmatrix} \hat{y}_1(t-1) \\ \hat{y}_2(t-1) \end{pmatrix} + \begin{pmatrix} \psi^0\varsigma(t) \\ v(t) \end{pmatrix}$$

$$(10.14)$$

and, with $P_M(\cdot)$ probability 1,

$$(\varsigma, v)(0, \omega_P) = 0 \text{ and } E\{(\varsigma, v)(t, \omega_P) \mid \hat{y}(0), \ldots, \hat{y}(t-1)\} = 0. \quad (10.15)$$

It follows from these equations that the short-run dynamics of spot and forward rates in the two universes are different. The common trends, and hence the long-run dynamics, of the exchange rates in the two data universes may also be very different. In the upper data universe the common trend is a multiple of $\hat{y}_2(0) + \Sigma_{0 \leq s \leq t-1}\delta_2(t-s, \omega_P)$. The $\delta_2(t)$ are TPD distributed. How the TPD distribution of $\delta_2(t)$ is related to the RPD distribution of $\varphi\eta(t)$ is uncertain since the assumption about accurate observations says nothing about the relationship between the RPD and the TPD. In the lower data universe, the common trend is a multiple of $\hat{y}_1(0) + \psi^0\Sigma_{0 \leq s \leq t-1}\zeta(t-s, \omega_P)$. According to my deliberations in chapter 7, the MPD distribution $\zeta(t)$ equals the RPD distribution of $\eta(t)$. Hence, the MPD distribution of $\psi^0\zeta(t)$ may be very different from the TPD distribution of $\delta_2(t)$. Since I do not know the relationship between the RPD distribution of $\psi^0\eta(t)$ and the TPD distribution of $\delta_2(t)$, I cannot determine in what way the long-run dynamics of spot and forward exchange in the two universes differ.

The statistical analyses Goldstein and Anundsen carried out in the two universes were also very different. Still, the inferences about social reality that one may draw from their analyses are related in interesting ways.

Anundsen's estimate of the dynamics of spot and forward rates in the franc–dollar market is a congruent econometric model. Also, if the observed spot and forward rates are accurate observations of the theoretical spot and forward rates, an analogue of theorem T 7.5 in chapter 7 is empirically relevant in the empirical context that Anundsen's analysis determines. Specifically, the researcher in charge cannot reject the hypothesis that there is a pair of orthogonal second-order random processes, $\{\delta(t, \omega_P); t \in N - \{0\}\}$, such that my observations satisfy equations 10.12 and 10.13. But if that is so, my observations also satisfy equation 10.13 and the following two equations:

For all $t > 0$, $\hat{y}_1(t) = \hat{y}_2(t-1) + \delta_1(t)$ and $\hat{y}_2(t) = \hat{y}_2(t-1) + \delta_2(t)$.   (10.16)

Moreover, according to my OxMetrix 7 program and my analysis of equation 7.49 in chapter 7, the researcher cannot reject the hypothesis that the $\delta_1(t)$ and the $\delta_2(t)$ are normally distributed. Judging from the scatter diagram in figure 10.1, he may also not be able to reject the hypothesis that there is a constant φ such that $\delta_2(t)$ in $P_P(\cdot)$ measure has the same distribution that $\varphi\delta_1(t)$ has in $P_P(\cdot)$ measure. If that is so, the researcher cannot reject the hypothesis that $\hat{y}_1(t)$, $\hat{y}_2(t)$, $\delta_1(t)$, and $\delta_2(t)$ in the upper data universe satisfy analogues in $P_P(\cdot)$ measure of the conditions that I delineated in the last four axioms of Γ_T—that is, A4, A5, and the conditions concerning the $\eta(t)$ in A6 and A7.

Goldstein's estimate determines an econometric model that satisfies equations 10.14 and 10.15. His estimates also satisfy equations 10.15 and the following two equations:

$$\hat{y}_1(t, \omega_P) = \hat{y}_1(t-1, \omega_P) + \psi^0\varsigma(t, \omega_P),$$

$$\hat{y}_2(t, \omega_P) = \hat{y}_1(t-1, \omega_P) + v(t, \omega_P).$$
(10.17)

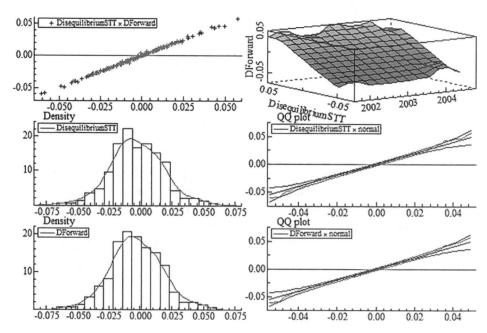

Figure 10.1
Graphs for DisequilibriumSTT ($= \hat{y}_1(t) - \hat{y}_2(t-1)$) and DForward ($= \Delta\hat{y}_2(t)$).

From these equations and from G1–G5, I find that if I let ω_P be a vector in the support of the given MPD and define $(y, \lambda, \eta, u)(t)$ by the equations

$$u(t) = v(t, \omega_P),$$

$$\psi\eta(t) = \psi\varsigma(t, \omega_P),$$

$$\varphi\psi^\circ,$$

$$\lambda(t) = \hat{y}_1(t, \omega_P),$$

and

$$y(t) = \hat{y}_1(t - 1, \omega_P) + (\psi)^{-1}(\hat{y}_1(t, \omega_P) - \hat{y}_1(t - 1, \omega_P)),$$

I can use the MPD distribution of the right-hand variables of the latter equations to calculate the RPD distribution of (y, λ, η, u) that the given MPD distribution of $(\hat{y}_1, \hat{y}_2, \varsigma, v)$ determines. In that way I use the estimated MPD and the bridge principles to construct a model of the theory universe in which the RPD distribution of the variables $y(t)$, $\lambda(t)$, $\eta(t)$, and $u(t)$ satisfies the last four axioms in Γ_T—that is, A4–A7.

What have the two analyses taught me about social reality? The positive analogies in the theory universe established by the analysis in the lower data universe are the same as the positive analogies in the data universe established by the analysis in the upper data universe. These positive analogies are of two kinds. One kind is described in A4 and A5 and in the parts of A6 and A7 that relate to $\eta(t)$ without reference to any particular probability measure. It matters not that that the data variables have the TPD distribution and the theory variables have the RPD distribution. The second kind of positive analogy comprises all the theorems that can be derived from A4, A5, and the parts of A6 and A7 that relate to $\eta(t)$—again without mention of a particular probability measure. For example, spot and forward rates are linearly cointegrated second-order random processes with cointegrating vector (1, –1). It matters not that the observed dynamics of spot and forward exchange differ in the two data universes.

On the surface, it appears that the statistical analyses in the two data universes in chapter 7 yield the same information about the characteristics of spot and forward exchange in social reality. However, there is a subtle difference in the basis on which this information rests. In the upper data universe, under the assumption that the researcher has accurate observations of his theory variables, the researcher cannot reject the hypothesis that there is a true value of φ and a true distribution of $\delta_1(t)$ and $\delta_2(t)$ such that in P_P measure the quadruple $\hat{y}_1(t)$, $\hat{y}_2(t)$, $\delta_1(t)$, $\delta_2(t)$ satisfies analogues of axioms A4 and A5 and the conditions concerning $\eta(t)$ in A6 and A7. Thus, in the upper data universe the researcher may claim that his empirical analysis gives him good reasons to believe in the positive analogies of social reality which his theory describes. In the lower data universe, the family of data-admissible models of the MPD and the pertinent bridge principles determine a family of models of Γ_T each member of which is empirically relevant. Hence, in the lower data universe the researcher can claim, on the basis of his empirical analysis, to know that the positive analogies which his theory describes are empirically relevant in social reality. To him it is not relevant whether any one of the empirically relevant models of Γ_T has the same φ and the same variances of the error terms as the true model in the upper data universe.[5]

Suppose next that theory T is deemed empirically relevant in one of the universes and not in the other, as in the example from experimental economics in chapter 3, the theory of the Permanent Income Hypothesis in chapter 3, and the theory of a perfectly competitive market for a triple of exchange rates in chapter 8.

I begin with the example from experimental economics, in which I picture social reality as a room with an urn full of balls and two serious men—a blindfolded man and me. The urn contains 1,000 identical balls. Some of the balls are red, others are blue, and the actual number of blue balls is unknown. The blindfolded man picks from the urn 250 balls at random and with replacement. I am to determine the proportion of red balls in the urn. (Why I need to know is not relevant!)

My null hypothesis is that the proportion of red balls resides in the interval [0.5, 0.6]. In the upper data universe I reject this null hypothesis because the confidence region around my maximum-likelihood estimate of the true proportion contains too many points. I do that even though the econometric model that the estimate determined is a congruent model of the TPD! In the lower data universe, I accept the null hypothesis because the confidence region around my maximum-likelihood estimate has a non-empty intersection with [0.5, 0.6]. I discover, also, that the same confidence region contains [0.5, 0.6] and constitutes a data-admissible confidence region around the estimated MPD. From this it follows that the bridge principles in the example are valid in the Real World, and that each of the probabilities in the interval

[0.5, 0.6] is empirically relevant. In the given context, it is irrelevant for me which one of these probabilities represents the actual proportion of red balls in the urn.

In the permanent-income example, social reality is represented by the way consumers function in the imaginary city of OS: They use their income to pay for consumer goods. I generate a random sample of observations of consumer income and expenditures in OS in accord with the probabilities in table 3.2. The purpose of the sample is to see if Friedman's Permanent Income Hypothesis is empirically relevant in the city of OS.

In section 3.4 the Permanent Income Hypothesis was deemed empirically irrelevant in the lower data universe. In this case, the 95-percent-confidence region around the estimate of the MPD is not data admissible. It contains a congruent econometric model, but it does not contain a data-admissible model of the MPD. From this it follows that the bridge principles are not valid in the Real World, and that there is nothing about the behavior characteristics of the theory variables that one can infer from the empirical analysis. In the upper data universe, the theory was deemed empirically relevant. In this case, the assumption that the value of α is 0 implies that the value of Friedman's marginal propensity to consume, β, is 0.6859. Except for that and the positive analogies mentioned by the Γ_P axioms, the empirical analysis has nothing to say about the behavior characteristics of consumers in OS—the present social reality.

In chapter 8 social reality is the market for Swiss francs, US dollars, and euros during the period for which I have observations of the rates at which the three currencies were exchanged. André Anundsen (in the upper data universe of figure 2.1) and Harald Goldstein (in the lower data universe of figure 2.1) analyzed the same data by different methods. The dynamics of the market for the three exchange rates that Anundsen's statistical analysis establishes are very different from the dynamics of the same market that Goldstein's statistical analysis determines. My theory of a perfectly competitive market for three exchange rates in chapter 8 is deemed empirically irrelevant for the empirical context that Anundsen's analysis creates in the upper data universe. Consequently, the dynamics of the three exchange markets in the upper data universe carry little information about the behavior characteristics of the three exchange rates in social reality. In contrast, my theory is deemed empirically relevant for the empirical context that Goldstein's analysis establishes in the lower data universe. Therefore, the dynamics of the three exchange markets in the lower data universe carry interesting information about the dynamics of foreign exchange in social reality.

Goldstein's estimate of the MPD determines one empirically relevant model of Γ_T. In this model, the y(t) constitute a non-linearly cointegrated second-order random process that is not linearly cointegrated. Now, according to theorem T8.5 in chapter 8, ŷ is linearly cointegrated of order C(2, 2) with cointegrating vector a = $(a_1, a_2, 0)$ if and only if Ẍ , relative to $P_T(\cdot)$, is linearly cointegrated of order C(2, 2) with cointegrating vector a. Also, it follows from theorem T8.3 that Ẍ is linearly cointegrated of order C(2, 2) if and only if there is a pair (a_1, a_2) that satisfies the equation $(a_1, a_2)\varphi$ = 0. It is, therefore interesting that there are empirically relevant models of Γ_T in which the three exchange rates are both linearly and non-linearly cointegrated. Here is an example that I owe to Harald Goldstein.

E10.8
Harald Goldstein has proved that the two matrices

$$\varphi^* = \begin{pmatrix} 0.11002 & 0.22168 \\ 0.93448 & 1.88371 \end{pmatrix} \text{ and }$$

$$\Psi^* = \begin{pmatrix} 0.25218 & 0.17783 \\ 0.81928 & 1.85650 \end{pmatrix}$$

belong to the confidence region D' that we constructed in chapter 8. It is also a fact that the vector a* = (1, –0.11768) approximately satisfies the equation

$$a^*\varphi^* = 0.$$

Hence, there is a data-admissible model of the MPD in which ŷ is both linearly and non-linearly cointegrated in the lower data universe.

In chapter 8 I demonstrated that a data-admissible mathematical model of the MPD and pertinent bridge principles determine one empirically relevant model of Γ_T. By replacing ψ^0 and φ^0 with ψ^* and φ^* in my proof in chapter 8, I can produce an empirically relevant model of Γ_T in which the exchange rates are both linearly and non-linearly cointegrated, and the linear cointegrating vector is (a*,0) This cointegrating vector is very different from the cointegrating vector in the upper data universe.

The empirical relevance of the theory of foreign exchange that I developed in subsection 8.2.2 implies that the positive analogies of foreign exchange that are expressed in the Γ_T axioms and the theorems that one can derive from them are characteristics of foreign exchange in social reality. The fact that there is an empirically relevant model of the axioms in which $\ddot{X}$ is linearly cointegrated implies that there exist in social reality linearly cointegrated efficient markets. That is a novel insight.

Suppose that theory T is deemed empirically irrelevant in both universes. Two examples are the test of the Permanent Income Hypothesis in chapter 5 and the case study of female participation in the labor market in chapter 4. These examples are interesting from several points of view.

In the first example, I use ideas that Frisch developed in his 1934 treatise on confluence analysis to formulate a factor analysis test of the Permanent Income Hypothesis. In this analysis, Friedman's permanent components of income and consumption become so-called systematic variates, and Friedman's transitory components become accidental variates. Both the systematic and the accidental variates are unobservables that live and function in the Real World—in the present case, the data universe. In a commentary on the meaning of confluence analysis, Haavelmo (1950, pp. 262–263) identifies Frisch's systematic variates with his own true variables. In doing that he justifies my placing Frisch's analysis in the upper data universe in figure 2.1. In the upper data universe confluence analysis provides me with an extraordinary example of how different the present-day-econometrics treatment of errors in variables and errors in equations is from the formal-econometrics treatment of inaccurate observations of variables in Frisch's model world.

In the second example, I present a case study in which the empirical relevance of a family of qualitative response models is at stake. Specifically, I confront a Probit family of models with data on female participation in the 1980 US labor force. The theory is rejected in both data universes. This rejection leaves open the possibility that a different family of models might be relevant in the same empirical context and the possibility that the same family of models might be empirically relevant in a different empirical context (e.g., the 2006 US labor force). To illustrate the possibilities, I confronted a different family of qualitative response models with artificially generated data. In the lower data universe, the estimate of MPD was not data admissible. However, the 95-percent-confidence region around the estimate contained both a congruent econometric model and a data-admissible model of the MPD. Hence the theory was deemed empirically relevant in the lower data universe. In the upper data universe, the theory was deemed empirically relevant in the sense that the data did not give the researcher reason to reject the theory's empirical relevance. Since in this case the theory was not intended to delineate positive analogies of social reality, the empirical relevance of the theory carries no information about interesting characteristic features of social reality.

So far I have discussed how differences in the understanding of the essence of an economic theory affect applied econometrics. The example of a scientific explanation in econometrics in chapter 9 adds important new insight to this discussion. In chapter 9 the problem is to give a logically and empirically adequate explanation of a stylized fact that Hall et al. observed in the Treasury Bill market. Heather Anderson's analysis in Stigum 2003 demonstrates that the stylized fact is empirically relevant in the context the TPD determines. My scientific explanation demonstrates that the stylized fact is empirically relevant in the lower data universe too. Here the important thing to notice is that the TPD in the upper data universe and the MPD in the lower data universe share the positive analogies of Treasury Bill behavior that Hall et al. observed. Other characteristics of the TPD may be very different from the salient characteristics of the MPD.

My explanation of HAG's Dictum exemplifies the strictures of an SE2 scientific explanation. It also brings to bear my understanding of the essence of an economic theory. The theory delineates certain characteristics of social reality that an economist has found interesting and nothing else. My explanation explains the whys and wherefores of a stylized fact concerning the US money market and nothing else. The fact that the TPD and the MPD differ exemplifies Bas van Fraassen's interesting remark (1980, p. 98) that whether a theory explains some fact or other is independent of whether the real world as a whole fits the theory.

10.4 Formal Econometrics and Econometric Methodology

I have written this book to provide ideas for meaningful discussions of the use of theory in applied econometrics. For that purpose I have presented case studies that demonstrate the usefulness of the axiomatic method in econometrics and contrast the methodology of present-day econometrics with the methodology of formal econometrics. In the process I have raised serious questions concerning the empirical relevance of standard qualitative response models, and I have questioned the little room that current ways of analyzing cointegrated economic time series leave for economic theory in the empirical analysis.

10.4.1 The Axiomatic Method

The chapters in this book bear witness to the usefulness of the axiomatic method in econometrics. They do so in different ways, depending on the use to which the method is applied. For example, in chapter 2 the path from income in OS in E2.2.1 to a perfectly competitive commodity market in E2.2.9 illustrates how an efficient search for interesting models in applied econometrics can be carried out. In chapter 3, examples from experimental economics, the Permanent Income Hypothesis, and simultaneous equations illustrate how and why the meaning of empirical relevance differs in the two data universes in figure 2.1. In chapters 7 and 8, the axiomatic formulation of a theory-data confrontation illustrates how auxiliary variables can be used to carry out an analysis of positively valued time series with currently available software programs.

10.4.2 The Contrast

Formal econometrics is a name for empirical analyses carried out in accordance with an axiomatized theory-data confrontation. When one looks back at the case studies, it becomes clear that the main differences between the empirical analyses of present-day econometrics and those of formal econometrics originate in the researchers' perceptions of the essence of an economic theory. A present-day econometrician identifies his theory variables with Haavelmo's true variables and carries out his theoretical analyses as well as his empirical analyses in the upper data universe in figure 2.1. He may, but need not, assume that his observations provide accurate measurements of the respective true variables. Whatever he assumes, his assumptions are accounted for in the TPD—the true probability distribution of the data variables.

In formal econometrics, the researcher in charge identifies his theory variables with imaginary matters in Frisch's model world, formulates his theory in a theory universe, and carries out his empirical analysis in the lower data universe in figure 2.1 He uses bridge principles to describe how his theory variables are related to his data variables. These bridge principles may, but need not, claim that the researcher has inaccurate observations of his theory variables. No matter how inaccurate the observations are, the bridge principles and the probability distribution of the theory variables—the RPD—induce a probability distribution of the data variables—the MPD—that may be very different from the TPD.

A present-day econometrician uses the TPD as a basis for statistical analysis and presumes that there is one and only one true model of the TPD and, hence, that each of the parameters of which he obtains estimates has a true value. The inferences about social reality that the econometrician gains from his statistical analysis are the inferences of a mathematical statistician. For example, in a hypothesis test he will claim either that he has no reason or that he has good reasons to reject the empirical relevance of his null hypothesis. If he does not reject the hypothesis, he may claim that his statistical analysis gives him good reasons to believe in the existence in social reality of the positive analogies about which his theory deliberates.

A formal econometrician uses the MPD as a basis for empirical analysis and presumes that the MPD has as many true models as there are models of the RPD and the bridge principles. His parameter estimates, therefore, are estimates of the parameters of any one of the many true models of MPD. To gain information about social reality, he delineates a 95-percent-confidence band around his estimate of the MPD and uses the data-admissible models of the MPD in this confidence band and pertinent bridge principles to determine a set of empirically relevant models of his theory. The information about positive analogies of social reality that the set of empirically relevant models provides constitutes the inference about social reality that the researcher's statistical analysis yields.

10.4.3 Qualitative Response Models and Cointegrated Time Series
In working with the case studies in the book, I have discovered two problematic aspects of current econometric methodology that ought to be discussed. One of them concerns the possible empirical irrelevance of the standard qualitative response models. Such models surface in analyses of situations in which individuals are asked to choose from among a finite set of alternatives; e.g., a high school graduate's choice of whether to enter college or search for a job. Suppose that I have a finite number M of observations of Americans who graduated from high school in June of 2003. My observations tell me whether a student has entered college in the fall of 2003 and what his or her salient socioeconomic characteristics are. My problem is to ascertain how a high school graduate's socioeconomic characteristics influence his or her choice whether or not to enter college. To address that problem, I develop a standard univariate qualitative response model with $k + 1$ variables, $y^* \in \{0, 1\}$ and $x^* \in R^k$, and two equations:

$$\Pr.\{y^* = 1 \mid x^*\} = F(\alpha + \beta x^*) \tag{10.18}$$

and

$$\Pr.\{y^* = 0 \mid x^*\} = 1 - F(\alpha + \beta x^*). \tag{10.19}$$

Here $y^* = 1$ if a graduate has entered college and 0 otherwise. The components of x^* record the graduate's socioeconomic characteristics, $F(\cdot): R \to [0, 1]$ is a cumulative probability distribution function, and $\alpha \in R$ and the components of $\beta \in R^k$ are constants. I assume that I have accurate observations of y^* and x^* and proceed to estimate the values of α and the components of β with the help of LIMDEP 9.0's software program for Probit models. These estimates and the derivatives

$$\partial F(\alpha + \beta x^*)/\partial x^*_i = F'(\alpha + \beta x^*)\beta_i, \quad i = 1, \dots , k \tag{10.20}$$

provide me with answers.

My case studies in chapter 4 give me good reasons to believe that the information I gather from equations 10.20 may be meaningless. Here is why. In the present case, the pair (y^*, x^*) for the United States in 2003 has a well-defined discrete probability distribution, $P(\cdot)$, whose values I can estimate with my data. The probability distribution of the pairs (y^*, x^*) determined by the estimated marginal P-distribution of x^* and the estimated model in equations 10.18 and 10.19 may be very different from $P(\cdot)$. If the latter distribution does not lie within a 95-percent-confidence region around my estimate of $P(\cdot)$, I will deem equations 10.20 meaningless. In subsection 4.2.2 I subjected the Probit model of female participation in the US labor force to such a test; it failed badly.

The second aspect of present-day econometric methodology that I find problematic is the way econometricians analyze cointegrated time series. I detailed my concern in example E6.2.3; I will paraphrase it here: Let $X = \{x(t, \omega); t \in N\}$ be a p-dimensional second-order random process. Suppose that X is an $I(1)$ ARIMA process that satisfies the equation

$$\Sigma_{0 \leq i \leq n} A_i \, x(t - i, \omega) = \eta(t, \omega).$$

with $A_0 = I$ – the p-dimensional identity matrix. Suppose also that $\eta(0) = 0$ and that the family of vector-valued random variables $\{\eta(t, \omega); t \in N - 0\}$ is a purely random process, with mean 0 and finite covariance matrix C with positive diagonal elements, that satisfies the equations $E\{\eta(t) \mid x(0), \dots , x(t - 1)\} = 0$, where $t > 0$. Then there exist matrices, Π and Γ_i, $i = 1\dots , n - 1$, such that the characteristics of X can be expressed with a model of Søren Johansen's fundamental error-correction formula,

$\Delta x(t, \omega) = \Pi x(t - 1, \omega) + \Sigma_{1 \leq i \leq n-1} \Gamma_i \Delta x(t - i, \omega) + \eta(t, \omega).$

Also, X is linearly cointegrated of order C(1, 1) if and only if the rank of Π, r, is positive and less than p. If $0 < r < p$, there exists a pair of p $\times$ r matrices, α and β, of rank r such that $\Pi = \alpha\beta'$ and such that the family of vector-valued random variables $\{\beta'x(t, \omega); t \in N - \{0\}\}$ constitutes a wide-sense stationary process. One example of such a process is the two-dimensional I(1) ARIMA process that I discussed in example E6.2.3 in chapter 6, in which

$\Delta x_1(t, \omega) = \eta_1(t, \omega)$

and

$x_2(t, \omega) - x_1(t - 1, \omega) = \eta_2(t, \omega), t \in N - \{0\}.$

In a model of Johansen's error-correction formula, these two equations take the form

$\Delta x(t, \omega) = (0,1)'(1, -1)x(t - 1, \omega) + \eta(t, \omega), t \in N - \{0\}.$

Consequently, X is cointegrated of order C(1, 1) with cointegrating vector (1, −1). In the present case, why do we insist that x(t) is cointegrated when we equally well could have insisted that $(x_1(t - 1), x_2(t))$ is cointegrated? Figure 6.2 and tables 6.2–6.4 provide reasons for my asking the question. It is true that the cointegrating vector is the same. It is also true that their long-run dynamics are the same. However, their respective error terms—$x_1(t) - x_2(t) = \eta_1(t) - \eta_2(t)$ and $x_2(t) - x_1(t - 1) = \eta_2(t)$—and their short-term dynamics are different. How different the short-term dynamics can be is displayed in figure 6.2 for the present model.

The preceding remarks apply to the two models in equations 10.12 and 10.16 as well. The cointegrating vector of the latter two models is the same, and their long-run dynamics are the same. Also, the differences in the short-run dynamics of the two models in equations 10.12 and 10.16 are as prominent as the differences in the short-run dynamics of the models in equations 10.21–10.23. Tables 7.9, 7.11, and 7.13 and Anundsen's analysis in the appendix to chapter 7 bear witness to that.

I believe that an exclusive use of the error-correction formula to search for cointegrating relations in economic time series is problematic. It may hamper a researcher's ability to draw meaningful statistical inferences about social reality from such data. My discussion in this chapter of Harald Goldstein's and André Anundsen's empirical analyses in chapter 7 gives a good idea of what I have in mind. In that discussion, I used equation 10.16—and not equation 10.12—to infer what Anundsen's results told me about interesting aspects of social reality. Similarly, I used equation 10.17—and not equation 10.14—and the bridge principles to infer what Goldstein's results told me about interesting positive analogies in social reality.

Notes

Chapter 1

1. An axiom system is said to be consistent if it does not harbor contradictory assertions.

2. Here I have adopted John Searle's definition of facts as it appears in his explication of truth in *The Construction of Social Reality* (1995, pp. 211–213).

3. According to Bjerkholt and Dupont-Kieffer (2010, p. 22), Frisch drafted the fundamental idea of the constitution of the Econometric Society and stated that its goal was to "promote studies that aim at the unification of the theoretical-quantitative and empirical-quantitative approach to economic problems and that are penetrated by constructive and rigorous thinking."

4. In Haavelmo's 1944 treatise (p. 7), the *true* variables are variables in the real world with which a researcher identifies his theory variables.

5. Frisch describes his model world on p. 32 of Bjerkholt and Quin 2011. I quote Frisch's description in chapter 2 of this book.

6. There are good reasons for including prices as arguments in the utility function—for example, the idea that the quality of a commodity is judged by its price (Veblen 1912; Scitovsky 1945; and Kalman 1968). The justification given in my 1990 book for having current prices as arguments of $V(\cdot)$ originated in Stigum 1969a. There, as in the 1990 book, I developed a dynamic theory of consumer choice under uncertainty in which the consumer's choice of first-period budget vector was shown to satisfy the conditions of a consumption bundle in a certainty theory with current (and past) prices as arguments of $V(\cdot)$. In my 1990 book this result is stated precisely in theorem T 30.3.

7. The theorems I am referring to here are due to Richard Olshen and Henry McKean. Olshen (1974) established the theorem for integrable exchangeable random processes in Kolmogorov's axiom system. McKean established the theorem for super-exchangeable random processes on a full conditional probability space as it appears in Rényi's probability theory. (See theorem T 18.10 in B. Stigum 1990.)

8. For an application to economics of the view of scientific theories attributed to Balzer et al., see Klein 1998.

9. In table 1.1 I follow Allais in insisting that $P(\cdot)$ be an additive probability measure. In uncertain situations, like the one in E1.3.2, the $P(\cdot)$ of an investor who shades his probabilities is likely to be superadditive. For example, the $P(\cdot)$ of an investor who shades his

probabilities, overvalues low probabilities, and undervalues high probabilities might look like this: $P(\{\omega R\}) = 1/3 + \tau$, $P(\{\omega Y\}) = P(\{\omega B\}) = 1/3 - 3\tau/2$, $P(\{\omega R,\omega Y\}) = P(\{\omega R,\omega B\}) = 2/3 - \tau/2$, and $P(\{\omega Y,\omega B\}) = 2/3 - 3\tau$. (See Shafer 1976 and B. Stigum 1990 pp. 317–330 and 445–455.)

10. I learned of positive and negative analogies from reading Keynes' 1921 treatise on probability.

11. I discussed von Neumann and Morgenstern's theory and the subfamily of models that I put in the Interpretation of Theory box on pages 349–351 of Stigum 1998. Von Neumann and Morgenstern gave a statement and a proof of their fundamental theorem on pages 617–628 of their 1953 book *Theory of Games and Economic Behavior*.

12. For a good example of Allais' work, see Allais 1979.

13. I discussed the axioms of the certainty theory of the firm in microeconomics on pages 224–226 of Stigum 2003. The eighth axiom, N8, imposes conditions on the undefined terms that ensure the existence and uniqueness of the firm's input-output strategy in arbitrarily given price-wage situations.

14. In discussing Keynes' General Theory I have included the price level as one of the theory's undefined terms. That makes sense to me even though Keynes (1936, p. 39) deemed the concept vague and unnecessary. The reasons for the inclusion are given on pages 123–128 of Stigum 2003.

15. It is interesting that chart 2B in Brady and Friedman 1947 lends support to Duesenberry's Relative Income Hypothesis, and it is relevant that in 1990 I tested the empirical relevance of Friedman's theory and of Modigliani and Brumberg's theory (B. Stigum 1990, chapters 26 and 27). Friedman's theory failed the test; Modigliani and Brumberg's passed. On pages 691–693 of my 1990 book I sketched a non-formal explication of the controversy that Keynes' theory caused. I used Friedman's theory for the explanation. The empirical relevance of the explanation hinges on the empirical relevance of that theory.

16. I have in mind Leontief's *The Structure of American Economy, 1919–1929*, Haberler's *Prosperity and Depression* (1937), Tinbergen's *Business Cycles in the United States of America, 1919–1932* (1939), Keynes' critique of Tinbergen's methods (1947), Burns and Mitchell's *Measuring Business Cycles* (1946), Koopmans' "Measurement without Theory" (1947), Wolpin's *Limits of Inference without Theory* (2013), Samuelson's *Foundations of Economic Analysis* (1947), Solow's *Growth Theory: An Exposition* (1970), Allais' many articles on the empirical irrelevance of the expected utility theory (e.g., "The General Theory of Random Choices in Relation to the Invariant Cardinal Utility Function and the Specific Probability Function"), and Debreu's *Theory of Value* (1959).

Chapter 2

1. I owe the idea of a toy economy to a lecture that Robert Solow gave in Oslo on his way back from the 1987 Nobel festivities in Stockholm. However, I am not sure that Solow will accept the way I use his idea here. To me the toys in a toy economy are abstract ideas. They are not the products of some toy factory in social reality.

2. I have listed three conditions for a branch of knowledge to be a science and insisted that economics in 1944 satisfied the first two conditions. For arguments in support of my contention, see pages 8–11 of B. Stigum 1990.

3. Figure 2.1 is a version of figure 1.1 in which I have added details that pertain to the present formal theory-data confrontation and omitted explicit references to the upper and lower data universes.

4. Spanos defines "statistical model" on page 415 of his 1989 paper; he lists sufficient conditions for a statistical model to be "statistically adequate" on page 416. Since I have not insisted that the TPD distribution of y is normal, the error terms in equation 2.10 need not be normally distributed. Hence, there are models of the axioms in which equation 2.10 need not be a statistical model in Spanos' sense of the term. In section 3.5 I will confront a family of models of Γ_T with artificially generated data relative to which the pertinent model of equation 2.10 is a statistically adequate statistical model in Spanos' sense of the term.

5. Here a *structural model* is taken to be a model of equations 2.1. A *structural parameter* is one of the parameters in a model of the first two of those equations.

6. The requirement the researcher's estimates must satisfy in order that they be declared theoretically meaningful sounds daunting, but my empirical analysis in section 3.5 demonstrates that the requirement is reasonable.

7. It is interesting to note that Haavelmo's view of econometrics is reflected in Christophe Bontemps and Grayham Mizon's discussion of data-generating processes and econometric models on pages 355–356 of their 2003 article "Congruence and Encompassing." Haavelmo's view is also adopted in the LSE approach to time-series analysis as described in Mizon's 1995 article "Progressive Modeling of Macroeconomic Time Series: The LSE Methodology."

Chapter 3

1. I have used OxMetrics' PcGive to compute the estimates that I record in tables 3.3–3.5. Detailed information about the meaning of the tables is given on pages 20–23 of the first volume of Doornik and Hendry 2009. Part.R^2 is the squared correlation between the relevant explanatory variable and the dependent variable, with all other variables held fixed. Also, in the tables, asterisks indicate the significance level of tests—one asterisk for $\alpha = 0.05$ and two for $\alpha = 0.01$. For example, the two asterisks in the normality-test line in table 3.4 insist that under the null hypothesis that the error term is normally distributed, the probability that the value of Chi^2(2)—that is, χ^2 with two degrees of freedom—is at least as large as 36.814 is less than 0.01. If there is no asterisk, the null hypothesis cannot be rejected. The value of σ is a measure of the standard deviation of the equation's error term. The hetero test checks whether the variance of the residual error term varies with the values of the explanatory variables of the equation. The RESET23 test is a Regression Specification Test that checks whether the fit can be improved by adding squares and cubes of explanatory variables to the original equation.

2. It is relevant here that the confidence intervals for β_{cy} and β_{yc} are, respectively, [0.471506, 0.5253746] and [1.3483, 1.49774]. From the last interval I obtain the following estimate of a confidence interval for $(1/\beta_{yc})$, [0.66767, 0.74168]. The estimated value of β, 0.6589, satisfies the relation, $0.5253746 < 0.6589 < 0.66767$.

3. The axioms in the present example have models in which prices and quantities of commodities can be negative. In the intended family of models of the axioms prices and quantities of commodities are positive. Figures 3.1 and 3.2 and equation 3.33 show that the intended family of models is not empty.

4. I gave a detailed description of the MPD distribution of y in chapter 2.

5. Here I take a family of models of the theory to be theoretically meaningful if there is a high probability that it contains the true model of the theory. The model of the theory that the estimated simultaneous-equations model determines is theoretically meaningful only if it is a member of a theoretically meaningful family of models of the theory.

6. I have recorded every sixth one of my 600 observations. All the observations of SALESYY were positive. Seven of the observations of PRICEY were negative.

7. Here OLS and FIML are, respectively, acronyms for *ordinary least-squares* and *full-information maximum-likelihood*. An introduction to PcGive's Autometrics is given on pages 71–80 in the first volume of Doornik and Hendry 2009. In the present case the Autometrics analysis ended up estimating the equations for SALESYY and PRICEY with OLS methods.

8. I gave a proof of the "if and only if" claim in this assertion in chapter 2.

9. For details concerning the derivation of H(a, ·) from the utility function that I have assumed to handle the given aggregation problem, see page 734 of B. Stigum 1990.

10. I impose this condition to make sure that the non-negativity of the data variables do not put restrictions on the range of η.

11. To keep my arguments as simple as possible, I ignore the fact that the triples of data variables in equation 3.43 can assume only positive values.

Chapter 4

1. Since the probability distribution of x^* does not appear in equation 4.3, the likelihood function in equation 4.3 is, strictly speaking, a conditional likelihood function. For a discussion of conditional likelihood functions, see pages 55–58 of Hendry and Nielsen 2007.

2. The researcher's equations 4.7 and 4.8 leave no doubt about the relationship between y and y^* and the accuracy of the observed values of y^* and x^*. This fact renders the researcher's models very different from the misclassified dependent-variable models that Aigner (1973), Hausman et al. (1998), and Lewbel (2007) discuss and the misclassified regressor models that Bollinger (1996) and Molinari (2008) analyze. In the kind of situations Aigner, Lewbel, and Hausman et al. consider, a woman in the researcher's latent variable model might have decided to enter the labor force even if $y < 0$. In situations such as those Bollinger and Molinari consider, the socioeconomic variables in the researcher's qualitative response model might have been misclassified.

3. I learned of the relevance of this remark from Erik Bioern.

4. I have borrowed the data from David Hendry and Bent Nielsen. For a description of the data, see page xi of Hendry and Nielsen 2007.

5. I have added the condition $\alpha \leq 0$ and $\alpha + \beta x > 0$ for some $x \in Q$ to the researcher's latent-variable model in subsection 4.1.2. In sections 4.2 and 4.3, that condition will help me contrast the empirical analysis in the lower data universe in figure 4.1 with the empirical analysis in the upper data universe.

6. An important caveat: Suppose that the standard statistical confidence region around the researcher's estimates of the parameters in equations 4.11 and 4.12 contains values of α and β that do not heed the restrictions that A3 imposes on them. The "appropriate"

confidence region will exclude such values of α and β. The researcher is asked to reject his estimates if the appropriate statistical confidence region does not contain any values of α and β that satisfy A3.

7. Here I have used the fact that

$$[\Phi(-\alpha^0 - \beta^0 v_j)p_j^0, (1 - \Phi(-\alpha^0 - \beta^0 v_j))p_j^0] = [(1 - \Phi(\alpha^0 + \beta^0 v_j))p_j^0, \Phi(\alpha^0 + \beta^0 v_j)p_j^0].$$

8. To have room enough for all the numbers in tables 4.2 and 4.5, I have dropped the last three digits.

9. Here I have added the condition $\alpha \leq 0$ and $\alpha + \beta x > 0$ for some $x \in Q$ to the researcher's standard qualitative response model in section 4.1. I imposed the same condition on the researcher's latent variable model.

10. Here, in line with standard tests of hypothesis, I insist that all the members of the confidence region around the maximum-likelihood estimates of α and β satisfy the condition $\alpha \leq 0$ and $\alpha + \beta x > 0$ for some $x \in Q$. In the case of the MPD, I included in the appropriate confidence region only those vectors that satisfy these inequality conditions.

Chapter 5

1. The original version of the present test of Friedman's Permanent Income Hypothesis was published on pages 679–700 of B. Stigum 1990. A short version of the test was published on pages 445–455 of Stigum 2003.

2. My deliberations in this section present the certainty version of Friedman's Permanent Income Hypothesis. To account for uncertainty, Friedman (1957, pp.15–16) suggested that it was sufficient to add a component to the argument of $k(\cdot)$ that constituted a measure of the ratio of a consumer's non-human wealth to his permanent income. On pages 700–719 of my 1990 book I develop a test of the uncertainty version of Friedman's hypothesis.

3. Strictly speaking, the assumption that the covariance of y_t and c_p relative to $P(\cdot \mid \Omega(g))$ is 0 is unnecessary, since it follows from APIH4 and the assumed orthogonality of y_t and y_p relative to $P(\cdot \mid \Omega(g))$. I have added the assumption in order to delineate properties of the MPD that are independent of the conditions that I stipulate in APIH4.

4. I sketch some of the mathematical details that underlie my factor-analysis test of Friedman's hypothesis on pages 687–691 and 694–697 of my 1990 book.

5. To derive the asymptotic probability distribution of my parameter estimates, I added the following assumption to the three axioms concerning the FRB sampling scheme in my 1990 book: As the number N of observations tends to ∞, for $i = 1, \ldots, 9$, and $g \in G$,

$$\lim_{n \to \infty} n^{1/2}(n(I_i \cap \Omega(g))/n - P[I_i \mid \Omega(g)]) = 0.$$

6. Strictly speaking, the confidence region determined by Wald's 95-percent-confidence limits is not an optimal choice. However, it is good enough for testing the empirical relevance of Friedman's PIH.

7. Here it is relevant that the estimates of both β and φ are positive and significantly different from 0. In table 4.7, $\Phi = (\sigma^2(y_p \mid g)/(\sigma^2(y_p \mid g) + \sigma^2(y_t \mid g))$ and $\varphi = \Phi \cdot b_{3f}$. I use the latter equality and the pertinent entries in the b_{3f} column in table 4.7 to claim that φ is positive and significantly different from 0.

8. Haavelmo's observations support my use of Frisch's ideas to exemplify the kind of empirical analysis that my first scenario in chapter 2 envisions.

Chapter 6

1. The probabilities that the researcher assigns to observing values of a consumer's disposable income differ from the true probabilities that I recorded in E6.2.1. The probabilities of y in E6.2.1 are TPD probabilities, whereas the researcher's E6.2.2 probabilities of y are MPD probabilities.

2. The ARIMA processes received their name in Box and Jenkins 1970.

3. I owe the condition $\Sigma_{0 \leq s < \infty} b_s \neq 0$ to Søren Johansen.

4. For a discussion of the short-run and long-run behavior of ARIMA processes, see B. Stigum 1975 and 1990.

5. I owe the idea of this example to Anindya Banerjee et al. (1993, p. 156).

6. The following discussion originated when Neil Ericsson pointed out to me that my time series of $x_1(t) - x_2(t)$—that is, of Spot(t) – Forward(t)—has a break at 2003w26.

7. It is relevant in the present context that the cointegrating vector in equation 6.10 is the same as the cointegrating vector in equation 6.11. The cointegrating vector of a theoretically meaningful cointegrating relationship will lie in the cointegrating space which the pertinent error correction formula determines. I owe this observation to Ragnar Nymoen and Søren Johansen.

Chapter 7

1. I learned of the relevance of UIP and CIP in this context from chapter 1 of Sarno and Taylor 2002.

2. Sarno and Taylor (2002, p. 35) established the validity of my equation 7.7 in their discussion of log-normally distributed variables.

3. Because of a missing forward rate, we changed one Wednesday to a Thursday.

4. This is a short version of Goldstein's analysis in Goldstein and Stigum 2009a.

5. Goldstein's bootstrap experiment is described in detail in Goldstein and Stigum 2009a.

6. Table 7.1 reports results from ADF tests for the order of integration of the US dollar–Swiss franc spot and forward rates. The optimal lag truncation was decided on the basis of the Akaike information criterion. Δ denotes the difference operator. The sample is 2001w28–2005w3.

7. Table 7.2 shows results from tests for lag reduction of the linear bivariate VAR for the sample 2001w23–2005w3. AIC is the Akaike Information Criterion. SC is the Schwartz criterion. Log.Lik. denotes the value of the log-likelihood. For the consecutive F tests, the numbers in brackets are p values.

8. Table 7.3 reports the results when we test for cointegration between the US dollar–Swiss franc spot and forward rates over the sample 2001w23–2005w3. A deterministic trend is restricted to enter the cointegration space, whereas a constant enters

unrestrictedly. In addition to reporting the eigenvalues, the table reports the p value of the asymptotic and small-sample-adjusted trace test. For the diagnostic tests, the numbers in brackets are p values.

9. Table 7.4 reports long-run coefficient estimates and tests for over-identifying restrictions of the cointegrating vector for the sample period, 2001w23–2005w3. The first panel shows the estimated cointegrating vector and loading factors when we normalize the cointegrating vector with respect to the spot exchange rate. In panel 2, we test whether the spot and one-week-forward rate are co-trending. Panel 3 shows the results when weak exogeneity of the one-week-forward rate is imposed. Panel 4 shows the results when we impose a unitary coefficient on the forward rate. The numbers appearing below the point estimates are absolute standard errors, and p values are reported in brackets after the test statistics for the likelihood ratio tests for over-identifying restrictions.

10. Goldstein carried out his analysis of spot and forward exchange rates with mean adjusted observations. With mean adjusted data and Anundsen's arguments one ends up with a VECM without the constants, with αSpot = −0.966389, and with the standard deviation of αSpot equal to 0.07259.

11. We are grateful to Neil Ericsson for suggesting that we consider a subsample analysis of this kind.

12. I have tried and failed to invent a meaningful bootstrap experiment for the probability distribution of φ.

13. Anundsen wants me to add that the views of the foreign-exchange market that he presents in his empirical analysis are his own and not the views of the Bank of Norway.

Chapter 8

1. Good references are Allen 2003 for one-, two-, and three-dimensional random walks, Goldstein and Stigum 2009 for generalized random walks, and the data we analyze in section 6.3 for non-linearly cointegrated economic time series. Here a generalized random walk is taken to be a random walk with an innovation process whose members are moving averages of orthogonal second-order random variables that need not be independently and identically distributed.

2. Good examples are the test statistics developed by Breitung (2001), Karlsen et al. (2005), and Choi and Saikkonen (2008).

3. Chapter 23 of Stigum 2003 contains a good example of the kind of scientific explanation that I have in mind. There Anderson et al. give a scientific explanation of why observations of Treasury Bill yields in the United States. Money market are linearly cointegrated with ten cointegrating vectors: $(-1, 1, 0, \ldots, 0)$, $(-1, 0, 1, \ldots, 0)$, $\ldots$, $(-1, 0, \ldots, 0, 1)$.

4. For example, Juan-Carlos Escanciano and Alvaro Escribano, in their interesting 2007 survey article on non-linear cointegration, insist that an I(0) process is a short memory in the mean covariance stationary process with positive and bounded spectral density. Moreover, an I(d) process, with d a positive integer, is a second-order process, X, whose d^{th} difference series, $\Delta^d X$, is an I(0) process. Aparicio Acosta et al. (2002) suggest an interesting variant of Granger's E1.3 definition of I(0) and I(1) processes. Specifically,

they insist that a second-order process, X, is short-memory if $\lim_{T \to \infty} \Sigma_{0 \le h \le T} |\text{cov}(x_t, x_{th})|$ is finite. X is long-memory if the given limit is infinite, and X is an I(d) process if it is long-memory and d is the smallest real number such that $\Delta^d X$ is short-memory. Here d need not be an integer. In E1.2 and in the present paragraph, I take a second-order process to be long-memory in the mean if and only if it is not short-memory in the mean.

5. Inasmuch as there is no stipulated upper bound on the finite means of a second-order process, c_t, $t \in N$—the sequence of constants that characterize a degenerate process—may be all alike, bounded, or unbounded.

6. I owe these two examples to Harald Goldstein.

7. Myklebust et al. (2002, pp. 98–102 and 107–109) insist that two generalized integrated Markov processes (GI(1)), X and Y, are f-cointegrated if $\{f(x_t, y_t); t \in N\}$ is stationary. One of the models of $f(\cdot)$ that they mention is $f(x, y) = x/y$, $y > 0$.

8. For an authoritative account of linearly and polynomially cointegrated processes, see chapters 3 and 4 of Johansen 1995. For a formal discussion of polynomially integrated processes and related error-correction models, see Gregoir and Laroque 1993.

9. This is a short version of the analysis presented in Goldstein and Stigum 2009b.

10. We owe these conditions to Timo Terasvirta. Their relevance is discussed at length in Nakatani and Terasvirta 2008.

11. Bollerslev, Chou, and Kroner (1992, p. 17) mention several studies that have found the constancy of s to be a reasonable empirical working hypothesis.

12. In an earlier version of his analysis (Goldstein and Stigum 2009b), Goldstein observes that estimates of pertinent parameters need not be identified. For example, when $\varphi = \psi$, which we call the COMFAC hypothesis, neither Φ nor Ψ, and therefore neither φ nor ψ, is identified. Also, if a row in the ARCH matrix A is 0, then the corresponding row in the GARCH matrix B will be unidentified, as will the corresponding constant w term—at least in terms of the approximating stationary and ergodic process. To judge from table 8.1, the first possibility is of no concern to us. However, the estimated values of the components of A and B are disconcerting. To check whether the estimates are as expected, Goldstein carried out a profile log-likelihood analysis of his estimates and concluded that there probably is no GARCH effect present in the $z_2(t)$ series, and that there does not seem to be evidence in the data for the presence of volatility effects in the $z_2(t)$ series. The latter is in accord with the results reported in table 8.1.

13. The choice of a 95-percent-confidence band here is in accord with the way we delineate the intended family of data-admissible mathematical models of the MPD, IM_{MPD}, in our empirical analysis in subsection 7.3.3.

14. For a discussion of the existence of fourth-order moments in GARCH(2,2) and GARCH(1,1) models, see He and Terasvirta 2004.

15. In an earlier draft of Goldstein and Stigum 2009b, Goldstein proved the consistency of his parameter estimates under the assumption that his likelihood function had only one maximum. Under the same assumption, he also established the asymptotic normality of the estimates.

16. There is a snag in the argument we used to show that a pair (φ, ψ) in a COMPAC solution to equation 8.62, in which $\varphi = \psi$ belongs to D'. If $\varphi = \psi$, then φ and φ are not identified. The asymptotic distribution behind D' may not be justified under the COMFAC

hypothesis for lack of identification. We take a somewhat simplified approach to this problem, however, by arguing that, formally, there are values of (φ, ψ) in D' arbitrarily close to the COMFAC without being exactly COMFAC (thus ignoring the potential problem that the asymptotic distribution may be a poor approximation for parameters near the COMFAC solution). On that basis, we can then still insist that all (φ, ψ) such that $\varphi = \psi$ be incorporated in the set D.

17. Table 8.4 reports results from ADF tests for the order of integration of the franc–euro (E1) and euro–dollar spot exchange rates (E2). The optimal lag truncation was decided on the basis of the Akaike Information Criterion. Because of the allowance for a maximum lag length of 8 in the first differences of the tests, the sample starts in 1999w11, although we have data from 1999w1.

18. Table 8.5 summarizes the residual diagnostics of a bivariate fifth-order VAR when it is estimated on the sample 1999w6–2006w36.

19. Table 8.6 gives results from tests for lag reduction of the linear bivariate VAR for the sample 1999w6–2006w36. AIC is the Akaike Information Criterion. SC is the Schwartz criterion. Log.Lik. denotes the value of the log-likelihood. For the consecutive F tests, the numbers in brackets are p values.

20. Table 8.7 reports the results when we test for cointegration between the franc–euro exchange rate and the euro–dollar exchange rate. A deterministic trend is restricted to enter the cointegration space, whereas a constant and the dummies enter unrestrictedly. In addition to reporting the eigenvalues, the table reports the p value of the asymptotic and small-sample-adjusted trace test. For the diagnostic tests, the numbers in brackets are p values.

21. Table 8.8 reports long-run coefficient estimates and tests for over-identifying restrictions of the cointegrating vector. The first panel shows the estimated cointegrating vector and loading factors when we normalize the cointegrating vector with respect to the franc–euro exchange rate. The second panel shows the results when weak exogeneity of the euro–dollar exchange rate is imposed.

22. Table 8.9 reports the results obtained when we estimate the conditional equilibrium correction model in equation 8.44 by OLS. Autometrics is used to reduce the dimensionality of the model. A constant and the levels variables are restricted to enter the final model.

23. Anundsen wants me to add that the views of the foreign-exchange market that he presents in his empirical analysis are his own and not the views of the Bank of Norway.

Chapter 9

1. Originally, Hempel (1965, p. 248) insisted that "sentences constituting the explanans must be true."

2. For an interesting account of the applicability of Hempel's DNS in the social sciences, see M.H. Salmon 1989.

3. The ideas for this example come from pages 595–598 of Stigum 1995.

4. Allais used his experiments to advance his own theory of choice under uncertainty. In chapter 18 of Stigum 2003 the interested reader can find two formal versions of Allais'

theory and a formal theory-data confrontation in which the empirical relevance of Allais' theory is tested against the empirical relevance of the expected-utility theory. I discuss a model-theoretic formulation of Allais' theory in section 1.3 of the present volume.

5. In this context Marcia Stigum's penetrating account of the US money market is relevant. (See M. Stigum 1990.)

Chapter 10

1. For a discussion of the first-order predicate calculus, see chapter 20 of Stigum 2003.

2. "The Real World" is the name of a possible world that plays a central role in a given situation; e.g., an exchange market during a specified period of time or the consumers in an imaginary city.

3. Here the Real World may be the group of students from which I have drawn my subject.

4. These estimates are taken from the "All" line in table 28.1 of B. Stigum 1990.

5. An interesting aspect of this example that should not go unnoticed is that the dynamics of the exchange market in the two universes are very different. I have not been able to demonstrate that the I_{IMP}—the pertinent confidence band around Goldstein's estimates—is data admissible. Hence I cannot claim that my bridge principles in the present example are valid in the Real World.

References

Aasnes, J., E. Bjoern, and T. Skjerpen. 1993. Engel Functions, Panel Data, and Latent Variables. *Econometrica* 61: 1305–1422.

Aigner, D. J. 1973. Regression with a Binary Variable Subject to Errors of Observation. *Journal of Econometrics* 1: 49–60.

Aldrich, J. 1989. Autonomy. *Oxford Economic Papers* 41: 15–34.

Allais, M. 1979. The So-Called Allais Paradox and Rational Decisions under Uncertainty. In *Expected Utility Hypotheses and the Allais Paradox*, ed. M. Allais and O. Hagen. Reidel.

Allais, M. 1988. The General Theory of Random Choice in Relation to the Cardinal Utility Function and the Specific Probability Function. The (U,θ) Model. A General Overview. In *Risk, Decision, and Rationality*, ed. B. R. Munier. Reidel.

Anderson, H. M. 1999. Explanation of an Empirical Puzzle: What Can Be Learned from a Test of the Rational Expectations Hypothesis? *Journal of Economic Methodology* 6: 31–59.

Anderson, H. M. 2003. Explanation of an Empirical Puzzle: What Can Be Learned from a Test of the Rational Expectations Hypothesis? In B. P. Stigum, *Econometrics and the Philosophy of Economics*. Princeton University Press.

Anderson, T. W. 2003. *An Introduction to Multivariate Statistical Analysis*, third edition. Wiley.

Anderson, T. W., and H. Rubin. 1956. Statistical Inference in Factor Analysis. In *Proceedings of the Third Berkeley Symposium on Mathematical Statistics and Probability*, ed. J. Neyman. University of California Press.

Aparicio Acosta, F. M., M. A. Arranz, and A. Escribano. 2002 A Model-Free Cointegration Approach for Pairs of I(d) Variables. Working paper, Department of Statistics and Econometrics, Universidad Carlos III de Madrid.

Arrow, K. J. 1965. *Aspects of the Theory of Risk-Bearing*. Yrjö Jahnssonin Säätiö.

Balzer, W., C. U. Moulines, and J. Sneed. 1987. *An Architecture for Science: The Structuralist Program*. Reidel.

Banerjee, A., J. J. Dolado, J. W. Galbraith, and D. Hendry. 1993. *Co-integration, Error Correction, and the Econometric Analysis of Non-Stationary Data*. Oxford University Press.

Berger, P. L., and T. Luckmann. 1966. *The Social Construction of Reality*. Anchor.

Bjerkholt, O., and A. Dupont-Kieffer, eds. 2009. *Problems and Methods of Econometrics: The Poincaré Lectures of Ragnar Frisch, 1933*. Routledge.

Bjerkholt, O., and A. Dupont-Kieffer. 2010. Ragnar Frisch's Conception of Econometrics. *History of Political Economy* 42: 21–73.

Bjerkholt, O., and D. Qin, eds. 2010. *A Dynamic Approach to Economic Theory: The Yale Lectures of Ragnar Frisch, 1930*. Routledge.

Bollerslev, T. 1990. Modelling the Coherence in Short-Run Nominal Exchange Rates: A Multivariate Generalized ARCH Approach. *Review of Economics and Statistics* 72: 498–505.

Bollinger, C. R. 1996. Bounding Mean Regressions When a Binary Regressor Is Mismeasured. *Journal of Econometrics* 73: 387–399.

Bontemps, C., and G. E. Mizon. 2003. Congruence and Encompassing. In B. P. Stigum, *Econometrics and the Philosophy of Economics: Theory-Data Confrontations in Economics*. Princeton University Press.

Bontemps, C., and G. E. Mizon. 2008. Encompassing: Concepts and Implementation. *Oxford Bulletin of Economics and Statistics* 70, Supplement s1: 721–750.

Box, G. E. P., and G. M. Jenkins. 1970. *Time Series Analysis: Forecasting and Control*. Holden-Day.

Brady, D. S., and R. D. Friedman. 1947. Savings and the Income Distribution. In *Studies in Income and Wealth*. National Bureau of Economic Research.

Breitung, J. 2001. Rank Tests for Nonlinear Cointegration. *Journal of Business and Economic Statistics* 19: 331–340.

Brockwell, P. J., and R. A. Davis. 1987. *Time Series: Theory and Methods*. Springer.

Burns, A. F., and W. C. Mitchell. 1946, *Measuring Business Cycles*. National Bureau of Economic Research.

Cagan, P. 1956. The Monetary Dynamics of Hyperinflation. In *Studies in the Quantity Theory of Money*, ed. M. Friedman. University of Chicago Press.

Carnap, R. 1956. *Meaning and Necessity*, second edition. University of Chicago Press.

Cartwright, N. 1989. *Nature's Capacities and Their Measurement*. Oxford University Press.

Castle, J. L., J. A. Doornik, and D. F. Hendry. 2012. Model Selection When There Are Multiple Breaks. *Journal of Econometrics* 169, no. 2: 239–246.

Choi, I., and P. Saikkonen. 2008. Tests for Nonlinear Cointegration. Working paper, University of Helsinki.

Cootner, P. H. 1964. *The Random Character of Stock Market Prices*. MIT Press.

Cramér, H. 194. *Mathematical Methods of Statistics*. Princeton University Press.

Dale-Olsen, H. 1994. Produksjon I busstransportsektoren. Department of Economics, University of Oslo.

Davidson, R., and J. G. MacKinnon. 1993. *Estimation and Inference in Econometrics*. Oxford University Press.

Davison, A. C., and D. V. Hinkley. 1997. *Bootstrap Methods and Their Applications*. Cambridge University Press.

Debreu, G. 1959. *Theory of Value*. Wiley.

Dhrymes, P. J. 1986. Limited Dependent Variables. In *Handbook of Econometrics*, volume 3, ed. Z. Griliches and M. D. Intriligator. North-Holland.

Dickey, D. A., and W. A. Fuller. 1979. Distribution of the Estimators for Autoregressive Time Series with a Unit Root. *Journal of the American Statistical Association* 74, no. 366: 427–431.

Doornik, J. A. 2009. Autometrics. In *The Methodology and Practice of Econometrics*, ed. J. L. Castle and N. Shepard. Oxford University Press.

Doornik, J. A., and D. E. Hendry. 2009. *Econometric Modelling, PcGive 13*. Timberlake Consultants.

Duesenberry, J. S. 1949. *Income, Saving, and the Theory of Consumer Behavior*. Harvard University Press.

Dufrênot, G., and V. Mignon. 2002. *Nonlinear Cointegration with Applications to Macroeconomics and Finance*. Kluwer.

Duhem, P. 1981. *The Aim and Structure of Physical Theory*. Atheneum.

Dunford, N., and J. T. Schwartz. 1957. *Linear Operators, Part I: General Theory*. Interscience.

Efron, B. 1982. *The Jackknife, the Bootstrap, and Other Resampling Plans*. Society for Industrial and Applied Mathematics.

Ellsberg, D. 1961. Risk, Ambiguity, and the Savage Axioms. *Quarterly Journal of Economics* 75, no. 4: 643–669.

Engel, E. 1857. Die Productions- und Consumtionsverhältnisse des Königreichs Sachsen. *Zeitschrift des statistischen Bureaus des Königlich Sächsischen Ministerium des Inneren* 8–9: 28–29.

Engle, R. F., and C. W. J. Granger. 1987. Co-integration and Error Correction: Representation, Estimation and Testing. *Econometrica* 55: 251–276.

Ericsson, N. R., and J. G. MacKinnon. 2002. Distributions of Error Correction Tests for Cointegration. *Econometrics Journal* 5: 285–318.

Ericsson, N. R., and E. L. Reisman. 2012. Evaluating a Global Vector Autoregression for Forecasting. *International Advances in Economic Research* 18: 247–258.

Escanciano, J. C., and A. Escribano. 2009. Econometrics: Nonlinear Cointegration. In *Encyclopedia of Complexity and Systems Science*. Springer.

Feller, W. 1957. *An Introduction to Probability Theory and Its Applications*, second edition, volume 1. Wiley.

Feller, W. 1966. *An Introduction to Probability Theory and Its Applications*, volume 2. Wiley.

Fellner, W. 1961. Distortion of Subjective Probabilities as a Reaction to Uncertainty. *Quarterly Journal of Economics* 75: 670–689.

Ferber, R. 1965. The Reliability of Consumer Surveys of Financial Holdings: Time Deposits. *Journal of the American Statistical Association*, March: 148–163.

Ferber, R. 1966. The Reliability of Consumer Surveys of Financial Holdings: Demand Deposits. *Journal of the American Statistical Association*, March: 91–103.

Florence, J. P., D. F. Hendry, and J. F. Richard. 1996. Encompassing and Specificity. *Econometric Theory* 12: 620–656.

Friedman, M. 1953. The Methodology of Positive Economics. In Friedman, *Essays in Positive Economics*. University of Chicago Press.

Friedman, M. 1957. *A Theory of the Consumption Function*. Princeton University Press.

Frisch, R. 1926. Kvantitativ formulering av den teoretiske økonomikks lover. *Statsøkonomisk Tidsskrift* 40: 299–334.

Frisch, R. 1929. Correlation and Scatter in Statistical Variables. *Nordic Statistical Journal* 1: 36–102.

Frisch, R. 1933. Propagation Problems and Impulse Problems in Dynamic Economics. In *Economic Essays in Honour of Gustav Cassel*. Allen and Unwin.

Frisch, R. 1934. *Statistical Confluence Analysis by Means of Complete Regression Systems*. Universitetets Økonomiske Institutt, Oslo.

Goldstein, H. E. 2003. On the COLS and CGMM Estimation Methods for Frontier Production Functions. In B. Stigum, *Econometrics and the Philosophy of Economics*. Princeton University Press.

Goldstein, H. E., and B. P. Stigum. 2009a. Methodological Problems in Analysing the Dynamics of Foreign Exchange. Department of Economics, University of Oslo.

Goldstein, H. E., and B. P. Stigum. 2009b. Nonlinear Cointegration in Foreign Exchange. Department of Economics, University of Oslo.

Gourieroux, C. 2000. *Econometrics of Qualitative Dependent Variables*. Cambridge University Press.

Gourieroux, C., A. Montfort, and A. Trognon. 1983. Testing Nested and Non-Nested Hypotheses. *Journal of Econometrics* 21: 83.

Granger, C. W. J. 1981. Some Properties of Time Series Data and Their Use in Econometric Model Specification. *Journal of Econometrics* 16: 121–130.

Granger, C. W. J. 1991. Some Recent Generalizations of Cointegration and the Analysis of Long-Run Relationships. In *Long-Run Economic Relationships*, ed. R. F. Engle and C. W. J. Granger. Oxford University Press.

Granger, C. W. J. 1995. Modeling Nonlinear Relationships between Extended-Memory Variables. *Econometrica* 63: 265–279.

Greene, W. H. 1997. *Econometric Analysis*, third edition. Prentice-Hall.

Greene, W. H. 2003. *Econometric Analysis*, fifth edition. Pearson.

Greene, W. H. 2007. LIMDEP Version 9.0. Econometric Software.

Gregoir, S., and G. Laroque. 1993. Multivariate Integrated Time Series: A Polynomial Error Correction Representation Theorem. *Econometric Theory* 9: 329–342.

Haavelmo, T. 1943 The Statistical Implications of a System of Simultaneous Equations. *Econometrica* 11: 1–12.

Haavelmo, T. 1944. The Probability Approach in Econometrics. *Econometrica* 12, supplement: 1–115.

Haavelmo, T. 1947b. Methods of Measuring the Marginal Propensity to Consume. *Journal of the American Statistical Association* 4, no. 237: 105–122.

Haavelmo, T. 1950. Remarks on Frisch's Confluence Analysis and Its Use in Econometrics. In *Statistical Inference in Dynamic Economic Models*, ed. T. C. Koopmans. Wiley.

Haavelmo, T., and M. A. Girshick. 1947. Statistical Analysis of the Demand for Food: Examples of Simultaneous Estimation of Structural Equations. *Econometrica* 15: 79–110.

Haberler, G. v. 1937. *Prosperity and Depression*. League of Nations.

Hall, A. D., H. M. Anderson, and C. W. J. Granger. 1992. A Cointegration Analysis of Treasury Bill Yields. *Review of Economics and Statistics* 74: 116–125.

Harvey, A. C. 1989. *Structural Time Series Models and the Kalman Filter*. Cambridge University Press.

Hausman, J. A., J. Abrevaya, and F. M. Scott-Morton. 1998. Misclassification of the Dependent Variable in a Discrete-Response Setting. *Journal of Econometrics* 87: 239–269.

He, C., and T. Terasvirta. 2004. An Extended Constant Conditional Correlation GARCH Model and Its Fourth-Moment Structure. *Econometric Theory* 20: 904–926.

Heckmann, J. J. 2001. Micro Data, Heterogeneity, and the Evaluation of Public Policy: Nobel Lecture. *Journal of Political Economy* 109: 673–748.

Hempel, C. G. 1965. *Aspects of Scientific Explanation and Other Essays in the Philosophy of Science*. Free Press.

Hendry, D. F. 1995. *Dynamic Econometrics*. Oxford University Press.

Hendry, D. F., and J. Doornik. 2009. *Empirical Econometric Modelling Using PcGive*, volume I. Timberlake.

Hendry, D. F., and H.-M. Krolzig. 2003. New Developments in Automatic General-to-Specific Modeling. In B. P. Stigum, *Econometrics and the Philosophy of Economics*. Princeton University Press.

Hendry, D. F., and B. Nielsen. 2007. *Econometric Modeling*. Princeton University Press.

Hendry, D. F., and J. F. Richard. 1989. Recent Developments in the Theory of Encompassing. In *Contributions to Operations Research and Economics: The XXth Aniversary of CORE*, ed. B. Cornet and H. Tulkens. MIT Press.

Hendry, D. F., S. Johansen, and C. Santos 2008. Automatic Selection of Indicators in a Fully Saturated Regression. *Computational Statistics* 33: 317–335.

Hoover, K. D. 2010. Worlds Apart? A Review of Bernt P. Stigum's *Econometrics and the Philosophy of Economics: Theory-Data Confrontations in Economics*. *Research in the History of Economic Thought and Methodology* 28A: 299–305.

Joereskog, K. G., and D. Soerbom. 1978. Liserel IV, Analysis of Linear Structural Relationships by the Method of Maximum Likelihood. Department of Statistics, University of Uppsala.

Johansen, S. 1988a. The Mathematical Structure of Error Correction Models. *Contemporary Mathematics* 80: 359–386.

Johansen, S. 1988b. Statistical Analysis of Cointegration Vectors. *Journal of Economic Dynamics and Control* 12: 231–254.

Johansen, S. 1992. A Representation of Vector Autoregressive Processes Integrated of Order 2. *Econometrica* 80: 188–202.

Johansen, S. 1994. Testing Weak Exogeneity and the Order of Cointegration in U.K. Money Demand Data. In *Testing Exogeneity*, ed. N. R. Ericsson and J. S. Irons. Oxford University Press.

Johansen, S. 1995. *Likelihood-Based Inference in Cointegrated Vector Autoregressive Models*. Oxford University Press.

Johansen, S., and B. Nielsen. 2009. An Analysis of the Indicator Saturation Estimator as a Robust Regression Estimator. In *The Methodology and Practice of Econometrics*, ed. J. L. Castle and N. Shepard. Oxford University Press.

Juselius, K. 2006. *The Cointegrated VAR Model: Methodology and Application*. Oxford University Press.

Kallenberg, O. 1997. *Foundations of Modern Probability*. Springer.

Kalman, P. J. 1968. Theory of Consumer Behavior When Prices Enter the Utility Function. *Econometrica* 36: 497–510.

Kant, I. 1781. *Critique of Pure Reason*. Doubleday, 1966.

Keynes, J. M. 1921. *A Treatise on Probability*. Macmillan.

Keynes, J. M. 1936. *General Theory of Employment, Interest and Money*. Harcourt Brace.

Keynes, J. M. 1939. Professor Tinbergen's Method. *Economic Journal* 49: 558–568.

Keynes, J. M. 1973. "Letter to Roy Harrod, July 4," In *Collected Writings of John Maynard Keynes*, volume 14. ed. D. Moggridge. Macmillan.

Klein, E. 1998. *Economic Theories and Their Relational Structures: A Model-Theoretic Characterization*. Harcourt Brace.

Knorr Cetina, K. D. 1981. *The Manufacture of Knowledge*. Pergamon.

Kolmogorov, A. 1933. *Grundbegriffe der Wahrscheinlichkeitsrechnung*. Chelsea.

Koopmans, T. C. 1947. Measurement without Theory. *Review of Economics and Statistics* 29, no. 3: 161–172.

Kripke, S. A. 1963. Semantical Analysis of Modal Logic. *Zeitschrift für Mathematische Logik und Grundlagen der Mathematik* 9: 67–96.

Kripke, S. A. 1971. Semantical Considerations of Modal Logic. In *Reference and Modality*, ed. L. Linsky. Oxford University Press.

Kuznets, S. 1952. Proportion of Capital Formation to National Product. *American Economic Review* 42: 507–526.

Lansing, J. B., G. P. Ginsburg, and K. Braaten. 1961. *An Investigation of Response Error*. Bureau of Economic and Business Research, University of Illinois.

Lawley, D. N., and A. E. Maxwell. 1971. *Factor Analysis as a Statistical Method*. American Elsevier.

Leamer, E. E. 1984. *Sources of International Comparative Advantage*. MIT Press.

Lehmann, E. L. 1986. *Testing Statistical Hypotheses*, second edition. Wiley.

Leontief, W. W. 1941. *The Structure of American Economy, 1919–1929*. Harvard University Press.

Leontief, W. W. 1953. Domestic Production and Foreign Trade: The American Capital Position Re-examined. *Proceedings of the American Philosophical Society* 107: 332–349.

Lewbel, A. 2007. Estimation of Average Treatment Effects with Misclassification. *Econometrica* 75: 537–551.

Lewis, D. 1973. *Counterfactuals*. Blackwell.

Ling, S., and M. McAleer. 2003. Asymptotic Theory for a Vector ARMA-GARCH model. *Econometric Theory* 19: 280–310.

Luce, R. D., and P. Suppes. 1965. Preference, Utility, and Subjective Probability. In *Handbook of Mathematical Psychology*, ed. R. D. Luce, R. R. Bush, and E. Galanter. Wiley.

Luetkepohl, H. 1993. *Introduction to Multiple Time Series Analysis*. Springer.

McFadden, D. L. 1984. Econometric Analysis of Qualitative Response Model. In *Handbook of Econometrics*, volume 2, ed. Z. Griliches and M. D. Intriligator. North-Holland.

Mill, J. S. 1836. On the Definition of Political Economy. Reprinted in *The Collected Works of John Stuart Mill*, volume IV: *Essays on Economics and Society*, ed. J. M. Robson. University of Toronto Press, 1967.

Mill, J. S. 1843. On the Ground of Induction. In *A System of Logic Ratiocinative and Inductive, Collected Works of John Stuart Mill*, volume 7, ed. J. M. Roberts. University of Toronto Press. reprinted in 1973

Mincer, J. 1974. *Schooling, Experience, and Earnings*. National Bureau of Economic Research.

Mizon, G. E. 1984. The Encompassing Approach in Econometrics. In *Econometrics and Quantitative Economics*, ed. D. F. Hendry and K. E. Wallis. Blackwell.

Mizon, G. E. 1995. Progressive Modelling of Macroeconomic Time Series: The LSE Methodology. In *Macroeconometrics: Development, Tensions, and Prospects*, ed. K. D. Hoover. Kluwer .

Modigliani, F., and R. Brumberg. 1955. Utility Analysis and the Consumption Function: An Interpretation of Cross-Section Data. In *Post-Keynsian Economics*, ed. K. K. Kurihara. Allen and Unwin.

Molinari, F. 2008. Partial Identification of Probability Distributions with Misclassified Data. *Journal of Econometrics* 144: 81–117.

Montague, R. 1974. *Formal Philosophy: Selected Papers of Richard Montague*, ed. R. H. Thomason. Yale University Press.

Mosteller, F., and P. Nogee. 1951. An Experimental Measurement of Utility. *Journal of Political Economy* 59: 371–404.

Myklebust, T., H. A. Karlsen, and D. Tjoestheim. 2002. Nonlinear Unit Root Processes and the Problem of Nonlinear Cointegration. In *Essays on Uncertainty: Festskrift til Steinar Ekerns 60-årsdag*, ed. P. Bjerksund and Ø. Gjerde. Norges Handelshøyskole.

Nagel, E. 1961. *The Structure of Science*. Harcourt Brace.

Nakatani, T., and T. Terasvirta. 2008. Positivity Constraints on the Conditional Variances in the Family of Conditional Correlation GARCH Models. *Finance Research Letters* 5: 88–95.

Nerlove, M. 1958. Adaptive Expectation and Cobweb Phenomena. *Quarterly Journal of Economics* 72, no. 2: 227–240.

Olshen, R. 1974. A Note on Exchangeable Sequences. *Zeitschrift für Wahrscheinlichkeitstheorie und verwandte Gebiete* 28: 317–321.

Phillips, P. C. B. 1991. Optimal Inference in Co-integrated Systems. *Econometrica* 59: 282–306.

Phillips, P. C. B., and J. Y. Park. 2001. Nonlinear Regressions with Integrated Time Series. *Econometrica* 69: 117–161.

Pratt, J. R. 1964. Risk Aversion in the Small and in the Large. *Econometrica* 32, no. 1/2: 122–136.

Press, W. H., S. A. Teukolsky, W. T. Vetterling, and B. P. Flannery. 1992. *Numerical Recipes in C: The Art of Scientific Computing*. Cambridge University Press.

Projector, D. S. 1968. *Survey of Changes in Family Finances*. Board of Governors of the Federal Reserve System.

Projector, D. S., and G. S. Weiss. 1966. *Survey of Financial Characteristics of Consumers*. Board of Governors of the Federal Reserve System.

Rényi, A. 1970. *Foundations of Probability*. Holden Day.

Salmon, M. H. 1989. Explanation in the Social Sciences. In *Scientific Explanation*, ed. P. Kitcher and W. C. Salmon. University of Minnesota Press.

Salmon, W. C. 1989. Four Decades of Scientific Explanation. In *Scientific Explanation*, ed. P. Kitcher and W. C. Salmon. University of Minnesota Press.

Samuelson, P. A 1947. *Foundations of Economic Analysis*. Harvard University Press.

Samuelson, P. A. 1953. Consumption Theorems in Terms of Overcompensation Rather Than Indifference Comparisons. *Economica* 20: 1–9.

Sargan, J. D. 1964. Wages and Prices in the United Kingdom: A Study in Econometric Methodology. In *Econometric Analysis for National Economic Planning*, ed. P. E. Hart, G. Mills, and J. K. Whitaker. Butterworth.

Sarno, L., and M. P. Taylor. 2002. *The Economics of Exchange Rates*. Cambridge University Press.

Scitovsky, T. 1945. Some Consequences of the Habit of Judging Quality by Price. *Review of Economic Studies* 12: 100–105.

Searle, J. R. 1995. *The Construction of Social Reality*. Penguin.

Scheffe, H. 1959. *The Analysis of Variance*. Wiley.

Shafer, G. 1976. *A Mathematical Theory of Evidence*. Princeton University Press.

Silvapulle, M. J., and P. K. Sen. 2005. *Constrained Statistical Inference*. Wiley.

Sismondo, S. 1993. Some Social Constructions. *Social Studies of Science* 23, no. 3: 515–553.

Solow, R. M. 1970. *Growth Theory: An Exposition*. Clarendon.

Spanos, A. 1989. On Rereading Haavelmo: A Retrospective View of Econometric Modeling. *Econometric Theory* 5: 405–429.

Spanos, A. 2012. Revisiting Haavelmo's Structural Econometrics: Bridging the Gap between Theory and Data. Paper presented at Trygve Haavelmo Centennial Symposium, Oslo, 2011.

Stigum, B. P. 1967. A Decision Theoretic Approach to Time Series Analysis. *Annals of the Institute of Statistical Mathematics* 19: 207–243.

Stigum, B. P. 1969a. Entrepreneurial Choice over Time under Conditions of Uncertainty. *International Economic Review* 10: 426–442.

Stigum, B. P. 1969b. Competitive Equilibria under Uncertainty. *Quarterly Journal of Economics* 83: 533–561.

Stigum, B. P. 1972. Resource Allocation under Uncertainty. *International Economic Review* 13, no. 3: 431–459.

Stigum, B. P. 1975. Asymptotic Properties of Autoregressive Integrated Moving Average Processes. *Stochastic Processes and Their Applications* 3, no. 4: 315–344.

Stigum, B. P. 1990. *Toward a Formal Science of Economics*. MIT Press.

Stigum, B. P. 1995. Theory-Data Confrontations in Economics. *Dialogue: Canadian Philosophical Review* 34: 581–604.

Stigum, B. P. 1998. Scientific Explanation in Econometrics. In *Econometrics and Economic Theory in the 20th Century*, ed. S. Strøm. Cambridge University Press.

Stigum, B. P. 2003. *Econometrics and the Philosophy of Economics*. Princeton University Press.

Stigum, B. P. 2004. A General Equilibrium Input-Output Trial: The Empirical Relevance for Norwegian Trade Flows of the Heckscher-Ohlin Conjecture. Presented at International Conference on Input-Output and General Equilibrium: Data, Modeling and Policy Analysis, Free University of Brussels.

Stigum, M. L. 1990. *The Money Market*, third edition. Dow-Jones-Irwin.

Stock, J. H., and M. W. Watson. 1993. A Simple Estimator of Cointegration Vectors in Higher Order Integrated Systems. *Econometrica* 61, no. 4: 783–820.

Tinbergen, J. 1939. *Business Cycles in the United States of America 1919-1932*. League of Nations.

Toulmin, S. 1953. *The Philosophy of Science: An Introduction*. Harper & Row.

Tse, Y. K. 2000. A Test for Constant Correlations in a Multivariate GARCH Model. *Journal of Econometrics* 98: 107–112.

van Fraassen, B. 1980. *The Scientific Image*. Clarendon.

Veblen, T. 1912. *The Theory of the Leisure Class*. Vanguard.

von Neumann, J., and O. Morgenstern. 1953. *Theory of Games and Economic Behavior*. Princeton University Press.

Willassen, Y. 1984. Testing Hypotheses on the Unidentifiable Structural Parameters in the Classical "Errors-in-Variable" Model with Application to Friedman's Permanent Income Model. *Economics Letters* 14: 221–228.

Wolpin, K. I. 2013. *The Limits of Inference without Theory*. MIT Press.

Yoo, B. S. 1986: Multi-Cointegrated Time Series and a Generalized Error-Correction Model. Discussion paper, University of California, San Diego.

Zellner, A. 1971. *An Introduction to Bayesian Inference in Econometrics*. Wiley.

Index